1/5 13 + 6.

WARTIME CHRONICLE

UNIFORM WITH THIS VOLUME:

CHRONICLE OF YOUTH
War Diary 1913–1917

CHRONICLE OF FRIENDSHIP
Diary of the Thirties 1932–1939

VERA BRITTAIN

Diary

1939–1945

WARTIME CHRONICLE

Edited by Alan Bishop
& Y. Aleksandra Bennett

LONDON
VICTOR GOLLANCZ LTD
1989

First published in Great Britain 1989
by Victor Gollancz Ltd
14 Henrietta Street, London WC2E 8QJ

Vera Brittain's diary © the literary executors
for the Vera Brittain Estate, 1989; compilation
and editorial matter © Alan Bishop and
Y. Aleksandra Bennett, 1989

British Library Cataloguing in Publication Data
Brittain, Vera, *1893–1970*
    Wartime chronicle: diary 1939–1945
    1. English literature. Brittain, Vera, 1893–1970.
    Correspondence, diaries etc.
    I. title   II. Bishop, A. G. (Alan Gordon) *1937–*
    III. Bennett, Y. Aleksandra (Yvonne Aleksandra) *1953–*
    828'91209

    ISBN 0–575–04517–5

Typeset at The Spartan Press Ltd,
Lymington, Hants
and printed in Great Britain by
St Edmundsbury Press Ltd, Bury St Edmunds, Suffolk

CONTENTS

ACKNOWLEDGMENTS

We would like to thank all who helped us in the preparation of this book: the Librarian and Staff of Mills Library, McMaster University, Hamilton, Ontario – and especially the Staff of the Library's William Ready Division of Archives and Research Collections (which holds the Vera Brittain Papers); Paul Berry and Geoffrey Handley-Taylor, Vera Brittain's Literary Executors, and Shirley Williams, her daughter; the Social Sciences and Humanities Research Council of Canada; the Humanities Faculty, McMaster University; Manon Ames, Mark Bostridge, Fred Bottley, Desmond Bowen, Winifred Eden-Green, Robert Goheen, Deborah Gorham, Frances Montgomery, Mark Phillips, Richard Raiswell, Richard Rempel, Howard Whitten; Livia Gollancz; and our families and friends.

ABBREVIATIONS, ACRONYMS AND NAMES

A.A.:   Anti-aircraft
A.B.C.A.:   Army Bureau of Current Affairs
A.F.S.:   Auxiliary Fire Service
A.P.F.:   Anglican Pacifist Fellowship
A.R.P.:   Air Raid Precautions
A.T.S.:   Auxiliary Territorial Service
A.W.:   Alex Wood
Amy: Amy Burnett
B.E.F.:   British Expeditionary Force
B'm: Birmingham
B'mouth: Bournemouth
C.B.C.O.:   Central Board for Conscientious Objectors
C.O.:   Conscientious Objector
C.O.R.B.:   Children's Overseas Reception Board
Ch.Ch.:   Christ Church College, Oxford
Clare: Clare Leighton
D.H.:   *Daily Herald*
"D. of J.":   "Day of Judgment"
E.G.:   Winifred Eden-Green
Edith de C.:   Edith de Coundouroff
Ellen: Ellen Wilkinson
Endsleigh Street, 6 Endsleigh Street: PPU Headquarters
F.A.U.:   Friends' Ambulance Service
F.O.:   Foreign Office
F.o.R.:   Fellowship of Reconciliation
F.U.:   Federal Union
G., Gordon: Vera Brittain's husband, G.F.G. Catlin
G.L.:   George Lansbury
George, G.P.B.:   George Brett
H.O.:   Home Office
"H.w.H.", *H. with H.*:   *Humiliation with Honour*
Helen: Helen Mayo
I.L.P.:   Independent Labour Party
I.o.W.:   Isle of Wight
I.V.S.P.:   International Voluntary Service for Peace
J., John: John Brittain-Catlin
J.H.:   James Hudson
J.M.M.:   John Middleton Murry

K.H., Stephen K.H.:   Stephen King-Hall
L.C.C.:   London County Council
L.L., L.P.L.:   Leonard Lockhart
L.N.U.:   League of Nations Union
L. of N.:   League of Nations
L.P.:   Labour Party
L'pl: Liverpool
M., M.S.J., Margaret, Margaret S.J.:   Margaret Storm Jameson
M.E.W.:   Ministry of Economic Warfare
M.o.I., M. of I.:   Ministry of Information
M.U.:   Mothers' Union
Max: Max Plowman
Mrs. E.G.:   Winifred Eden-Green
N.P.C.:   National Peace Council
O.U.:   Oxford University
p.c.   postcard
P.L.:   Park Lane
P.N.:   *Peace News*
P.P.U.:   Peace Pledge Union
P-plane: Pilotless aircraft (flying bomb, robot, doodlebug)
Phyllis: Phyllis Bentley
R.A.M.C.:   Royal Army Medical Corps
R.A.O.C.:   Royal Army Ordnance Corps
R.I.I.A.:   Royal Institute of International Affairs
Rache: Lovat Dickson
Ruth: Ruth Colby
S., Shirley: Shirley Brittain-Catlin
S.M., Stuart: Stuart Morris
S'ampton: Southampton
T. & T.:   *Time and Tide*
T. of F.:   *Testament of Friendship*
T. of Y.:   *Testament of Youth*
U.D.C.:   Union of Democratic Control
U.N.R.R.A.:   United Nations Relief and Rehabilitation Administration
Univ.:   University College, Oxford
V.G.:   Victor Gollancz
w':   with
wh.:   which
W., Winifred: Winifred Holtby
W.E.A.:   Workers' Educational Association
W.E.G.:   Winifred Eden-Green
W.I.L.:   Women's International League for Peace and Freedom
W.K.S., William: William Kean Seymour
W.V.S.:   Women's Voluntary Service
Y.P.:   *Yorkshire Post*

INTRODUCTION

I

THIS DIARY PROVIDES a dissenting perspective of the Second World War on both the international and home fronts. In years overshadowed by war, Vera Brittain endeavoured to live by her pacifist faith, and sought the radical reordering of society and its values, and the elimination of force — be it political, economic, psychological or sexual — from human affairs. Brittain's domestic and world visions demanded cataclysmic change.

The strength of her diary lies however in its ordinariness. This is the diary of an upper-middle-class woman. Its entries reveal deeply-engrained class perceptions and attitudes, reflective of the degree to which class differentiation, separateness and often antagonism characterised inter-war British society. Vera Brittain accepted, and profited from, the social, educational and other advantages of membership in her class. Yet at the same time she also unreservedly involved herself in the support and promotion of causes with potentially revolutionary implications. The consequent paradox of her position runs as a continuous thread through her diary.

A second paradox is evident in the account Brittain gives of "her war". The diary illustrates the extent to which Hitler's bombs contributed to the creation of a more egalitarian and pluralistic British society, whilst simultaneously demonstrating the degree to which the upper levels of that society "enjoyed" a qualitatively different war from their "social inferiors". Brittain's experience reflects the transitional phase through which British society was passing, as the experience of total war melted down and reformed many societal patterns, attitudes and expectations, accelerating dramatically the beginnings of the welfare state.

Yet the theme of ordinariness may be taken too far. Vera Brittain was not a typically representative figure of the upper middle classes, or of any other class. Brittain, indeed, was atypical in that she belonged to an activist minority, possessed of a highly-developed sense of political consciousness which — in her own case — was expressed in her resolute commitment to the pacifist movement. In this, of course, there is still another paradox: the minority to which Brittain belonged stood four-square in the established political, religious and humanitarian tradition of British Dissent, which had an equally long tradition of drawing an important element of its leadership from the middle and upper classes.

During the Second World War, as a leading member of Britain's most prominent pacifist organisation, the Peace Pledge Union, Vera Brittain was undoubtedly identified with "the trouble makers". She argued in favour of a negotiated peace with Hitler, she was a powerful critic of saturation bombing (also called area, strategic and mass bombing), she was an outspoken advocate of food relief for the malnourished populations of Nazi-occupied Europe, and she was an unwavering supporter of independence for colonial peoples. Above all, Brittain was tireless in her commitment to pacifism, a faith which had, by 1936, subsumed her socialism and her feminism, and informed every aspect and action of her life.

The first wartime campaign in which Vera Brittain was involved was the P.P.U.'s "Stop-the-War" campaign. Her advocacy of a negotiated peace was not inconsistent with Munich, nor was it an illogical response to the strange period of the "phoney war". Indeed, the suggestion of a negotiated peace was supported by numbers of pacifists, liberal internationalists and even by some conservatives. When, at Casablanca in 1943, Roosevelt and Churchill adopted unconditional surrender, Brittain argued that such a policy would only serve to harden the resolve of the Axis populations, and that the avoidance of a fight to the finish was of paramount importance. In January 1945 she was to write: "When the history of this age comes to be impartially written, I believe that 'unconditional surrender' will be shown as the greatest blunder ever made by blind and obstinate statesmanship."

But the essentially liberal and humanitarian arguments of the advocates of a negotiated peace were undermined by the clearly totalitarian features of Nazism. The fate of the Jewish people, and of those others who perished in the Nazi death camps, faced the pacifist movement with a critical dilemma. As John Middleton Murry was to note in *Peace News*:

> If the Nazis have really been guilty of the unspeakable crimes circumstantially imputed to them, then — let us make no mistake — pacifism is faced with a situation with which it cannot cope. The conventional pacifist conception of a reasonable or generous peace is irrelevant to this reality.

The second, and equally controversial, campaign in which Vera Brittain was involved, was that against saturation bombing. The protest was headed by the Bombing Restriction Committee of which a prominent Quaker, Corder Catchpool, was the founder. The B.R.C. was formed in 1942, growing out of the Committee for the Abolition of Night Bombing which had been established in the summer of 1941. Brittain's protest was primarily an ethical one, against what she saw as the immoral killing of civilians; but it also challenged the premise that area bombing would break German morale, shorten the war and thus save lives. Brittain's individual contribution to the campaign against area bombing was considerable. Her most important written piece was a pamphlet entitled *Seed of Chaos*, which was published in England in 1944, and received little attention, although it did provoke savage criticism from George Orwell. Extracts were, however, also published in the United States, and twenty-eight leading American clergymen added their names to a postscript supporting Brittain's critique of area bombing.

Recent scholarship has tended to vindicate the stance adopted by Brittain and the B.R.C. On the subject of aerial bombardment, and the collapse of morale, Solly Zuckerman has written:

> As we now know, bombing at a hundred times the intensity of anything ever suffered by European cities during the Second World War at no moment broke the spirit of the people of Vietnam against whom the American forces were fighting between 1964 and 1973.

George Orwell himself, reporting for the *Observer* from Germany, in April 1945, wrote that "To walk through the ruined cities of Germany is to feel an actual doubt about the continuity of civilization."

The third campaign to which Vera Brittain was deeply committed was the Food Relief Campaign of the Peace Pledge Union. On the outbreak of war in 1939 a British blockade of continental Europe had been initiated, and the F.R.C. sought to gain governmental permission for controlled food relief for Nazi-occupied territories, most notably Belgium and Greece. As in the protest against area bombing, the arguments of the critics were posed at two different levels. First, they were levelled at the immorality of visiting suffering upon the civilian population of occupied Europe by means of the blockade. Second, they were directed at the premise underpinning the policy, namely that starvation and famine would induce revolt, just as area bombing would break morale. Critics considered it of vital importance to avoid placing civilians in the intolerable position of choosing between existence and Nazism on the one hand, and starvation and liberation on the other.

The issue of food relief raised questions about the nature of total war and the place of morality and humanity in the wars of the twentieth century: did traditional Christian values have any place at all? In 1944, however, under the chairmanship of Vera Brittain, and through the tireless work of Roy Walker as Organising Secretary, the P.P.U.'s Food Relief Committee did win the permission of the British Government to send 1,000 tons of food to Greece every month.

By involving herself in these three campaigns, Vera Brittain also assumed an extensive administrative commitment which obliged her to attend innumerable executive and organisational meetings, in addition to speaking engagements around the British Isles. Furthermore, Brittain used her pen to heighten public awareness of the issues raised by the campaigns. Her output of letters, articles, pamphlets and books was, by any measure, prodigious, whilst her capacity for work, and her ability to organise her time, were quite remarkable. In addition to those undertakings, Vera Brittain also spoke at public gatherings for the P.P.U., maintained an extensive private correspondence, and still found time to work, speak and write for the cause of Indian independence. She had a long-standing commitment to the Indian cause since — as she understood it —

the struggle against war, which is the final and most vicious expression of force, is fundamentally inseparable from feminism, socialism, slave emancipation and the liberation of subject races.

Vera Brittain's unstinting efforts on behalf of the Indian independence movement, and her close links with the women's movement in India, earned her an invitation to attend the All-India Women's Conference as British delegate in December 1941. The British Government refused, however, to allow Brittain the necessary exit permit, on the grounds that "the Congress Party would make propaganda hostile to the Government from your views on the war". Mrs Vijaya Lakshmi Pandit, then President of the All-India Women's Conference and later Indian High Commissioner, commented that the British Government's

decision was unfortunate. At this critical period in the relationship between the people of India and those of England, human contacts are important. Miss Vera Brittain would have forged another link in that chain of friendship between our peoples which this organisation has been trying to create.

Vera Brittain's commitment to pacifism clearly exacted a high personal cost, yet her wartime diary may not stir much personal sympathy in the contemporary reader. Her complaints about crowded, late-running trains, and the absence of dining-cars, seem somewhat out of place in view of the national emergency. Similarly, her ability to frequent restaurants enabled her to circumvent some of the vexations of food rationing. Yet it should be remembered that Vera Brittain travelled about the country and maintained a punishing personal schedule because she had the courage of her convictions and tried to live by them.

If Brittain's diary is, in places, banal and even petty, her consistency and tenacity of purpose can only command respect. Indeed, the survival of the British peace movement is probably owed, in no small measure, to the wartime work and witness of groups like the P.P.U. and individuals like Vera Brittain. In the crucible of war they kept the nineteenth-century tradition of moral protest vigorous, and continually reminded those who would listen of the threat posed by war to the very existence of Western civilisation.

The young supporters of the Committee for Nuclear Disarmament who marched from Aldermaston at Easter, or the pacifists [led by the aged Earl Russell], who sat down in Trafalgar Square, were the heirs of the Peace Pledge Union of the thirties. Their actions, however strange, suggested no spirit of indifference to the deepest spiritual problems of the age.

Such was the legacy of Vera Brittain.

Y.A.B.

II

Although *Wartime Chronicle* stands firmly on its own as a record of the Second World War, it is also the final volume of a trilogy. Like its companions *Chronicle of Youth* and *Chronicle of Friendship*, this book is an abridgment of diaries now in the Vera Brittain Papers of McMaster University Library, Hamilton, Ontario. To form it, some 150,000 words have been reduced by more than a third through the omission of passages considered redundant or of little general interest. Editorial principles established in the preceding volumes have been retained, but some innovations (such as occasional interpolations in the text, to bridge gaps, and the addition of a list of abbreviations and names) have been occasioned by this diary's idiosyncrasies.

As a trilogy, the three books record not only major events in modern history but the maturing of a complex and influential personality. The idealistic, ambitious girl of the 1913–17 diary, in her early twenties, was a feminist inspired by the writings of Olive Schreiner. Her struggle to achieve higher education was counterpointed with the evolution of her love for Roland Leighton — until both were interrupted by the Great War. Then her diary becomes a poignant account of pain and endurance: Vera Brittain, V.A.D. nurse, daily struggling to control her emotions, and to ameliorate physical sufferings caused by the vast conflict that took from her Roland Leighton and then two other young men at the centre of her life. By the time her only brother, Edward, was killed in 1918, her diary, not surprisingly, had lapsed under the torment of her losses. *Chronicle of Youth*, for all its sharp observation of fact, has the firm focus and emotional power of a novel.

When Vera Brittain started again to keep a diary regularly, in 1932, she was in her mid-thirties, married, mother of two children, established as a writer and journalist, and on the eve of achieving international fame with an autobiographical study based on her earlier diary — *Testament of Youth*. Armed with her Oxford M.A. in Modern History, her clarity in exposition and argument, her skill as a public speaker, she also worked hard through the 1930s in the service of feminism and peace (as her many speeches and articles attest). This Vera Brittain seems intimidatingly competent and confident, a brash career-woman; only her close friend Winifred Holtby understood her continuing inner vulnerability, her need of warm appreciation and sharp criticism. At the centre of *Chronicle of Friendship* is Brittain's relationship with Holtby. But again death and war were poised to break apart her world: Holtby died in 1935, and by then feminism had given ground decisively to pacifism in Brittain's journalism — for a second world catastrophe was imminent.

The Vera Brittain of this third diary is primarily a public figure, juggling an array of responsibilities and undertakings. Her entries are generally shorter than those in the earlier volumes; and among other indications of haste are the many abbreviations and rapid summaries. The immature, fulsome style of her first diary, the firmer and more serviceable style of the 1930s, modulate now into urgent plainness and, occasionally, jotted notes. Yet Brittain's great virtues as a diarist are more then ever evident: her responsiveness to changing events (sharpened by a historian's appreciation of cause and effect), her determined truthfulness, her ability to seize on telling fact and detail. Her accounts of the London Blitz, of the effects of bombing on other places she visited (like Coventry), convey vivid immediacy and authenticity. It is as if the background of the earlier diaries has forced itself to the foreground. The external, the facts of total war are seldom out of sight.

Yet links with the earlier diaries are strong. Throughout, we are reading the words of a professional writer. *Chronicle of Youth* described Brittain's determination to fulfil that vocation. Her love for Roland Leighton owed much to the facts that he was a poet and a fastidious stylist, and had writer-parents. And her love for Winifred Holtby owed much to their writing partnership, in which mutual encouragement and criticism were central. *Chronicle of Friendship* was, to a large extent, a record of literary events and relationships. As it ended, in August 1939, Brittain had recently, as Holtby's literary executor, prepared *South Riding* for publication, and had just completed her biography of Holtby, *Testament of Friendship*.

Wartime Chronicle also focuses frequently on Brittain's writing, which was amazingly prolific despite (and because of) her frenetic work as a pacifist throughout the War. Much of it was, of course, directly in service to the pacifist cause — the two hundred "Letters to Peace Lovers"; most of her many articles; *Humiliation with Honour* (an argument for pacifism in the form of letters to her son, 1942); her powerful short treatises *One of These Little Ones* (against the Blockade, 1943) and *Seed of Chaos* (against saturation bombing, 1944); the anthology she undertook with her husband, *Above All Nations* (1945). Less directly connected with her pacifist work was her fine personal account of the Blitz, *England's Hour* (1941). She was thwarted in attempts to write biographies of George Lansbury and Amy Johnson, but did write an ambitious novel indirectly connected with her pacifism, *Account Rendered* (1945), and was writing her final novel, *Born 1925* (1948), as the War ended. All this in six years, under the often-nightmarish conditions of wartime!

Account Rendered was based on the experiences of a doctor, Leonard Lockhart, who was shell-shocked in the First World War and killed his wife just before the Second began. Brittain's willingness to be a witness on his behalf, when he was tried for murder, is just one instance in this diary of her profound acceptance of responsibility for colleagues, acquaintances and servants, as well as family and friends. As a girl she had railed against the much greater domestic demands made on her, because of her sex, than on her brother. Paradoxically, perhaps, she grew up with an intense commitment to personal duty and, as an adult, no matter how busy she was, never wavered in fulfilling her high sense of obligation in relationships with others.

Despite irritation, and occasional anger, her concern for the welfare of her mother and husband was constant, and expressed in many practical ways. Sending her two young children to America in 1940, after the fall of France, was an anguished decision, and one she regretted; but it was taken out of responsibility, out of urgent, protective love (for, apart from the more obvious dangers her children faced in wartime England, Brittain knew that the family of a prominent pacifist was unlikely to survive long after the expected invasion of England by the Nazis). Her pain when the repeated denial of an exit permit (occasioned by her pacifist activities) made it impossible for her to visit the children, her intense worrying over the question of their return over U-boat-infested seas, are movingly obvious.

This is not, then, a bloodlessly objective record. There are diaries in which the domestic and personal dominate; there are diaries in which the public and political dominate: this diary melds what are often considered to be diverse matters, for that was Vera Brittain's way. Even in her P.P.U. work, her sense of personal responsibility always complemented the wider social responsibility that, in driving her to attack those who ordered the blockade and saturation bombing (including Churchill), exposed her to contumely. When Stuart Morris fell from grace in the P.P.U., she did not pass on the other side, but did all she could, at considerable cost, to help him; and, for the sake of the cause, she managed to work productively with prickly individuals like John Middleton Murry. In this diary one sees a hard-earned maturity controlling, equably and productively, a complicated life: a woman whose strength of will and sharp intelligence are balanced by compassion and aspiration. She can plough like steel through opposition, but she can also pick herself up weeping from the floor.

Her vocation as writer, her sense of duty and her respect for relationships, run through the three diaries in this trilogy; and impinge on what had become the cause of her life. *Chronicle of Youth* shows us why she became a pacifist. Though at the outbreak of that war she was swept up in the jingoistic euphoria of her compatriots, and remained for many years under the spell of Rupert Brooke, she had also been influenced by Olive Schreiner's pacifism, and she responded to war-caused suffering with a wide and deep compassion. In the early 1930's she moved ever closer to a full pacifist commitment, which she made in 1937, under the influence of Dick Sheppard. Once a member of the P.P.U., she gave herself unstintingly to its work for peace. The forms and extent of that work are never far from the centre of *Wartime Chronicle*.

For that reason we have chosen to end this Introduction by reprinting an article Vera Brittain was writing when this diary begins, in August 1939, just before the outbreak of war. It explicates the origins and the fervent but practical nature of her pacifist faith, and against it one can judge the thoughts and actions recorded in her diary.

A.G.B.

III

WHAT CAN WE DO IN WARTIME?

I am often asked when I first became a pacifist.

It is always difficult to recall the exact moment of "conversion" to a faith or a point of view, even though that conversion may transform the past with the illuminating power of revolution, and put the whole future in a different perspective.

But I do remember the period at which I ceased to take the Great War for granted as an "act of God", and my service in it as my unquestionable duty to the British Government.

In August 1917 I should normally have just completed my third year at Oxford. Actually, I was in a camp at Etaples, nursing German prisoners after two years of war service. My only brother had recently been sent from the Somme to Ypres, where his regiment was taking part in the opening campaign of the long agony now known to historians as the Battle of Passchendaele.

One day, when I had just finished the gruesome and complicated dressing of a desperately wounded prisoner, a disturbing thought struck me. Wasn't it somehow odd that I, in Etaples, should be trying to save the life of a man whom my brother up at Ypres had perhaps done his best to kill? And didn't that argue the existence of some fundamental absurdity in the whole tragic situation?

My misgivings were increased by the tolerant, friendly attitude towards the prisoners of our own wounded Tommies, who dropped in of an evening with packets of cigarettes from the canteen, and seemed to feel no trace of the arm-chair hatred which had been so rampant at home. I had never been much impressed by the propagandist articles which described "the Huns" and "the Boches" as devils incarnate and ourselves as angels of light. But I now began to think on definitely pacifist lines — though I did not then recognise them as such. By the time that I went on night duty in a British hut at the same camp four months later, I had definitely ceased to regard the War as an instrument of God or even of human justice.

In this hut we had sent down to us, almost as soon as they left the field, the first mustard gas cases from the Battle of Cambrai. There were about a dozen of them. I cannot remember how many survived, but the proportion was not high. Their plight made me write, in a letter home, my first angry protest against war-time hypocrisy.

> I wish those people who write so glibly about this being a Holy War . . . could see a case — to say nothing of ten cases — of mustard gas in its early stages . . . The only thing one can say is that such severe cases don't last long; either they die soon or else improve — usually the former; they certainly never reach England in the state we have them here, and yet people persist in saying that God made the War, when there are such inventions of the Devil about . . .

To-day we who lost our friends and lovers between 1914 and 1919 are faced with the bitter fact that all the suffering and service of those nightmare years failed completely in their purpose. Far from smashing German militarism and making the world safe for democracy, their long-range consequence has been to smash German democracy and make the world safe for militarism. The war to end war has resulted in a greater fear of war than the world has ever known. The attempt to smash militarism by force has led to more of it — and not in Germany and Italy alone — than at any period of history. The Europe that was to be made safe for democracy has only 150 million people living under democratic governments, and 350 millions under different forms of despotism.

If we are indeed to be faced with another emergency, our only hope of releasing mankind from perpetual cycles of devastating war will lie in avoiding the emotional ferocity which produced the Treaty of Versailles. In this form of reconciliation the service of pacifists to prisoners can play an important part. I know of no better lesson in the fundamental similarity of human nature, and the urgency of curing its fatal tendency to periodic self-destruction. But it is not the only form of such service. There are many other kinds, which can be carried out not only during a war, but in order to maintain the friendly relationship of peoples in time of peace.

Pacifists divide into two main varieties. The first is the uncompromising type whose protest against war takes the form of complete non-cooperation with the State and a resolute endurance of its consequences. These are the martyrs of the movement, who testify by their own suffering in prisons and concentration camps to the fact that neither force nor violence can break the resolute human spirit.

But a large number of pacifists are not of this order. Judging by letters that reach me from anxious correspondents, the writers do not feel that they could serve under a government in war-time, or do anything to further, even indirectly, the purposes of war. Many have taken a pledge not to do so. But at the same time they have a sense of obligation to the community of which they are part, and feel unwilling to remain completely passive while the world is in turmoil. Among them are highly intelligent persons with vigorous bodies and trained minds, who would suffer intensely and even be driven to the verge of madness by prolonged inactivity during a period of tension. How, they demand, can they serve society without lending themselves to the purposes of militarism?

It is, of course, difficult even for the most uncompromising pacifist to withdraw completely from all connection with war when the conduct of a war is the leading purpose of the world in which he lives. Every income-tax payer contributes not only to armaments, but to the salaries of Cabinet ministers and other government servants who are deliberately using those armaments to destroy their fellow-men. Conscientious pacifists can cause themselves much purposeless suffering by painful inquisitions. All that a pacifist can undertake — but it is a very great deal — is to refuse to kill, injure or otherwise cause suffering to another human creature, and untiringly to order his life by the rule of love though others may be captured by hate.

There are two main forms of national service which pacifists, both in and out of war, can undertake. The first method — an obligation upon both active and non-cooperative pacifists — is that of acting as perpetual evangelists for peace and conciliation. In wartime, and even during a period of tension, this is a harder task than it sounds. It involves finding out and telling the truth — which Lord Ponsonby has called "the first casualty in war-time" — at a moment when every device of propaganda is being employed to conceal or distort it. This form of service is probably the most valuable which can be undertaken by writers, preachers, speakers and other exceptionally articulate pacifists. Inevitably, for the duration of war or tension, they will have to face loss of reputation, of income, and even of their means of livelihood — a price paid during the Great War by many courageous pacifist-writers, such as Bertrand Russell and Laurence Housman.

The second form of service, which can be undertaken by any intelligent and able-bodied person, is that of relief and reconstruction work under such unofficial organisations as the Society of Friends. The relief of pestilence and famine, the organisation of hospitals, the distribution of food and clothing, the comforting of prisoners, both at home and abroad, the rebuilding and repairing of ruined cities and villages, all come within the scope of this active pacifism.

A full and useful account of the pacifist reconstruction work in the last War has been drawn up for the Council of Christian Pacifists by Miss Ruth Fry, under the title of "Pacifists and the Call for National Service". This pamphlet rightly emphasises that relief work of the type described need not be confined to a period of general war. Quite apart from national battlefields such as those of Spain and China, there are, at all times and in every country, "depressed areas" where pacifists could find ample scope for reconstruction, and lonely individuals who would receive a new lease of life from inclusion within a pacifist fellowship. The community is always with us, and the pacifist is its servant.

One final and specialised type of national pacifist service could, it is true, operate only during or immediately after war. This is the task of seeking out ways for shortening the conflict, hastening negotiations, and laying the foundation of a just and lasting peace. During the Great War, leading peace-lovers from many countries — not all absolute pacifists, but all agreed that fighting should cease — met in neutral cities, made proposals for peace by negotiation, and discussed the bases of post-war agreements. The little that was good in the Treaty of Versailles came out of their advice, and the worst evils from disregarding it. Had their counsel been heeded in 1916, the two bitterest years of war would have been eliminated and the world would never have had to confront the recent months of terror — consequences of a crushing defeat and a Peace dictated by cumulative animosity in which the early ideals of the War were lost.

The wartime negotiators failed because they received insufficient support from their own countries, and least of all, perhaps, in England. It therefore seems clear that the success of such preliminary peace-making depends less upon the leaders who initiate them, than upon the strength of the movements behind those leaders. This in its turn results from the influence which the rank and file of pacifists can exert upon their friends and neighbours.

At all times the pacifist's task is to act as a leaven of peace and gentleness throughout his society. But in time of war and crisis he becomes not less, but more, important. So long as war can still be prevented — and this is right up to the moment that the bombs begin to fall — it is the pacifist who will prevent it by determined sanity and the refusal to be swept off his feet. And if war comes, it is again the pacifist whose level-headedness, power over others, and ability to keep in touch with both sides, can alone guarantee the next generation against another Versailles.

VERA BRITTAIN, AUGUST 1939

Diary 1939–1945

1939

Thursday August 24th   Lyndhurst
Terms of German–Russian Pact published; contains clause guaranteeing
that neither power will join an alignment of Powers against the other.

Were told in Lyndhurst that 'phone has been going all day with people
booking rooms in hotels, etc. Shops begging us to lay in stocks of tinned
food so that they have more room for storage. Played with children with
heavy heart; they were at edge of Forest running a "Bracken Club", and
had collected a little stock of blackberries on a tree trunk. Very thrilled
with their game. Just before tea came wire from Ruth Colby offering to
take children; wired back explaining had arranged to keep them here.

Evening wireless (to which I listened at a house outside Bank) &
evening paper reported Chamberlain speech in Parlt. Strangely reminiscent of Sir Edward Grey's 25 years ago. Danzig taken over by Nazis.
Papers full of instructions what to do in war-time. Close thundery day,
oddly silent & oppressive.

Friday August 25th
G. rang up at 9.30, arriving Brockenhurst 9.52; went straight there with
car & met him. Ran into Lyndhurst & had a drink at the Crown; talked for
an hour about his activities in London — promotion of "Anglo-Saxon
Tradition", schemes for a job in Ministry of Propaganda, etc.

Nothing very definite in papers. "Left" flabbergasted by Russian *volte-
face*. French & British military missions returning from Moscow.
W.N. Ewer revealed that Russians had wanted to occupy two Polish
provinces in return for aid.

Saturday August 26th
Morning news that the Tannenberg Rally is off — hardly tactful for
Germans to celebrate their 1914 victory over their dear friends the
Russians! Evening news said Nevile Henderson flying from Germany
with a "plan" from Hitler which is certain to be rejected.

Lovely mellow day. In afternoon walked with G. into Lyndhurst &
watched the Crisis personified in the stream of traffic along the road —
buses full of troops, long distance "Relief" buses carrying civilians, small
cars filled with luggage, cots and prams, large furniture removal vans,
motor-cyclist dispatch riders, etc. Just before Seymours arrived, G. & I

strolled down to the Roman bridge in the Forest. Water tinkling gently, lovely light on the surrounding heather, kissed him standing on the bridge, thinking how remote war seemed for that quiet place.

Sunday August 27th

News much the same. Hitler plan rejected here, British sending over alternative proposals. Children all being evacuated from London, etc. to-morrow.

Lovely warm day. Walked in forest & talked finance with William in morning. He left soon after tea to drive back to London, & I walked into Lyndhurst with G.; then we met Rosalind at the Emery Down Inn for a drink. William rang up about 9.30 to say Hitler had summoned the Reichstag etc., etc.; news jittering on in the usual way.

Monday August 28th

Spent morning answering letters & doing odd jobs for G. After lunch he went back to town from Brockenhurst. John, Shirley & I saw him off. Queer feeling about going to London or seeing other people go just now — as if it were the front.

A train full of children (being evacuated from Southampton to B'mouth?) went through when we were in the Station. Evacuation rehearsals going on in all large cities.

British cabinet writing a note to Hitler. Troops from New Forest rumoured to have crossed Channel. *Europa* from N.Y. passed S'ampton without stopping. Rumour at S'ampton says that *Bremen*, ordered by wireless to turn round in mid-Atlantic, was compelled to go on by over 1,000 rampageous American passengers. All Americans leaving England.

Tuesday August 29th

Beautiful day. World in condition of tension & deadlock while prepara-tions for war and "defence" continue everywhere. Hitler writing long reply to British note. Much secret coming & going bet. England and Germany. German-Russian Pact not ratified yet.

Answered letters, mowed lawn, played with children. Odd having to stand by them till Sept. 21st with so much going on. Parenthood inconvenient in crises — or rather motherhood. Took John to see *Pygmalion* at Lyndhurst Cinema. The "news" which preceded the main film was a fortnight or three weeks old, as it often is in these little places. One picture showed the British military mission starting out for Soviet Russia! Though the operator wound up this part to full speed, it was still possible to see the smug, smiling faces of the British representatives & hear the narrator's suave comment: "And we wish them every success in their friendly negotiations with the Soviet Government." I waited for the reaction. Would it be boos, hisses? It came — a spontaneous & unanimous outburst of derisive laughter. Truly we are a wonderful people.

Wednesday August 30th
Still deadlock. Communications passing between Hitler & British Cabinet. Hitler wants good relations with Britain, but is obstinate over Danzig. We don't want war but are obstinate over our pledge to Poland. Queen Wilhelmina of Holland & King Leopold of Belgium have offered themselves as mediators. Millions of lives seemed to hang on the chance of somebody finding a "face-saving" formula which will enable Hitler to say he has got Danzig without involving us in "another Munich".

Spent all day drafting memorandum on a personal Peace Letter. Walked into Lyndhurst this evening with children. White lines & sides being painted on main road in preparation for black-outs.

Received anonymous letter from Glasgow asking me to "do something" from someone who has obviously never attempted to do anything herself!

Thursday August 31st
Met G. at Lyndhurst Road; train half empty, station quiet. Walked & talked with him after lunch re his schemes for book, etc., & internat. situation. Showed him my Memorandum as sent to Canon Morris, re Peace Letter. He approved & thought it workable.

Evacuation schemes for children announced to-morrow. People asked not to travel.

Friday September 1st
When G. & I were in Lyndhurst this morning announcement came through that Germany had attacked Poland & crossed frontier. "Total war" now seems inevitable. Spent rest of day trying to realise it and decide how to protect the children & what to do with ourselves. Felt slightly sick all day — as when people die — and didn't know how to eat. Saw number of evacuated children coming in to Emery Down but none at Lyndhurst or Bank so far. Called on the Woman Officer for Bank & offered to be a Blood Donor; she has a large half-empty house and was expecting 4 evacuated children but so far none had come.

Nothing new by late wireless except the usual long string of announcements re black-out, recruits, A.R.P. etc.

Saturday September 2nd
G. decided to take a cross country train — the 12.46 to Rochdale, as people there telephoned yesterday that Selection Conf. was still being held. Went in with him to Southampton. Station a pandemonium full of children being evacuated & large numbers of young men presumably joining regiments. Platform tickets temporarily suspended & no one not travelling allowed on platform. No cross country trains running so G. had to go to Rochdale by London after all & took the Waterloo train that was just leaving. He got his A.R.P. "mobilisation" notice just before leaving & was still uncertain when he went whether to report at Chelsea or Lyndhurst. It

took ages to get out of S'ampton owing to stream of traffic. Entire docks surrounded by balloon barrage. Most large ships had departed but *Empress of Britain* was there, steaming as though just about to leave.

Large thunderstorm. Went wet walk with John in Forest. Ultimatum went to Germany asking her to leave Poland (Germany says war never formally declared); by late news no reply had been received & Arthur Greenwood, who evidently wanted to plunge into war the moment Poland was entered, commented bitterly in Parlt. on the length of the period of suspense. Mussolini has apparently issued invitations to a Conference wh. we refuse to attend unless Poland is evacuated.

Sunday September 3rd

First thing this morning the news was still indefinite & I half decided to go up to London to the P.P.U. Hyde Park gathering organised for to-night. Then at 10.0 the B.B.C. made the "important announcement" that an ultimatum asking Germany to leave Poland would expire at 11 a.m. — and if no answer had been received, Mr Chamberlain would speak at 11.15. At that time we turned on the wireless again & heard his statement that from 11.0 this morning a state of war existed between England & Germany. His voice sounded old & trembled — and suddenly, as I sat on the camp bed in the study listening between the two children, I found that the tears were running down my cheeks — I suppose from some subconscious realisation of the failure of my efforts for peace over 20 years, for I had expected the announcement. Poppy hugged me & all but licked my face like a puppy. I rang up the P.P.U. & Canon Morris answered; said they might want me to do my weekly letter, & also a Pacifist Service Corps was going to be organised in wh. I might take part. Went out in the forest; in the sunny quiet of the gorse & heather it was impossible to take in the size of the catastrophe. To comfort myself, wrote an article for *Peace News* called "Lift Up Your Hearts". At night G. telegraphed from Rochdale that Morgan, not he, is selected.

Monday September 4th

News broadcast this morning that the liner *Athenia*, with abt. 1,400 passengers aboard, including 300 Americans, had been torpedoed off the Irish coast abt. 200 miles out. She remained afloat for some hours & everyone was saved except those killed by the explosion. French campaign developing. To-night news came through that our R.A.F. had flown right across Germany from West to East & came back, dropping not bombs but pamphlets! The airmen were not detected & returned safely. 6 million pamphlets were dropped altogether.

Took the children into Bournemouth this morning to buy school clothes & get their hair cut. People hurrying through the streets carrying their gas-masks. Bealeson's quite a pandemonium because most of the men had been called up & the girls were working in departments unfamiliar to them. When we got back to Lyndhurst John pointed out six balloons which we could see from here. They are evidently being extended from S'ampton round the coast.

Tuesday September 5th
Met G. at Brockenhurst at lunch-time. Ticket collector reporting rumours of raid on S'ampton. G. who passed through saw no sign of any such thing.

G. reported at Lyndhurst A.R.P. to-night as instructed by Chelsea — but Arthur Greenwood & Sir S. Hoare are interesting themselves in a job wh. may take him to U.S.A. next month in a liaison capacity. Very pathetic note from Margaret Storm Jameson to-night; she is desperate about Bill.

Lovely day; made into such a mockery by the wireless announcements. There is now a balloon barrage between us and the Coast, and amid the stars to-night was a terrific constellation of searchlights from Calshot. British bombed Kiel to-day; retaliation probably expected.

Wednesday September 6th
Rumours of an air raid early this morning but probably nothing but rumour. Lyndhurst A.R.P. standing to.

Children playing round Highland Water; Shirley fell into stream.

G. & I walked twice into Lyndhurst. Discussed finance, & appointing guardians for the children. Wrote Margaret S. J. asking her to be one.

Thursday September 7th
Another lovely day. Raid yesterday reported as airplanes approaching East Coast but driven off. French said to have broken through Siegfried Line. Germans rapidly mopping up Poland.

Letter from Ministry of Information asking me, as author valuable to them, to refrain from other national service till instructed. Can only reply that as pacifist can be useful only in so far as information contributes to peace.

Conversation with Canon Morris on phone re idea of Letter; welcomes it, but says Max Plowman has similar one about a magazine! Arranged to meet him & talk to-morrow before Executive.

Friday September 8th   London
Went up to London to attend P.P.U. Council & see Canon Morris. Train very deserted; had coffee & Bovril in restaurant-car before they are all taken off next week. Brilliant hot day; ran into London under shining galaxy of barrage balloons. Parted from G. in Whitehall & went straight to Edwardes Square. Looked serene & lovely as ever in spite of air-raid warning yesterday. Wonder how long it will remain so.

Went to Euston Rd. by 73 bus; A.R.P. shelters & piles of sandbags everywhere; also large notices *To the Trenches*. Yet somehow it seemed more tolerable to be near danger & *know* what was happening to one's self & others, than to be in the country with everything slowed down & wild rumours rushing round. G. said that S'ampton on evacuation day was the only English town he had seen wh. reminded him of Madrid in the Spanish War.

G. & I had Canon Morris to lunch with us & got his support for the personal letter idea. Oswald Garrison Villard from U.S. also staying at the Ambassador's Hotel (had come on a peace mission & arrived to find War). He lunched w' H.N. Brailsford — & joined us later for coffee. Long P.P.U. Council afterwards to discuss situation. Letter scheme endorsed; also Pacifist Service Corps to be founded. General approval for co-operation w' Min. of Information on peace-making only.

Very hot day. Dinner & spent night at Edwardes Square.

Saturday September 9th   Lyndhurst

No alarms last night. Slept soundly bec. very tired. Directly after breakfast went down to Cheyne Walk; dismantled pictures etc. & recovered copies of Wills. At 11.45 went to see Percy Bartlett of the Fellowship of Reconciliation & got his support for the letter idea too.

Lunched Edwardes Square; caught 3.30 at Waterloo & met W.K. Seymour on way to spend night with us. He takes typical war-propaganda attitude (Germans are "Huns", Hitler a "Teutonic brute") & insisted on arguing nearly all the way down in train till G. & I were nearly mad. Children very glad to get us back. Didn't see much of Seymour as both too busy getting our letters written & drawing up memoranda.

Germans reported in Warsaw. French into German territory; Saarbrücken surrounded. More millions of propaganda leaflets dropped by British R.A.F.

Sunday September 10th

No special fresh news. Announced on wireless that we must prepare for a long war. Everyone expects months of deadlock once Poland is overcome.

Monday September 11th

Proofs of *Testament of Friendship* arrived from Macmillan.

Letter from Margaret S.J. in afternoon consenting to be guardian in case of need. Worked at letters in shelter all day. Drew up scheme for guardians & alterations in Will & sent to Rubinstein.

Germans fighting in Warsaw; partly pushed back by Poles. City on fire.

Tuesday September 12th

British troops now in France. Grim description in *Evening Standard* of burning towns in Poland & air bombing of Warsaw.

Spent all day drafting & typing specimen letter to peace movement. Sent it off to Canon Morris by evening post, & a copy to G.

At dinner time G. telephoned that cable had come from Colston Leigh urging me to come out & lecture all autumn & winter! G. also said Ministry of Information wished he had accepted the Cornell job & wanted him to go to U.S.A. for the duration of the War! Whole aspect of going [to] U.S.A. would certainly differ if one was officially sent. Life unspeakably full of complications & upheavals.

Began correcting proofs after dinner. Another lovely day — very hot in afternoon, with cool wind. War seems to have an extraordinarily uplifting effect on the weather.

Wednesday September 13th
Took children to Southampton to get applications for renewal of re-entry permits; specially necessary in case of trip to U.S.A. I was glad to get them out again, for there is no doubt about the docks being a military objective. Many small gunboats, cruisers, etc. were in the harbour, & in the Cunard-White Star dock was the *Mauretania*, painted steel grey and so completely camouflaged that from a distance we thought she was a battleship. Balloon barrage overhead in grey sky. S'ampton looked deserted except for main streets, & sandbags everywhere gave it the air of a place in the front line.

Thursday September 21st
Took John back to Malvern by car. Got caught in fleet of army lorries which exhausted our diminishing supply of petrol — & Burnett had to get more from a garage fortunately not too far away. John rather subdued & quiet, but when we got to the Downs School he said goodbye with equanimity & walked in with me quite calmly loaded up with coat, suitcase, drawings & gas-mask. Mr Hoyland took me into his study for a talk. I mentioned our possible service in America; he fully understood, & undertook to be responsible for John in the Easter holidays if I wished. We drove straight back stopping only for tea at Cirencester. Burnett drove splendidly & did not even seem very tired — but I felt cramped, dizzy & deaf after spending the best part of 12 hours in an Austin 7.

Friday September 22nd
Felt extraordinarily desolate all day without the children. House very quiet. Answered letters all day. Walked to Lyndhurst for stamps in morning, and after lunch went to the children's "submarine" — the big fallen tree in the wooded glade over the brow of the nearest hill — and pictured the children's small ghosts playing there. Have decided it is just selfishness wh. makes me wish in these days that they had never been born; it isn't so much the fear that they will suffer, as reluctance to suffer more myself through my love for them. Every dear human relationship which

makes one long for life turns one into a potential coward & makes courage more difficult.

Letter from Canon Morris about his matrimonial complications, & a wire from the W.I.L. asking for a 500-word article for their news-sheet.

Sunday September 24th
Spent morning inserting some of the corrections suggested by Phyllis, Margaret & Creech Jones into proofs of biography. Proofs all afternoon; then tea with G. at Mrs Drury-Lowe's. Pleasant fire; good tea; usual jumping dogs.

Went for walk with G. Very quiet afternoon; no wind stirred the interlacing boughs of the beeches in the woods. Coming back, we passed the little group of cottages at the corner of the glade; a smell of peat-fires came from them, mingled with the scent of flowers & ripe red apples. In the corner garden was a riot of large dahlias — orange, crimson, yellow & scarlet. In the lane a little boy was twisting himself on a swing above a wood-pile. I remarked to G. how much more tragic the war seemed down here than in London; the contrast is so poignant between the lovely, serene, stable, civilised things which are the real essence of people's lives, and that cruel unnecessary violence, carnage & destruction that threatens their very existence.

Death of Sigmund Freud announced on wireless this morning.

Thursday September 28th   London
Spent all day at Cheyne Walk with Miss Sweet (voluntary secretary from P.P.U.) copying addresses for Peace Letter from fan-mail files.

After tea walked over Albert Bridge to have a look at Old English Garden. Still lovely as ever; massed with Michaelmas daisies in all shades of purple & mauve, taller than myself. Very bright sunset sky; amazing view from bridge of barrage balloons all over London, the more distant ones looking like pearl beads floating in the sky. Thickest conglomerations over City.

Saturday September 30th
Warm day with cold wind. Able to finish correcting proofs of *T. of F.* in garden.

Papers trying to make out that the Hitler–Soviet pact isn't important and doesn't alter anything — especially the papers which made out in favour of Soviet alliance with Britain that Russia was impregnable & her resources endless. Reichstag summoned by Hitler for Tuesday.

Sunday October 1st
Large editorial in *Sunday Express* about U.S. suspicions of us owing to "hush-hush" methods of disseminating news. Implication, that Americans are disappointed because we haven't so far provided them with

disasters which could be photographed & give them a thrill — whereas the Germans have! Also implied fear that the Americans are suspicious of us because they think the Govt. is going to make peace instead of "fighting to a finish" and "destroying Hitlerism"! I only wish I thought it was.

After tea made rough draft of next "Peace Letter" — urging everyone to express their opinion about ending the war before it is too late. Lloyd George in *Sunday Express* urged careful consideration of Hitler–Stalin terms by Govt. with full sense of responsibility. Garvin in *Observer* blundering on with fulminations about continuing the war — apparently whatever happens & whoever is in the last resort to blame.

Wednesday November 8th

Worked till lunch; at 1.45 saw Dr Millais Culpin at 1 Queen Anne Street as result of definite request to contribute to Dr Lockhart's defence. Again we talked for nearly an hour about shell-shock & its psychological effects.

Went on to office to answer letters and help send out circular letter. Attended Committee of Pacifist Research Bureau — a good deal of time-wasting discussion as usual. Dr Alfred Salter wanted me to stand as pacifist candidate at Macclesfield where there is a by-election against a Tory. I was very reluctant but he tried hard to persuade me. (Later he had to advise me not to attempt it, as the Macclesfield Labour vote turned out to be a "booze vote" not at all likely to be given to a pacifist.)

Thursday November 9th   Birmingham

Went to Birmingham for big P.P.U. meeting. The hall was packed. Didn't feel I spoke as well as usual. Spent the night at the flat of Mrs Phillips, a Birmingham P.P.U. worker separated from her V.C. husband bec. he cannot agree to her pacifism.

Saturday November 11th   Glasgow

Met at Glasgow by President of W.I.L. Took me to her nurses' club & gave me excellent breakfast. Then ran me out with the U.D.C. Scottish secretary & another friend to see the Trossachs. It was a pouring wet day but I did get some idea of the mist-covered hills.

At luncheon at the nurses' club met a little party of W.I.L. members; then went to St John's New Church where I had a truly magnificent audience of W.I.L., P.P.U. etc. & spoke for nearly an hour.

Monday November 13th   London

At 10.0 Margaret Storm Jameson arrived, to stay for 5 weeks. Gave her John's room & the nursery for her study.

At 11.30 went to Baird Lewis & ordered a minimum collection of clothes for my American tour; a new black & gold luncheon dress with bright coloured tassels; new black day jumper with vivid trimming; gold-embroidered cerise evening jumper, & several renovations.

Dictated replies to about 20 P.P.U. letters.

Tuesday November 14th
Evening, visited Roger Eckersley at B.B.C. & he took me along to see Edward Murrow (the American rep. of Columbia Broadcasting who does work here similar to Raymond Green serving on the other side). Mr Murrow turned out to be a near-pacifist who was anxious for me to go over & counteract effect of Duff Cooper etc.

Wednesday November 15th   Nottingham
Spent morning in office dictating letters. At 5.0 went to Nottingham from Marylebone to attend the Lockhart trial as a witness for the defence. It seemed incredible that only a year ago I stayed with the Lockharts in Beeston & now he was being tried for Molly's murder. When I went into the Ladies' Cloakroom at the top of the stairs to tidy up, I remembered how Molly Lockhart had taken me there before we all three dined together in the hotel grill-room & remarked as I was putting my hat straight: "What a lovely hat!" (It was a navy one with a big bow at the back & a veil.)

Thursday November 16th
Mr Varley arranged for Mr Coles & myself to attend opening of the Assize. Mr Justice Singleton entered with much impressiveness (tired but not inhuman face with humour about the eyes) & the Clerk to the Court made the opening announcements. First 5 cases tried & quickly dealt with as all pleaded guilty — perjury, child assault, buggery, wounding with intent to harm, bigamy. Then came a case where prisoner wished to be defended. Judge appointed Counsel & while he went down to study case, called "Leonard Phipps Lockhart". I gripped the front of the bench as Leonard came up from below & took his place in the dock quite close to us. He stood up & when charged answered firmly "Not Guilty". He looked tired & harassed but all his friends said he appeared much better than at the early proceedings when he "looked like a little old man." Wore well-cut blue suit; black hair neatly brushed back. Case for prosecution, outlining facts, opened by Mr Sandlands.

Friday November 17th
Case for Lockhart's defence opened by his counsel, Sergeant Sullivan. Then Leonard was put into the box; made a magnificent witness, but it was like watching a crucifixion. Was taken through his life from 1918; recounted black-outs of memory at the front, at Exeter hospital, & failure to recollect anything of the tragedy of Sept. 1st till it came back to him as a vague dream in prison. Broke down twice — once when asked if his marriage had been happy. His patent sincerity obviously impressed puzzled jury (all men) of Nottingham tradesmen.

Afternoon occupied with medical witnesses for defence testifying to effect of "dissociation". After cross-exam., attempt to get Leonard acquitted was abandoned so Mr Bedford & I not called.

Saturday November 18th
Case for defence concluded with hearing of the prison doctors from Leeds & Lincoln, who supported medical testimony that L.L. was in state of "dissociation" when he agreed to the suicide pact. Mr Sandlands & Sergeant Sullivan made their closing speeches; then Judge began masterly summing up, beginning by explaining state of law on suicide pacts. In afternoon he resumed; went through the medical testimony; court cleared of public when it became obvious that no death sentence would be passed. Jury returned after only 20 mins. & brought in expected verdict of "Guilty but Insane". Judge sentenced L.L. "to be detained as a criminal lunatic during his Majesty's Pleasure". Leonard threw his head back as though ready to face a new life & said "Thank you my Lord for a most patient hearing."

Sunday November 19th   London
Mother's 71st birthday. Lunched with her & gave her a diamanté brooch which also made two clips.

Had tea also & left directly afterwards to speak at Leighton Park School; evening address in chapel to the boys. Lovely moonlight evening. Talked to boys about maintaining decent values; avoiding hatred; not being triumphant over sinking of U-boats, Blockade, etc. Endeavoured to explain what these things really meant in terms of human life.

Sunday papers (*Express, News of the World, Mirror* etc.) contained sensational articles about the Lockhart case, absurdly trying to write up L. as a "real life Dr Jekyll & Mr Hyde".

Wrote to him in the morning at Lincoln Prison (where he has returned for a few days) to congratulate him on his remarkable carriage throughout the trial; offered to keep him in touch with the world of literature & to go & see him when he was ready for visitors.

Tuesday November 21st   Exeter
Left 1.30 for P.P.U. meeting at Exeter. Arrived at tea-time; given tea in town café by a family. Lecture in Labour Hall; excellent friendly audience (unexpected). Chairman, tho' L.N.U., sympathetic & excellent.

Wednesday November 22nd   Burnham
Lunched with Mrs Turner, the wife of a bricklayer. Her husband came in later & sat talking to me for half an hour in the small sitting-room. A most intelligent man & a convinced pacifist.

Went on to a rather dreary women's meeting with a young Salvation Army woman in the chair.

Thursday November 23rd   London
Had Roger Eckersley & Guy Chapman to dinner; Margaret of course
there too. She said Villard, back from Germany, talking at Friends' House
yesterday, had prophesied quiet during the winter but an attempt to
demolish English beginning with May & lasting 3 months.

Friday November 24th   Portsmouth
Spoke at Portsmouth (P.P.U. meeting). Large rather dark hall, nearly full.
Made quite good speech, not very controversial, & got little of the expected
opposition.

Dr Inman (the psychologist & friend of Dr Millais Culpin, whom I met
at Portsmouth when speaking two or three years ago) had asked me to stay
the night. Got there abt. 9.0. Sat in front of fire eating sandwiches &
talking to Dr & Mrs Inman (a large very tall woman with white hair & I
should say a tendency to be jealous of her husband). Finally she & their
guest, a young married woman, went to bed; & Dr Inman & I sat up till
3 a.m. talking about his theories, discoveries & cases, Dr Millais Culpin
whom he knows well & who started him on psycho-analysis, the Lockhart
case which I related. There are not many people with whom it is possible to
talk for six hours on end.

I am convinced that the discoveries of the next century will be in this
unexplored field of the mind.

Saturday November 25th   Swanage
Came to Swanage from Portsmouth to see Shirley. Very wild blustery
evening with cold heavy rain. Shirley looks quite well but lovely brown
colour of the summer has gone.

Miss Hascroft of the W.I.L. asked me to go to-day to cremation of Mrs
Swanwick, who committed suicide last week by overdose of medinol owing
to War. Could not bec. of seeing Shirley.

Monday November 27th   London
Spent afternoon in P.P.U. office dictating answers to letters. Now have
over 1,300 subscribers to Letter.

Wednesday November 29th
Howard Lewis finished drawing me; after lunch took drawing to
Macmillan to be photographed. Saw Lovat Dickson; learnt they had
changed my publication date to Jan. 5th bec. of New Year holiday in
Scotland; protested violently on ground I should have left or be leaving by
then; got it put back to Jan. 1st.

Thursday November 30th   Liverpool
Left at 1.0 (Euston) for lecture on "Autobiographies" at Gt. George St.

Chapel, Liverpool. Only lower part occupied as evacuation etc. had greatly depleted the lecture audience; contrast to last two occasions that I lectured at the Chapel when floor & galleries were packed with about 1,400 people. But they said it was the biggest audience they had had this season.

News of Soviet attack on Finland; Helsinki bombed.

Friday December 1st   London

News of resignation of Finnish government & negotiations for an armistice after 15 hours' attack.

There was a letter for me from Dr Lockhart, who has now gone to Broadmoor. It was written in pencil, thanked me for mine, said he was now going to keep his eyes on the future and was determined to "get back" — which he repeated in a note he asked me to pass on to Dr Millais Culpin (their ration of letters being limited). Said he was sorry to leave the Lincoln Prison officials (who came in relays to say goodbye to him) but was glad to get to open spaces again & was finding much peace in the beautiful surroundings of Broadmoor. Continued that he would like to have my book & to see me — so I wrote asking the Medical Superindt. if I might come on Thursday week.

Saturday December 2nd

Spent morning in office dictating replies to the week's letters — & corrected proof of Letter No. 10.

Home for late lunch. Beautiful though cold day; went for a walk over the bridges. Spent evening clearing up letters & writing Letter No. 11 (about the P.P.U. Women's Crusade, the founding of the W.I.L., and a memoir of Mrs Swanwick).

Christmas number of *Good Housekeeping* out, with the article on Winifred made up of serialised extracts of *Testament of Friendship*.

Monday December 4th   Accrington

Got the 10.20 train to Manchester for lecture at Accrington (Blackburn). Bitterly cold day & train; no heat at all till after Rugby.

Met by Mrs Higham's car (Hilda Noble, one of my pupils at St Monica's; plain girl then, but now, at 32, smart & attractive). Taken to luxurious house, very warm & beautifully furnished; comfortable bedroom & bathroom to myself; faces Lancashire hills. Sat with her & her nice young husband (the owner of a cotton-mill), drinking sherry before the fire till dinner & at last felt warm. Taken with them 7 miles to Accrington. Spoke to Accrington Arts Club, wh. they had founded, on "A Personal Confession"; interval in middle for tea. Club rather like an American Women's club. Little theatre in wh. I lectured was quite packed. Pink footlights. Lecture seemed appreciated.

Tuesday December 5th   Harrogate
Hilda Higham drove me to the station for half an hour by train to Barnsley where Dr Kathleen Rutherford (Stuart Morris's beloved) met me in a car; plain, sensible, fortyish, intelligent, chairman of Harrogate pacifist group. Drove me (with a patient she had taken for treatment at Barnsley) 40 miles over the hills to Harrogate; snow lying deep on hills at top but snowplough (which we met) had already been over. Wonderful effect of blue sky, & later reddish afternoon light over snow.

Stuart Morris arrived about 6.0 & after an early supper we went to the meeting — a crowded basement room at the Imperial Café as no halls or hotels are now available in Harrogate (all commandeered by Govt.). Many Civil Servants in audience. Stuart took chair, I spoke, & we both answered questions.

Wednesday December 6th   Bradford
Breakfast in bed; Stuart Morris & Rutherford family talked to me as I ate it. Letters included several from Macmillan abt. *T. of F.*, review copies, jacket etc.; one from Broadmoor giving permission to visit Dr Lockhart; one from Edward Murrow saying he is trying to arrange a broadcast for me in U.S.A. At 11.30 Stuart returned from going on rounds witth Dr Rutherford & we went for an hour's walk out to pinewoods on edge of country. He talked of his personal problems; hopes to marry Dr Rutherford but it involves double divorce as she was married early to a London specialist with whom she only lived 3 months.

Dr Rutherford & her mother gave a lunch for me at a small Harrogate hotel — very pleasant; about a dozen guests; & then Stuart took me down to catch the Bradford train. Dr Frost (tall Irishwoman, widow, one son) drove me to meeting at Friends' House; we got there late owing to getting lost in black-out. Large hall, quite full in both gallery & floor. Spoke quite well — well received.

1940

Tuesday January 2nd   London
Testament of Friendship published. Magnificent review in *Y.P.* — good also
by Robert Lynd in *News Chronicle*.
  Definitely decided abandon Clipper owing delays, & go U.S.A. by
Vulcania.

*Vera Brittain sailed for New York from Lisbon on January 5th. Gordon Catlin met her
(he had been in North America since November), and, separately or together, they
travelled widely for over two months — dining with Bertrand Russell in Los Angeles
and with Charlie Chaplin and Upton Sinclair in Pasadena. Both in the United States
and Canada, Brittain gave many lectures, often to University students on the topic
"Youth and War"; and a question about her activities was asked in the House of
Commons during her absence. She and Catlin returned to England in the* Vulcania,
arriving in mid-April.

Saturday May 18th
News very grim. "Battle of the Bulge" still developing round Sedan. Constant and somewhat over-emphasised warnings not to listen to rumours of
breaks-through and possible Allied defeat suggest that the rumours have
some foundation in fact.
  Struggled all day to write an article for the W.I.L. *News* on American
opinion. Could not concentrate for the thought of all the young men —
British, French, German — being blown to pieces in France. After tea
G. & I walked to Kensington Gardens — trees all shades of fresh vivid
green, blossom out in full, chestnuts, red & pink & white may, laburnum (vividly gold after the long winter), lilac, wisteria. Saw the Dutch
garden — a glorified version of the little gardens in Holland of which so
many have been ruined — a blaze of crimson tulips & purple iris.
Incongruity intolerable of the loveliest spring for years & no heart to
appreciate it.

Sunday May 19th
Another perfect sunny day, presumably helping Hitler's advance in
France. Unbroken fine weather for over ten days now. G. & I worked in
morning & afternoon, after listening to broadcast about terrific battle still
going on. After tea went to Cheyne Walk. Again, as in autumn, took

remaining pictures off walls, filled bath with water & made other preparations for fire-fighting.

Back to Edwardes Square for supper; seems useless trying to persuade Mother to move from London as she can't visualise anything really happening here, & is determined not to. Before broadcast news to-night, Winston Churchill made a speech, not minimising the extreme gravity of the situation, and emphasising that the Blitzkrieg from which other countries have suffered would be upon us as soon as the situation stabilised in France. Broadcast news which followed described — in complacent B.B.C. voice — as ghastly a storm of mechanised battles, bombed oil tanks at Hamburg shooting flames 10,000 ft. high, etc., as one could have imagined in the worst nightmare conceivable.

The Blitzkrieg, destroying what the men of the past built up with infinite exertion — towns, art, literature, civilisation itself — is a betrayal of the whole human race.

Usual anti-pacifist attacks in the newspapers etc. to-day. Those who opposed war & for 20 years tried to save the world from what is happening to it now are described as "the enemy guard". In Bristol Cathedral a Canon tries to square the Gospel with the present violence — says it was written in the midst of a military society, but failing to point out that it was directed *against* that society.

My God — let us say if we must that we have no choice but to do as we are doing, but don't let us call it Christian.

Monday May 20th
Morning at P.P.U. — went as adviser for an hour to Women's Peace Campaign. Dorothy Evans, on Committee, taunting me with having been a pacifist "after the event" in the last War — as though at 20 one had formulated one's views.

News getting worse all day; Germans in & around St Quentin. Gamelin dismissed as G.O.C. in France; Marshal Weygand replacing him. French line broken.

Tuesday May 21st
News came to-night that the Germans have taken Amiens, Arras & Abbeville & are trying to encircle the British Army in the N.E.

This morning again brilliant summer weather — though the wind was east & cold. Hitler's weather. Went to Euston at 10.30 to see my guaranteed refugee, Alfred Saueracher, & his family off to Liverpool to sail to-morrow. Saueracher visibly moved both at our seeing him off & at the news — which made us feel that he was the lucky one. Then went to Café Royal & met Margaret Storm Jameson & G. We had coffee at Stewart's & talked for two hours about the situation & the children — what, if anything, to do for the best. News steadily getting worse all day. Streets empty except in middle of afternoon. Everybody quiet but faces looking white & strained.

After lunch rang up Roger Eckersley & made an appointment for lunch to-morrow. Had a long conversation about the attack on pacifists in the Press, etc., as probably engineered by the real Fifth Column as a screen for their activities. Had my hair washed after tea; may as well be bombed with clean hair as dirty.

Wednesday May 22nd

Visited Kensington police to find whether Vera Z. could go with mother to Bournemouth. Permit needed from there. All over dinner (with G. absent) Mother put me through it for making her go to Bournemouth till I felt exhausted.

Bill to mobilise entire nation (i.e. to make every man & woman work as wanted, and have full rights over property) put through Parliament. Attlee & Morrison on the wireless to-night, both gravely — Attlee on the new Bill, Morrison on urgency of supply. A Bill is also being put through to punish spies & traitors with death. Occasional sounds of guns.

Thursday May 23rd

Germans up to Channel ports; fighting round Boulogne. Saw Mother off to Bournemouth by the 9.30 from Waterloo. Went at midday to George Lansbury's Memorial Service at Westminster Abbey — "Memorial Service for the Human Race" it might have been. Strange irony of service for a pacifist on such a day, especially as at same moment Dr Wood, Stuart Morris & Maurice Rowntree were being tried at Bow Street for the poster: "Wars will cease when men refuse to fight. What are You going to do about it?" Many wet eyes & strained faces at Westminster Abbey — especially during singing of "From death's dread sting" and "Jerusalem".

Gerald Bailey joined us for lunch & told us Cyril Joad had written a virtual recantation in yesterday's *News Chronicle* saying that nothing now mattered but victory. Went to P.P.U. & discussed trial with Maurice Rowntree, Stuart & Dr Rutherford; the magistrate (Sir Robert Dummett) has apparently made up his mind adversely in advance.

News to-night of rounding up of Brit. Union of Fascists & arrest of Captain Ramsay, M.P.

Friday May 24th   Lyndhurst

Got up early, shut up 37 Edwardes Square, breakfasted at Lyons, went to Cheyne Walk & from there to Passport Office & Min. of Information on G.'s business; then to Waterloo. Barricades & heaps of sandbags everywhere; barbed-wire entanglements round Govt. offices in Whitehall; large machine-gun dump below Admiralty Arch guarding road to Buckingham Palace.

Got 11.30 train down to Lyndhurst for a few days; illusory peace of the countryside made me realise how extreme has been the tension of the last week in London. Country covered with rhododendrons & white may; bluebells in the Forest, but I learn that all over it are searchlights, anti-aircraft guns, dumps of rifles, etc. Anti-parachute corps not yet organised here & police very lethargic. Ordnance maps displayed *outside* the windows of Lyndhurst shops. No aliveness to Fifth Column possibilities whatever.

The King spoke on the wireless to-night (Empire Day) — dull, heavy, uninspired, full of platitudes. Sir Oswald Mosley announced by morning papers as arrested yesterday.

Saturday May 25th

Germans now said to be in Calais but some indications that this is Nazi propaganda. Wireless no longer announcing movements and places in the battle for fear of giving information to Germany about troops cut off & unable to communicate.

Sunday May 26th

News still grave & obscure, but Garvin's article in the *Observer* makes it clear that the whole Maginot line system collapsed and that the Germans pushed through from Sedan to Boulogne in four days. They are said to be not yet in Calais, but the wireless has stopped saying where they are. There will be some recriminations when this War is over.

Coming back from the post at Bank to-night, G. & I decided that those most to blame were (a) the Communists & near Communists, like Gollancz & Laski, who urged hatred of Germany on us in the name of Soviet Russia; (b) foolish pugilistic Liberals like Geoffrey Mander & Stephen K.H., who were provocative with no sense of responsibility, & wanted us to guarantee small powers all over Europe without knowing whether we could; (c) the Francophiles like Vansittart & Duff Cooper, who tied us to French policy & over-estimated France's military strength.

Rain this morning. Walked with G. to the small Catholic church at Lyndhurst as the most tolerable way of celebrating a day of National Prayer. Heard a simple sermon by the local priest, much less militaristic than Cardinal Hinsley's radio address.

Monday May 27th

News now being virtually withheld, but said to-night to be "very grave". Gap between British & French armies widening. One lives in a kind of confused & terrible fog, in which we know nothing but realise that what there is to know must be bad.

On G.telling me that Lord Lothian had discussed with Cordell Hull (as reported in *The Times*) the possibility of America taking large numbers of British children, I sent him both an airmail letter & a cable urging scheme & offering collaboration.

Went over to Bournemouth & back by coach to see Mother — expected her to be against the idea of staying, but found her surprisingly cooperative — pleased with the small hotel that she has found and ready to remain for the present.

Tuesday May 28th

Very grim news broadcast by M. Reynaud at 8.30 this morning — the Belgians on the order of the Belgian King capitulated at 4 a.m., thereby leaving open to the Germans the road to Dunkirk by which supplies had gone to the British Army. Obviously the Belgian Army in three weeks had been battered to death, but the French military spokesman called the surrender "treasonable" & the *Evening Standard* to-night wrote angrily of "King Quisling". The news dominated the day, making certain the loss or evacuation of the 700,000 B.E.F. in France. In a short statement to the House at 4.30 Winston Churchill said we must "suspend judgement", but that grave & heavy tidings must be our lot in the next few days. To-night Duff Cooper in a wireless address admitted that the Army would have to be evacuated. Attempted invasion of these islands now almost certain. Feel sick at heart when I think of John & Shirley, & can only pray that the tide of war will roll over their heads without harming them.

Wrote next week's circular letter to-day & sent it off in case normal life & work soon ceases to function.

Wednesday May 29th   London

Came up to London by early train; staying at Cheyne Walk. Burnett came up later in afternoon to do the housework.

B.E.F. being evacuated from Dunkirk under cover of terrific rearguard action by French.

After dictating letters to Miss Wall went along to see Lovat Dickson, who told me that in spite of crisis my book is still selling 150 copies a week. Also, Foyle's do still want *T. of F.* for the Jan. Book of the Month.

G. had talk with Jean Monnet of the Anglo-French Coordination Committee, who thinks all London should be evacuated to make it more possible to defend this country.

Thursday May 30th

Spent morning somewhat unprofitably — but in afternoon went to P.P.U. and had long discussion with Mrs Richardson of the Pacifist Service Corps about the possibility of organising local assistance columns from pacifists with First Aid or other qualifications.

B.E.F. still being shipped back from France. Outlook for invasion here very gloomy. Signposts being moved from all roads by Ministry of Transport.

Friday May 31st

Tens of thousands from B.E.F. getting back across the Channel hungry, tired, half-clad, and in any kind of boat that will take them, bombed all the time. Thank God I don't know anyone with the Army this time.

Unprofitable morning; then went to P.P.U. & worked on Pacifist Ambulance Scheme with Mrs Nancy Richardson & with Miss Wall & Mrs Eden-Green. On to a meeting arranged by the N.P.C. to examine position of pacifists under Defence Regulations.

Both felt jaded, tired, chaotic, so after tea at the Euston Hotel walked in Regent's Park amid shaded mauve pansies and lupins in many delicate colours. Desertedness of everything gave impression of Sunday. Since most of the iron railings had gone for conversion into armaments, the Park looked like a vast green field, very fresh & vivid. A few elderly people were sitting in chairs, a few young people sailing in boats with striped sails. Such an illusion of peace. I felt as though I were watching the funeral of civilisation elegantly conducted. So the Roman Empire must have appeared just before the barbarians marched in.

Asked Stuart Morris to-day who was writing G.L.'s life.

Saturday June 1st
Evacuation from Dunkirk still proceeding. Caught early afternoon train for Hithewood, Sydenham Hill, for P.P.U. Council. Just before I left G. was on telephone to Victor Finney, L.G.'s secretary, who told him that the news was so bad (I concluded of casualties in the B.E.F.) that Duff Cooper & Harold Nicolson were at their wits' end how to convey it to the public.

Travelled to Hithewood with Laurence Housman, Stuart Morris, John Barclay, Sybil Morrison etc. Lovely house with beautiful garden on top of hill; fine view of London & innumerable barrage balloons. John Barclay in course of discussion spoke of terrible conditions in France as told him by a journalist who had come home bec. not allowed to tell the truth — of fears of cholera in Holland owing to destruction of water supply, of bodies ground to human pulp by tanks. Had been in Sunderland, where local minister had visited 300 men of local regiment in hospital. 900 had gone out; the rest were dead. These may be rumours, but in present terrible conditions seem probable.

Sunday June 2nd   Lyndhurst
Council discussions continued, this time in garden where red & pink rhododendrons were in full flower. Very hot day. Soft occasional thumping of guns in distance gave unreality to the discussion of policies and principles. Definite split as usual in P.P.U. between the "practical men" who wanted to carry on aggressive propaganda with view to demonstration of their own integrity, and the "intellectuals" (e.g., John Middleton Murry) who wished to establish "nuclei of resistance to tyranny" which would enable the ideas we believe in to survive even in a totalitarian world, and instead of challenging, meet challenge only when it came. I agree with

the latter position, & spoke saying that the reason [for] my own failure to convince & that of others in spite of apparent popular success had still to be thought out. There seems no point of contact between the two groups.

Returned home at 5, tea with G., back to Allum Green at 7.30. Some evacuated troops from Dunkirk came into Waterloo as we had supper while waiting for train & were loudly cheered.

Monday June 3rd
Last night when just about to go to bed, we heard the windows rattle & quite suddenly anti-aircraft guns very close to us opened up against an aeroplane which we heard overhead. G. & Burnett looked out of the door & saw the aeroplane caught in a searchlight; it showed a light on its tail and we concluded from this that it was British. But we still don't know for certain, as bursts of anti-aircraft gunfire continued in the far distance till about 2 a.m.

Very hot beautiful day. Most of the B.E.F. home & French soldiers are now coming. All roadside signs have been removed for fear of invasion by parachutists, to prevent them from knowing where they are. Lyndhurst this afternoon was full of stranded motorists inquiring their way. I walked in about tea-time to try to see Mr Ashford of the New Forest District Council about the possibility of rendering local assistance. G. went over to Winchester to see about Vera Z.'s status as an alien; then joined a meeting of local anti-parachute volunteers.

Tuesday June 4th
Huge American mail this morning; had hardly got it sorted before I had to leave for Bournemouth to see Mother. Though a little inclined to complain about loss of occupation in running her house, she really looks better than she has done for weeks & obviously has acquired more companionship than in London. We discussed the question of finding temporary work for Vera Z. who is forbidden Hampshire by police regulations.

Bournemouth full of very tattered-looking French & Belgian soldiers, with an occasional Moroccan with red fez amongst them. Odd to see in Bournemouth the same kind of cosmopolitan assemblage of troops as I used to see in Valletta during the last War. One or two did not hesitate to relieve themselves on the spotless Bournemouth pavements, but in the beautiful Park a tiny fat English boy sprawled over two recumbent French soldiers who were obviously enjoying the game.

Churchill announced to-night over 300,000 of the B.E.F. saved; 30,000 lost. No camping to be allowed within 10 miles of coast in E. Scotland & coast of South England.

Wednesday June 5th   London
Came up to London by early train; G. had an appointment at noon with

Hore-Belisha; I went to the house, dictated letters, saw Vera Z., etc. Very hot lovely day; countryside looked perfect as we came through, perfumed with elder and field-flowers.

On morning wireless & in papers news of a great new German offensive on the entire 120 miles of front — obviously a thrust for Paris. Looks like the next new objective before our turn comes. We lunched Basil Mathews to talk over the general Anglo-American situation. Like Hore-Belisha, he appeared deeply overcome by the general gravity of the situation. Told me Priestley & Vernon Bartlett are broadcasting every evening to U.S.A. Bartlett good, but Priestley will only do more harm than anything else.

Went on to P.P.U.; John Barclay full of terrifying stories of a German break-through which he said he had from Kingsley Martin. Tea with Lovat Dickson & Dan Macmillan to discuss the possibility of a biog. of George Lansbury.

Thursday June 6th   Swanage
Went to adjourned hearing of the P.P.U. poster trial at Bow Street at 10.30. Stuart Morris said he had heard the Govt. don't want to press the prosecution & so it appeared. Magistrate & Attorney General took tolerant attitude; result "Bound Over". Later I offered to pay the costs, assessed at about £30. Found whole proceeding an inspiration wh. helped to clear my own thoughts.

Snack lunch with G. at Prince's; had hair done at Marshall's; then joined G. at H. of Commons to advise Megan Lloyd George on her American broadcasts. She gave us tea on the Terrace. Rhys Davies came up to me & expressed alarm about the situation. Defences still holding, but tragic series of coastal air-raids on England last night.

Down to Swanage for Shirley's half term by late slow train.

Friday June 7th
Hotter & brighter again than ever; Swanage looking beautiful in the heat.

While strolling along the front saw Shirley bathing with the other Oldfeld children; she raced along the sands calling to us, looking very fit and brown. We went up to Oldfeld for the school play, *The Admirable Crichton*, and found it as boring as usual to be a parent in this respect, though the children did it well. Shirley (not in play) a little shy & seemed to have no use for us — as always when she sees us at school.

Strolled with G. on headland beyond hotel and remarked on strange unreality of the lovely landscape, because only an illusion of tranquillity. I remembered the same feeling in the last war, espec. when watching the camouflaged ships in Cornwall in 1918. Felt as though my life were a recurring decimal — constantly repeating experiences.

Woken during night by explosion, searchlights and aeroplane overhead

— after telling G. what a relief it was to spend 3 nights where we weren't likely to have raids.

Saturday June 8th
G. fetched Shirley to hotel for breakfast; then went back to Oldfeld to get her friend Susan Colbrean to spend day with us. Had the two children on the beach all morning. Both bathed. Shirley very pretty now with her brown skin setting off her bright blue eyes & fair hair.

Germans pressing hard & pushing the French slowly back towards Paris despite the tank traps. Large scale air-raids on England yesterday; few casualties.

Sunday June 9th   Lyndhurst
More blazingly hot than ever. *Sunday Express* reports this as the finest & hottest spring for ten years, after the coldest winter for 45.

Had Shirley for breakfast again; then went up to the school to see the Hicksons. We discussed with them the possibility of their taking Shirley for August, to free me for some kind of service. They also mentioned the remote possibility of moving the school to Canada in event of invasion, since nowhere in England wld. be much safer than Dorset. Feel meanwhile considerable confidence in the Hicksons & their excellent air-raid shelter.

Took Shirley after lunch to see Corfe Castle (destroyed in the Civil War as a Royalist stronghold). Back to Beach Café for tea; then took Shirley back to school. Said goodbye to her at the gate and turned round to watch her walking up the hill with her gas-mask & the toys G. had bought her — a stalwart, self-possessed little creature in a red and white check frock (the one I brought back from U.S.A. in 1937, now lengthened to its last lap). Such an effort to bring a child through its first ten years of life — and now for what? I wondered what I should have seen & done before seeing her again.

Monday June 10th
Italy entered the War to-day. Mussolini made the announcement in a speech at 6 o'clock and the fact was given in the middle of the 6 o'clock broadcast . . . And 22 years ago on Saturday Edward was killed fighting for Italy. What a damned silly ironic folly War is, making the greatest fools of those who fight it. I hope they'll take care of his grave among the pines on the Asiago Plateau.

This morning, having decided that the various responsibilities I carry (so many that I hardly realise half of them till confronted with the prospect of farming them out to other people) really are hardly compatible with full-time service to the nursing machine, I went down to Lyndhurst & offered myself & my experience (plus Burnett & car) to the local Council; also the suggestion of a pacifist service unit. Instead of the Mr Ashford I expected to see, found also an ex-Admiral & a Colonel who blew up at the word "pacifist" and was prepared to treat me as "Fifth Column" until somewhat disconcerted by my war experience. After abt. 10 mins. argument we began to discuss practical details and it seems I may get some casualty work to do.

Wrote letters all day; my circular letter now in debt. At 9.0 Duff Cooper broadcast a foolishly insulting speech about Italy.

Tuesday June 11th

At 12.15 a.m. last night heard Roosevelt broadcast a grand-sounding speech from the University of Virginia, pledging America's resources to the help of the Allies, and describing his efforts to negotiate for Italy if she would only keep out. Italians to-day bombed Malta, but without doing much damage. Meanwhile the Germans are pressing down on Paris. Refugees from villages further north are sweeping through it; the Bourse & several Ministries as well as innumerable private residents have moved into the provinces.

Italians being rounded up in London; many interned.

All the time Roosevelt was speaking, the Germans kept cutting in on the radio with a broadcast of the Horst Wessel Song and their national anthem.

Wednesday June 12th

Steady evacuation of Paris going on towards the South. The Germans are now within 30 miles of it. Places in Italian Abyssinia & Libya have been burned by S. African & British air forces; also Genoa & Turin. So the crazy game goes on.

Spent most of to-day writing Circular Letter No. 34 — about Italy, Edward, & what pacifists shd. do now total war has come.

Lovely day again; not quite so hot. Further mention of possibility of evacuating children to Dominions mentioned on wireless to-night. Princess Juliana & daughters already in Canada.

Air-raid alarm sounded here at 1 a.m. "All Clear" half an hour later.

Thursday June 13th

Germans very close to Paris. A newspaper reporter broadcast this afternoon a grim description of the roads leading south from Paris tight jammed for 30 miles. Moral: if caught by an invasion, stay put. Fighting 17 miles from Paris to-day.

Letter to-day from Rache Dickson reporting "some success" over the interview abt. the Lansbury biography — but further diplomatic steps to be taken.

Further press paragraphs about children going to Dominions. Attack yesterday by Viscount Elibank in H. of Lords on Prof. Ogilvie of the B.B.C as a "pacifist".

Further defence measures announced on the wireless to-night. Church and chapel bells now to be rung only as a warning of the approach of air-borne enemy troops — a strange use for the instruments designed to summon the faithful to worship their Lord. People to be discouraged from visiting, except on business, the East and South Coasts from The Wash to Sussex.

Friday June 14th   Colwall
Left Lyndhurst by early train. In London for two hours; telephoned Mother, who is back there, & Rache Dickson, who said Raymond Postgate wanted to do a Lansbury biography but not for two or three years — & anyhow would only sell about 700 copies if he did. Arranging for me to meet the agent Watt, as representative of the family, on Monday. Went to P.P.U. to supervise new Letter appeal for an hour.

Caught 1.45 train; early editions of evening papers proclaimed Germans already in Paris wh. has been declared an open town. Train very hot & crowded with troops. Got to Colwall at 5.48 & found Mrs Dendy, the proprietress of the Horse and Jockey and born a Frenchwoman, in tears at the fall of Paris & saying to me "Your nation has let us down". Reynaud this morning broadcast a new appeal to U.S.A. for further help.

Colwall village charming as usual. Not able to see John to-night.

Saturday June 15th
Paris completely in hands of Germans; swastika flying from Eiffel Tower. Twenty-two years ago to-day Edward was killed on the Asiago Plateau. What futility! John is so like him, & to what has he been born?

Daily Mail this morning outlined scheme for sending 100,000 children to U.S.A., not Canada. Wrote promptly to Col. Wedgwood offering help & saying J. & S. might take advantage of it.

Took John into Malvern by train; went over Priory, climbed to top of tower and looked at lovely country stretching from Worcester to Wales & giving same too-poignant an impression of false tranquility as the past five weeks all over England. "Look thy last on all things lovely," wrote de la Mare. What will this country be like soon? Local evening paper full of sinister information; denial that France will make a separate peace suggests she will. German communiqué claims rout of French Army & capture of 200,000 prisoners.

Sunday June 16th
Roosevelt's answer to Reynaud promised redoubled export of munitions so long as Allies resist, but "only Congress can declare war". Usual expression of sympathy & non-recognition of German occupation of France. No fresh news on morning wireless or in Sunday morning papers. Two months since I returned from U.S.A.; seems more like 2 years.

Weather broken at last; wet, grey morning.

Thursday June 20th   London
Evacuation-to-Dominions-&-U.S.A. scheme published in Press. Put in application for J. & S. to go. Queues of 1,000 people outside Cook's building in Berkeley St. Rather irritable official broadcast at night saying movement of whole population never contemplated & only a few could go.

Bombs last night on several towns including Cardiff— the first visit to the S.W.

As it was for other parents, the question was agonising: whether or not to send their children — John and Shirley were twelve and nearly ten years old — on a dangerous journey to isolated safety. "There seemed no right decision to be made," Vera Brittain wrote later; "whichever course I took would involve bitter regrets." But their children would be looked after by close friends in the United States (the Colbys and George Brett). Moreover, German invasion seemed imminent — and Brittain could be in no doubt of the likely consequences, for her and her family, of the Gestapo's arrival in England.

Wednesday June 26th
Children sailed from Liverpool

Thursday July 4th
Heard children's boat had arrived.

Thursday August 15th
Beginning of Blitzkrieg. Siren 7.30 p.m. Croydon raided.

Friday August 16th
Siren 12.0. Siren 5.0. (Wimbledon & Maldon raided).
Wrote article for *Peace News* while morning raid going on.

Saturday August 17th
No sirens.

Sunday August 18th
Siren 1.0. Siren 5.0. (South London raided).

Tuesday August 20th
First night, *Take Back Your Freedom*. Most important critics there, including Desmond MacCarthy & Agate.
Obvious flop. Glad W. not here to see this.
No sirens.

Friday August 23rd.
Siren 3.30 a.m. Got up & went to basement.

Lunched with Mrs J.L. Hodson & toured with her round devastated areas of Maldon & Wimbledon.

Saturday August 24th
Siren 8.30 a.m. Suburbs raided.
  Siren 3.55 p.m. Suburbs.
  Siren 11.45 p.m. City bombed for first time. Went out on to Embankment with G. & Burnett & saw huge glow of the City fire in sky like a flaming sunset.

Sunday August 25th
Siren 10.30 a.m. Siren 12.30 midnight. After the All Clear, searchlights on the horizon S. of Battersea Park & sickening crash of falling bombs.

Monday August 26th
Siren 3.30 p.m. Siren 9.30 p.m. Six-hour night raid over London — longest yet. Crashes all night. Spent most of it in cellar.

Wednesday August 28th
Creech Jones to lunch.
  Siren 9.0. All-night raid. 3 bombs on Burton Court (two delayed action). Heard one of them whistle past window when in bathroom.

Thursday August 29th
No siren. G. packing for U.S.A.

Friday August 30th
G. left for Glasgow by 4.50 from Euston to get his boat. Face devastated with anxiety as he left; realised how foolish I had been not to go with him. Air-raid warning just as his train left; I went straight down Euston Tube & was kept there an hour.
  Siren 12.0 noon. Siren 3.30. Siren 4.30. Siren 9 p.m.
  Persistent explosions all night. Lay awake deciding that if G. rang me from Glasgow in morning I would ask him to stay till Sept. 10th & go with him.

Saturday August 31st
Sirens 8.30 a.m., 10.40 a.m., 1.0 p.m., 5.30 p.m., 10.0 p.m., 12.0 midnight.
  Waited all day for wire from G. Letter from Crewe but no wire. No 'phone in morning so could not change plans & go with him. Felt desperate.
  Decided move to Edwardes Sq. — at least a little less lonely to be with Mother.
  Wire finally came from G. to say he did not get to Glasgow till noon — but caught boat (*Cameronia*).

Felt too miserable for words — realise how much I depend on him now he has really gone.

Sunday September 1st
At Edwardes Sq. Exasperating but less lonely. Sirens 11.0, 2.0 p.m.

Monday September 2nd
Letter from G., explaining late arrival at Glasgow. No actual raids on train — but it arrived 4 hours late at Crewe. Did some writing on book.
Sirens 8.10 a.m., 4.24, 10.34.

Tuesday September 3rd
Sirens 10.30 a.m., 2.50 p.m., 11.35 p.m.

Wednesday September 4th
Siren 9.30 a.m. (35 since Aug. 15th), 1.45 p.m., 9.5 p.m.
After this last warning, saw array of searchlights in SW & flares falling from sky.
Spent night in basement; persuaded Mother to have it strengthened as very fragile.

Thursday September 5th
Blitzkrieg getting steadily worse.

Friday September 6th
Worse & worse. Lack of sleep getting very hard to bear.
Siren 5.20 a.m., 8.40 a.m., 12.57 noon, 6.0 p.m., 8.55 p.m. (45), 11.35 p.m.
Most of night in basement as usual.

Saturday September 7th
Wrote all morning. P.P.U. Council meeting in afternoon. Didn't hear siren just before I left; strolled calmly through Hyde Park wondering why people were standing about in groups; by the time I got to Hyde Park Corner whole city was shaken by roar of guns and I saw about 12 German 'planes in the sky above the docks with shrapnel bursting all round them. After watching a minute or two took a taxi; from top of Edwardes Sq., wh. I reached safely, saw columns of smoke rising into sky from direction of docks.
Decided *not* to go to bed too early after supper but work despite siren, when suddenly it went. Had just taken dress off & was going downstairs in dressing gown when Vera Z. called Mother & me to look at the glow of fire over the City. We had just gone into the drawing-room when suddenly there was a terrific roar & a crash; the house shook like a ship in a rough sea. We turned to rush downstairs when there was a second & louder

crash, & we were practically *blown* down into basement — where we sat all looking very green, & listening to tinkle of falling glass. I 'phoned the police who came in later & said that the bomb had fallen — not on us, as I imagined, but on 29 Warwick Gardens, which lost its roof & is practically in ruins down to ground floor. We had several panes of glass damaged by bomb splinters but most escaped thro' being open.

Church bells rung as if for invasion.

Sunday September 8th
Terrible night — 10 solid hours of bombing from 8.0 p.m. to 6.0 a.m. German bombers circling overhead — now far — now nearer, with bomb crashes as they came. One very loud one broke glass in shelter window, already shattered by previous night. Between 2.0 & 3.0 bombs seemed to drop every 5 minutes. Lay in shelter most of night face downwards with pillow over my head. Worst night yet.

In afternoon (& also early morning) went round & saw damage done last night. Warwick Gdns. was a devastated area — no glass anywhere. House at corner of Pembroke Gdns. & Earl's Court demolished — windows all round broken; clock & windows smashed on St Philip & St James's Church.

Monday September 9th   Woking
Beaufort St. shelter bombed in night — 50 people killed. Felt appalling still after shock of Saturday & Mother looked worse. Decided that effect of nightly bombing ever since Aug. 15th was just too much — & rang up Bentley Carrs to ask if we could go to Woking for a few days' rest — not from danger as the bombers are constantly over there, so much as noise. They urged us to come at once.

In afternoon got ready for train. Storm Jameson telephoned & urged me to remain away from London till my book is finished; said she couldn't have written a line there. Agreed. Taxied to Waterloo; found it closed (Vauxhall Bridge [had] been bombed). Took taxi on to Clapham Junction; part of area round station sealed off for delayed-action bomb; air-raid alarm sounded on station, but we went on; ran into raid, train bombed & machine-gunned, people running for their lives; got on to floor. Changed at Surbiton — reached Woking half-dead, and SLEPT.

Tuesday September 10th
Spent day at Woking — suffering violently from reaction. Answered letters — but couldn't pull myself together to get on with my book until after tea.

Early siren — a bomb explosion occurred near here about 8.30. Bombers and searchlights overhead all night.

Have taken Fräulein & child in for the moment, as the block of flats in which she lives was demolished by a time-action bomb.

No news of Gordon — though I should have heard yesterday. Cabled George Brett that I was still unhurt and would be glad to have cabled news of G. & the children.

Wednesday September 11th

Went up to town by car. During drive saw the most wide-spread & devastating damage from Kingston onwards — though certainly nothing to the City & the East End. As we got towards Chelsea the railed-off streets increased — till Chelsea itself seemed the worst hit of all. A bomb had fallen opposite lovely Lindsey House at the other end of Cheyne Walk where I had tea with the doctor's family who recommended Oldfeld — others had caught Swan Court & there were craters in practically every street leading down to the Embankment.

Fixed all the family — persuaded Amy to come to Woking & Fräulein to Cricklewood; then went to Edwardes Sq. & told Elsie to go home as soon as I could get a flat & take Vera.

Thursday September 12th

Terrible night of noise from guns — between 3.0 & 4.0 a.m. stood in window & watched terrific Blitzkrieg (as I thought) over London — flashes & balls of fire in air, blue explosions as though from falling bombs. Thought London at least being demolished — but wireless next morning said much less raid damage done than usual, owing to increase in intensity of London barrage. So terrific firework display more guns than bombs.

Helen Mayo rang up to say she had found me a flat — so decided to go up to London to-morrow. In morning they rang up from Cheyne Walk to say there was at *last* a cable from Gordon. "Safely in — benedictions — anxious you safe." Also two delightful letters from children & another from Ruth Colby. Spent most of day answering these & writing to Gordon.

Friday September 13th   London

Took car early to town. At Esher a raid warning sounded. We drove on through it. Rainy day — low ceiling of cloud — our journey very dangerous as we afterwards learnt that bombs had dropped all morning in Fulham & Kensington — through wh. we drove. Far more streets up than 2 days ago — some in Fulham so thick with broken glass as to endanger car.

Further events:

(1) Daylight raid went on till after lunch — saw 3 German bombers low over flats. One brought down in City.

(2) Mother went to Edwardes Sq. & found maids had gone. Got on to P.P.U. & gave new whereabouts.

(3) Burnett rang up to say delayed-action bomb dropped this morning in Cheyne Court.

(4) Bombs on Buckingham Palace. Also just opposite B.B.C. — heard it scream here & bang just before second afternoon warning.

(5) Raid damage terrible in Chelsea & Kensington. Sick feeling of seeing lovely familiar places damaged.

(6) Mother went back after second warning & got safely to Woking. Cloudy ceiling all day — imposs. go out far. Lack of air & exercise terrible feature of War.

(7) Dined Helen Mayo's. Back just in time for siren. Terrific night of gunfire.

Saturday September 14th

Spent morning trying to fix up American visit & answer Leigh's cable. Got to passport office just before morning raid — saw damage to Buckingham Palace & front of Westminster Abbey. Immense detours now necessary in Central London. Whole side of John Lewis down — new building. At passport office, after long wait, found passport safely there but still polite uncertainty about exit permit — though this virtually promised. Felt sick & tired — as G. wouldn't have gone without me if he had thought any doubt about it.

Was kept by a raid warning in basement of building in Vict. St. for a time — but got home easily by lunch. Wrote letters all afternoon; sent twice into basement by raids. Incendiary bomb fell on roof of building on opposite side of street to this about 5 p.m. A bad day for raids — lots of low clouds.

Sirens to-day: 9.28 a.m., 11.04 a.m., 3.50 p.m., 6.19 p.m., 7.49 p.m., 9.39 p.m. (lasted only 13 minutes). Quite good night in basement, slept well for once. 2,000 tons bombs so far dropped on London — German news agency.

Sunday September 15th

Incendiary bomb still smoking away on roof opposite. Got up 7.15 a.m., had bath, went for early walk in lovely sunshine & at last got some fresh air after having had to stay under cover for almost whole of two days. Barrage balloons flying very high — a new device.

11.30, what sounded like a time bomb went off. Strong wind getting up — may save us if it goes on. (*Sunday Express* & *Observer* report Hitler all ready for invasion on other side Channel.)

12.15 noon — Siren — Planes over almost immediately — Hear bombs — then guns, then crumbling sound — hear from porter 2 minutes later that plane has been blown up by our guns — descended over Oxford Circus — Pilot baled out. Noise of terrific battle overhead. Jubilant savage remarks of some people in this block of flats (Italian-born man & American wife) positively nauseating.

Wrote a chapter of book. Evening raid started about 8.15 & never let up till 4.30 a.m.

Monday September 16th
Five sirens.

Went along to Grosvenor House and put in application to be "volunteer escort" when I do go to America.

Extremely kind letter from George Brett about children — offering to pay John's tuition at St Paul Academy. Replied assuring him that I — or my estate — would repay him after War. Rang up P.P.U. & was answered by John Barclay who said Friends were starting relief committees in East End. Felt I ought to help with this.

Had Rache Dickson to tea; he agreed that my book could be written at intervals & published later than November.

Back to flats for dinner & early siren. Terrible night; nearly struck. Bombs on Langham Place, Gt. Portland St., Park Crescent etc.

Tuesday September 17th   Mortimer
Four or five sirens.

Margaret came up for day — told me it was nonsense my remaining in town for no particular reason instead of writing — urged me to come with her for nights. Meanwhile rang up John Hoyland abt. relief work in East End — he invited me to Committee at Kingsley Hall at 3.0.

Still no news of exit permit — passport office just stone-walling. Bomb in Chelsea still not gone off. At 2.0 went to East End with Margaret, via Liverpool St., then taxi. Got there all right, sat & listened to Committee discussion, mainly about what remained to be done, putting pressure on Govt., etc. Raid on, so whole discussion happened in dug-out.

To get to Paddington, we ordered a taxi; it was a nightmare journey like one of Wells' most terrible fantasies. Went along Mile End Road, then through City. Dislocation appalling everywhere; yawning gaps where buildings had been; immense detours, huge traffic blocks, piles of rubble, craters in street. Made me feel too sick for words.

Got out to Mortimer without a raid but stood all way in train. Margaret's house pleasant red brick, large garden. Went to bed at once & slept for first time properly since Woking. Rang up Mother, who wept, poor dear, and wanted to be with me. 'Planes over house but did not hear them.

Wednesday September 18th
7 sirens.

Back to London in morning; seemed to spend all day trying to telephone, but still no decision from passport office. Rang up Chelsea — bomb still not gone off — but Vera very bravely went there & fetched my three coats.

Extraordinary look of West End; Bond Street all devastated; Walpole's burnt out; people standing round in groups gazing.

All Clear went as I drove to Paddington but I just missed the 4.45 & another siren went before the 5.15 — so we crawled at 15 miles an hour through all the military objectives W. of London.

Thursday September 19th
Back in town; visited passport office; saw the man I had hitherto spoken to on 'phone; usual polite stone-walling.

Walked back from Piccadilly to Langham Place through Regent St. Not one dignified shop without windows smashed & structure blackened; in one antique furniture store whole plate-glass window was smashed but two elegant yellow porcelain vases stood untouched on their stands. Street ankle-deep in glass; air filled with smell of burning wood. Passers-by moving aghast beneath dangerous walls w' glass falling round them in showers as they moved. Weary policeman repeating in kind of helpless resignation: "Naw then, show a little commonsense, cawn't yer?"

Rang up Chelsea again; bombs still not gone off.

Friday September 20th
Up to town; got in fairly early. Had tooth out at 11.0; a few moments of oblivion almost desirable. In my dreams seemed to hear terrific bombardment & came round to hear actual siren wailing. Lay for hour in Helen Mayo's basement while she put through calls to Passport Office & Cook's. Exit permit still undecided; told Cook's must cancel Saturday booking.

Brought trunks with me to keep at Reading. Mouth sore; very tired after gas. Went to bed immediately & slept.

Saturday September 21st
Spent all day writing next Peace Letter. Beautiful day. Went for walk round lanes with Margaret after tea.

Vera Z. rang up to say cable from Gordon, reporting children well & in good spirits; going on to Kansas.

Rache Dickson, passing by in morning, advised me on strength of a lunch with a Home Office official to put in for exit permit again on purely domestic grounds.

Sunday September 22nd
In morning drafted the "And so — Farewell" chapter of my book. Very painful writing.

Wireless news of general bombings everywhere.

Monday September 23rd
Ship torpedoed in Atlantic with 85 evacuee children.

Up in London again. Siren just as I arrived held up work — but got to Cook's, filled up new exit permit application & forms, with ticket, left these at Passport Office, then went on to Chelsea. Expected to find house laid flat, but was surprised at being able to get in without obstruction; bomb had apparently gone off over week-end & Chelsea looked more in order than it did ten days ago. Got out two best pictures, war diaries, MSS of *S. Riding* & *T. of F.* & some warmer clothes. Evidently much bombing all round as plaster fallen from ceilings & all rooms covered with dust. Burnett had left everything in uproar; evidently in midst of cleaning when made to leave.

Creech Jones telephoned; met him at Stewart's just after 3.0 & discussed exit permit question & whether I am on "black list". Then called at C.O.R.B.; everyone rather depressed, but work proceeding. Two of the lost children had been torpedoed before, on earlier boat.

Got 5.15 to Reading; dragged rescued pictures & books up by bus. Overwhelmed with misery of present world.

Wednesday September 25th
Moved into attic; worked on "And So — Farewell" Chapter in morning.

In afternoon Passport Office rang up to say my exit permit to U.S.A. *refused*. No explanation.

Went down to Reading & cabled G.

Friday September 27th   Oxford
46 more people saved from *City of Benares* — including 6 children, Miss Counts & Father O'Sullivan.

Came to Oxford for chapter of my book. 10.40 train finally came in just before 12.0. Went very slowly; got to Oxford about 1.15. Amused myself drafting letter to Harold Nicolson.

Found Oxford crammed — 15,000 people more than normal; evacuees from East End & Kent. Somerville (no evacuees) a haven of peace; quite difficult to find anyone; finally discovered I was at Maitland No. 10 — near my first room as a student in 1914.

Invited to coffee by Miss Darbishire; while there windows suddenly shook, bombs obviously dropped in distance (later heard it was Boars Hill). We all moved into hall & became very friendly. Miss Darbishire obviously nervous; Miss Farnell's sister & I, being London veterans, did our best to give reassurance.

Saturday September 28th
Wandered all over Oxford again, after marvellous luxury of breakfast in bed. Visited the evacuee depot at the Majestic Cinema; talked to two women from Poplar & Plaistow; then helped in kitchen & made friend w' the W.V.S. women, who told me all about how the place started.

Learnt present conditions of undergraduates. Much less change than in last war apart from crowding of town with evacuees. Term beginning in a fortnight; about half the normal University will be up.

Sunday September 29th   Mortimer
Learnt that Mother had rung me up to say that 37 Ed. Sq. had been ruined by bomb wh. fell just inside railings.

Tuesday October 1st   Stoke-on-Trent
Left for Reading on way to Potteries; went via Birmingham; very slow tedious journey, crowded with troops. Alfred Haigh met me. Walked over hill to house.

V. tired. Glad to go to bed early in such a peaceful place. Thought how Jessie's life & pleasant house seemed quite unchanged by war, wh. has crushed mine.

Wednesday October 2nd
Busy day in Potteries; saw over our own paper mills.

Not much air-raid damage to be seen anywhere.

Thursday October 3rd   Mortimer
Left Haighs early; long weary day travelling back to Reading. Eventually arrived to find huge mail, which included definite refusal from Passport Office of both my applications for exit permits, and a cable from G. to say he was writing Morrison (who is now Home Sec.) about it.

Friday October 4th   London
Met Mother in Kensington; went on to 37 Edwardes Square — really very grim; bomb had fallen exactly opposite, just inside square railings; windows & doors gone; ceilings down; fire in front hall had destroyed curtains & carpet. Real desolation; structure & furniture mostly intact. If Mother had been there, the shock [would] have killed her.

Raid started just before I left for Chelsea; spent abt. 2 hours in W.K. Seymour's Bank with gunfire overhead; lunched with him opposite at Harper's but he brought me back to Bank & insisted on returning for tray with half cold coffee & Welsh rarebit! Got tired of waiting; went to Chelsea & got out G.'s blue suit & jewellery, children's miniatures etc. Gave key of house to A.R.P. Wardens at Hall of Remembrance, who would not accept offer of house for homeless even for day or two bec. it wasn't safe!

Very noisy night; heavy gunfire till midnight while I wrote letters to Ruth & G.; about 11.30 huge time-bomb fell in Albany St., dropped like stone, shaking flats.

Saturday October 5th   Mortimer
Stayed in town till evening. Got hair washed at Marshall's v. comfortably in morning; then went on to skin specialist, Dr Brain (passing two houses completely wrecked in Harley St.) & learnt that what I had was "chronic dermatitis", aggravated by the effect of the bomb blast. He gave me a sedative X-ray treatment, prescribed some drugs, and said that what I really suffered from was overwork & I must try to take 2 weeks' complete holiday in N. Wales.

Monday October 7th
Letter from G. in morning — written Sept. 23rd & reporting children very
well & happy; anxious about me & exit permit. Replied giving full account
of permit negotiations.

Worked on "England's Hour" most of day. Walked alone through lanes
in afternoon & for short walk with Margaret in evening. Lovely day; blue
sky; chestnuts yellow in sunshine; cherry trees & ampelopsis scarlet.
Aeroplanes flying all the time overhead.

For first time for weeks, daily papers report that London had *no raids*.

Tuesday October 8th
Very nasty early morning raid, in rush hour. Just getting to Paddington at 9
a.m. when train stopped in very middle of line & looking up I saw green
circle of condensed smoke which Nazi airmen now put round themselves
(presumably to show their location to reinforcements); Nazi 'planes were
in the middle dropping bombs. Seemed very near Paddington, but learnt
later that it was Charing Cross area. Many casualties.

Mrs Eden-Green turned up fairly early & I gave her letters. Lunched
her & Sybil Morrison, who told me of her experiences in Holloway —
filthy, bad food, no shelter in raids, etc. Went on to P.P.U. Exec.; everyone
much below their best through raids. Long argument about whether
pacifist service units ought to do propaganda as well as relief. Gave Nancy
Richardson £10 for the work.

Got in to find cable from G. saying he couldn't return till end November
& urging me to go to the Lakes — wh. is much too far & lonely.

Wednesday October 9th.
Wrote all day at Mortimer. Long letter to G. in morning; then walked
during afternoon amid winds & wet flying leaves & thought all the time of
G.P.B. In the lane beside the common met a little girl about ten or eleven,
with fair hair. She reminded me of Shirley, so I smiled at her, & rather
shyly she smiled back.

Thursday October 10th
Revised chapters so far written; took them by bus in afternoon to
typewriting office in Reading for first typing.

Cabled Gordon suggesting possibility of cabling Ellen — who goes to
Home Office — about my permit. Margaret who came back from a P.E.N.
meeting reported that the P.E.N. is approaching the Foreign Office.

Friday October 11th
Beautiful day. Got out a bit on to heath & lanes, but spent most of the day
on my "London Under Fire" chapter.

Mother going to Dawlish to-day by car.

Received cheque for £506 from Macmillan for *T. of F*. Another £500 paid

me by Rache last month. Altogether book has made £1,306 in this country
alone since publication.

Telegram from Mrs E.G. saying difficulties over my Letter; tried to
telephone but no luck.

Sent in article for *Peace News* on Reprisals.

Saturday October 12th

Finished "London Under Fire" & wrote the "Anniversary" chapter.

Got on to Mrs E.G. in morning; found printer objected to details about
my Midland travels; said he could submit paragraphs to M. of Information.

Sunday October 13th

Mrs E.G. 'phoned that M. of I. not likely to pass my material — so
arranged for her to come down here for day to-morrow with pages to rewrite
so that I could get on with my book instead of travelling all day.

Worked on the "Training Centres" chapter which I find *very* dull, and
started the "Country Visit" one. Afternoon talk with Margaret about
writers who are "fakes". Feel sure I am one myself, but she said *T. of Y.* was
one of the most honest books ever written.

London's 200th raid occurred last night.

Tuesday October 15th

Wet but warm & lovely country day. Not much time to go out — wrote
"London's Hour" chapter & sent this and the "British Morale" one to be
typed. Got up to date with letters. Guy back from London reported that
St James's, Piccadilly, had been demolished — also the tailors, Burton's,
opposite, and the Vicarage next door. More difficult than ever to get
about, but insisted that London had much more light & air with so many
buildings down.

Full moon; Nazi planes going over early.

Wednesday October 16th   Cambridge

Went up to town by 8.15 with Margaret & Guy. Went to flat & learnt that
B.B.C. had at last been hit; walked round to look at it. Bomb had dropped
through 3 floors, then burst & torn a great jagged hole right in middle of
building. (Various listeners last night said they heard it crash & the
announcer hesitate a moment.) All over width of Portland Place, bricks
and fragments of MS. about the news were scattered.

Walked over to Endsleigh St. (past Maples, wh. was still smoking) &
joined Stuart Morris, Laurence Housman & Dr Herbert Gray who was
driving us to Cambridge. Got out far more easily than I expected; didn't
see very much damage; about the worst was Camden Town Station, wh.
was wrecked. Lovely colours on way to Cambridge; found on arrival that it
had been bombed the night before & manager of elec. light works killed, off

Trumpington Rd. Found I was staying with Alex Wood. Lunched there, then went on to Christ's College where Canon Raven received us. Had Forethought Committee discussions in warm pleasant room like small Common Room.

Friday October 18th   Mortimer
Back to London. Dr Gray put us down at Golders Green. Mothers & children already queuing up for Tube at 11.30 a.m. with mattresses, thermoses, etc.

Saw wreckage of St James's, Piccadilly, with only front wall standing — tower & roofs gone. Blackened skeleton of tailors' shop opposite.

Friday October 25th
Worked all day at the two Oxford chapters of book. Nice letter from George dated Oct. 8th comparing London situation to life at front in last war & deciding London more constantly dangerous.

Rache Dickson turned up in late evening — brought MS. of "England's Hour" back. Much pleased with MS. as a whole but wants me to lengthen & strengthen some of the early chapters. Asked Guy if I could borrow his *Times* — agreed though somewhat grudgingly. He always alarms me; manner suggests contempt for everyone but especially for myself.

Like my dear son I was born both timid and conscientious — the worst possible combination of qualities in a world where only toughness matters.

Several bombs dropped somewhere in this district about 10 p.m. House shook & windows rattled. Gunfire persistently on & off all night.

Saturday October 26th
Much vague & menacing news on wireless & in papers, about Hitler's conversations with Laval & Pétain. Unification of Europe seems to be going ahead (as J. Middleton Murry said it would) whether we like it or not. 'Planes, gunfire, searchlights, all creating a disturbance around here as usual from supper-time till midnight.

Sunday October 27th
Finished revision of typescript for Rache who picked it up at 5 p.m. Started "Industrial Midlands" chapter.

Lovely afternoon walk in woods; colours like an American autumn.

Vichy talks proceeding. *Empress of Britain* said to have been sunk.

Monday October 28th
Finished "Industrial Midlands" chapter; 14 pp.

Italy invaded Greece — thereby presumably started war in Near East. News of *Empress of Britain* confirmed.

Lots of heavy bombers going over between 9.0 & 10.0 but didn't hear any bombs — possibly too busy.

Tuesday October 29th
Letter from George Brett to say he, G. & Colston Leigh were corresponding on how to get me to U.S. to join my family — also from Agatha Harrison re invitation to India.

Greece said to be "holding out".

Wednesday October 30th
Worked all day at "Living Dangerously" chapter. Only went out for short walk over fields after lunch. Letter from Gordon; still appears to have v. little realisation of what we have been through since he left.

Thursday October 31st
Was revising "Living Dangerously" chapter when numerous bombs fell in neighbourhood this morning. Very wet day; got tremendously wild in afternoon.

V. nice letter from George — ending with usual injunction to keep underground during air-raids, and request for a new photograph.

Friday November 1st
Drove all round London with Margaret for $5\frac{1}{2}$ hours, looking at damage for chapter called "The Ruins of Troy".

Agatha Harrison came to lunch and we discussed India. Told her of the prohibition on my movements. She will approach Amery, Lothian, Mathews.

Got back to Reading after dark, very tired. Huge constellation of search-lights like Jacob's Ladders all over the sky as we went up in the bus.

Monday November 4th
Finished "England's Hour"; except for revisions. Worked all day except for $\frac{1}{2}$ hr. walk in rain in middle of afternoon. Wrote 23 pages — Prologue, Epilogue, & most of "Forever London". 70,000 words since mid-August, in spite of war & lost fortnight in September after the bomb of Sept. 7th.

Tuesday November 5th
Air-raids again on London last night & to-day. Margaret in town for annual P.E.N. meeting. Could not go as had to revise chapters written yesterday & take to Miss Mason in Reading for typing.

In Reading saw small curly-haired boy of about 3 being cuffed by hard-faced woman — obviously not his mother, probably the woman with whom he is billetted. Couldn't bear it — so followed them along Main Street & finally said to child, "Hullo, old sweet — what's the matter?" Child, astonished at being spoken to kindly, stopped crying. Woman looked rather ashamed & said: "He's been a rude boy — you've got to chastise them sometimes or there's no discipline." I just said: "I can't bear to see a child crying like that — espec. in the street." Hope it did some good. Could have wept to think how these unfit people have small children to look after, & I can't even care for John & Shirley myself.

Sunday November 10th
Handed "England's Hour" over to Rache Lovat Dickson.

Thursday November 14th
Terrible raid on Coventry during night. Between 8.0 p.m. & midnight, sky over Berkshire like hive of gigantic bees with the 'planes going over. Anti-aircraft barrage going all round countryside. At midnight watched shells bursting like rockets almost above the house.

Friday November 15th   Dawlish
Went down to Dawlish to spend week-end with Mother at Sefton Hotel.

Monday November 18th   Mortimer
Returned Reading. Journey back quite quick & easy; got lunch on train.

Friday November 22nd
Mother left Dawlish for Carbis Bay.

Sunday November 24th
Second inoculation for typhoid-tetanus. Told Dr Simmons to call on me for First Aid etc. if ever there was a severe raid on Reading.

Saturday November 30th
Drove with Margaret to Lyndhurst; put cottage in hands of Sawbridge with instructions to let. Worked all day removing food stores & putting things into Shirley's little room.
   Another severe raid on S'ampton began about an hour after we left it.

Sunday December 1st
Yet another terrible raid on S'ampton. Thousands made homeless & escaped into New Forest — just as I foresaw when I tried to start relief units there & got no encouragement from the New Forest Council. Fire- fighting services called from Reading.

Tuesday December 3rd
In London for the P.P.U. Executive. Beforehand did shopping, discussed publicatn. of *England's Hour* & exit permit, India, etc. with Lovat Dickson at Macmillan's office, & had Sybil Morrison to lunch at Marshall & Snelgrove's. At Executive usual discussion abt. public meetings & "caution" arose & I told Roy Walker that if we were a set of poltroons we shouldn't be in that room. In midst of meeting, a telephone call reported a telegram from Creech Jones saying "Regret application refused". Reported this third refusal of my exit permit to the Executive, wh. later passed vote of sympathy with me & proclaimed itself ready to give me publicity whenever I thought fit.

Friday December 6th

In London to see Creech Jones. Went to P.P.U. & talked over sitn. with John Barclay, Stuart Morris & Sybil Morrison. Met Agatha Harrison for 20 mins. at Express Dairy in Whitehall. Then went Montagu House & saw Jon. He reported reactionary stupidity on part of Home Office. My enemy not really Morrison but Peake. Morrison grumbles about "these literary people" trying to go to America & be comfortable; when Jon points out that when I could have stayed I deliberately came home & went through the Blitz with everyone else, Peake said that by doing that, or by failing to accompany the children, I put myself out of a category! They really object to my opinions — & to the question asked abt. me in the House — but won't admit it even to Jon. J. advised me to make direct appeal to Lothian; also get Harold Macmillan's help if possible. Lunched at Marshall's; in middle of lunch Ellen Wilkinson came in; saw me, looked uncomfortable, and hurried away after brief word of greeting; obviously had bad conscience.

John Barclay in morning talked about Coventry wh. he had just visited. Official figures quite out by the Town's own estimate; they say 4,000 dead & 9,000 injured. Chief shelter was under Woolworth's & other buildings in main street. Hundreds were trapped there & later buried when burning buildings collapsed on top of them. When town took census, 23,000 people had disappeared; most of these left town during night while raid was on & no one there knows where they have gone. Two thirds of town's war production smashed. Barclay produced a pamphlet issued by the local P.P.U. group urging not reprisals but a negotd. peace.

Got back to find cable from Gordon to say he was taking early December Cunard sailing immediately. Long to have him but do wish he hadn't decided to come at this dangerous time — after my cables saying he wasn't to come immediately.

Saturday December 7th

Bitter cold day. Wrote numerous letters, chiefly re G., in morning.

Proofs of *England's Hour* — first 30 pp. — arrived.

Sunday December 8th

Still very cold. Wrote long letter to Stuart M. re P.P.U. policy, showing how Bournemouth meeting wh. provoked Page-Croft's question had ended my work in America & prevented my accepting the India invitatn. by reason of [denial of exit permit].

Evening wireless reported raids on London starting again. Many incendiaries dropped.

Gordon Catlin, after several months in the United States, was travelling back to England in the liner Western Prince *when it was torpedoed by a U-boat. More than twenty people died, but he and most of the passengers survived several dangerous, uncomfortable days in lifeboats and a freighter before reaching England just in time for Christmas.*

1941

Sunday January 26th   London

Wendell Willkie arrived in England from Lisbon with staff. G. went to Bristol in hope of meeting them; had a few words with Cowles.

Spoke for Reginald Sorensen at Walthamstow at a dull meeting of the Labour Pacifist Fellowship. No tea & very wet day.

Tuesday January 28th

G. & I breakfasted at Dorchester with idea of his making contact with Wendell Willkie. Sent up his card at 9, told to go up, found Willkie still in bed, had conversation while he read letters & stormed through the 'phone at the Min. of Information — which he is obviously trying to escape from. Got back to flat about 11.0; walked to early lunch at Stewart's through raid, with guns popping over the park.

At 2.30 saw Roger Wilson (a young Quaker recently dismissed from the B.B.C. for pacifist views, who is now running the Friends' War Service Committee). We discussed my joining the Friends' Ambulance Unit & doing a supervisor's job in a large model shelter under Lloyd's in Leadenhall St. I said I would like to take it on, & he promised to arrange for me to go there & see it. Had early tea at Friends' House as there was another raid on & guns were noisy. Four raids altogether to-day but heard no bombs drop.

At 6.0 Rache Lovat Dickson called in for sherry, bringing page-proof copy of *England's Hour*. Said he had already ordered a second 5,000 to be printed, & if Smith's & Boots' libraries gave a good order, would do yet another 5,000 making 15,000 altogether.

Wednesday January 29th

Went to Kingsley Hall in Bow in time for lunch. Talked with Patrick Figgis about evacuation of children; then lunched with him, Dorothy Hogg & four young settlement workers in the upstairs sitting-room. In afternoon attended a moving little service for women in their Meeting Room. After tea we went round taking soup & cocoa to shelters just after siren had gone, signalling a fire-Blitz. The first, trench shelter, in Bromley-by-Bow recreation ground, was inches under water & dripping from the ceiling. The guns began to sound while we were in it, & during the ten minutes' walk to Glancus Rd, real Blitz was on — noisy guns, sky lighted with flashes, glow of a fire further East, bombers sounding overhead. I was really frightened when a visibly-lighted train ran over a railway bridge just as we reached it & the bomber swooped low — but the bomb-crash was distant. Glancus Rd only a little less damp than the other, & rowdier. Guns stopped as we moved from there to a warmer but more dangerous shelter under a church.

Thursday January 30th

Long morning talk, after breakfast, with Pat Figgis — about the needs of the Settlement, & the conquest of fear. Then made notes of the conversation & of yesterday's experiences.

A morning Blitz on when I started back; guns in Bow so loud as I walked along the Bow Rd that I sheltered for a moment in the Post Office — then went on, as it seemed so much less terrifying than the previous night. Raid on all the time as I travelled home by Underground — but heard no bombs, only guns.

Had Fred Warburg to lunch at Dorchester to discuss a 30,000 word book wh. G. might write on Fed. Union for a series of his.

Back to find annoying letter from Margaret, wanting me to move my things from Mortimer; glad to be able to tell her I hope to work for the F.A.U. Batch of preliminary press-cuttings from various papers about *England's Hour*. Wrote my tenant, Mrs Newman, asking if I could put my Mortimer belongings at the cottage. Letter from Mother describing experience of Blitz at St Ives; two bombs caused a good deal of damage & shook local morale owing to absence of shelters.

Friday January 31st

Rache telephoned that advance copies of *England's Hour* were ready, so spent afternoon signing presentation copies. Pleasant-looking red book with striking red & black photomontage cover.

To Dorchester again after tea with G. to see if Willkie had come back from visit to Dover, but he did not appear. G. says he & I were down to breakfast with Willkie last Wednesday, but as invitation never materialised, we must have been crossed off the list (presumably because of my pacifist beliefs) by one of the officials always present. Left a copy of my book for Willkie. Rache showed me a very favourable description of it in the bulletin issued for American booksellers by Virginia Kirkus, putting it on top of that week's non-fiction list.

Alerts nearly all day from breakfast time till dusk & a good deal of gunfire. 'Plane swooping low over Leicester Square just as I arrived at Macmillan's office about 2.30.

Saturday February 1st

At 6.0 set out for Leadenhall St. to begin the job in the shelter under Lloyd's which the Friends' Ambulance Unit has offered me, as soon as the person now doing the work (Miss Noel Honeybunn! some name) moves from it to work on the evacuation of children. The shelter is 5 mins. walk from the Bank station (the one smashed in the Blitz of Dec. 29th) and is under about 10 stories of steel & concrete. It is air-conditioned & the plant works reasonably well; it is also equipped with lavatories, canteen, bunks etc., as the Friends use it as a model shelter. There is a recreation room on the ground floor where everybody stays unless the Blitz is bad. About 200 shelter there — men, women & children. Most of the women are Lloyd's own office cleaners & are good, decent persons. There is quite a job to be done as friend, counsellor & nurse for minor ailments. Seem to spend much of the evening taking temps., binding cuts & giving doses of cough mixture. Tea for everyone (more like supper) at 7.30. Two young F.A.U. men also always there. No Blitz last night, though fine & starry.

Sunday February 2nd
Came back to breakfast in flats from City shelter; sharp cold morning. Learned later from Roger Wilson that job cannot develop further for the present as Friends are too short of funds to start the child evacuation scheme yet — so Miss H. will continue with shelter job she created.

Joined G. in afternoon at Kingsley Hall for afternoon service & shelter work. Lovely atmosphere of Meeting Hall (brown walls & daffodils on platform table) — "safe where all safety's lost" in the heart of Poplar. Stayed for the Communion service (tho' we didn't actually take the communion); Corder Catchpool stayed too. Later we all had tea together in the Club room with crowds of young people — afterwards visited same shelters as before, leading community singing & handing round tea. No Blitz this evening. G. & I got back to flat via District Railway about 11.0.

Monday February 3rd
Signed presentation copies of *England's Hour* all morning at Macmillan's office.

At 5.30 went down to Bermondsey with G. to help in the shelter work; I went round on the municipal mobile canteen (a very elegant one, presented from America). Visited surface shelters, shelters under warehouses, & finally an amazing place beneath Spa Road arches (part of the 500 railway arches running from London Bridge to New Cross to carry trains over once marshy ground). About 1,000 people sleep there in comparative warmth & dryness, regardless of trains that roar over their heads. Their only ceiling is the railway arch reinforced in places with tin. Saw every variety of man, woman and child, & all kinds of bedding mostly filthy. But the size & loftiness of the place saves the atmosphere from becoming as appalling as it is in the Tubes. Outside these arches, a very fit-looking & intelligent twelve-year-old boy, who was like an East End version of John, turned up to help wash the cups & serve the drinks. Very cold in the canteen. It was a snowy evening with a clouded moon. Driving in uncertain light through devastated parts of dockland gave me queer feeling of being back 25 years on the Western front. No Blitz during canteen serving. A very short Alert came while we were being driven home by an A.R.P. worker to whom we gave a drink at the flat.

This morning a letter came from H.N. Brailsford, telling me that Mrs Leighton died on Jan. 28th in Aylesbury Hospital & was buried on the 30th. I would have gone had I known in time. At the end her mind was in total eclipse. He gave her (unknown) age as 75. How much of the past vanishes with her! She lived alone with a savage [dog].

Wednesday February 5th
Spent all morning finishing Letter No. 50. In afternoon took it in bitter East wind to Brock the printers in the Harrow Rd. This seems to be almost a "safe" area; hardly a house was down in the entire mile of dreariness that I traversed. Saw only one little burnt-out shop, presumably damaged by an incendiary bomb.

Came back to struggle with mass of correspondence. G. went to Bermondsey to help again with the mobile canteen. Blitz started soon after he left; guns sounded continually and there were one or two crashes as I wrote to Mother & Clare in my flat. Sent Clare the cutting about her parents from the *Star*, & the little notice I wrote for *The Times* which it evidently is not going to put in. G. returned about 10.30, quite all right but covered with snow, which was falling heavily. "All Clear" sounded soon afterwards.

Thursday February 6th
Letter from Storm Jameson thanking me for gift of my book dedicated to her and prophesying immense success for it — which is quite an exaggerated notion of the probable results of anything so slight.

Friday February 7th   Coventry
G. & I went to Coventry, to stay with P.P.U. Group & see effect of Blitz on city. Found it by far the worst damaged place I had seen yet. Whole centre of city laid flat, except remnants of the Market tower & Coventry's 3 characteristic spires wh. rise serenely undamaged in the midst of desolation. One stands on the hillside & looks downwards at a mass of bricks, charred wood & twisted girders where the main shopping centre was. In the midst of it some gruesome-minded wit had stuck a white corpse-like dressmaker's bust on a stick. Cathedral just a shell — no roof; only ten feet of surrounding stone wall with bits of shattered stained glass sticking to remains of stone window frames. Of other two big churches, one was damaged & other (like the Town Hall) oddly untouched. The rest was as though one stood in Piccadilly Circus & saw everything between one's self & Trafalgar Square laid in ruins. Inside Cathedral where King had stood was a board marked "G.R., November 16th". Raid was on the

14–15th. It started about 7 p.m. & continued for about 12 hours; the din never ceased & left everyone dazed. Further out towards the circumference of the town was damage just about every 50 yards and then about every 100 yards. Many factories demolished or burned down, including Armstrong-Siddeley & Daimler. Extent damage due largely to 2 catastrophes: (1) the defences ran out of ammunition after 2 or 3 hours, never expecting a Blitz of that size; (2) the chief water-main was hit early in the evening & the water-supply for fire-fighting failed. They might have saved the Cathedral but just had to watch it burn. About $\frac{2}{3}$ of the city's industry was temp. destroyed & about one third permanently.

Saturday February 8th   Birmingham
Went by bus from Coventry to Birmingham. Centre of city very much damaged, espec. buildings round New St. station. Cathedral (dark grey Hanoverian affair) had had its roof burned away; debris still lay on floor giving a more squashed appearance than totally ruined Coventry.

Struck me as worse than London: small arms factories are scattered all over city & so many are demolished. Also looked worse because B'm is an uglier city; London's parks still manage to look lovely whatever happens. B'm had continuous small raids from August onwards. Worst in Nov. & December; worst of all 3 was on Dec. 12th. Immense amount of shops burned. Great deal of damage (factories) in Bradford St.; also at University; Medical School & Education Building destroyed.

Lunched at a town café & then took tram to Friends' House for meeting. Smaller & less zestful by far than Coventry.

Monday February 10th   London
Harold Laski came to lunch; thought G. should be sent officially to U.S.A. by M. of I. but without salary to give him greater independence. I agreed I could act as Treasury if allowed to lecture but explained exit permit situation. He had not heard of it — said it was "fantastic", & that he would talk to Morrison about it. Showed him copy of *England's Hour*. G. & I wondered [about] real reason for this outburst of apparent benevolence.

Margaret forwarded delightful cable from Phyllis: "I saw John and Shirley on Tuesday, their lovely characters and talents are thriving in favourable air."

Lovely day; mild & sunny. Walked in Park after Laski went. Made up speech for W.I.L. & wrote letters all evening. Air-raid warning at about 10.0; All Clear an hour later. Brilliant night; real bomber's moon.

Macmillan passed on cable from Sweden asking for translation rights of *England's Hour*.

Tuesday February 11th
England's Hour published to-day but no apparent repercussions; didn't see

it anywhere or have any messages — tho' agreeable letter of thanks came from Harold Nicolson & Geoffrey Shakespeare & a non-committal one from Ellen.

Went to Friends' House, heard the two visiting American Friends, Henry Cadbury & Robert Yarnall, talk about Blockade. Were very frank on wickedness of Govts. — ours as much as the German. Gave confidential picture of our Govt.'s intransigence on subject & their efforts to overcome it. Two other American Friends are simultaneously in Germany.

Short Alert during night but no noise. Slept soundly in shelter of flats for first time.

Wednesday February 12th
Letters all morning. Spoke to W.I.L. Luncheon at Friends' House on Women Peace-Lovers & their work to-day. Intentionally small affair; about 40 present.

Thursday February 13th   Manchester
Took midday train to Manchester, got lunch on train, met at London Rd station; [taken] to the Friends' meeting house by way of Portland St., which certainly has been badly Blitzed (great street of warehouses formerly filled with cotton). At Friends' Meeting House spoke to good-sized P.P.U. group; then went to Chorlton to spend night with my host & hostess Mr & Mrs George Gibb.

Friday February 14th   Hull
Breakfasted early & went out in car to see more of Manchester. Immense amount of damage at Exchange Station, wh. is out of action. Cathedral (back knocked down) & Victoria Hotel (burnt out). Saw also ruins of Free Trade Hall & Manchester Exchange. At 11.0 signed copies of my new book for about half an hour at Sherratt & Hughes shop, wh. had a good display in the window. From there drove to the University. Lunched there w' students & then spoke and answered questions for an hour. Spoke on origins of my pacifist belief in last War & the analogy bet. pacifism & early Christian Church. Caught 2.25 train to Leeds & 5.10 from there to Hull where I lecture to the Lit. & Phil. Society to-morrow. Got in just before black-out time to Royal Station Hotel. Everything quiet during dinner, but very noisy guns between 9.0 & 10.0 followed by heavy shake of a distant bomb.

Saturday February 15th
Raid not over till 3.15 a.m.; aeroplanes hovering over Hull half night. Dozed half-dressed on bed till All Clear; then undressed & slept till another siren woke me at 6.45 a.m. Alarm lasted for an hour. There was another of about same length at midday.

Had breakfast rather late; newspaper told of hundreds of incendiary bombs dropped on London. After breakfast walked along to Brown's bookshop in King Edward St., met the manager & signed numerous copies of *England's Hour*. Lectured after lunch to Lit. & Phil. Society in their own Institute on a "Personal Confession" — an informal sort of talk which started with childhood & school days, went on to War & after & contained a good deal about Winifred; also much that was in effect pacifism & got applauded. Had tea with some of them afterwards; then went & spoke again for ½ an hour to the Hull P.P.U. group at their Dick Sheppard Centre. Everybody talking about raid of last night; Hull *Daily Mail* contained long account of damage & casualties (none fatal). Siren again, 7.30 p.m.

So far v. little damage in Hull.

Sunday February 23rd   London
At 3.0 went to Dick Sheppard Club to read from *England's Hour*. Meeting packed. Nearly £8 taken in collection.

Long discussion with G. ended in conclusion that I shouldn't leave the P.P.U.

Saturday March 1st
Tiny note from E.M. Delafield remarked on the "generosity" of my previous note with the quotation from Ephesians, though she thinks all considerations of that kind (e.g. charity, forgiveness) must be postponed till we've won the war! Wrote her a longer more difficult letter about her son whom Margaret S.J. says *was* killed in action.

Bundle of press-cuttings about book — number of favourable reviews from provincial press, but a very abusive letter from Lorna Lewis in *Time & Tide* following up Delafield's review.

Three Alerts after dinner — one long crash during the first as though from a landmine.

Sunday March 2nd
Perfect spring day. Gold & white crocuses and snowdrops out in Hyde Park. As though a comment (which it doubtless is) on the coming of campaign weather, Hitler's troops have entered Bulgaria, and one more small country has fallen to the Axis. How much of this would have happened if we had not guaranteed Poland & gone to war?

This afternoon went down to Kingsley Hall again for the discussion, service & tea. Found that the Letter "appeal" had brought them in over £50 so added another £10.

Friday March 7th   Plymouth
Left for St Ives with G. Got off train at Plymouth; met by Mrs L. Cowling

of the P.P.U. Saw some damaged houses round station; then taken to tea. No damage in main Plymouth streets. Mrs C. said docks still undamaged too, and no shortage of food. Cold wet day. Taken on train by Mrs C. to see damage at chief hospital in one of main parts of town. Waited a long time; then Medical Superintendent appeared. Took me hospital; one ward had been "Blitzed" with one or two casualties, also a store-section. We went upstairs here & stood among the ruins. Very rickety. Odd how some glasses & cups were quite untouched. Taken on by Mrs C. to see a damaged part of the town near the gas works. After the worst Plymouth raid in December, the city had no electricity for a long time & has still no gas.

Went on in a bus to see Plymouth Hoe. In pelting rain Mrs C. showed me across Plymouth Sound the island airfield which is frequently bombed. She described seeing, on night that Swansea was raided, 50 German aeroplanes flying low over Plymouth Sound; then 40 minutes later on the News heard the Sirens sounding over Bristol. 'Planes destined for S. Wales or Bristol fly over Devon or Cornwall. Mrs C. (very strenuous woman who kept me constantly walking in the rain in bitter wind) also told me that Lord Astor is Mayor of Plymouth this year; was not at his house on Plymouth Hoe (she showed it me, in a terrace of substantial-looking grey houses) with Lady Astor & Ellen Wilkinson, who was staying there for the night — presumably inspecting Plymouth shelters. She also told me that the skilled workers in Plymouth docks (repairers of ships etc.) said they would make the war last ten years if they could — it has given them all jobs.

Finally after waiting a long long time at tram stop got a tram to Friends' Meeting House; arrived too late for any meal except a cup of coffee & biscuit during speech. Spoke for 1½ hours (speech & questions) feeling very tired, cold & wet, tho' there were some intelligent questions which cheered me as I went on (speech was to the Plymouth P.P.U. group). Got out of hall to find black dark night & pouring rain. No siren or apparent likelihood of raid. Taken by tram to Westminster Hotel & left there. At last got a meal (they had kept dinner for me; it was then about 9.30!). Having been soaked for 3 hours, expected to wake up with another attack of lumbago but oddly enough was all right.

Saturday March 8th   St Ives
On to St Ives to join G. Very bleak cold day. Tea with Mother & Belle. Spent most of day unpacking & getting ready to write various articles.

Cable from Fred M. Payne of Toronto *Star Weekly* asking me to do article (3,500 words) on London shelters.

Monday March 10th
Finished, typed & sent article to Nancy Pearn for *Daily Herald*. Papers

reported fairly heavy raid on London on Sunday night & many casualties among dancers at a London restaurant which got a direct hit. Guessed this to be Café de Paris by death reported of the Café de Paris restauranteur Neil Poulson.

Later Pearn, Pollinger & Higham confirmed that it *was* the Café de Paris, & Edith de C. told me that 160 people were reported killed there.

Saturday March 15th
Letter from J. Middleton Murry asked for article for *Peace News*. At first wrote saying I only wanted to do book reviews till India business settled. Then moved by wireless last night to write article on the Presentation of News which I sent Express.

Wednesday March 19th
Finished & sent off Letter No. 53.

News of a heavy raid on Hull (which I foresaw owing to all the reconnoitring that went on when I was there). Also casualties of Clydeside & Merseyside raids last week given as very heavy — 500 deaths in Clydeside, 500 in Merseyside; 500 injured in Merseyside, 800 in Clydeside. (The usual "500" which I now realise from visits to Blitzed areas represents the "official" figure for a big Blitz. Actual casualties are obviously far more.)

Had hair washed at Preed's little shop in the town; done by new assistant who told me she had just come here from Birkenhead & was in the Blitz there last Wednesday. Said the raid was on the north (poor area) of Birkenhead; that the City fathers had made no adequate arrangements & 10,000 homeless people were now sleeping in stations and shelters. Local authorities hopelessly Conservative. According to her, 3 miles of docks were virtually obliterated, and 50 landmines fell last Wednesday in the area. She saw two of them coming down herself. Owing to the number of falling parachutes, town thought the invasion had begun.

Thursday March 20th
Five letters from St Paul came all together, two of them duplicates. Lovely letters & drawings from the children. Also very nice letters from Ruth — promising to keep them for duration if necessary & educate Shirley if worst came to worst (George educating John).

News on wireless of heavy raid on London last night, with many casualties. No details of districts.

An Alert here soon after nightfall; just after dinner windows shook several times from distant sound of bombs dropping & we heard German 'planes going over. Then came 5 louder detonations of bombs dropped perhaps 5 or ten miles away. All Clear went about midnight.

Friday March 21st
Worked on balcony in perfect sunshine. This place more like the Riviera
than the Riviera itself, but I find its beauty intolerable in the midst of
catastrophe — & shall be glad to get back to London even though I get
through far more work here than I can ever do there in the midst of callers,
appointments, telephones & bombs.

Guns sounding from sea all morning. St Ives like a perfect pastel
painting against a grey-blue sea and a pale cobalt sky with pinkish-tinged
clouds.

Worked till 3.15; then went by bus with G. to Zennor. Usual fine
Cornish church; must be beautiful village in summer but to-day bleak &
no tea obtainable. Got a lift back to St Ives on a coal lorry.

Saturday March 22nd
News of yet another big raid on Plymouth last night. Fires said to be still
burning.

Started weekly letters to children and Ruth. Found Ruth little brooch
shaped like a butterfly and Shirley round one with a hare's head on, for
Easter.

Monday March 24th
Rumours about Plymouth flying round town. Heard one woman say: "The
centre of Plymouth is all gone and there are no policemen left." (The police
station was hit.) Decided to drive over to-morrow and see.

After dinner walked up in misty rain to Wilfred Wellock's meeting at
Hillesvenn. Quite a good P.P.U. crowd there for a small place. W.W.
spoke of the inevitable breakdown of civilisation after the war — the
famine period after short boom. If he is right, *we* were right to send the
children to America.

Tuesday March 25th
Drove over to Plymouth from St Ives. Passed streets railed off for bombs at
Redruth. Not much damage in Devonport, but signs of Blitz began as soon
as we approached the Hoe. Guns & debris all over the place. Pavilion on
shore burnt out. Whole place pervaded by smell of burning and wet wood.
Duke of Cornwall Hotel looked burnt out. Elegant terrace where Astors
lived much damaged. Blitzed motor-cars lying about in debris like
discarded bully-beef tins of last war.

Started to look for Mrs Cowling's house. Two men living in a damaged
row of houses called "The Terrace" directed us towards it but said we
should find it burnt out. I climbed over rubble on planks, between Blitzed
cars, & in the window saw Miss Piper, the director of staff at Dingle's
Stores & Enid Cowling's employer. She had been at my meeting,
recognised me and called me in. She had taken over the house as Dingle's
temporary office, and she, Enid Cowling & another member of the staff

were making plans for starting again — as Dingle's was destroyed. Enid
Cowling told me that they were all safe tho' they hadn't known it till the
evening.

Everyone in Dingle's temporary office was very cheerful, though the
Cowlings had lost everything.

Wednesday March 26th   London
Left St Ives & got London train from St Erth in pouring rain. Not much
delay at Plymouth despite North Road Station being badly damaged.
Wrote small article & diary in train.

Thursday April 3rd   Langham
To Max Plowman's place, The Oaks, Langham, nr. Colchester (community centre founded 1936 by John Middleton Murry & others) for
weekend while G. goes north for a ten days' speaking tour for Federal
Union.

Given a bare but pleasant single room looking south over wide Essex
field from top of The Oaks. Daffodils in bloom everywhere. Went to bed
early being tired & slept well. Evacuees not yet come to house; everything
very peaceful. Had dinner in kitchen. Shown round by Kenneth Wray,
who is now Warden here.

Monday April 7th   Doncaster
Travelled up to Doncaster by 4.0 train; tea on train; then sat in carriage
with a grandmother & two charming small boys a little younger than John
& Shirley, travelling for holidays to Retford from their school evacuated to
Dartmoor.

Met at Doncaster by Mrs McGregor & Mrs Gates, Chairman &
Secretary of the Women's Luncheon Club. Doncaster looked quite
unimpaired & they told me they had had no bombs there, but one or two at
Bentley which caused a few casualties & made several families homeless.

Alert late at night but no noise anywhere near; everyone seemed rather
nervous however!

Tuesday April 8th   London
Breakfast alone with Mrs McGregor; then set off by car with her to
Armthorpe to visit local elementary school of which I am a "patron",
together with Sybil Thorndike & Phyllis Bentley. Shown all over the
admirable Modern School, with its long low buildings and angle windows;
then girls (mostly miners' daughters) were gathered together & I made
them a short speech. They sang "Jerusalem" & I spoke again for a few
minutes, telling them how it was sung at Winifred's Memorial Service &
bidding them remember her whenever they heard it. Then on to Doncaster
Women's Luncheon Club, where I spoke to record attendance of about
160. Club has grown greatly since I first addressed it in 1934. Spoke on

"The American Scene since the War" for 40 mins. They all seemed pleased. Fee £12.12.0. I congratulated them on providing a reason for people to meet wh. had nothing to do with the War.

Back to London by 3.25 train; got to London in reasonable time, but train played outside King's Cross for about an hour. Got to flat just before black-out. G. in Leeds tonight. Dined alone & read letters. Alert went at 9 p.m. & there was no All Clear till after 4.0. Heard no bombs, but guns went at frequent intervals. Didn't get to sleep till about 4.30 a.m.

Wednesday April 9th   Langham
Back to Langham after tremendous rush of work. Everyone in the house preparing for the evacuees, who arrive to-morrow. Very cold.

Evening Standard said Germans pressing hard down Vardar Valley. 9 o'clock wireless reported fall of Salonika as announced in Churchill's speech this afternoon. Talk starting again about our "necessity to defend Egypt" — after our reverses against the Nazis in Libya. Wireless also announced another heavy raid on Coventry & many casualties feared.

Thursday April 10th
Evacuees finally turned up at 5.30, having been taken to Southend by mistake of driver. Mostly old people from Bermondsey, Bow and Bethnal Green. One blind man, one lame; one hunchback woman among them. Told stories of being bombed out of homes. Said: "Well, we never expected to be welcomed by so many kind people."

Served at dinner. Most of the evacuees left half of the stew given them, but seemed pleased none the less. One old woman said: "I'm not going to leave this rich place where they give you late dinner."

Poor Langham — rich! Dorothy & I spent all morning in Colchester buying mats, chamber pots & other oddments.

Had supper late after serving. Wireless reported another heavy raid on Birmingham. 'Planes going over.

Friday April 11th
Milder & rather rainy. Large number of more able-bodied evacuees volunteered after breakfast to do washing up & cleaning wh. enabled me to get on with own work.

Went for walk [by] myself after lunch. This country very like Holland; wide horizons, pageants of cloud, wealth of spring flowers. Lanes now filled with celandines; gardens full of daffodils & primroses. Lines of daffodils in Langham Garden; some under trees near white bee-hives. Walked up a little lane past a derelict farm left to go to ruin, at top found an old woman cultivating a lovely little garden filled with daffodils & grape hyacinths. She looked ancient enough but said her employer was 93! & she & her husband did the garden.

Had supper with the C.O. farm boys at the Little Cottage; very warm & comfortable.

Saturday April 12th
Milder day, for first time really like spring. I could live very happily here, away from the worst sorrows of this war, if I were not moved by an inner compulsion to travel about the country and find out, on the spot, the truth of the suffering that it has caused in order that I may record it some day in the sequel to *T. of Y.* — "Testament of Experience".

After usual housework, spent morning & afternoon on letters, one to Margaret S.J. who asked in a note this morning whether my book was in the U.S. best-seller list yet. Actually, a copy of the *Herald Tribune* for March 9th showed it half way up the non-fiction best-sellers.

Sunday April 13th
Easter Sunday. Usual housework in morning. When it was done, wrote to John & Shirley, telling John that by my new Will I shall appoint him my Literary Executor from the time he is 21, if need be.

Max got me together a box of vegetables, including leeks & onions, to send to Mother in Cornwall. Went for a walk after lunch but it had blown up cold; came back to garden & at Max's invitation picked daffodils in bud & forsythia to take back to London.

German 'planes over this part of Essex this morning, & guns firing.

Monday April 14th   London
Returned from Langham by 9.37 train. Many people about at Liverpool St. & in Piccadilly; most of them seemed to be keeping Bank Holiday as usual.

At flat found cable from the Toronto *Star Weekly* asking for articles on bombed cities & England's children; also cable from American Friends' Service Committee requesting me to speak at Summer Institutes.

Took Mother's box of vegetables to Paddington after lunch; then started on letters. Expected G. about 5.30, but he did not arrive till nearly 9.0. Said Warburg had turned down his Federal Union book despite contract; we discussed ways & means of getting it published.

Beautiful evening; vivid sunset just before he came, reflected in blunt noses of barrage balloons, made their tips glow like fire opals all over the sky. They really did resemble jewels, as Villard said — or perhaps even more silver fish floating in mid-air gradually shading into iridescent goldfish. Beautiful moon but no raid.

Tuesday April 15th
Worked most of day on Fortnightly Letter No. 54, on Virginia Woolf. (I had a very sad letter about her yesterday from Dame Ethel Smyth, to whom I wrote; promised to go down soon & see her at Woking.) After

lunch dropped in to Macmillan's office to see proof of half-page advt. of American reviews wh. they are putting for me into *T. of T.* & *Spectator*. Went on to Friends' House for a small group meeting on India arranged by Agatha Harrison & addressed by Arthur Moore, Editor of the Calcutta *Statesman*. G. put in for reservation for passage to America in Sept. for both of us in hope that H.O. *may* reverse decision.

News nearly all bad. Libyan campaign reversed; Germans over Egyptian frontier tho' Tobruk still holding out. News of Balkans confused. "Leaders" in both *Evening News* & *Standard* striking same kind of note as at time of collapse of France last summer. Another fine evening; raid warning at 11 p.m., noisy guns for a time. Alert not till about 4.30. Little sleep.

Thursday April 17th
Raid which began at 9.0 last night turned into the war's heaviest Blitz on London. Hundreds of 'planes were over us, & dropped bombs every few seconds all round London but chiefly on the West End areas — retaliation for our raids on Berlin's centre & Unter den Linden on Wednesday last week. It was worse than the raids of Sept. 7th–8th, tho' being with G. & the people from these flats I minded less than when I was crammed with Mother & the two maids into the little basement of Edwardes Square. In fact I can't say I really minded at all; there were hours between 12.0 & 4.0 when I accepted the fact that we might not live through the night, yet I felt entirely detached & perhaps rather dazed — almost as if I were looking on at someone else's affair. When the bombs came near, this whole building rocked like a ship at sea.

Eventually we went down to the basement shelter & found that nearly everyone else had done likewise. It was less noisy down there, but we felt the shudders of the earth from the dropping bombs & heard glass falling all round. The mixed collection of foreigners & English people behaved very well. No one screamed or even murmured. The Naval officer who is Warden here kept going round. At last, after what seemed an eternity, the All Clear went at 5 a.m. — after 8 solid hours of it.

Went up to the flat & heard what I thought was heavy rain. Put out light, pulled back black-out; saw what I had thought to be rain was a broken water main pouring down the road. The bright half moon still shone — & suddenly, away to the left, I saw the sky bright from innumerable fires & buildings. It looked as if all St James's & Whitehall were burning.

I got G. up from the basement, & we both dressed quickly & went out. Piccadilly had had the worst of the Blitz & was indescribable; we walked ankle deep in glass, bricks & mud, & had to walk through piles of debris. Went to see if Prof. Allan Nevins was all right at the Athenaeum Club, but found later he had spent night at B.B.C. Walked all over West End & centre; saw Charing Cross Hotel burning from the top, Christies' on fire all over (Spink's next door was saved just in time by the arrival of the fire engine), Fortnum & Mason's burning from the top, 3 huge crumps in Piccadilly roadway, a landmine fallen into crater opposite St James's Church. Hardly a building in Piccadilly was undamaged. Air smelt of burning wood & broken gas mains. Clouds of smoke everywhere. Part of Admiralty Arch knocked off. Had some coffee & porridge at Lyons wh. had been crowded all night (in Coventry St.). Glass, bits of buildings & burning wood showering down all over; walked in middle of street. Prof. Nevins came to breakfast; talked eagerly of British courage & American support for us.

Later we went to Chelsea to see if our house was still there & found the district terribly damaged. Heaps of debris all over in familiar streets. House alright except that bomb on roof across road had blown in whole of one nursery window — not only glass & wood, but brickwork as well. Had fallen as a solid mass into nursery, yet only one pane was damaged & other window intact. Walked further along Embankment & saw a terrible sight. Chelsea Old Church, that lovely landmark, had been completely demolished; it had fallen in on itself & was quite unrecognisable; also many surrounding houses had gone & Crosby Hall was badly damaged. Heard later that 5 fire-watchers were killed there.

Later went on to a meeting of the Nat. Peace Council, held at P.P.U. bec. Friends' House was damaged. Stuart Morris v. tired, had been out in Blitz picking up corpses on stretchers. Joined in this by various soldiers & sailors, brought back one sailor for a drink of lime juice who was much astonished to learn where he was. Went to bed early. Couldn't get anyone on telephone all day, as in September. Two short Alerts during night but slept too deeply to be much disturbed by either.

Saturday April 19th
Had sandwich luncheon party in flat to discuss educational development of community idea. Those who came were John Middleton Murry, Richard Murry his brother, Mary Gamble, the Plowmans, Wilfred Wellock, &, very late, Pilgrim Francis [Roberts]. Richard Ward also there. Satisfactory talk; then we all departed, except G., to go to the Annual General Meeting of the P.P.U. & listen to reports & criticisms of them.

Very noisy raid started again just before 9.30; early bombs shook this place & we heard one whistle loudly as it came down quite close. Another very near shook flats, as last Wednesday. Raid still in progress at midnight. Went on till 5.0 as before. Slept on floor at back of room with head under table.

Sunday April 20th
In morning saw soldiers digging for time bomb just inside Park railings exactly opposite our window. Had slept latter part of night quite calmly with it there. Must have been the one which screamed down & we never heard go off. Learnt from papers & wireless that raid had been only a little

less heavy than Wednesday's but had been on the East End & docks again—hence less noisy with us, though bad enough.

Back to P.P.U. Annual General Meeting for most of day. Usual division in speeches (including their own) between John Middleton Murry's philosophical policy & Roy Walker's activist one. At end, proposed a resolution supporting Bishop of Chichester's letter in *Times* last Thursday advocating offer by British Govt. to abolish night bombing if German Govt. would do the same. To my surprise got it over with only 7 dissentients by advocating importance of supporting Church when it *did* do something decent, & by mentioning that reprisal raids on Berlin arranged by Govt. officials occupying safe shelters or going every night to country came back as further reprisals on heads of people in Bermondsey & Bow. Bermondsey delegate seconded.

Worse news from Greece. Greek capitulation probable. No raid on London.

Monday April 21st   Langham

W.E.G. came & I dictated letters all morning. Then rushed out to Manfield's to get long-needed new shoes. Coming back along Conduit Street, saw plaque perched on pile of debris: "George Canning (dates) lived here". Remarked to woman who said it was terrible, that Canning could hardly have foreseen what would happen to his house. Woman welcomed idea of reprisals on Berlin & we got into an argument wh. made me late.

At flat found Sir William Rothenstein, invited to lunch, already there. Strange, ugly, intelligent little monkey of a man in blue Air Force uniform. Present job is largely going round aerodromes as official artist, painting them & their personnel. He said he would be glad to paint my portrait—later suggested 100-guinea fee wh. though not much for him is a bit stiff for us, but G. is determined to have it done & hopes Mother will help. Rothenstein wants me to spend a few days at his place in the Cotswolds so that he can paint me at his own studio.

Hastily packed when he had left, but owing to masses of debris & detours similar to those of last Sept. caused by last week's raids, we missed the train to Colchester for Langham. Took nearly 3 hours to reach Colchester. Went via Gilea Park & Shenstone, changing at both, instead of usual route. First part of line like going through a devastated city. Everything not Blitzed before seemed to be Blitzed now. In one place a flour mill had been bombed & the flour scattered over the surrounding area, covering everything with a greyish white mud.

Tuesday April 22nd

Worked most of day on Aberystwyth oration. G. went around the place on his own & helped in various ways. In afternoon walked as far as Langham Church but couldn't get in. Saw view of Stour Valley that Constable painted.

Wednesday April 23rd
Langham. Finished preparing Aberystwyth Oration. Walked with G. in afternoon to Valley of Stour. By stream found pumping station guarded by only 2 workmen rolling lawn!

Gloomy news; Greek capitulation; King gone to Crete; our own forces fighting rearguard action.

Thursday April 24th   Shrewsbury
Took the early train from Colchester which gave me 1½ hours to get the 11.5 for Aberystwyth. But owing to further damage on line (one rumour said due to exploding of a time bomb, another that 17 trucks fell over in the night) I missed train, as we had to go round Chigwell loop.

Found Paddington badly damaged by bomb wh. wrecked restaurant & waiting room on Platform 1 on Wednesday night last week, filling Station approach with debris. 14 killed. Another bomb destroyed 3 houses in Bishop's Rd, including the Y.M.C.A. hostel.

Friday April 25th   Aberystwyth
Caught 10.35 train from Shrewsbury on to Aberystwyth. Beautiful bright day though cold. Slow journey through Wales, but enjoyed the beauty of the late spring. Railway banks covered with primroses, anemones & celandines. Going into this unbombed, unimpaired country from England was like entering another world.

At Aberystwyth the Anglo-Greek girl research student in psychology, Helle Georgiadis, who had arranged for me to give the Oration to University College, London, met me with a fellow student, Jean Ross. Went with the two girls for short walk along the sunny front; then changed, had tea, & met the Provost, Sir Allen Maner.

At 6.0, after a speech by Sir Allen commemorating members of the College who had died during the year, I gave the Foundation annual Oration on "The Shape of the Future". The hall was crowded with students from London, & Wales; also cadets from the Army & R.A.F. (a purely voluntary attendance). They listened attentively, without shuffling, & hardly anyone left, which showed their interest, but though everyone seemed pleased afterwards I did not feel it was one of my best speeches; there was too large a space between the platform & the audience for easy contact. Going back, the students told me that my predecessors as Foundation Orator had been Lord Cecil, Dean Inge & Anthony Eden. I was the first woman to be invited.

After sherry we went on to a town café (all hotels crowded with Army, R.A.F. & University) for a dinner where I sat next the Provost & talked to him. Prof. John MacMurray, with whom I had a short conversation, also there. Helle Georgiadis told me I had "said so much more" than Anthony Eden, who was "woolly".

Saturday April 26th   London

Took the 10.5 back to London. Cold, bright, windy day. The Welsh country looked beautiful in the clear sunshine. Found something almost too poignant for endurance at this time in the lambs leaping in the meadows, the late buds, the blue ruffled streams, the herons & wild swans, the tall green & brown hills, the flowering blackthorn, palms, & gorse. Passing lovely little secure tranquil places such as Borth, Yorys-las & Glondyfi, felt a cowardly longing to retire there for the duration & write. News as usual as bad as it can be; "Empire forces" still retiring in Greece, & Germans down to Corinth.

Got back to London for late dinner-time. Usual mass of mail. Saw on posters that we had raided Berlin again.

Sunday April 27th

After lunch took 25 bus to Bow (as railway out of action) & went to Kingsley Hall. Found yet more damage, espec. at Hell's Corner, where the school used as a fire station was demolished by a direct hit yesterday week, killing all the members of the Beckenham A.F.S. which had just arrived (about 17 of them) to help with the East End fires. They had a mass funeral yesterday, but found the last of them (headless) last night.

I had had a cowardly shrinking of the soul in going to spend the night there, as I felt certain that being Sunday we should get a reprisal raid for Berlin. Gave the discussion group my talk on "Methods of Expression in Wartime", wh. seemed to interest them; then had tea & talked to a pacifist unit group from Hounslow, working from Trinity Hall. About 8.30 started out with Dorothy Hogg visiting shelters & helping with services there. Shelters much fuller since recent Blitzes. As we walked, darkness came on; between the grotesque skeletons of wrecked buildings in twilight, had sense of being back in Verdun or Peronne during the last war.

At 9 a.m. Churchill made a wireless speech on the situation, especially in the Mediterranean; we had to get on with our job & couldn't listen, but we heard fragments of it coming out of the little houses that still had wireless sets. Spent the night at the Children's House in bed put for me in a study. To our surprise no Blitz, not even an Alert. Slept soundly.

Monday April 28th

After breakfast Patrick Figgis read prayers in a little ante-room off the mission hall, which is still unusable owing to demolished doors & windows. As we knelt I looked up & saw a copper vase filled with double white jonquils standing on the ledge in front of the cracked window panes. Thought as so often: "Even Hitler cannot stop the spring". Queer how much flowers mean in this damaged city — the daffodils blooming near bomb-craters in the Parks, the magnolia trees in flower in the debris-filled gardens of abandoned houses in Kensington & Chelsea. The jonquils, in the house where Gandhi stayed, were a reminder that life springs eternal from death, hope from catastrophe.

Wednesday April 30th   Birmingham
Went to Birmingham by the 2.10 for lectures at Friends' House for the W.I.L. on India, & at Bournville Works.

Stuart Morris had telegraphed me earlier in the day asking if I would give him a message for his campaign as a pacifist in the King's Norton by-election. In addition to Peto, the Govt. candidate, there is now a "bomb Berlin" candidate too. One of the Birmingham papers had a cartoon about what it calls the two "freak" candidates. Many members of the W.I.L. had wanted me to stand — but I wouldn't have.

My fellow speaker at the India meeting was Krishna Menon, who was moderate for him. Good audience — much better than the London one.

Thursday May 1st
Driven over to Coventry. Recent Blitz did not appear to have altered what I found on my first visit except that same sort of damage was more extensive, & more houses & factories gone. Cathedral ruins tidied up; was able to go inside as bricks all swept into heaps round edges. Charred & twisted wooden cross still stood, a grotesque travesty, before where the altar had been. The Guildhall still stood tho' it lost its roof in the recent Blitz. Officials there said that the two nights together were not so bad as the first big raid.

Got back for lunch; spent afternoon walking round the Cadburys' lovely garden — filled with daffodils, primroses & rare rock plants round a pool on the lawn. After tea the chauffeur took me to Bournville where I lectured on "The Future", to a very keen picked group of Cadbury's women workers in an atmosphere pervaded with the warm smell of chocolate. They seemed familiar with my book & brought several to be signed. At 9.0 listened to 3 accounts of the Greek evacuation, on the wireless. An Alert sounded about 11.0; several Nazi planes over but no bombs.

Friday May 2nd   London
Back from Birmingham by 9.0 o'clock train. Had conversation on it, with Donald Soper, who had been lecturing in B'm at some Methodist function. He gave me coffee in the restaurant. We discussed the P.P.U. & Stuart Morris's election campaign at King's Norton, which Soper thought a mistake. He is now living at Kingsway Hall, wh. is a rest centre. His wife & 2 boys are in Lincoln. He said they were suddenly machine-gunned one day by a Nazi 'plane on a station, but not much upset by it.

This afternoon went to Peter Jones & dictated letters. Then on an impulse walked round Chelsea & was made so sad by all the smashes that I felt I never wanted to live there again. Land mines have destroyed a block of flats facing Burton Court & the little new houses, Cheyne Place, in

Royal Hospital Rd., which hardly has a sound house. The little green & white house at the corner of Swan Walk & Royal Hosp. Road is wrecked, also the Victoria Hosp. for Children in Tite Street where Baba had her operation just before Hitler marched into Prague. Our house still serene; brought some branches from the garden back to the flat.

Saturday May 3rd
News of a rising against us in Iraq under Axis-dominated Premier, Rashid Ali. Query: Did we or did we not break our treaty with Iraq wh. according to a hurried reading appears to allow us to take troops through, but not to leave them there? Also query: Will the Arabs in Palestine take the opportunity to rise against the Jews?

Worked hard all morning & most of afternoon on letters & review of Housman's book *The Preparation of Peace* for *Peace News*.

Colonel Josiah Wedgwood & Mrs Wedgwood came to dinner; we took them to Shepherd's. The Colonel tho' in his 70th year has grown a moustache & looks 10 years younger. He is going to U.S.A. by *boat* on Tuesday, & we discussed mainly this. He wrote to Churchill & hence had no difficulty about fixing it all up through the M. of I. Jos. Wedgwood poured scorn on the Home Office's attitude towards me & said he would speak to Halifax.

Sunday May 4th   Langham
Last night third of three heavy raids on Merseyside; same method apparently being adopted as at Plymouth, which has had 5 major raids in 9 nights, reducing much of the city to rubble.

Went off by 10.0 train to Colchester for a management committee of the Community Centre (on which I have just been put) at 3.0. G. going later to Oxford, then Sheffield (Monday), then Manchester.

Train to Colchester unimpaired this time but slow. Beautiful day; country looked perfectly lovely in what was really early morning as we changed to yet another "summer-time" hour last night — which was a short one for me as there was a raid (apparently reconaissance as I heard no bombs) in which raiders dropped flares.

Committee meeting in garden under trees. Garden in first day of warm spring sunshine so lovely as to be almost heartbreaking. Shrubs all coming out; one budding Japanese sycamore with pale flamingo-coloured leaves looking like a Japanese print against the blue sky. Daffodils fading but lawns pied with daisies; coloured primroses & blossoms everywhere.

Listened to news with Plowmans at 9.0 & went to bed early. Many 'planes over & a good deal of gunfire — also it seemed by shaking of windows that some bombs were dropped not far away. Nothing new on News, but an appalling post-script by Mr Menzies, the P.M. of Australia, who has just left, giving an "appreciation" of English women whose terms would have been old-fashioned in the last war.

Monday May 5th   London

Returned from Langham by 9.37 train. Had hair "permed" at Marshall's by an assistant called "George" — some kind of naturalised foreigner whom I should judge to be an ex-Italian. Didn't much like him (tho' not for this reason) but there is no choice nowadays.

In flat alone as G. absent. An Alert went about midnight; All Clear about $\frac{1}{2}$ hr. afterwards. Bright moon, clear sky but no further trouble. Went to bed about 2.0.

Tuesday May 6th   Bath

Got the 1.55 from Paddington for Bath. Driven to Friends' House, where I spoke to a crowded public meeting on "The Shape of the Future". Meeting enthusiastic despite usual proportion of dissentients. Rather a sub-enthusiastic Chairman — a schoolmaster — who added to my usual doubt whether public meetings are worthwhile just now.

Wednesday May 7th

Breakfast in bed kindly given me by Mrs Mottram. Dressed & went down to town (long pleasant walk downhill in cold sunshine). I learnt a good deal about Bath, which seems to be as typical as any spa could be of reception towns taking the war comfortably. It had about 60,000 inhabitants before war; now has between 80,000 & 90,000. Many people from Bristol here, & others still living there come over to do their shopping owing to Bristol's loss of shops. Bath dominated by Admiralty (Naval staff & civil service) who swank. Preface orders in shops or restaurants with remark: "I'm Admiralty" — much to annoyance of normal residents, of whom many have left. Others were turned out of hotels in wh. they had lived for years when Admiralty took them over. Restt. was crowded. Tables have to be reserved for lunch if any hope of service. Ample choice of food. Prices higher than London. Tables so crowded that 2 women shared ours. One, elderly, with saggy discontented face, complained because just what she wanted was not there. "What, no lamb! You don't mean to say the lamb's finished! I can't stand these made-up dishes!"

After lunch took bus to Bristol; met there by a charming young P.P.U. girl, Kathleen Tucker. Had tea with Kathleen & Eric Tucker at their house on the edge of a housing estate wh. got the force of the Good Friday Blitz. The taxi-driver who drove us lived there too; he acted as assistant to an undertaker in his spare time & did a good deal of digging people out — talked of one street where he found "27 bodies & 5 sackfulls of human remains". Smokes a pipe while working. Both the taxi-driver & K.T. told me of Churchill's reception here. He did not really come bec. Bristol was bombed but to the Univ. to get an hon. degree with Winant the U.S. Ambassador. When they realised the Blitz was on, his train was stopped outside Bristol at 5 a.m. & he was taken in when the Blitz was over. Went straight to Grand Hotel & had a slap-up breakfast when many people in

Bristol were homeless & hungry. Local paper made a good deal of this. When Churchill got to the housing estate where the bombs had just fallen, he was met by an angry procession with a placard: "We're tired of Churchill & his cigar. Give us peace." It had to be put down by police. Taxi-driver said you don't feel patriotic after being bombed.

After tea the Tuckers took me to Friends' Hall, where we had a v. good meeting, lasting till 8.0 — a big group meeting. Then I got a 9.0 train back to Bath.

Later heard guns in distance & learnt that Bristol did have a Blitz tho' not a big one. Main attack on Clydeside and Merseyside again.

Thursday May 8th   Chalford

Very cold. After a tedious journey via Mangotsfield and Gloucester, reached Chalford & was met by Sir William Rothenstein, to stay 3 days for my portrait. Driven to his charming grey house Far Oakridge, overlooking a beautiful valley & wood of spring trees. Was given a pleasant bed-sitting room through the dining-room with a wood fire. After dinner sat over sitting-room fire talking & looking at Sir W. R.'s drawings.

Friday May 9th

Sir W. R. started the portrait with trying to find a satisfactory pose & doing preliminary drawings. House v. cold as weather like Feb. & food somewhat scarce. Old man obviously a skinflint domestically tho' generous in his charges as an artist. Between paintings he took me for one or two walks, espec. into valley just below where Sir Stafford Cripps has just built a new house. Fields & lanes full of primroses, anemones, cowslips & bluebells. John Rothenstein turned up at tea-time from Upton-on-Severn to wh. the Tate Gallery wh. he directs is evacuated.

Saturday May 10th

In morning Sir W. R. at last did a drawing that satisfied him. G. turned up about tea-time from lecturing to troops in Manchester. Had a Blitz there (Old Trafford & Eccles) on Wednesday night. The Rothensteins all took to him, espec. John, who is a Fed. Union enthusiast, having been at Pittsburgh & Lexington University.

Sunday May 11th   London

Woke up to lovely morning — first warm day in Cotswolds. Rumours from morning wireless spoke of another big raid on London last night.

Sir William painted me again in morning. After lunch (less meagre than usual) we all talked over coffee in the garden, & then G. & I wandered with John Rothenstein through an exquisite spring field filled with cowslips & talked of his & G.'s ideas of the outcome of the War & the hope of some form of Fed. Union as a solution.

Got a late afternoon train direct from Chalford to Paddington. Train was hardly late & ran into station without much delay though we passed several Blitzed coaches on the line. But as soon as we drove through the streets we noticed signs (as the Cotswolds air-raid warden had warned Sir William & me during our walk) of another really big raid. Two huge craters in Park Lane roadway near the Dorchester had blown in windows & doors of houses between Dorchester & Piccadilly. Flats still undamaged, but Mac. the valet told us it was as bad as the Wed. raid.

Three Alerts during Sun. night, so not much sleep.

Monday May 12th

G. left early for King's Cross to lecture at Middlesbrough. Went out to dictate letters at Peter Jones, & visit Bank, & saw everywhere evidences of Saturday's heavy raid. All the windows were blown out of St George's Hospital, & next after a few houses by Hyde Park Corner station came the Alexandra Hotel where the bomb, destroying the roof, fell through & exploded in the basement, killing or trapping the people sheltering there. It was a grim sight, as the tree in the Park opposite was covered with tattered garments blown from the windows of the hotel & hanging from the branches — scarves, pullovers, socks. Torn papers & bits of stone from the hotel were scattered in the Park itself. All day the rescue squad ambulance was in front of this building & also before a big crash in Clarges Street where two or three houses went down. As always after a big raid in dry weather, the air was full of dust & bits of debris, particularly near the damage. In Sloane St., saw that Holy Trinity had lost its roof. Found Chelsea had not suffered this time.

Later, after working on huge mail till tea, came back from Macmillan's where I had to sign a book, via Westminster, & saw the scarred & blackened face of Big Ben — still telling the time on all its clock faces despite large gash on the one facing Victoria St. Noticed also the smashed roof of Westminster Hall with Cromwell's statue still unharmed & imperturbable before it. Everywhere in Victoria St. were long queues waiting for buses, as all rail transport was again upset. Walked all the way back to flat.

Stuart Morris came to supper, which we had at the Berkeley Buttery to get privacy. We talked about his election, & laid plans for the implementing of my A.G.M. resolution about night bombing, by the Council. Stuart had had magnificient meetings; told his supporters to ponder the significance of the Cross they put on their voting papers. He also told me (not on first hand authority) that during Sat. night's raid the Dean of Westminster sent for Churchill, showed him damage to Abbey & said: "Where is all this going to end?"

Alert just before midnight; not over till 3 a.m.

Late letter from George Brett indicated failure of his efforts to persuade our Embassy at Washington to let me do a lecture tour.

Tuesday May 13th

Much excitement because morning papers record escape by 'plane of Rudolf Hess, Hitler's deputy, from Nazi Germany; landed unarmed near Glasgow on Saturday night.

Letters & telephone calls all morning. Arranged to do another article for *D. Herald*, on "Shall We Learn from our Second Lesson?" (chances of spiritual revival after this war cf. with last).

At 2.0 went to Reading for a P.P.U. meeting at the University. Good meeting of students in a lecture-room; spoke to about 100 on "The Future".

Wednesday May 14th   Dagenham

Drafted *Daily Herald* article. After tea went to address Annual Meeting at Kingsley Hall, Dagenham (large housing estate near Ford's Works). Muriel Lester started Settlement because workers at first so isolated. Still (after 20 years) not many amenities in shape of shops, cinemas etc. Spoke on "The Future" to crowded meeting. Long & tiring question period. Went to bed soon after (after signing several books). Quiet night; no siren or bombs.

Thursday May 15th   London

Gruesome-looking damage now in areas off Strand, round Covent Garden. Found Odham's Press much bricked-in on the outside corridor — but inside where works & store-rooms must have been was nothing but an open arena of wreckage — the usual twisted remnants of gardens all mixed up with charred or saturated paper machine-rolls & large dumps of flat paper equally spoiled.

Decided after long discussion with G. to leave Margaret S.J. out of my Will altogether except for small legacy, owing to complete lack of sympathy shown in recent letter. Don't want someone who disagrees with my views on most vital points to be in charge of either children or books.

Friday May 16th

Finished Letter 57; wrote it most of the day after morning much interrupted by 'phone calls & correspondence. As it was a beautiful spring day, wrote in Green Park during the afternoon, sitting on a seat at edge of one of the bomb craters.

G. & I dined at Café Royal; long talk with little foreign waiter (French or Italian) describing bombs on his home, etc. Said he had presentiment about last Saturday's raid & changed his fire-watching night so as to be "at home with the missis" in a little house off Soho.

Alert about 11.30 p.m. & some heavy gunfire. Decided to get sleep if possible so went down to shelter for only 3rd time since we came to flats. Did sleep but came back before All Clear went, about 4.30. Bright waning moon.

Saturday May 17th   Oxford
Dictated some letters at Peter Jones; then long visit to bank; put in cheque from Macmillan. Also transfd. £200 of latest cheque into deposit account, & got out £150 for P.P.U. in cash.

Went on to P.P.U. Council meeting at 2.30. Usual long & rather wearisome discussion on policy after minutes taken & elections made (I was re-elected to the Executive). But some interesting introductory speeches by Bill Grindlay, Alex Miller, J. Middleton Murry, Max Plowman & Andrew Stewart; also a poor one by Roy Walker. After the tea interval brought up questn. of my resolution supporting the Bp. of Chichester's letter & got it referred to the Exec. for further action.

Got 7.40 train to Oxford to spend night there with G. who had gone to a Fed. Union Research Institute Conference. Lovely to get an evening hour in Oxford; city sweet with blossom. Spent night at queer little pub called Castle Hotel near Station. Siren in night v. loud — but All Clear soon after.

Sunday May 18th   London
Got early train back to London to go on attending Council. Sunday papers full of speculations about Hess, who has now been "faded off" the front page of the daily papers.

Had very belated breakfast at the Paddington Hotel & went on to Council. We spent rest of day till 4.0 discussing report of the "Developt. Committee" to allocate 25% of the diminishing income to area developt. & adjourned the matter in the end for further discussion — also I proposed a fundamental discussion by the next Executive of the Women's Committee, raised by D. Evans & S. Morrison.

Took taxi to Bow to get there in time for their 6 p.m. Memorial Service to their treasurer Ben Platten, who was killed yesterday week while doing a fire-watching job. It was all espec. tragic as Ben (the *D. Herald* Chief Account.) was only relieving a friend for the night & was killed by one of our own shells. His legs were blown off & two woman ambulance drivers killed with him. His wife, a First Aid worker, in the local hosp., found his dead body behind a screen while attending other patients before anyone told her he was dead. She went straight out into Epping Forest & was there all night among the bombs. Ben's ashes were in the urn in the little chapel & lovely flowers before them.

Monday May 19th
Letters all morning; then walked up Bond St. to do small amount of shopping & found huge smash of last Saturday had brought down whole corner of Bond St. & Bruton St. where Speight's was. Even pedestrians couldn't get through so I turned off into Savile Row & found most of that gone too. Back into Bond St. via Conduit St. wh. is also now mostly rubble. Even the most familiar streets are ceasing to be recognisable; I keep saying to myself: "What *was* this?" & forgetting what was there. Struck again by

the usual incongruity of Western Front ruin & almost next door beautiful
flowers & smart hats in the still standing Bond St. shops. I thought nothing
could be worse than the *acres* of ruin wh. I passed in the taxi & on the top of
the bus coming back from Bow yesterday (I found Bow Church reduced to
rubble as Dorothy said), but this bit of the West End rivals them. Finally
arrived at Spiller's in Wigmore St. to have my glasses re-screwed, & found
that their premises too had been wrecked at the back by incendiaries &
high explosives, & my usual man & his typist were carrying on behind
boarded up doors in a shop wh. looked as though it were only held together
with string. But they took my glasses for repair. Query: What is the effect
on one's mind of constantly walking about amid the utter ruins of lovely or
familiar things?

Tuesday May 20th
Saw Jennie Adamson M.P. by appointment at the Ministry of Pensions
where she is P.P.S. to Sir Walter Wormsley — & got material for the
Toronto *Star Weekly* for my article on "Orphans of the Blitz" to whom she
is official "foster-mother". She was spruce, direct & friendly as ever. I
gathered I was privileged in getting the interview wh. many newspapers
demand & can't get. She gave me a very interesting account of her own life
— the total family record must be one of the most remarkable in the
country.

   Back to flat in time to give a cocktail to Mary Adams (Mrs Vyvyan
Adams) who had telephoned offering to give me information about the
Home Office attitude towards myself. When she came she explained her
new readiness to help by telling us that she has now resigned from the M. of
I. owing to the constant hampering of its work & refusal to accept
suggestions of criticisms by older departments. She told me that the
opponent of my going to U.S.A. is really Peake, not Morrison, & that the
real snag is my membership of the P.P.U. & possible questions in the
House — not, as Margaret S.J. thought, my Circular Letter or anything I
write. She agreed, however, that no person of integrity could give up their
convictions & activities for the sake of personal interest. We discussed
possible methods of getting over the difficulty & she said she would try to
arrange for me to see Peake.

Wednesday May 21st   Swindon
Finished 3,000 word article for Toronto *Star Weekly*, typed it & sent copy
off to Jennie Adamson to look over, as promised. Final copy of my Will
came for engrossment. Felt great relief at now having desired arrangements for children in legal form.

   Got 5.12 train to Swindon for a P.P.U. group meeting; arrived a little
late thanks to an oil train (wh. we passed later) being on the line, so was
obliged to go straight to meeting & speak. Good sympathetic crowd (abt.
180) & some useful questions.

Thursday May 22nd   Chalford

Had not to leave for Chalford till 11.25, so had a late breakfast & talked to Mrs McKinley about her work for evacuees at the local Friends' House. Swindon had only had 2 lots of bombs since the Blitz began & is now so full of evacuees & extra Great Western workers that it has been made by Act of Parlt. one of the "closed towns" where no one not normally resident there can stay for more than 3 days without special permission.

Day less hot & sunny than yesterday but countryside beautiful — new leaves out everywhere & fields filled with buttercups & cowslips. Met at Chalford by car. Sat in afternoon to Sir Wm. Rothenstein to usual sound of aeroplanes perpetually flying overhead from the many aerodromes near. Wireless news from Crete sounded menacing in evening; intimation that we have withdrawn our air force from airfields there means that the Imperial troops will be completely at mercy of the Luftwaffe & that the island must fall to the Germans sooner or later. Sir Wm. told me that Jan Masaryk of Cz. himself told him that at time of Munich he had been obliged to advise Chamberlain to "sell" the Czechs owing to our lack of preparation.

No enemy activity on country during night.

Sunday May 25th   Langham

Spent Sunday at Langham. Cold rainy day. Max ill with severe gastric chill. Started article on London Missions. After lunch saw the Adelphi Players, directed by Richard Ward, act 3 of the *Little Plays of St Francis* very well indeed.

News of the sinking of HMS *Hood* in a battle with the *Bismarck* off Greenland (sunk by a shell fired from 13 miles away).

Monday May 26th   London

Back from Langham by 8.15 a.m. train. W. Eden-Green came & I dictated letters. Began to feel mouldy & suspected I had caught milder variety of chill which laid Max Plowman low over week-end. But according to schedule spent evening in Stepney. Visited first the temp. Friends' Institute at Ratcliffe; then walked for miles round Wapping & Shadwell on the river bank opposite Bermondsey & Rotherhithe.

Tuesday May 27th

Still feeling sub. Couldn't get much done in morning. 2 p.m., P.P.U. Executive, at which I (a) outlined possibilities of campaign against night-bombing of civilians & was supported by J. Middleton Murry & Literature Committee who are reproducing Max Plowman's *Adelphi* article "Bomb the Bishop"; (b) got position of Women's Committee, which I have always opposed as typifying an out-of-date type of feminism, defined & finally wound up. I was supported by Mary Gamble & Nancy Browne.

Tea at Euston Hotel; then spent evening in Bethnal Green & Hoxton visiting the Quaker Bedford Institutes there.

Sinking of the *Bismarck* reported in evening papers.

Wednesday May 28th

4.30 a.m., Roosevelt speech declaring unlimited national emergency in U.S.A.

Gastric chill persisting; felt too mouldy to eat anything worth mentioning all day. But went with G. to his Federal Union Luncheon at Gunter's off Park Lane. Speakers were Prof. Newall (who treated Fed. Union as though it meant an Anglo-American War Alliance), & Mackay, who made an excellent forward-looking speech. Sir Wm. Beveridge, in the chair, was poor, & talked a good deal of wishful-thinking stuff about what we wouldn't & would permit the Germans to do after the War.

At 6.30 went to Walthamstow to look over the Educational Settlement for my Bedford Institute report. Spent about 3 hours seeing dressmaking, art, Esperanto & other classes. V. tired. Got back about 10.30.

Thursday May 29th

Stayed in bed all day to get better of gastric chill. Dull & rainy. Miss Lemon came in afternoon to take down letters.

Increasingly bad news of fighting in Crete. Canea reported taken. German parachutists with green-painted faces landing in thousands. 20,000 said to have been killed & 10,000 drowned trying to land by sea. Max Schmeling, the champion boxer who was among them, was killed. More Germans attacking Egypt.

Proofs of G.'s book *One Anglo-American Nation* arrived from Andrew Dakers.

Sunday June 1st

Pleasant warm Sunday. No raid. Walked with G. in Green & St James's Parks. Plenty of people doing the same — staying put. Beautiful flower beds in St James's Park now almost on edge of bomb craters, but still cultivated. Saw various Govt. officials, including Zilliacus, in Park.

Monday June 2nd

Evacuation of Crete reported in morning papers.

Went to Labour Party Conference in afternoon. Heard a discussion, which was, in effect, a row over the disaffiliation of the King's Norton Labour Party wh. refused to support any of the candidates in the recent election — including the Govt. candidate, thus breaking the party truce.

Quiet Whit Monday in London. City seemed full, but no crowds.

Tuesday June 3rd   Chalford

Attended Labour Party Conference in morning. Rhys Davies had evidently made a pacifist speech before I came, & I heard violent criticisms of it by Ben Tillett. Memorandum criticised by Richard Stokes M.P. & Davies of Leek. Philip Noel-Baker replied for the Executive & the gathering of yes-men voted for the Memorandum with the huge majority that one would expect.

Went down to Chalford by 6.30 train for two more sittings to Sir Wm. Rothenstein.

Wednesday June 4th

Sat to Sir William all morning. Portrait making real progress towards a likeness. He told me Hugh Walpole had stayed here and they liked him tho' they had never read or owned any of his books. Sir Wm. also thought the Obituary of him in *The Times* a mean attack. Priestley wrote protesting against it to-day.

Motored into Cirencester with Sir Wm., who was visiting an aerodrome 2 miles beyond, & visited the lovely parish church of St John the Baptist. Perfect afternoon. Churchyard typical of poignant mingling of war & spring. Copper beeches glowed red brown in sun, lilacs just flowering. But the two largest stained glass windows in the church were boarded up, looking like blind eyes, & the sky was filled with the uneasy sound of brown bombers like huge malignant beetles flying overhead. The grass near the church was cut, though pied with daisies, but the far end of the churchyard was left to riot, & tombstones 100 years old were gradually being submerged by a rising sea of grass, cow parsley and dandelion clocks, with tulips & a few late bluebells struggling to survive amid the tangle. The lacy shadows of the trees were flung by the sunlight across the tombs & white butterflies danced in the air.

Death of ex-Kaiser announced on wireless.

Thursday June 5th   London

Had a sitting with Sir Wm. and got midday train back to town.

Got in to find G. out & a mass of letters — two from Ruth, one from John & some drawings. Opened a letter in a hand I didn't recognise & found it was from Mary Gamble saying that they were all in great distress because Max was taken ill again suddenly on Monday & died on Tuesday afternoon — of pneumonia. Felt dazed & overwhelmed myself — but had to pull myself together as F.W. Ogilvie and Mary came to dinner. It would have been a pleasant enough evening if I hadn't been thinking all the time about Max and the phrase: "The wind passeth over it and it is gone."

Friday June 6th

Jon Creech Jones came to lunch & we discussed the possibility of my seeing Osbert Peake through Mary Adams, & general situation re U.S. — also possibilities of jobs for G. in govt. departments.

Short glider raid; bombs dropped without an Alert at 2 a.m.

Saturday June 7th   Langham

G. & I went to Max's funeral at Langham. Travelled there by the midday Saturday train from L'pool St. with Stuart Morris, Maurice Rowntree, Frank Middleton & the Barclays. Mary Gamble met us at Colchester & drove us to Langham. It was a wonderful June day after the long cold spring, with The Oaks' garden a radiance of flowers in sunshine — lilac, laburnum, may, roses & poppies all out together. We went to the Plowmans' little cottage, where Max's coffin was laid on the floor with flowers over & around it. I added my little sheath of ophelia roses & lilies of the valley to the rest. Dorothy & Piers were both there, brave & self-contained. In the big garden various people were wandering about looking dazed & unhappy — Richard Ward, Richard Murry (J.M.M. had been down for 2 days but didn't stay for the funeral) & various old evacuees. At 3.0 a little procession of cars (Mary Gamble took us again) followed the coffin through may-scented lanes. In the beautiful church we sang "The strife is o'er, the battle [done]" (as at G.L.'s Memorial Service), the psalm "I will lift up mine eyes unto the hills", "Now thank we all our God" & listened to the lesson "I saw a new heaven & a new earth". In the churchyard where the birds were singing we stood in the long grass round the grave & saw the coffin lowered (Piers helping). Finally we sang "Jerusalem" — Piers with his arm round Dorothy. Back at Langham Dorothy said to me: "He's very much here still", & I promised to come back more than ever. Wrote some paragraphs about Max for *Peace News* while a huge lantern moon rose. But it was soon covered with clouds & we had no raid.

Sunday June 8th   Sidcot

Left Paddington with G. at 10.30. Travelled together to Bristol, where I changed & got on to the Cheddar Valley line to Winscombe for my speech to Sidcot School. Met by Mr & Mrs Hutchinson; taken for drive over Mendip Hills & through Cheddar Gorge, which reminded me of the Topley Pike & Miller's Dale district near Buxton but is still deeper. Right at bottom of gorge is the Cliff Hotel looking out on an artificial lake made by the streams from the many caves. Had tea very pleasantly with a party of assistant masters & mistresses at their house. At 7.0 came the evening meeting at Friends' House. After hymns & readings I spoke for about 20 minutes — starting about Max as a pioneer, & going on to the future — but as always with children felt I was not very successful.

Monday June 9th   St Ives

Travelled from Sidcot to St Ives. *News Chronicle*, bought at Bristol, reported landing of British, Imperial & Free French troops in Syria, wh. now looks like becoming the battlefield. Bristol–Plymouth train stopped nearly everywhere. Heard air-raid siren at Exeter. Wrote up arrears of diary in train. No restaurant car.

Had two hours to wait in Plymouth so walked round the town to see aftermath of the big Blitzes. Went down what was the street where Dingle's & Harrison's were (George St.) & found nothing but ruins. Worse than Coventry. Landmarks completely gone; only things left in centre the big red bank building (damaged) & the clock (now charred with its face bashed in) which marked centre of that once fine town. No hotels or restaurants left & very few food shops. Joined train again at North Road station (only place where any sort of food kiosk). Talked in carriage to an old man (looked like a fisherman) who came from Penzance & said it was bombed last night. G. met me at Curtin Ferry & walked with me to Idris. Walked with Mother in lane after supper.

Tuesday June 10th

Beautiful day. Country all round superb. Spring & summer flowers all out together. Hill behind Idris covered with wild rhododendrons in all shades of pink & puce, lanes filled with may, campions, late bluebells, garlic, budding foxgloves, bird's eye, Star of Bethlehem, elder coming into flower. Garden at Idris full of pinks & periwinkles. Superb scent everywhere.

Letter came from Agatha Harrison enclosing cable from President of All-India Women's [Congress] cordially inviting me to attend the Conference in December. This will re-raise whole question of my exit permit & right to leave the country. Second invitation puts me in a very strong position.

Wednesday June 11th

Dull wet day. Typed letter No. 59 in morning (comparison bet. Hugh Walpole & Max Plowman, especially as regards the subject of forgiveness, wh. Max offered as a matter of course and Walpole was never capable of).

Wrote Agatha Harrison about India — saying I thought there wasn't much hope but suggesting plans.

No special war news. Our Syrian advance continues, & usual disputes are taking place between Hitler & Vichy.

Quiet night, no Alert. Grey with rain but not dark because of concealed full moon.

Thursday June 12th

Better day — started wet, gradually cleared tho' wind cold. Started report for Quakers in morning — "The Bedford Institutes in London's Blitzkrieg". G. depressed by a non-committal letter from the Ministry of Home Security wh. did not say for certain that he would be able to get his exit permit for U.S.A. this autumn — though he had some pleasant letters from Lord Sankey & George Gibson of the TUC about the advance copies of One Anglo-American Nation. So we splurged on a bottle of wine at the café.

Sat on the shore in the sun after lunch, where I bound up the leg of a plucky little girl (about Shirley's age but dark) who had gashed her knee.

Long letter from Ruth enclosing a short one from John echoing his determination to study art by himself for the present and not have a master to impose a style on him. Ruth says he has grown 3 inches in a year — & that Shirley has grown too, & is more slender & prettier. Damn this hell war.

Spent rest of day sitting in garden writing report on Quaker Settlements & did ¾ of it.

Friday June 13th   Oxford
Two Alerts during night; noise of 'planes overhead in early morning; guns from coast sounding heavily in bright moonlight. In night had idea for a book of contemporary portraits called "The Quick & the Dead" — six living people, six dead ones.

Left Carbis Bay to go to Oxford with G. Fine day again. Walked up hill behind Idris with Mother before leaving. Guns still sounding.

Very long tedious journey to Oxford though day increasingly fine. Would have been beautiful if I could have stayed at St Ives. Reached Oxford after 8.0 & got a late dinner at the George Café. All foliage very late; may still out & laburnum in full bloom as it usually is at the beginning not the end of term. Looked over Magdalen Bridge to dark water where G. & I used to punt on summer evenings in the early days of our engagement. Life was better then — but it seems odd sometimes to have been deeply in love with two men but to have married a third who wasn't either of them.

"Alert" in night & much noise of 'planes.

Saturday June 14th
Sat in Castle Hotel all morning finishing Report on Bedford Institutes for the Quakers in the little lounge. G. & I met Frank Pakenham in the Mitre for cocktails before lunch. Told me he had written a political play wh. V.G. is probably publishing. Lunched with G. v. late at Randolph Hotel second sitting — the only place we could find as Oxford is more choc-a-bloc than ever & the food situation becoming difficult. Uneasy sound of aeroplanes overhead all the time. Trudged back to Castle Hotel & started to type report; then back to Univ: for tea with Sir W. Beveridge & Mrs Mair (reason for my visit as G. wants a job out of Beveridge thro' Greenwood). Back to Castle Hotel for more typing — then returned to 129 High St. for small dinner of O.U. Labour Club where Laski speaking. Sat by Frank Pakenham & Prof. Dodds. F.P. related to me supposed daily prayer uttered by Churchill: "O God, I thank Thee for making me P.M. I thank Thee for making me P.M. in the greatest hour in England's history; & grant that the war may last as long as I live."

Sunday June 15th   Langham
Had queer dream in night; thought someone on staff of American *Who's*

Who wrote to notify me that they were going to remove my name, as a writer whose main characteristic was her work for peace was not worth putting in just now. G. says I said in my sleep: "What's the good of living when one's so frustrated & ineffective?" But I don't feel like that by day; I just take each thing as it comes & try not to think too much about the complete shattering of my life since a year ago. And two decades ago. To-day is the 23rd anniversary of Edward's death on the Asiago Plateau. He would be 45 now. I still miss him & never more than in these days when he would have been a source of the stability & support which I can get from no one in England now.

Left Oxford at 10.30 by tedious trains (a change at Didcot) to get to Colchester for the meeting about Langham's future now that Max (another stabilising & kindly influence) is dead. Dull warm day, with flickers of sunlight. Got up to Langham in hired taxi just in time for meeting; J. Middleton Murry & others there.

Monday June 16th   London

Dorothy Plowman came up to my room before I was dressed & started talking about Max — also showed me a most pathetic letter written by Piers to his friend about how much he loved Max. Travelled back to London with J. Middleton Murry & Mary Gamble.

Back to flat to find a huge accumulation of letters — ever since last Thursday. Spent rest of day fighting my way through them. Hot lovely day, just because I am back to London from country. G. turned up from Oxford just before lunch.

News of Hitler–Soviet negotiations; Germans prevailing on Turks to sign an economic pact & preparing to put pressure on Russia.

Corrected proofs of Letter No. 59. Andrew Dakers dropped in for tea to discuss final publication with G. of *One Anglo-American Nation*. Good comments now from Sankey, Amery, Beaverbrook & Gilbert Murray.

Tuesday June 17th

Up early. Dictated letters to Miss Lemon till 10.30; then went to P.P.U. executive at 11.0. Routine business of no special interest. Back to Athenaeum Court as Rache Lovat Dickson had had to postpone our luncheon engagement to tea.

Rache described effect of paper shortage on reissue of classics (e.g. Hardy) as it isn't worth doing unless you issue 10,000 copies for a long period — but the paper now is so bad that no one would buy the particular edition after the War. We discussed my suggested volume of portraits of 6 living & 6 dead characters, but he was doubtful about my title of "The Quick & the Dead". After dinner G. & I went to Battersea to discuss with Agatha Harrison possible approaches to the India Office regarding my invitation again to the All-India Women's Conference.

Wednesday June 18th

Lunched as a Guest of Honour at Foyle's Luncheon (subject "Books & Freedom") to give publicity to the Booksellers' Provident Institution. My letter enclosing the £5 I sent in advance was read out with great approval by the President, William Longman, though without my name. J.B. Priestley spoke, beginning with the importance of salvaging all paper, & going [on] to show how much better books kept the spirit of democracy alive than newspapers, the B.B.C., or public meetings, all of which were more subject to different forms of authoritarian control. Called at American Embassy & found permit still hadn't arrived.

Thursday June 19th   Nottingham

Met at Nottingham by young Marion Cox, the P.P.U. Group secretary — a pretty, delicate-looking girl who had had a blood transfusion the day before. Coming into the station saw much evidence of the Nottingham Blitz a month ago, & again walking from it. Damage chiefly round there & in the poorer quarter of the town stretching for three miles. It didn't compare with Sheffield or Manchester, but Mrs Cox told me that 350–500 people were killed.

Crowded meeting; gave usual speech on "The Shape of the Future".

Friday June 20th   Chalford

Comfortable journey back to London in luncheon car though lunch itself is now beginning to show signs of deterioration. No sherry or gravy to be had; sausages all bread. Fortunately food doesn't interest me much, & rations less.

Found G. perturbed after interview with Harold Nicolson wh. suggested that he might not get exit permit for U.S.A. in autumn & led him reasonably to suppose that some of my pacifist pitch had spilled over on to him. He showed me a letter he had written Nicolson recapitulating his long American experience & status there, & his refusal of the 1939 offer from Cornell on Lothian's advice. Got 6.30 from Paddington for Chalford.

Saturday June 21st

Got up to beautiful day with cool breeze. Garden at Far Oakridge exquisite now; passion flowers & clematis of all kinds in bloom; honeysuckle out, roses beginning. Cotswold Valley now in full summer; all trees out, air full of meadow scents everywhere. Grass long on both lawns & fields because gardener has left. Buttercups & daisies all over lawn; powder-blue butterflies & small fritillaries flitting everywhere. Portrait good & obviously like but seems to me to get my features at their ugliest angle & my face at its thinnest. Everyone much more agreeable this time. Is it because I brought more than my rations & a bottle of sherry?

Sunday June 22nd

To my breakfast (in bed) Lily, the maid, brought a note from Lady

Rothenstein, who listens to the early morning wireless, to say that Hitler declared war on Russia at 5.30 a.m. this morning. Also reported fall of Damascus to Allied & Free French troops. Sat to Sir William in morning; another lovely day, hotter than ever. Sunday papers, wh. arrived at midday, full of speculations regarding significance of Germany's attack (put forward with all the usual propaganda excuses) & its consequences for us. It seems evident that: (a) the original Pact was a way of keeping Russia quiet when a war on two fronts might have been disastrous for Hitler; (b) fear of a stab in the back by Russia while invading us is Hitler's real reason for wishing to demolish Russia first. Russian resources probably a secondary consideration.

Sat in garden all day, trying to make this week-end a rest wh. would make me feel less tired & fitter for work. Later weather reports gave temp. to-day as 91 — the hottest June day ever recorded in England.

Tuesday June 24th   London
Went along to C.O.R.B. after easily getting certificate of evacuation of children from Cook's. She fixed everything up for me quickly, including the 66 coupons (which I am allowed for clothes for each child & of which I was the first recipient). But total value of *all* parcels sent during year, including birthday gifts, must not exceed £10 per child. Sent off Shirley's birthday present (Spanish night-dress case).

Afternoon, attended P.P.U. Committee to decide reallocation of budget & staff.

Wednesday June 25th
Took chair at W.I.L. Luncheon at Friends' House for Mme. Magda Yvois-Peters, a Belgian speaker. We discussed Cammaerts' book vindicating the King of the Belgians, of which there was a reveiw & leading article in to-day's *Times*. She fully agreed with the rightness of the King's action in saving his people.

Another lovely day. Walked back from the luncheon & spent rest of day drafting Letter No. 60, on the Russian invasion & Churchill's wireless speech. Cabled the children, as it is a year to-morrow since they sailed: "Loving thoughts on anniversary of your leaving England warmest thanks to Ruth and Woodard. Mummie, Daddy."

Thursday June 26th
12.15 midday, met Agatha Harrison, Mrs Corbett Ashby & Miss Solomon of the British Commonwealth League to discuss possibility of my going to India to the Conference for the liaison group. To my surprise I convinced them easily that I would go only as a reconciler & that my views on the war would be no obstacle. Found only sympathy, no opposition.

Friday June 27th
16th anniversary of our wedding. G. gave me a beautiful red lacquer cigarette box bought at St Ives (carved wood, red outside, black inside). I gave him [an] intaglio ring, but we went to Spink's to look at the others & we decided to change it for the darker red 1st century A.D. Roman intaglio for which they charged me only £1 more.

News about Russian frontier very obscure. Both sides telling lies for all they are worth and claiming to have destroyed hundreds of aeroplanes and tanks. The lull here seems uncanny, and almost more productive of apprehension than regular raids — though the usual foolish parents seem to be bringing their children back to London in the way they always do when raids decrease.

Saturday June 28th   Winchester
Charming cablegram from Ruth on our wedding anniversary (which I suppose she has learnt from one of my books), intended to arrive yesterday. It says that Shirley has already gone to camp. John still at St Paul till after July 4th (Independence Day), then going to camp as well. He sent his love with theirs. My dear sweethearts! how I do ache to see them.

Had an early lunch & went down to Winchester for a P.P.U. group meeting. Mr Seeger drove me to a house which Mr Lucas, Master at Winchester College, shares with 3 other masters. It was a little group meeting held in the drawing-room. The day was warm enough for the garden, which looked charming, but Mr Lucas explained to me that he & the other masters were keeping pigs in the garden as a contribution to the national effort, & he wasn't sure that the smell of the pigs would assist the success of the meeting.

Sunday June 29th   London
Very beautiful hot day. Left just before 11.0. Had good look at Southampton — more Blitzed than at Christmastime & later. Station had had recent heavy smash — also the large warehouse near the docks. No ships to be seen. Between S'ampton & Brockenhurst, New Forest looked perfect. Our familiar stations — Lyndhurst Rd, Brockenhurst — filled me with acute nostalgia for the children & the cottage.

Meeting at 3.0; large crowd; gave usual speech; tea after (Friends' Hall). Felt more miserable than ever going through New Forest in lovely evening light; couldn't help dwelling on my lost children & a story told me of small girl called Jean, aged 10 (youngest of 3, two boys much older), sent to Canada bec. so precious & lost on the *City of Benares*. Her poor mother was found the other day in the woods near Bournemouth weeping her heart out bec. Jean is dead & a little boy who refused to go when she went was still alive.

Monday June 30th

Lunched at Café Royal with James Laver to discuss our joint article for *Home & Garden* on "Conversation To-day". He is living near Cambridge with family & enjoying the war running round making speeches for the Nat. War Savings Committee. His museum job is in abeyance for the duration as the treasures have been moved into the country.

Long cigarette queue outside "State Express" shop in Piccadilly after lunch. Managed to get 200 Turkish from Martin's — also a ¼lb. box of chocolates from Page & Shaw. General muddle everywhere over fish & eggs. Bomb crater in road by St James's, Piccadilly, now nearly mended; buses running along the road — after over 2 months.

Tuesday July 1st

Still a long string of names in *The Times* In Memoriam column commemorating young men killed at the battle of the Somme 25 years ago when Edward was wounded. Noticed 2 which have been in all these years — W. N. Hodgson & Eric Jellicoe, nephew of the Admiral. Like Edward, they would now be 45.

Very hot. Sat in Park after lunch working on the Laver article & other things. Still haunted by story of little girl lost from *City of Benares*. I do wish the children would write oftener — though I know it must be tiresome for them. Couldn't help weeping about them as I sat in the Park.

Wednesday July 2nd

Russo–Nazi battle now 200 miles deep; Germans claim to have captured Minsk & Lwow (latter admitted by Soviet). Very much belated sea-mail letters (March 27th & April 1st) arrived from Ruth, enclosing drawings from the children & two of J.'s Easter term reports. The letter was not censored. What it can have been doing all this time I just can't imagine. Thank God for cables.

Very hot day. Must be nearly 90° again, if not over. We have now had unbroken fine weather since June 7th. Mother writes that baths are rationed at St Ives.

Thursday July 3rd

Went to Baird Lewis & arranged for various renovations to clothes. Putting two old fur coats into one; no material needed & hence no coupons. Had tea with Marjorie Roberts at Forum Club. She told me how the former Red Cross "chief" of her Hospital Library work had left for another job & his place had been taken by Major Bullock, Lord Derby's son-in-law. Gradual strained relations between Bullock & herself had now ended in her dismissal (on absurd grounds of "inefficiency", "being familiar with Lord Hamilton", etc.) & she could not understand it after 11 years' service in wh. she practically created the job. When she told me that she had talked peace & reconstruction with Major B. & had actually shown him a

P.P.U. pamphlet tho' she is not a member, I remembered that the Derbys ousted Chamberlain & it dawned on me that she was being got rid of as an "appeaser" (Major Bullock evidently not realising she was Jewish). I explained all this to her & later sent her an introd. to Caroline Haslett.

Friday July 4th
Went to Helen Mayo at 10.45 to have stoppings done. She had got rid of lease of 92 Portland Place & moved opposite to a very nice flat at 71. She showed me all over it. The building was considerably blitzed by a bomb wh. fell opposite on May 10th. Helen & Andy were away that night, but Miss Gaskell the secretary was there. She had been watching wardens putting out incendiaries when the bomb fell; bits flew across the room, & it blew the wardens to pieces. Part of one of them landed on the cot of a 3-weeks-old baby which had been put for comparative safety into the hall of an adjacent house. Baby unhurt but the porter at 71 had his leg blown off. Miss Gaskell saved him from bleeding to death by rushing out & finding a doctor who had walked home with his wife from the theatre; they had had to fall flat 15 times on the way & had just done so again. He saved the man while Miss G. attended to his wife.

Saturday July 5th   Northampton
More frustrated than ever by 3 depressing communications — (1) cable from Toronto *Star Weekly* saying shelter article excellent but other two required alteration (evidently editor does not realise censorship difficulties); (2) from Ruth Baker saying that there has been a crisis at Langham & the Wrays have gone; letter from Kenneth Wray suggesting that this was due to a row with Dorothy; (3) from Owen Clover, saying he had spoken to Roger Wilson on my behalf but there is nothing doing in Ambulance or other work for Friends at the moment, & I'd better wait till Sept. when the position will be clearer.
    Letters at last from Ruth & the children; excellent description of the film *Fantasia* from Shirley; emphatic statement of disinclination to go to Eton (with which I sympathise) from John. Wrote long letter to Ruth & a short one to the children — to whom I had already written last night. Left by 7.5 train to go to Northampton.

Sunday July 6th   London
Spoke at the monthly breakfast of the Northampton P.P.U. group; chairman first read passage about minorities from Dick Sheppard's *Some of My Religion*. Spoke for about an hour to crowded audience at Friends' Hall — wh. included Richard Murry (J.M.M.'s brother) and a little girl of 12 who was introduced to me just before I spoke — Pamela Holtby. She so resembled Winifred that people with copies of *Testament of Friendship* were exclaiming at her likeness to the portrait in the book. Her father is some kind of cousin of Winifred's father. The child — a most charming

unaffected creature who seemed as pleased to meet me as I was to see her
— had the same blue eyes, fair hair, long face, & long thin arms & legs.
Also the same look of eagerness! I couldn't stop looking at her. She might
have been Winifred's daughter.

Returned to London in carriage with a party of theatre people to find
that *Sunday Express* had splashed a review of G.'s book on its middle page &
had wired asking him to their luncheon for Raymond Gram Swing, who
arrived in London on Friday having crossed the Atlantic in a bomber.

Monday July 7th
Extremely hot. Almost too hot to walk outside comfortably; must have
been up in the 90s.

Mary Gamble came to tea & we discussed problems at Langham & the
Wrays' departure. While she was there a summons came from the
Admiralty for G. to take his destroyer trip on June 19th. So we arranged to
give up the flat that day; G. to go whenever the boat leaves & I to take our
belongings to Langham.

German–Russian news still obscure and inconclusive.

Charming letter from Jim Putnam (posted actually on 27th June) saying
that the children were going to them on July 17th for a month & then to the
Bretts about Aug. 20th. Jim said that Colston Leigh didn't want any
English lecturers this year since the Institute of Internat. Educatn. had
queered the pitch by getting all sorts of distinguished people who go over to
do propaganda at merely nominal fees.

Tuesday July 8th
Another long & painful P.P.U. Executive.

At 10.0 went to Savoy to see Raymond Gram Swing. He was tired &
overworked though as agreeable as always, & left most of the talking to us.
We walked back from the Savoy. G. had his fortune told for amusement
this afternoon. Teller said that someone very close to him was interested in
art & every sacrifice should be made as the person was very good! Dear
John.

Wednesday July 9th
Agatha Harrison rang up before breakfast to tell me that Mrs Corbett
Ashby had seen Mr Amery yesterday & he had agreed to see me — the first
major official to do so. At breakfast came a letter from the India Office
making an appointment for 3.30 on Monday.

Thursday July 10th
Visited American Embassy & got verdict that my re-entry permit
certainly lost at sea, owing to obstinacy of Washington State Department
in refusing to use airmail. Had to make a new deposition & make new
application to the Bank of England for 6 dollars to pay for cost of new

permit & extension. Total expenditure another 9 dollars — nearly £3 at present rates. Embassy said some people had had their permits sunk twice.

Delightful letter from George Brett about (1) children, (2) my Will. He was much pleased with 6 weekly reports sent him by Ruth from John's school & described John as "a bright young man".

Friday July 11th

Chores again. Shopping, journey to Chelsea to fetch shoes, 3.15 dental appointment. In morning wrote fortnightly Letter No. 61, on the Church & War, & left it with porter for Brock.

Very very hot. Heavy sweltering heat like New York; made one sticky all over; temp. must be in nineties. Flat insufferable, walking impossible. Had gastric attack at bedtime, almost certainly due to heat.

Russians apparently still holding Germans.

Saturday July 12th

Went to Brighton for the day though feeling wobbly from last night's gastric attack. Morning heat as great as ever; Pullman train (sadly fallen from former glories; had sardine on toast and tinned grapefruit for lunch) absolutely sweltering.

Met at Brighton by Dr Hendry, chairman of P.P.U. group; got in without difficulty, tho' I was reminded at the Victoria booking office that it was a restricted area. Walked slowly along the sea front with him; freshness of air divine after London. Very strange to see the quite empty, wired & fortified front. Made Brighton seem a very desirable place to stay — quite an idea. One or two bomb craters in town but no blitz evidence. Norfolk & Old Ship Hotel's still functioning, though Grand & Metropole closed. Spoke to the P.P.U. group at 3.0; had tea with Dr Crow, & returned by the 5.8. Driven to station by tanned, good-looking young woman known as "Nan"; she suddenly told me that her husband, a doctor & specialist in anesthetics, had been killed in Crete. She had a daughter aged 11 — is now trying to sell his practice at Worthing.

Sunday July 13th

After tea took 25 bus to Kingsley Hall; on the top, saw City & East End ruins even better than usual. Arrived with $\frac{1}{4}$ hour to spare before the 6.0 service; saw Dorothy Hogg, who told me that Patrick Figgis had had a breakdown & been away nearly a fortnight, returning Tuesday. He was suddenly overcome with severe headaches during a service & could not go on. Dorothy Hogg, as I commented, has carried on right through from the Sept. Blitzes without breaking down, but she thought that Patrick had been more distressed by being ousted from his church owing to his pacifist convictions than by any Blitz. Bow Church now a heap of ruins amid trees but services still continuing somehow. Had dinner with G. at Berkeley

Grill — later we had a talk at the Dorchester with John Wheeler-Bennett who is staying there.

Monday July 14th
News of actual treaty of alliance signed with Russia yesterday, but the B.B.C. still won't play the *Internationale*! The Russian & German claims (which say they are almost at Kiev) as incompatible as usual — but Sunday papers had almost optimistic articles by Garvin & John Gordon. I think this unwise. People here will slack more than ever if they imagine things are going better. Personally I don't even want to begin to hope till there is unassailable reason for it. Lunched at Athenaeum Court & at 2.15 heard Churchill make one of his vindictive radio speeches, at a County Hall luncheon which succeeded a parade of the Civil Defence forces. He talked about "inflicting on them the torments they have inflicted on us," and gloated over the sufferings of German civilians under our bombing — to say nothing of our own civilians when the reprisals come back. The speech was about on the moral level of an Old Testament Hebrew tribal leader. Gone is the comparative decency, since Churchill became Premier, of our distinction bet. the Nazi leaders & the German people.

Tuesday July 15th
Long letter (sea-mail) from Ruth — about John's painting, Shirley, isolationism etc. — of which I have never had the airmail. This letter was April 20th, but the postmark was "St Paul, June 12th"!
   Had pleasant dinner party — David & Mrs Low, Christina Foyle, Colonel Claborne of the U.S. Embassy. G. depressed because he thought Christina had initiated too much talk on pacifism. Low shared my views on Churchill's speech — said it showed evidence of our deterioration.

Wednesday July 16th
Finished dental appointments with Helen Mayo; she finished off the last three teeth. Asked me to phone her about Amery. Saw him at 12.15; not altogether unsatisfactory, even tho' I felt a fool & on verge of weeping all the time owing to ignominious position into which my views on war are constantly placing me. Took large dose of sal volatile but it wore off long before the interview. Amery was kind, gave me half an hour of his time (on busy day when papers reporting new pronouncement to be made on India), seemed really sorry to have to catechise me, but felt however I behaved there would be a balance of disadvantage as Congress party would make propaganda capital out of my views on the war.

Thursday July 17th
Was a guest of honour at the Foyle Luncheon "Women in Peace & War". Other guests were Jennie Lee, Virginia Cowles, Polly Peabody, Mrs Sieff, Diana Wynyard, Lilian Braithwaite. Over 1,000 people present in the

Grosvenor House Ballroom. Three terribly flat & boring speeches made by Mrs Tate, M.P., Lady David Douglas-Hamilton (Prunella Stack — a self-satisfied young woman with a complacent voice who enunciated more platitudes than I have ever heard put together before) and Lady Londonderry — who looked younger than she said she was (she described herself as "one who ought to be a great-grandmother if her children had done their duty") but made the longest & dullest speech I have ever heard from a woman. At the end I said to Rebecca Sieff: "We now take a deep breath & come to the surface." Sat next to Jennie Lee, & to the former Editor of the *Frankfürter Zeitung* (name Cohen) who is now editing *Die Zeitung* for the refugee Germans here.

Saturday July 19th   Langham
Finished packing & gave up flat. Saw G. off at Euston for Liverpool to join his destroyer, for the observation trip & as correspondent for the *Yorkshire Post*. Then gathered up luggage at Athenaeum Court (1 trunk & 13 small pieces) & got midday train to Langham. Later G. telephoned from Liverpool & also wired that he had forgotten meeting he had promised to take for Creech Jones on Wednesday. Asked if I would get a F.U. speaker or take it myself. I said I would — later rang up Creech Jones & arranged to meet him on Wednesday, stay the night & give the lecture for G. Very wet stormy night.

Sunday July 20th
Quiet pleasant Sunday. Letters all morning, including the one to G.'s American lecture agent. Spent afternoon tying up the pink ramblers loosened by last night's wind and rain. Joe Watson from Durham, who has come with his wife & family to be "governor" here, strolled with me to the post — a very good choice on J.M.M.'s part. While I was tying up the roses, Frank Lea asked me if I would review *Into the Way of Peace* for the *Adelphi*, and also enclose slips about it in a fortnightly Letter. I told him I would.

Heavenly peace of the country after the heat & stuffiness of London. Evacuees in the White Room singing "Jersusalem" (10 p.m.).

Have just heard summary on wireless of the German-Russian war; a month of fighting finds the Germans still 150 miles from Leningrad & over 200 from Moscow. A delightful postscript by Raymond Gram Swing on his visit to London, commenting on our equanimity under Blitz. Shared fears seem less devastating than neuroses.

'Planes & 'planes going over for about an hour at midnight to bomb Germany.

Monday July 21st
Letter from Amery saying that "the Government of India" (which must be a convenient myth, as it couldn't have been consulted between Wednesday

& Friday, when he wrote me) felt that it could not reconsider its "carefully considered" decision about letting me go to India, & he didn't see how he could advise them to do so. Excuse the same as the previous one — that the Congress party would make propaganda adverse to the Govt. out of my views on the war. I wrote Agatha Harrison & Mrs Corbett Ashby pointing out (a) that the Congress party could make equal propaganda out of the refusal to let me go, (b) that Indian women were unlikely to give the same exaggerated emphasis to my views on the war as officials here.

After tea weeded half the front terrace, & after dinner sat on the back terrace drafting Letter 62.

Tuesday July 22nd   Weston-super-Mare
Long complicated journey from Langham to Weston-super-Mare, on increasingly warmer day.

At 7.0 went along to Friends' Meeting House; outside Amy & Burnett (very smart in Air Force Uniform) were waiting for me with Marian — who has become a really pretty strong-looking baby with fine blue eyes & lovely brown legs. They told me his training is finished & they don't know where he has to go next or whether she can join him.

Wednesday July 23rd   Leatherhead
Travelled back to London via Bristol. Took Underground to Victoria, had tea at Stewart's, sent off Shirley's birthday cable by telephone, & joined Jon Creech Jones at the H. of Commons at 5.0. His wife was waiting with the car & ran me down to their house at Leatherhead — a pleasant & convenient little modern house with a lovely view at the back over the Surrey hills.

After an early supper we went along to a local music school where I gave a W.E.A. lecture in G.'s place. The subject was "One Anglo-American Nation" so I spoke part of the time on Federal Union & the rest on America & the various reasons for her changes of opinion since the war. Despite the last-moment substitution of me for G., they had the biggest audience since the series began; room crowded & people standing outside the open window.

Thursday July 24th   Langham
Back to London with Jon on Green Line bus. Showed him Amery's letter, wh. he said must be regarded as a definite negative. He promised to try to see Amery at the House & ask him if any ulterior reason lay behind the one given. In London did various pieces of necessary shopping at Marshall's & Selfridge's. Took watch to Benson's to be repaired but they refused to take it — said impossible to get workers to do it now, though it only wanted cleaning. Had to buy an alarm clock at Selfridge's so as to have some idea of the time.

Got afternoon train to Colchester; had tea on train. At The Oaks found the usual mass of letters, mostly business, but one from Mrs Corbett Ashby said that she had been greatly enlightened about the Home Office attitude by the information that the P.P.U. was known to have Nazi agents among its members — & it was *this*, not the fact of pacifism, wh. made the intelligence depts. so suspicious. Decided to try to persuade Dr Wood to take up this matter with the Home Office, since nothing could be less compatible with Nazi doctrines than a pledge to renounce war.

Friday July 25th
Very strenuous domestic day, in intervals of which I wrote 19 letters, including one to Mrs Corbett Ashby asking if she could give me the source of the "Nazi agents" accusation regarding the P.P.U.

The "old ladies" who wash up have a day off on Fridays — so I washed up the breakfast & supper things; served lunch, & prepared the 9 o'clock tea. Very hot, lovely day; wrote most of my business letters under the trees.

Saturday July 26th
Papers report economic sanctions against Japan; her assets frozen here & in U.S.A. Germans seem still some miles short of their main objectives — Leningrad, Moscow & Kiev. Report in the *News Chronicle* of terrible raids by ourselves on Cologne — two cinemas and a main hotel destroyed, as well as many private houses. We can no more hit only "military objectives" than the Germans can. *When* will both the leaders and the ordinary people of the various nations realise just *what* they are doing, in destroying history's teasures in city after city? The sheer wastage now going on just beggars imagination.

Sunday July 27th
Dear Shirley's eleventh birthday — on Sunday for the second time since she was born on a Sunday. Never did I dream when the children went to U.S.A. a year ago that I should not see her before a second birthday had gone by. As I wrote to Ruth in my long letter yesterday, the grief I feel is not only due to missing the children's lovely mental and spiritual flowering to which I subconsciously looked foward all through the period of bathing & face-washing and pram pushing. It is due even more to the sense of being cruelly deceived by the government here; of having been first encouraged to go to U.S.A. to lecture, and then, when the children had gone beyond recall, told that I could not go again owing to pacifist opinions wh. I held just the same at the beginning of the war. As it is, I parted with the children for what seems likely now to be the duration of the war without having ever decided to do so, on the assumption that I should be going to America at frequent intervals & therefore it was better for them to be there than here.

In evening J. M. Murry arrived & made a speech on the Adelphi Centre, Joe Watson, the new Warden, taking the Chair. At end of meeting Watson, summing up, suddenly stated that the Adelphi Community must be run by the initiative of men only — every idea must go through "the mill of a man's mind" — & that women had "a different role" to play. I got up & instantly challenged this. J.M.M. put up Watson to reply — with the familiar Milton quotation "She for God in him". By this time the mixed audience was silent & intent. I got up again, said a partial equality was not true Socialism, & insisted that J.M.M. reply. He finally produced some mystical stuff about Blake's theories on the relationship of men & women, & I led him on to community in the post-war world. Much conversation followed the discussion. Had an impulse to leave next day but later thought better of it.

Monday July 28th
Quiet day. Avoided direct contact with Joe Watson who looked rather crestfallen — as though conscious of having dropped a brick! Felt quite sorry for him. Started drafting an article for *Peace News* on Women and Pacifism.

Wire from G. from Belfast, indicated he was back from destroyer trip; rather puzzled me as I expected him to return to Liverpool. Asked me to telephone him Liverpool midday next day.

Tuesday July 29th
Joe asked me to give a talk to the Centre on America — I suppose as amends. I said I would; also volunteered for fire-watching for house & village — so friendly relations restored. Decided not to go up to town for P.P.U. Committee for fear of starting the argument all over again with J.M.M.

Wednesday July 30th
Went up to town; met G. from his destroyer trip at Euston at 2.30. He & I dictated letters at Peter Jones's bureau. Returned to Langham together by evening train.

G. told me they went southwards towards Azores to pick up convoy returning from S. Africa. No adventures on way out — but when in submarine area on return journey, stayed with Captain on Bridge till about 4 a.m., then went down to Capt.'s cabin, wh. he used, for a short sleep. Awakened at 6.0 by tremendous explosion; assumed torpedoed again; went up on deck to find ship listing heavily & blazing hard. Fire put out; list corrected by flooding of cabins; destroyer limped back to Belfast under own steam. G. learnt she had not been torpedoed, but her sister destroyer, the *Brock*, making a sweep of the convoy, had accidentally rammed her in the grey dawn light! (This had happened before on another voyage!) The *Verity* was rammed in the engineer's cabin next to G.'s & also in the oil chamber. Collision miraculously failed to damage engineer, who was asleep in his cabin, but set fire to the ship very close to its stock of high explosives! Water & oil flooded in, damaging everything on cabin floor, including G.'s second-hand leather suitcase, wh. simply disintegrated with all its contents. He again lost his clothes — £30 worth — but small white suitcase of papers standing on cabin table was rescued. While standing on deck with it in his hand waiting to see if they had to take to the boats, someone told him he looked as if he had just come from Bond St. & was waiting to catch the 5.20 from Paddington. He got on well with the ship's officers who like him better than 2 previous B.B.C. visitors who drank too much.

Monday September 29th
Packing to return to London.
   Fire-watching at night — the second watch, 2.30 a.m. Called by Otto Ernst with a cup of tea. Between tours of the garden read *Hamlet* and an essay by Max Plowman on death.
   Would that at the end of the last War, at 25, I had started with the knowledge of the world, of literature, of myself, that I now have two decades later!

Wednesday October 1st   London
Came back to London from Langham with luggage. Met by G. at Liverpool Street. We moved into our new flat at Richmond, 67 Richmond Hill Court. Delighted with it. Lovely views over river in front & S. W. London at back.

Thursday October 2nd
Unpacking, shopping, straightening all day. Engaged a young married woman, Mrs Tibbetts, to come as daily maid for 2 hours each morning, and a part-time secretary, Gwen Paine, aged about 38, who came to see me in the afternoon.
   G. talking on Fed. Union at Earl's Court.

Friday October 3rd
More straightening & shopping. On sitting-room table in sunshine in afternoon, started to tackle accumulation of letters.
   M. of I. officials stone-walling & trying (having prevented G. from going to U.S.A.) to kybosh an Empire tour as well.

Saturday October 4th
Wrote Caroline Haslett & the Johnsons re possible book on Amy.
   G. & I walked in Kew Gardens. Moist, humid, dull. Autumn flowers still lovely. Few bombs have fallen here; pagoda & palm house are undamaged. Much more Blitz in Richmond itself. Several large houses

completely demolished behind these flats. Must have been some time ago, as sites are already grass-grown.

Read first chapter of G.'s autobiography & thought it excellent.

Sunday October 5th
Summer-time not ending; kept for 1 hr. Wrote numerous letters. Lovely day. This October weather almost incredible.

Argument about the "mercy ships" containing prisoners still going on between Britain & Germany. Germany has 1,200 of our wounded prisoners; we have only 150 of hers. Question of interpretation of the Internat. Convention.

Monday October 6th
Miss Paine arrived; proves an excellent secretary. Spent most of day dictating answers to accumulation of letters. We got through about 20, mostly quite long; & I then dictated others.

Germans leaving Leningrad alone for the moment (relatively); starting a new drive on Moscow.

Tuesday October 7th
Afternoon, P.P.U. Executive.

J. Middleton Murry gave me *carte blanche* to review any book I thought suitable for *Peace News* in anything from 200 to 1,000 words.

Charming letter from George Brett enclosing some beautiful snapshots of Shirley at their farm. Two, in a bathing dress, show her hair as fair as ever & her legs looking much longer & arms quite thin & lengthening. The others are all taken with the dogs; one, in which her arms are clasped round all three dogs together, wears an expression of ecstasy. George thinks she turns to animals partly because she is so much "smarter" than children of her own age that she has no use for them.

"Mercy ships" cancelled — we say for fear of German "breach of faith".

Wednesday October 8th
Got up early & went to Hatfield to see Miss Pauline Gower, the O.C. of the Women's Transport Auxiliary, for my article on "Women Pilots" for the Toronto *Star Weekly*.

Evening papers report Germans making progress towards Moscow; wedge driven into Timoshenko's army.

Thursday October 9th
Morning, made speech for Anglican Pacifist Fellowship. In afternoon (as new member of Anglican Pacifist Council, a position which I accepted due to my growing belief that the Church must revive itself from within) I gave it to the Anglican Pacifist Conference at the Oak Room in Kingsway Hall. Audience mostly clerics & church workers. Dr Percy Hartill in chair —

C. Paul Gliddon secretary. Spoke on need for banishing pessimism in peace movement; on need for constructive peace-making rather than negative method of mere war-resistance. Seemed to go down well. Paul Gliddon asked me before I left if I could turn it into a pamphlet; said I would try.

Went on to deadly & extremely boring Council meeting of Nat. Peace Council at Friends' House; concerned with scheme for taking over the New Commonwealth Institute & its *Quarterly*, and then with wording of a long N.P.C. commentary on the Atlantic Charter — which is unrealistic anyhow.

Friday October 10th
Peaceful day, no lectures or meetings. Completed 3,300-word article on Rationing, based mostly on collection of newspaper cuttings made over 3 months.

Cable from *Christian Century* (U.S.A.) asking if I would do article for Jan. number on the Christian Church in the post-war world. Offered $50. Accepted, as approve of the magazine, for which Villard writes.

By W.E.G.'s request, sent her a statement for presentation to the Min. of Labour officials at her interview on Monday (the 1914 group, with wh. she has just had to register) pointing out that though I paid her a full-time salary as my secretary, I allowed her to spend half her time on social work; that she also ran her home, so really was doing a full-time useful job.

Saturday October 11th   Langham
Took Federal Union lecture at Friends' House. Joad in Chair. Wasn't one of my best speeches — though on familiar topic "Shape of the Future" — as it was preceded by a luncheon with Sir John & Lady Mactaggart at 55 Park Lane in which *I* had one cocktail too many for complete clear-headedness (only two altogether — but they were stronger than usual!). But speech went down all right — followed by an interesting discussion in which girl pacifist in audience thanked me for making her own mind clearer.

Went on to Langham for week-end owing to 2-monthly committee tomorrow. V. dark night; a siren, but heard no bombs or guns.

Sunday October 12th
Morning, helped with vegetables in kitchen, worked in garden in sunshine. Turning colours of trees very beautiful. Sun as hot as summer while out. Mulberries almost all gathered, but pears & apples ripe, & many walnuts on ground. Hedges still thick with blackberries, but everyone has used up their sugar, so these late ones remain ungathered.

Monday October 13th   London
W.E.G. has had her interview & is to be allowed to carry on with her

present work — no pressure to change it. She had filed statement saying she was a pacifist.

Tuesday October 14th
Finished Rationing article. In afternoon Winifred Eden-Green & Derek Edwards came for a Conference on doing publicity for fortnightly Letter — which always has about £100 in bank, & could be expanded with output of additional effort. They only took 1¼ hours to reach Richmond from Blackheath. We ex-cogitated many new ideas which Winifred & Derek will gradually carry out. They stayed for tea with G. & me. W.E.G. said that the Min. of Labour official who interviewed her was v. sympathetic to her point of view.

When they had gone, G. & I went for short walk along towing-path by river. Lovely evening. I always think of Richmond now as the place that Father loved rather than the one where he chose to die. Beautiful sunset; river tranquil & fair in evening light.

Wednesday October 15th
Dictated letters in morning; gave G.P. rationing article to type, started next week's Fortnightly Letter (on frustration & depression of this War cf. with relative exhilaration of last; and on I.V.S.P. type of work as one solution).

Went to Caroline Haslett's office — the Women's Engineering Society & Electrical Association, at 20 Regent Street — & had a talk with her about the projected Amy Johnson biography. She told me many anecdotes about Amy — & Mollison's influence on her, and urged me to see the Johnson family if possible. Lent me several books; her secretary Miss Thomson also gave me much information. Caroline Haslett going to America on Saturday (by boat) so very busy, but she talked to me for about an hour & gave me tea. She herself arranged & financed Amy's memorial service. Said her own father virtually a pacifist — which accounts for her sympathy towards myself & the Letter.

Thursday October 16th
Moscow still holding but Government & officials have departed eastward.

Saturday October 18th
In morning, after various domestic chores, prepared in 2 hours my lecture on Winifred & her work, for Sheffield Educational Settlement.

Had hair washed in afternoon, packed for week-end, & then went with G. to a dinner at Sir John Mactaggart's flat — there met Cyril Asquith (once Ramsay Macdonald's secretary) & his wife — & a young soldier, a sergeant, whose company was called to Plymouth during the Blitz to help, & gave a grim account. Said about 1,100 people were killed the first bad

night. Meanwhile G., Cyril Asquith & Sir John discussed Federal Union
— to wh. Sir J. seems inclined to dedicate a little of his wealth.

We tried to get a hotel room so that I could go straight to my train in the
morning, but London crowded & even Athenaeum Court unable to take us
— so we had to go back to Richmond & walk up the Hill in darkness.

Sunday October 19th   Sheffield
Got up early, breakfasted St Pancras, caught 10.0 train to Sheffield. At
3.30 lectured under auspices of Sheffield Educational Settlement on
"Winifred Holtby & her Contribution to Literature", but such a crowd
came that they could not be accommodated in the Club room (which
anyhow was partly filled by a Soviet "exhibition" of books, pamphlets &
press-cuttings pasted on screens). So we moved over to an adjacent hall.
Lecture seemed to go well & please audience.

Monday October 20th   Doncaster
After lunch got bus to Doncaster. As I was getting off bus a young airman
in R.A.F. uniform stopped me & asked: "Are you *the* Vera Brittain — the
authoress?" I said: "Yes — I'm speaking here to-night." He said: "I've just
been reading a book of yours — I was interested seeing the name on your
suitcase."

Meeting at 7.0; packed bec. room small; abt. 200 people & others
standing outside windows. Organisers rather nervous bec. I gave a more
pacifist speech than they expected, on assumption that their advts. had
made pacifist nature of meeting clear — whereas they had only used my
name. Young chairwoman rather nervous but expected heckling did not
occur; only a few quite sensible questions. Large collection taken & all
available copies of my books & Letter sold. Loud sounds of gunfire as
meeting ended about 8.30; young Mr & Mrs Firth hurried me to their
home (he a C.O. who does night work at a bakery). Guns & searchlights
from Sheffield direction; uncertain whether bombs. All Clear just after
midnight.

Tuesday October 21st   Hull
Left Doncaster by 9.0 train for Hull — to spend 2 hours there in order to
see what has happened to it & to the P.P.U. group there. Had heard
rumours that Hull was most blitzed place in England — worse than
Plymouth — but this is untrue; Plymouth is much worse though Hull has
many ruins — chiefly in King Edward St. & Bond St. Their big Blitz
occurred one night last May, when some of the largest shops were bombed
out or burned.

Morning was beautiful. Found station & Royal Station Hotel undamaged. (They also had siren here last night from 8.30 till midnight.) Chief
things noticed:

(1) Opposite station you immediately see the gaunt burned-out skeleton of Hammond's, where Winifred & I often shopped & had meals, & where I spoke to the Hull Luncheon Club. Top floor café where I spoke now a few remnants of scorched stone open to the four winds.

(2) Completely undamaged, the large white granite War Memorial — "In memory of the men of Kingston-Upon-Hull who laid down their lives for their country in the Great War 1914–1918" — stands ironically in front of the burnt-out buildings of the Midland Bank & Sugg Ltd the Sports Suppliers — thus indicating the vanity of the sacrifice made by the men commemorated.

(3) The big Electricity Building to the left of the station has been damaged but not destroyed; boarded-up windows carry the notice: "Our window displays are reversed; come and see them from the inside."

(4) Found my way along wide, partly damaged but still recognisable thoroughfare to the Peace Centre at corner of Prospect St. where I spoke in February. Heard later that shop was not blown up or burned but damage done by blast wh. blew everything out of it, including a C.O. who had been sleeping there bec. he did not get on with his family. Being a heavy sleeper & rather deaf he did not notice the raid and was blown, bed & all, right out of the Centre. Was black as a cinder when he went home to his family but quite uninjured — a miraculous escape. To-day the words "The Peace Centre" remain undamaged above the blown-out lower floor where I had tea — no furniture or goods left there — only the usual swept-up debris of bricks, glass & torn paper. Upper room where I spoke similarly windowless. Door in lower room at back swinging on hinge.

(5) King Edward St. worst damaged of all; Co-op burnt out, also Brown's bookshop & many others. Kept wondering what Winifred & Mrs Holtby would have thought of Hull now. With his back to the ruins of the Co-op., the statue of Andrew Marvell, Hull's most famous citizen, stands serenely undamaged & scarcely even blackened.

(6) Went on as directed by notice on ruins to Brown's new shop at 24–26 George St., close by. Saw Mr Williamson the Manager, who told me that their shop was undamaged by the actual raid & only caught fire from the other buildings at 3 a.m. They lost all their stock of books, but no members of staff. Told me there was still a steady demand for *T. of F.* in the original 10/6 edition.

Sunday December 7th
Pearl Harbour.

Monday December 8th
U.S. in war.

1942

Thursday January 1st   London
What a New Year's Day! More countries at war than ever before in the world's history. Hong Kong gone; Sarawak going. Penang gone; war surging into Malaya; Rangoon and Singapore bombed. Manila burning, and the Americans fighting a hopelessly outnumbered battle in the Philippines. But in Russia the Nazis are still retreating — and in Libya. A year ago this country faced the Axis alone; now we have the United States, Russia and China as Allies. By next year — what?

Worked all day with Miss Paine on letters, etc. Collected folder and books for "Humiliation with Honour" to begin on to-morrow. After supper looked over the lovely illustrated edition of Whitman's *Leaves of Grass* which arrived for me yesterday for Christmas, from John, and wrote long letter to him, Shirley and Ruth.

Letter came from Mrs Nehru, President of the All-India Women's Congress, deploring the Govt.'s refusal to let me go there.

Friday January 2nd
Worked all day; Miss Paine typed my 3,000-word "England's Bombed Cities" article and I corrected and sent it off to the Toronto *Star Weekly* via Rache as usual.

Got chapter-headings for book done after tea. Copy of *Testament of Friendship* arrived from Macmillan to enable me to make the corrections for the new impression. Dreary bleak day.

Urged on telephone by Stuart Morris to speak at the Food Relief meeting on Jan. 24th which I refused yesterday. Prevailed on reluctantly to revise the decision.

Grim accounts in evening papers of fighting in Manila — in extraordinary contrast to complacency of articles on Japan and the Philippines in a newly-arrived copy of *Time* dated December 8th!

Sunday January 4th
Mild, pleasant, sunny day. Newspapers carry announcement that Wavell is appointed C. in C. of all forces in Far East. I like what I read & hear of Wavell. He took the first failure in Libya on his own shoulders. And, according to a quotation in the Richmond Parish Magazine (which I happened to see), he also said: "Think what a world we could make if we

put into our peace endeavours the same self-sacrifice, the same energy & the same co-operation as we use in the wastefulness of war."

Worked all day on "H. w. H." after tidying up the flat. In afternoon walked over to Richmond cemetery — which was much nearer than I expected — to see Father's grave. It was quite tidy, but the inscription is getting rather moss-grown & the sun-dial wants cleaning. Must see to it.

Tuesday January 6th
Went into central London; dictated to W.E.G. at Dick Sheppard House, then P.P.U. Executive.

Much upset by arrival of letter from Ruth, dated August 16th, enclosing clothes list for autumn for the children, and all too reminiscent silhouette drawings of their feet. Letter didn't even leave St Paul till Dec. 3rd. Wrote C.O.R.B. asking to fix some method by which this censorship by delay could be avoided where children concerned. Could have howled with grief and exasperation.

Wednesday January 7th
Met Joyce Wood at Piccadilly (little scholarship girl from Burslem, Staffs, who writes poems & sends me fan-mail letters; up in London for interview). No time to give her tea at Regent Palace as I intended, so took her to train at Euston; gave her cup of tea on station.

Wrote Letter No. 74; famine, & paper shortage for books.

Thursday January 8th
Very cold day but some lovely pale sun over the river. Went for walk by towpath after lunch, thinking partly of the children & partly of the Japs advancing on Singapore while the world's resources of tin and rubber are being destroyed. Roosevelt's budget was commented on in the papers to-day — the biggest war budget ever issued in the world — and the size of it made me realise more than ever the obligations that will be laid on American citizens and the importance of the children coming back if we can only get them. G. back late from Nuneaton.

Announcement in *Evening Standard* that we are at last to be allowed to make small contribution of £3 per child per month to children in U.S.A.

Friday January 9th
Japs advancing steadily down Malay peninsula. Tried to work but too much interrupted.

Amy, Burnett & Marian dropped in unexpectedly to tea, & Amy is coming once a week from now on to do mending, washing etc. Burnett said that though we heard little about raids, they had them on their aerodrome near Ramsgate 5 nights out of 7, and two nights ago a small village near Canterbury was completely demolished, with 15 people killed. He thinks more mass raids unlikely owing to strength of coastal defences. Works hard all day now as a fitter.

Saturday January 10th   Blackpool
Went to Blackpool to stay with Amy Johnson's parents for week-end. Journey not bad — got seat in corner so was able to do plenty of work. Only about an hour late. Met at Blackpool by Mrs Johnson — a most charming small woman just like a Dresden China doll as Caroline Haslett said. Taken to 141 Newton Drive — met Mr Johnson; kindly, bluff, Yorkshire, about 65. House warm, modern, most comfortable. Johnsons people of substance; the "Hull fishmonger" a Press canard. He has a big international business as a fish-merchant; has been 10 times to U.S.A. & 30 to Norway. His family has travelled, wife has had apartment in San Diego & cottage in Cumberland when recovering from breakdown. They own a house in Bridlington & another in Hull, as well as this in Blackpool where business was evacuated at start of war. Heard story after dinner (cocktails, soup, Dover Sole, cheese, coffee!) of Amy's ambitions; chance sight of Stag Lane aerodrome when acting as secretary in London to solicitors started her on her career. Parents gave her "Jason" at cost £600 with many misgivings lest sending her to death. No official support from any influential man except Sir Sefton Brancker who persuaded Lord Wakefield to help her.

An Alert while going to bed; distant gunfire.

Sunday January 11th
Spent all day looking at Amy's trophies, photographs etc. Family situation gradually became clear. Mr Johnson a solid, clever businessman with adventurous leanings; in '98 took part for 2 years in goldrush on Klondike. Mrs Johnson's family had beauty & a touch of wild genius somewhere. Amy the image of her mother. The four daughters all unusual, gifted, neurotic, makers of tragic marriages. Most normal the third, Molly, living next-door to parents; married to Trevor Jones, Town Clerk of Blackpool — has two baby daughters, at present doing all housework unaided.

Of other daughters, Amy, born 1903, was charming, brilliant, temperamental, keen on sports & outdoor achievements, could not stand cramped life of a typist. Unsettled for some years till she took up aviation. Her life a tragedy for 3 reasons: (1) Immediate exploitation by Press of her success in flying to Australia, bought by *Daily Mail* for £12,000. (2) Consequent lifelong lionisation by public, wh. turned her into species of film star instead of leaving her free to be a first-rate engineer & pilot, wh. was her ambition. She never expected this publicity; thought she would just fly to Australia & back, unnoticed, & say to officials at Stag Lane: "I've flown to Australia as I said I would; now give me a chance." Lionisation & publicity created jealousy of her throughout her life, and added to the official prejudice against her as a woman "trying to push into a men's monopoly", to prevent her from getting any kind of official recognition except initial C.B.E. (Request at outbreak of war to be given worthwhile work for R.A.F. produced decision that she could start as a "junior" who required 3 years' training! (3) Marriage to Jim Mollison, a real ne'er-do-well; only son who had a drunken father, is surly, ill-mannered, brutally neglectful of his widowed mother. Anxious only for publicity. Said to Wilcox & Anna Neagle about his part in the Amy Johnson film: "I don't care what you say about me so long as you keep talking." Lived on Amy; kept turning up & occupying her houses even after she had left him. She had several homes — a flat in Grosvenor House; and another at The Gateway, Kensington. Last house was an old mansion near Cheltenham.

The second daughter, Irene, born 1905, was sub-editor of Hull *Daily Mail* at v. early age. Ambitious, tied down by marriage, she had a brain-storm & gassed herself at 24 in 1929.

Youngest, Betty, only 22 now. Is equally neurotic, difficult, tempera-mental. Thinks she wants to write. I saw several short things of hers; very promising.

Monday January 12th   London
Johnsons saw me off at Blackpool by 10.0 train. During weekend, situation about the biography of Amy has become clear. Johnson family are concerned for Amy's reputation & want me to do the book owing to my literary standing. But Betty is keen to do a book, determined & obstinate, and Mr J. is afraid of the effect on her health of any opposition. I suggested she do her book first & be given a time-limit of a year, & said I would do nothing till she had finished & then see what material was unused. Mr J. called this arrangement "generous", but it seems to me obvious. Betty has no experience of handling material but can write a personal book. I have no personal experience of Amy, but can depict the tragedy of press exploitation & the struggles and influence of a woman pioneer.

Tuesday January 13th   London
Japs steadily penetrating Malay peninsula. Air raids on Singapore. "Pukka sahibs" on tin and rubber plantations no good at "scorched earth".

Snow on the ground; started to snow heavily in evening. "Shop-crawled" in search of rubber goods which will soon be unobtainable owing to loss of 85% of our rubber output in Malaya. Got a hot-water bottle in one shop, a rubber sponge at another, a pair of crêpe-rubber-soled walking shoes at a third. Otherwise, wasted day.

By afternoon post a beautiful hand-embroidered Chinese silk slip arrived from Ruth.

Wednesday January 14th
In flat all day but still did not reach book.

Wrote long letter to John, Shirley & Ruth after dinner. G. came back very depressed by an argument which developed in the Mactaggart Anglo-American group owing to their dislike of his Federal Union connections. I told him I thought them all a set of self-interested scoundrels in the group for their own ends, as I realised at the beginning, but he still thinks that when the scheme gets properly going he can balance them with some better personalities.

Thursday January 15th
G. rang up Nuneaton & found nothing doing there; constituency has decided to back National Executive Selections. I could have wept, he looked so miserable after yet another of this long chain of maddening setbacks.

Worked quietly all day alone in flat. Wrote my speech for the meeting on the 24th as also an article for *Peace News*; then got on to making notes & reading for my book at last.

Japs advancing steadily on Singapore. More & more columns in the Press about the unpreparedness of Malaya for war. Australia getting alarmed; I am more sorry than ever for the parents who evacuated their children there. Nazis still retreating along the Moscow–Smolensk road.

Learnt later that this was the coldest day in London since 1881. Temp. 10 above zero — i.e., 22 degrees of frost.

Friday January 16th
Growing row in Press about the situation in Malaya as the Japs advance towards Singapore, and the comfortable ease of the "pukka sahibs" with their contempt for the brown and yellow races who are now, naturally enough, "letting them down". This week's *Peace News* very forthright on the subject.

At 9 p.m. G. rang up from Stoke; thinks he may get reversion of one of the Pottery constituencies.

Saturday January 17th
Rang up Miss Lemon & got G.'s room booked at Kenilworth Hotel for F.U. Conference to-night. Shall be alone again as I have been all day — a not unusual situation now. Worked out grand idea in morning for sending my Fortnightly Letter to publishers on strength of book recommendations.

Went for walk alone in Richmond Park after lunch. Park snow-covered, freezing, everything ice-cold & deserted till I got near the Sheen Gate. Some people there, & a few small boys skating on a pond. Seems queer to be alone so much after our household of nine in Chelsea — which went down after the war began, till in Sept. 1940 I alone was left — with the Blitz for company.

Went through cheque books & found G. has had £574 from me since Xmas 1940; can't think what he spends it on with no rent, rates or domestic bills to pay. Couldn't concentrate on book.

Churchill back from U.S.A. by flying-boat; hope the criticisms are ready for him.

Monday January 19th
Another retreat in Malaya; Japs now almost on top of Singapore.

Started Letter No. 75 on retribution and the Nemesis of the Nations. G. in late. Snowing hard when we went out to diner. Conversation with Stuart Morris on efficiency of P.P.U. office; agreed not to bring it up at Executive.

Tuesday January 20th
No further decisive war news. Churchill proposes to stand up to critics in further 3 days' debate.

Went to P.P.U. Executive. Chief discussion about the Food Relief campaign (which Ponsonby proposes to raise in the H. of Lords). Usual row between John Middleton Murry and Roy Walker about the space given to the campaign in *Peace News*. Told Roy he was thinking too much about the campaign and not enough about the starving peoples for whom it was supposedly organised.

Six inches of snow on Richmond Hill which looks like a Christmas card with all its trees, or the outskirts of an American city. Snow too cold to melt, & almost untouched owing to lack of traffic since the Hill was bombed & Park closed to private cars. Snow on blitzed buildings here & in West End a melancholy sight.

Wednesday January 21st
Cold but brighter day. Snow lying hard; ground like iron. G. reported v. successful lunch & later talk with Major Braithwaite yesterday. Went off after luncheon to his A.B.C.A. affairs at Park Lane.

Some people at the hotel reported that an acquaintance had taken 24 hours to get from Glasgow over the weekend owing to the weather. No sleeper or restaurant on the train, though they managed to pick up food at one or two stations.

Worked all day at Letter No. 75 (on retribution); only got to book quite late. Letter from Phyllis welcoming possibility of the children's return if transport permits. Wrote her after supper explaining circumstances of their departure; also to both the children themselves.

G. telephoned late to say he was staying the night in Park Lane & reporting: "Tout va bien."

Jap. attacks on New Guinea & Bismarck Islands. Agitation in Australia. Archbp. of Canterbury retiring.

Friday January 23rd
Poured with rain all day, washing away the snow. Had Colonel Wedgwood — now Lord Wedgwood of Barlaston — to lunch at Athenaeum Court. He promised me a ticket to see him take the Oath in the

House of Lords. He had just gone when Miss Peggy Cox of the West Indies met me by appointment to talk about conditions there; she seemed astonished after her experience with officials that we not only saw her immediately but promised her prompt contact with the American Ambassador in order that something might be done about the bad effect in the West Indies of American colour prejudice.

Back to flat for tea; replied to Andrew Dakers' letter about "retribution" suggesting that I might write a pamphlet for wide distribution on lines of my Fortnightly Letter. Also wrote Arthur Wragg asking him to do a jacket cover for "Humiliation with Honour". Spent evening studying speech for to-morrow and reading up facts about the blockade.

Saturday January 24th

Jap. landings in New Guinea. Great agitation in Australia; demands for reinforcement and attack. How much of the British Empire will be left in six months?

Spoke at the London Group P.P.U. food relief meeting at the Aeolian Hall. Felt as though I were climbing a steep hill. Thought the audience must be indifferent or hostile, yet at the end they proved to be solidly behind us and unanimously backed the sending of a telegram to the Govt.!

The excellent bulletin "Famine" was on sale at the door & in the streets. After the meeting, Muriel Lester — still looking tired, & certainly having a busman's holiday by going there — spoke to me for a moment saying how glad she was that an effort was being made to rouse public opinion at last about the starving Belgians & Greeks.

Sunday January 25th

Walked with G. along towing path of river in both directions, but too cold for pleasure; bitter wind. G. showed me the lock across the river between Richmond & Kew bridges, & I suddenly realised to my great relief that Father couldn't have drowned himself in Richmond since his body was found at Isleworth on the *other* side of this lock, in August when the river is low. I always wondered how he persuaded a taxi to take him the long drive to Richmond in the middle of the night, and I think now he must have gone to Hammersmith Bridge, where he used to go & look over. I feel so thankful to know that our theory held for 6½ years is wrong, and that this shadow is lifted for me from lovely Richmond.

Monday January 26th

At home all day; working; many letters. Long one from Wm. K.S. discussing the literary executor question, to which I replied in detail. Also sent copy of Saturday's speech to Dr Nevin Sayre for possible publication in *Fellowship*.

Australia facing invasion. Low did striking cartoon on this — his native land. Rumblings of criticism precede the three-day debate at which Churchill proposes to force a vote of confidence. Hannan Swaffer in his *D.*

Herald column reports no cheers at cinemas when Churchill's picture appears on the screen. In the United States the report on Pearl Harbour fixes the blame on Admiral Kimmel and Lieut. Commander [Short], each of whom was dining-out the night of the attack assuming that the necessary precautions had been taken by the other. And the British Governt. announces its intention to lift the blockade to allow food for Greece! — though no one else.

Very cold again; bitter wind; frozen ground; thermometer must be very low.

Tuesday January 27th

Opening of large-scale debate on war. Churchill made long speech on general situation & asked for vote of confidence.

Worked on book notes in morning. Afternoon, met G. & went with him to Transport House for discussion on constituencies with George Shepherd. Shepherd friendly; informed G. how land lay at Nuneaton & in Potteries. Nuneaton slightly more hopeful than Staffordshire — but there didn't seem much to expect from either.

Back for more work. Sat up till 3 a.m. owing to 11.0–3.0 fire-watch. Quiet night; bright moonlight and stars. Read letters from German pastors written in prison. Thought of Father, & realised how fortunate I was to encounter Dick Sheppard & the P.P.U. when I did — to be now part of a Christian fellowship & within it to realise, through the Nemesis which has come to the erring nations, the working out of a moral principle in the world which would recompense good. This war has reversed, for me, the spiritual process of the last, which made me for the time a Rationalist.

Wednesday January 28th

Long letter came from Ruth, written Aug. 25! Usual lag, which I suppose I must now expect. Information in her letter that the F.B.I. in U.S. have been investigating her affairs because of her adoption of Dr Helene Stoecker, her elderly German refugee, suddenly threw light. As here in the panic days after the Fall of France, she is suspected of being a Nazi because she has befriended an anti-Nazi!

Went to House of Lords to see Lord Wedgwood taking the oath, after lunching at the Royal Empire Society with Mr Darkin Williams, Editor of the *Quiver*, to discuss an article I am doing for him on the effect of this War on the prospects of professional & industrial women. House of Lords ceremony a bit like an Oxford Investiture, as he was in full robes. When the ceremony was over one felt as if someone ought to clap — it seemed an anti-climax when the business just went on. Stayed for the debate & heard Lords Denham & Moyne speak, on conduct of the war. Lord Moyne gave dreadful details about Penang — wounded trapped in flaming ruins, all labour disorganised by raids, 1,000 casualties.

Thursday January 29th
Went to Leamington Spa to lecture at Pump Room on "A Personal Confession". Pouring wet cold day. Went for a cup of tea (by invitation) to Miss Gutteres who knew G.'s parents when he lived in Leam'ton. She said that neither should have been married to the other & that Mrs Catlin should never have been married at all — but should have had a career of social or political work; she had a sex inhibition, hated marriage & having children, & was never at all interested in G. till he was 7 or 8.

The lecture itself was rather heavy going, with a miscellaneous audience & in competition with Turkish baths, etc., but they all seemed pleased. Had tea after the lecture with Mrs Bailey & a small group of Leamington & Warwick pacifists. Did not get to Richmond & empty flat till 10.30.

Friday January 30th
At 4.0 went to Friends' House, Euston Rd, for Christian Pacifist two-day Conference on present perplexities & problems. No set speakers. Conducted from platform by Canon Raven (Chairman), Rev. Henry Carter (who is always excellent) & Percy Bartlett. First session turned on problems arising from our condemnation of both war & Nazism; question of whether people wanted an Allied victory in their hearts. Most people seemed to feel, as I do, that the victory of neither side would be best though it would mean a protracted war. I spoke on "Nazism" being an old evil, once known as "Reason of State", and not to be overcome by military weapons.

Saturday January 31st
Back at Conference by 10.0. This time in large Friends' Meeting House instead of small; it was *very* cold, which may have been reason why morning conference (on the kind of Christian Church we want to work for) was so poor. When discussions over, several people came up to me — among them Mary Ashford, my night sister in France in 1917, who is now a pacifist. She looks still quite young tho' she must be about 50 or more now, & I didn't recognise her when she spoke this morning. We had tea together at Euston; she told me that her nursing home in Hampstead had to be given up because of the Blitz. She now lives at Welwyn and takes one or two private patients in her own house.

News of war bad to-night; Malaya evacuated and all forces now defending Singapore itself.

Sunday February 1st
More heavy snow. Ground thickly covered. G. went off in the midst of it to a Rotary meeting (to-morrow) at Burton-on-Trent, followed by visits to Harrogate & Stoke.

Singapore awaiting heavy air-raids. The million people beleaguered there must feel much as we did after the fall of France, only worse. Only a miracle can save them now.

Monday February 2nd

Worked at home on correspondence and beginning of Letter No. 76. Snow lying too thick for much walking. Went out only for meals & to have hair shampooed in afternoon.

Finished Letter 76 in evening. Flat very cold; coal failed even for central heating, & snow too thick to deliver it. No hot water.

Wednesday February 4th

Much correspondence to dictate, including one to Rache who is quite obviously trying to head me off on writing novels as both safer & more profitable for persons with my opinions in wartime! I told him quite bluntly that neither safety nor profit were my main reasons for writing books, & that I was never likely to be moved to write more than an occasional novel.

G. rang up in afternoon to say that he was safely back but staying night in Park Lane. Very cold; heavy icy wind. Still no coal available for flats. At 5.30 I was picked up by an Army "utility" van, & conducted to a sort of one-man show debate (G. should have been there too but he got out of it) on America at the Greenford R.A.O.C. depot. Dined first in officers' mess; also treated to drinks now unobtainable by civilians — two sherries & a "Whisky Mac" after — which fortified me for the cold drive home.

Thursday February 5th

Changes announced in Government; Beaverbrook Minister of Production, Sir A. Duncan Minister of Supply; Harold Macmillan made Under-Sec. for Colonies & a P.C. Sir Stafford Cripps is not in & no real explanation is given for his refusal; it looks as though he were really going to have courage to lead the opposition & criticise the Government.

Bitter cold again; icy wind & more snow. Letter from W. E. Green reporting visit from police & inquiries about my Fortnightly Letter; I wonder if this is a preliminary to its suppression. Sounds like an investigation on "information laid" by someone. Shopped for household in afternoon. Feeling much depressed by constant cold weather, long period alone, complete absence of anything encouraging, & general fatigue from incessant work & late nights.

Noted the dreary look of Blitzed buildings (Richmond has many) half-covered with snow — snow on the ruined walls and on surviving remnants of "fittings" such as bookshelves.

Friday February 6th

Very cold. Many letters to dictate. Worked in flat all day, first on revision of *Christian Century* article as a pamphlet for the A.P.F.; then on article on women war-workers for the *Quiver*.

Wrote Ronald Kidd of the Civil Liberties asking whether I have any rights if police threat to my Letter develops.

Saturday February 7th

Wrote to John & Shirley after finishing article. Told them that I knew they were indeed "writing faithfully", for they were the best & loyalest children a mother ever had — as indeed they are. Told J. to read Ralph Ingersoll's *Report on England* for a vivid account of the Blitz.

Monday February 9th

Grimness of position at Singapore gradually becoming clear through the usual fog of censored news. Rationing of soap announced; buzz of talk among the women at the Ashburton indicated that it was more important to them than Singapore . . .

Cable from Dr Nevin Sayre of the U.S.A. F.o.R. asking for an article describing and evaluating British pacifism.

Tuesday February 10th

Better day. In afternoon walked by river. Letter from Miss Allen of the Civil Liberties said she thought it unlikely that my Fortnightly Letter would be suppressed; and that they would take up the matter at once if it were.

Singapore situation worsening. Work very difficult; 1940 tension back again. Criminal folly of those who started this war which we could have avoided becoming more & more self-evident.

In this mood of waiting I cannot write at all.

Wednesday February 11th

Japs already near, if not in, Singapore City. Dispatches from correspondents echo the noise, the terror; seem darkened with the smoke of a vanishing empire. American criticisms of us seem to be rising, endangering future relations. If we had had the sense to make peace when Hess offered it, our stock after resisting the Blitz would have been high.

Thursday February 12th

Work impossible to-day; news too grim. Singapore going, if not gone. Tension the same in my mind (though not apparently in that of most people here) as at the fall of France. American dispatches by Cecil King & Hanson Baldwin in *Evening Standard* both implicitly & explicitly condemn British policy & paint a black future. Australia calling up 45's; Sydney *Daily Mirror* plainly prophesying that soon little of the British Empire will be left . . . Japanese said to have crossed Burma river & to be threatening Rangoon. Kipling unknowingly prophesied this hour of our history when he wrote "Recessional". Everywhere voices asking more & more loudly: "Will Australia go? Will New Zealand? Will Burma? Will India?" This evening G. returned from lunch with Braithwaite M.P. & Vansittart (the Baron's brother) to say that within 6 weeks there will be a showdown, now preparing, in the H. of Commons, wh. will shake down the Government & perhaps Churchill himself.

The anguish of Singapore, its soldiers & civilians (who were deceived about the situation by our censorship until it was too late for them to escape), has been with me all day like a palpable presence. It is an overwhelming and sobering experience to have been born at the end of the prosperous Victorian era, and live to witness, while still only middle-aged, the collapse of that civilisation — thanks to two great Wars & the interests which brought them about.

Friday February 13th

More trouble for this unhappy country, more belabouring of politicians by the Press, because 3 German capital ships left Brest (where they had been bombed 100 times, apparently without any effect) & sailed straight up the Channel wh. no enemy fleet had done for generations. Protected by 200 'planes wh. were attacked by R.A.F., German ships escaped after we had lost 42 planes — & pilots.

Singapore still holding on, but its loss is assumed everywhere — & grim prophecies follow of the loss of Burma, perhaps India; the invasion of Australia & N.Z. Americans asking openly what we did with the armaments they sent, accusing us of sending Dominion, not British, soldiers to die.

Better day for work; impulse to do book.

Letter in *Times* from Compton Mackenzie, urging lifting of blockade to feed Greece.

Saturday February 14th

Most grim article by Alistair Cooke in *Daily Herald* speaking of hostile American reactions to British disasters. When Japan brought U.S. into the War I thought that there would be no Anglo-American recriminations, but if catastrophes continue it looks as if the British won't be very welcome in U.S.A. I hope John & Shirley won't hear these criticisms of their country — tho' God knows the criticisms are well deserved. Will the few of us who from Versailles onwards urged generous policies towards Germany — and towards the native populations under our Empire — wh. would have prevented all this, suffer from the tabu too, I wonder? Shall we be castigated by U.S.A. along with those who irresponsibly pushed this country into a major conflict & then mismanaged the war that they helped to create?

Had to abandon book for the moment and tackle the next Fortnightly Letter — No. 77 — wh. at least deals with the present situation. Finished it by evening & showed it to G. who approved.

Weather milder & misty, tho' still a cold wind. Tremendous row about the German battleships going on in the British Press.

Monday February 16th
Fall of Singapore officially announced in Premier's Broadcast last night &
in papers this morning. Papers full of attacks on Churchill for trying to take
too much on himself instead of devolving some duties on his colleagues.
Tension among the politically conscious as great as it was after the fall of
France (though apparently not among the rest, who are still discussing
soap).

Tuesday February 17th
Attended P.P.U. Executive at 2 p.m.; usual long discussion on famine
relief, ending in usual wrangle between J. Middleton Murry and Roy
Walker. Had very pleasant tea at Euston afterwards with Corder
Catchpool & his family to discuss how I could collaborate with the Friends
both during the war & after.

Wednesday February 18th
Papers this morning report another angry debate in the H. of Commons.
Churchill accused the House of "panic"; Pethick Lawrence queried this.
Churchill finally walked out while Gallacher was speaking, having been
compelled to promise an early debate on the war, & to give information
about the composition of the Court of Inquiry on the *Scharnhorst* &
Gneisenau.
   Four more letters from the children to-day! Two from John to Gordon,
one from John to me, one from Shirley to Gordon. J.'s letters are getting
most brilliant & original — as he is. He has now taken to *vers libre*!
   Went on to interview the Mr Wilkinson at the Min. of Health who is
trying to get shorter hair-dressing styles made popular as one means of
defence against typhus threats. I promised to give the idea what support I
could.

Thursday February 19th
Worked most of day on brochure for Adelphi Centre. Very cold; ground
hard & dry.
   Drafted a letter to the Home Secretary about recent visit of police to
Winifred Eden-Green. Dictated several letters to her over the telephone
this evening. One subscriber to the Letter sent me a cutting from the
Christian suggesting that the Nazis had bombed Bethel-bei-Bielefeld
themselves owing to the refusal of Pastor von Bodelschwingh to give up his
incurables for "mercy-killing".
   First air-raids by Japanese on Australia; heavy damage & presumably
casualties at Port Darwin.

Friday February 20th
Dictated numerous letters in rather a hurry before going into town.
Spent afternoon at Friends' House attending a conference of interested

organisations convened by the P.P.U. to discuss registration of the 16s to 18s & its implications.

Cabinet changes announced by Churchill. Main one is that Sir Stafford Cripps becomes Lord Privy Seal & Leader of the H. of Commons. Most people feel reconstruction not yet radical enough.

Japanese landings on Timor & Bali reported; now under 400 miles from Australia.

Saturday February 21st

Angry letter from M.S.J. saying I had "spoken ill" of her which up to a point is true, just as she has not only spoken, but written, ill of me. Personal differences of this kind are usually a 50–50 affair. Consulted G. who was helpful, wise & understanding about the whole affair. He is really my best friend as I with all my disadvantages am his. I replied to Margaret but took G.'s advice to do nothing about Middleton Murry through whom there has obviously been a hostile leakage of information. J.M.M.'s attitude to me changed from the moment I defended the position of the women at Langham instead of accepting the D. H. Lawrence idea (to wh. both J.M.M. and Joe Watson are enslaved) of a masculine *Herrenvolk* with an auxiliary chorus of women. To me and to many others (including G.) this is just another form of Nazism.

Bad day for work & *very* cold. Went out with G. for long trek in bitter wind after now scarce articles wh. meant going from shop to shop — soap powder, coal, cakes, etc. After dinner went with him to an American film called *Sergeant York* — the C.O. turned hero. Fine film, but based on a false interpretation of the "Render to Caesar" text.

Monday February 23rd

Many changes in Government announced. Stafford Cripps Leader of the H. of Commons & Lord Privy Seal. Most of the others doing musical chairs, but Margesson, Lord Moyne, Lord Reith & Arthur Greenwood completely dropped. No one knows what will happen now to the post-war planning (such as there was).

Decided to put pride in pocket & send Margaret a short note asking if we can meet and get on to an ordinary, even though not affectionate, plane again.

Work on "Humiliation with Honour" seems to become more & more impossible. Too much humiliation everywhere. May have to postpone & start novel, "Day of Judgment".

Tuesday February 24th   Wolverhampton

Devastating & furious letter from Margaret in morning calling me "disloyal", "untrustworthy", etc. Purely violent — and about as near reality as remark in previous letter that I had "rushed her things into an inaccessible store" was to the belated & reluctant removal of my belongings from Chelsea. Felt completely flattened out by violence — but got packed up in time to go for ten minutes to the service at St Martin's for the victims of famine. Then caught train to Wolverhampton.

Wednesday February 25th   London
Lectured Wolverhampton Women's Luncheon Club. Spoke on "Anglo – American Co-operation". Didn't feel it went down as well as usual; probably I was too pro-American for that audience.

Many letters but none of special interest, except one from Dorothy Plowman to say that the R.A.F. are taking much of the land round Langham & require the main house to be pulled down — wh. will probably destroy the Centre & Max's "University" idea.

Message from G. to say he is staying at Southgate, where he is lecturing, for the night, & won't be back. Tired and flattened. Only cheering thing a cable from St Paul saying that the children are well.

Thursday February 26th
Called first at the Haymarket offices of the American Committee for the Care of European Children. Saw their London representative who said that if the Colbys were on a "security" list owing to Dr Helene, they might be on it for the whole war.

Called at G.'s office & we went to the Dorchester together; he didn't think M.'s letter as devastating as I did, but thought her inhuman & wrong-headed, especially about the war, & urged me not to attempt to answer the letter.

Friday February 27th
Went to Friends' House to a Women's Commonwealth League Conference on India. Mrs Corbett Ashby spoke, & Agatha Harrison gave report on All–India Women's Conference — at which the President, Mrs Pandit, mentioned, & regretted, the refusal of my exit permit to go to India, pointing out that my presence would have been a reconciling, not an embarrassing, element.

Saturday February 28th
Weather suddenly become milder. G. in Hull. Went for a longish walk after lunch and sat for $\frac{1}{2}$ hour in sunshine on the Terraces. Saw two chaffinches and a bluetit. Spring smell of damp earth noticeable for first time, though pools & ditches still frozen in pools by the river.

Monday March 2nd
Roaring cold in head — either caught from someone or due to a sudden coming of milder weather. Day misty but gleams of pale sunshine. Coal now rationed but still unobtainable. Wrote my pamphlet for P.P.U. on "The Higher Retribution".

In the Terrace garden this afternoon I saw a tiny clump of snowdrops pushing their white spears through ground at the foot of a scarlet oak which would have been too hard for them to penetrate a week ago.

Fire-watching 7–11 p.m.

Tuesday March 3rd

Spent evening reading Victor Gollancz's excellent book against Vansittart: *Shall Our Children Live or Die?*

Java now in peril from Japs.

Wednesday March 4th

Did yet another copy of "The Higher Retribution" for Dr Nevin Sayre of U.S.A. & cabled him that it was coming.

Wrote Letter No. 78, on youth registration.

G. left early this morning to spend night in town & then 10 days on W.E.A. lectures in S. Wales. Made over £30 to him for expenses etc., leaving myself very short.

Heavy raid by R.A.F. on Paris last night. (Renault works now being used by Germans.) About 600 French people killed. This is another way, similar to the blockade, of making them love us.

Long letter from George Brett, describing his wartime committees; also assuring me that tho' his income is 40% of what it was he can still contribute to the children. Wrote asking what it was so that I could put it aside.

Thursday March 5th

Called in on G. at his office with his letters, socks etc., & we had a cocktail together before he caught his train to Swansea. Went on to Athenaeum Court and had lunch there with Jon Creech Jones (he as my guest). Jon emphasised the gravity of the present military situation; he did not contradict my view that the war should never have been allowed to begin — in our own interest quite apart from ideal considerations.

Friday March 6th

Conditions worsening in Java. First civilian casualty lists from Malaya & Hong Kong published in *The Times*. Long list; greatest number are the missing — always the most sinister, as in the Blitz here. I recall the gruesome item of the Bristol taxi-driver after the Blitz there — "five sackfulls of human remains".

"Observer's notes" (J.M.M.) point out this week the change of atmosphere in the H. of C. due to the sudden collapse of the Churchill legend. Churchill remains P.M. because there is no one else, but the faith in him as an inspired leader has gone.

Very cold again; snow; strong & bitter wind.

Saturday March 7th
Losing battle in Java nearing its end. Dutch, British, Americans hopelessly outnumbered. Batavia gone, Surabaya besieged, attack on Bandoeng — where the Government is — shortly expected. Doubtless we shall have similar conditions here before the end. Tragedy moves so swiftly from territory to territory that it is impossible to keep pace with it. The *Evening Standard* leader remarked to-night that in the S. African war it took the British $2\frac{1}{2}$ years to conquer the Boers, but the Japanese have conquered an Empire in $2\frac{1}{2}$ months.

Took chair this afternoon for a C.B.C.O. conference on the conscription of women; then went on to the P.P.U. National Council.

Laurence Housman told me at the Council that he found the same difficulty in writing in these days as I do — even his articles for *Peace News*.

Sunday March 8th
Newspaper filled with accounts of the tragedy of Java. The Juggernaut rush of events is overwhelming. It seemed just incredible that our Eastern Empire built up, however unjustly, over two centuries, should have vanished, with that of the Dutch, in $2\frac{1}{2}$ months. So much for Imperial power — a house built on the sand.

Monday March 9th
Dictated a few letters in morning, and thanks to Miss Paine's bright idea of ringing up the local fuel officer, actually got a promise of 1 cwt. of coal to-morrow from the Fuel Office as an "emergency ration".

Went to Friends House in afternoon to attend a Conference on Food Relief. Mr Dingle Foot spoke for the Govt.; Edith Pye & Roy Walker for the Friends & the P.P.U. Later several of us asked questions. Dingle Foot — rather an attractive youngish man — gave the plausible answers of a Parliamentarian, but seemed, I thought, a little embarrassed occasionally by his own position in the M. of Economic Warfare & the policy he was having to apply.

Tuesday March 10th
Sense of paralysis continuing and serious work impossible. Feel as if I were living in the midst of the "Decline and Fall" — only it is the British Empire this time, not the Roman.

Shopped in afternoon; was lucky in getting a good supply of cleaning materials; also registered for coal, but no great hopes of supplies were held out. Ration is now 1 cwt. a week.

Wednesday March 11th
Jap atrocities splashed over all the main pages of the daily papers, coupled with a good deal of hypocritical blah about the Govt. keeping it all back till it was confirmed out of consideration for the relatives of the victims. They

could spare the feelings of the relatives still if they wished, by keeping it out of the Press, but it serves their purposes too well. The effect of it on the common people in this country was seen immediately in a poster put up by a news-vendor outside the cinema on Richmond Hill: "WAKE UP ENGLAND. GIVE THE B JAPS A BLOOD BATH." It might be more becoming in us to refrain from righteous indignation over the Japanese until we have refrained from starving children on the Continent by our blockade.

G. telephoned asking me to meet him at his office at 7.0 and dine with him. We dined at the Café Royal Grill but it wasn't very successful as G. was suffering from the usual sense of frustration & non-collaboration owing to a breakfast with the President of McGill spoiled by the presence of Mr Andrews, and an invitation from Lady Astor to dine and discuss the Institute project with Lord Astor wh. was subsequently cancelled by telephone. Why? Unless Astor proposes to snaffle the idea & carry it through himself. Black dark rainy night; as I had come without a torch I spent the night with G. at 55 P.L.

Friday March 13th

Began writing Chapter 1, first draft, of "Humiliation with Honour". Have not by any means been through all the material I intended, but came to conclusion that to continue this would merely be a postponement of the painful effort of writing.

Went into town after lunch to get a front tooth stopped. Helen told me that her friend "Tanks" is missing in Libya. He didn't get on with his wife & I imagine that he & Helen were lovers. She looked faded & tired, I thought — though with the usual gay manner & conversation — but said she had an inner conviction that he was a prisoner with the Italians, not burnt up with his tank.

Saturday March 14th

Beautiful mild spring day. After working — very painfully — in morning on "H. with H.", I went for a walk along the towing path. Sunshine really warm; birds singing and a rich smell of earth in the fields beside the river. In the Terrace Gardens, snowdrops & crocuses were wide open to the sun.

A speech by Curtin & an article in the *Evening Standard* indicated that an early invasion of Australia by the Japs is expected. Australia again appealed to U.S.A. for effective aid.

Sunday March 15th

Another warm & beautiful day. Sunday papers contained accounts of the naval battle in the Java Sea before the capture of Java — a dreadful defeat in which the American, Dutch & our own naval losses have yet further worsened the Pacific balance of sea power. The *Exeter* & other ships just disappeared into a smoke screen put up by the Japs & were seen no more.

Monday March 16th

Actually a short Alert this morning — from about 11.0 [to] 11.15 — the 573rd in the London area. Later a few enemy reconnaissance 'planes reported to have been making their way towards London from the coast, & one got through.

Very busy day with a good many letters. One long one from Corder Catchpool to which I replied at length, on the possibility twice discussed with him of my joining the Society of Friends. He invited me to go to their house at Highgate for a weekend and talk it over. Certainly to be supported by the strength of the Friends' organisation would be a wonderful experience, and a great one for one if I were worth their having.

At last a letter from Ruth — & four from the children. Ruth's dated Feb. 2nd says J. is now 5 ft. 4 ins. tall — taller than me! Children ready to return here if & when we wish. Feel happier abt. them than I have for months.

Tuesday March 17th

Morning mail brought another long letter from Ruth, but this time one of the delayed ones from St Paul, date Sept. 15th. It was an important letter as it not only discussed J.'s character at some length, but told me the whole story of George Brett's offer to take Shirley. I read this in Marshall & Snelgrove's writing room, as I started off early taking the letters with me, and actually began to weep because [of] the real goodness & decency of both George & Ruth, & at the thought that my little girl had inspired such affection.

W. Eden-Green & I had lunch together & discussed the Letter; I also bought some white daffodils, yellow forsythia & two red roses for Helen Mayo in memory of "Tanks" & got W.E.G. to take them. Went on to P.P.U. Executive.

Wednesday March 18th

Wrote four more pages of Ch. 1 of "Humiliation with Honour". Difficult little book. Amy came as usual in afternoon. Wrote long letter to Ruth after supper.

Newspapers full of Australian preparations for invasion. Japs in New Guinea said to be preparing in force. The famous American general, MacArthur of the Philippines (whom George Brett so resembles), has left Bataan and flown to Australia to take charge of S.W. Pacific, 2,000 miles across Jap-dominated ocean, with wife & son. Australians must be feeling much as we did in July 1940.

Thursday March 19th

Went to West End to see Richard Murry's exhibition to write a 500-word notice of it for *Peace News*. First lunched at Marshall's & was somewhat depressed while eating my salad at the quick-lunch counter to note the number of fur-coated and bejewelled women who still apparently have plenty of leisure.

Went on to Bedford Square & was delighted with the little exhibition of 20 pictures, showing London's damaged buildings in all their variety of grotesque shapes and bizarre colours, by daylight, moonlight & twilight. One so pleased me — a little study called "Congested area" of one wrecked ghost-building standing in a desolate cleared area wh. reminded me of Bow — that though the price was 12 guineas I decided to buy it for John, as a memento of the Blitz and my contacts with Kingsley Hall & the East End.

Saturday March 21st   Dawlish
Went to Dawlish to spend week-end with Mother before bringing her to London for a fortnight. We went for a short walk before dinner; flowers at about the same stage as in Richmond, but buds more advanced.

We discussed G.'s and my surmises about the possibility of "camping out" in 2 Cheyne Walk but decided that the coal, gas & electricity rationing would make it finally impossible to run.

Sunday March 22nd
Very beautiful day. Spent most of it out of doors on three different walks — two with Mother & the third alone, when I went to get a few catkins from the walk under the arch beyond the Church. The crocuses — purple & gold — are thick in all the Gardens, & the catkins very plentiful, but most of them are out of reach, hanging like miniature lambs' tails against the blue sky.

Helped Mother to pack. Persuaded her to give G. the £100 a year she had offered me.

Monday March 23rd   London
Brought Mother to town from Dawlish by early 9.13 train. On Dawlish Station a little girl looked at the automatic sweet machines, insisted that they had chocolates in them; finally, to satisfy her, her mother pulled out the drawers & demonstrated that they were empty. Small child, aged about 8, looked terribly disappointed, & I remembered in my bag the little basket which was part of Shirley's present to Mother, with two of the marzipan fruits still left. I fetched it out & gave it to the little girl, thinking how much Shirley — with her passion for giving things away — would approve. Later I saw the little girl getting into the train with the basket held in her hand like a trophy. At Paddington G. met us, & I left Mother at the *Star & Garter* reasonably well satisfied with the hotel. She had tea at our flat first & was much impressed with it.

Tuesday March 24th
Spent day in town with Mother. First time for about a year since I have

visited West End shops in morning. Contrast [with] empty streets & shops during Blitz a year ago quite amazing. To-day, the luncheon-room at Marshall & Snelgrove's full by 12.30. Where do all these youngish-looking (presumably married) women come from & why do they have so much time to spare? I am *sure* that the atmosphere is different than that of the last war; that the tension I felt then was not only due to my being in hospital.

Wednesday March 25th
Dictated three days' letters, made brief draft of next Sunday's Peterborough lecture, then went to 55 Park Lane where we had the Ogilvies to lunch. They were obviously pleased to be asked. Mary is v. busy doing work under the Ministry of Health for day nurseries & nursery schools, but F. W. Ogilvie has had no job since leaving the B.B.C. & has obviously been badly treated. They both had a good deal to say about the evils of "monopoly broadcasting", the conservatism of the Corporation & the better system in the U.S.A. of diverse broadcasts through various advertising agencies.

Went on to Friends' House, had Corder Catchpool to tea to discuss launching of a campaign to counteract the growing Vansittart propaganda. Decided to begin with a Conference at Friends' House in May.

On returning alone to flat thought I heard burglar; got porter to come up & help me look through & do black-out.

Thursday March 26th
Few letters. Worked all day preparing a new "Shape of the Future" lecture for Peterborough Co-op on Sunday.

Usual dividend received from Brittain's. Had a 9% bonus added which would have raised it higher than usual but for income tax which is having a fortunate equalising effect; I should feel a bad conscience in having the money at all but for that.

Evening Standard reported that Herbert Morrison was "watching" *Peace News* as well as the *Daily Mirror*.

Sunday March 29th   Peterborough
Went to Peterborough to lecture to the local Co-op on "The Shape of the Future". Had an hour to spare before the lecture so was taken by the young man who met me to see Peterborough Cathedral — lovely and austere, with little colour; it seemed in my recollection not unlike Canterbury but of course much smaller.

I expected to be much heckled and criticised as I was by the Birmingham Co-op. & was also somewhat intimidated by the fact that my predecessors had been Joad & J.B.S. Haldane. Instead I had a most friendly and appreciative audience (rendered the more so by the supporting presence of about 40 of the local P.P.U. & Quaker Group). The organisers told me afterwards that it was much the best of the three lectures, asked me if I would give it again at an adjacent town called March, and inquired if I was ever free to deliver a series! One of the leading Friends introduced me after tea, commending the manner in which I had expressed the views for wh. we stood to a non-pacifist audience without controversy or provocation. I made a short speech on practical methods of subscribing to our values. The tea was followed by the ordinary evening meeting at Friends' House with the same man taking the meeting. At this I spoke briefly on "The Ordeal of British Pacifism" — the subject I had already thought out for the article set me by Nevin Sayre.

My train back was quite punctual & I was lucky in getting a carriage to myself. It had been such a beautiful spring day & so pleasantly spent that I did not feel tired, but must have been so for, just at the top of Richmond Hill up wh. I was perhaps walking too fast, I went semi-conscious & fell crash-down, hurting my left knee & tearing the one decent remaining pair of silk stockings. Was helped up by a young soldier, got to flat all right.

Monday March 30th
Much shaken by fall, leg very stiff, could not walk much or take advantage of pleasant sunny afternoon. Managed however to get Letter No. 80 (on Easter & plans for the future) written in time for Miss Paine to type it. Went to bed early (midnight).

Tuesday March 31st
Several letters from Macmillan by morning mail. One reported that [American] income tax on royalties earned by non-resident aliens had gone up to $27\frac{1}{2}\%$. This (with 50% tax here) means that one will only actually receive just over 20% of what one earns.

P.P.U. Executive this afternoon. At "emergency business" John M.M. reported Morrison's threat to *Peace News*.

Wednesday April 1st
Spoke on "Shape of the Future" to Baptist Ministers' Meeting in Southampton Row in afternoon. Hardly worth doing as so few were there owing to some theological conference.

Congress Party reported to be likely to refuse the Indian plan taken by Cripps.

G. went to Café Royal Grill to dine with Victor Gollancz in response to G.'s letter to V.G. about *Shall Our Children Live or Die?* I sent V.G. a message saying I was recommending his book everywhere. He told G. a story to the effect that when Eden was in Moscow, Stalin was telling him & Cripps his plans for post-war Europe. Eden interposed nervously: "But, M. Stalin, what about the Atlantic Charter?" Whereupon Stalin turned to Molotov and cryptically interpolated: "Ha, ha! The Atlantic Charter!" He continued to make this interjection at intervals throughout the conversation.

G. gathered that V.G. is now distrustful of the Soviet Union. He has obviously changed in the direction of magnanimity since his meeting in Chelsea abt. wh. I wrote to the *New Statesman*, thus initiating the severance of our business relations.

Fire-watching during the night 3 a.m.–6 a.m. Moon hidden but night light; bitter east wind.

Saturday April 4th
Took Mother to matinee of Emlyn Williams' play *The Morning Star*. About the first time I have been to a West End theatre for more than a year. The play was the story of the problems and love-affairs of a young doctor (played by Emlyn Williams) against background of the London Blitz. Blitz was very realistic; the air-raid night in the play reminded me of nights in Devonshire Street & at Athenaeum Court.

Discussions in India reaching critical stage — "neither hopeful nor desperate".

Sunday April 5th
Blowy showery Easter Day with intervals of bright sunshine. The daffodils are all out in the Terrace Gardens with pink prunus bushes in blossom amongst them. Took Mother to Kingsley Hall, where I had promised to go to tea & the service and give an evening talk on "Revolution". Patrick Figgis spoke at the service in the Mission Hall, which was decorated with daffodils — and very tidy and un-Blitzed-looking compared with my memories of it last spring. The Club room was crowded for my talk. I spoke of the War as a revolutionary situation — the result of deep revolutionary changes, and likely to be the source of more. Excellent & long discussion lasting till 9 p.m.

Double summer-time began.

Monday April 6th
Wind at gale force; intervals of sunshine. I went to Richmond cemetery in the afternoon to see Father's grave as it would have been his 78th birthday to-day. The cemetery seemed filled with spring flowers for Easter.

Wednesday April 8th
Collapse of India negotiations threatened (reading between the lines this seems to be due to the obstinacy of the War Cabinet, i.e. Churchill, in refusing even to consider the Indian defence demands). Last Sunday Gram Swing wrote in the *Sunday Express* that if the negotiations failed, Gandhi's name — as that of a believer in non-violence — would be the only Indian name still to count much in U.S.A.

Saw Mother off at Paddington by the 1.30. Had hair shampooed at Marshall's by Miss Low (who has just been away for 6 months having a baby). Picked up G. at 55 Park Lane & we had tea with his school and college friend Andreas Michalopoulos, now Greek Minister of Information, who also has an apartment in 55. He told us that B.B.C. regulations are now so asinine that he broadcasts to Greece through Moscow. Also that negotiations are in hand for removal of starving Greek children to Egypt or S. Africa; & that 7 Swedish ships have now begun to serve Greece with food.

Thursday April 9th
Large mail; dealt with it all morning. At tea-time went to Mayfair Hotel to see demonstration of "Liberty cut" sponsored by Min. of Health as anti-typhus measure. New line of country for me; place crowded with hairdressers, representatives of the Press (mostly hard-working women plainly dressed), and fashionable ladies in mink coats looking as if they'd never heard of the war. Several leading hairdressers talked on importance of shorter hair for women in present crisis. Demonstrations of "Liberty Cut" on different girls followed, including a showing of the "cut" itself. The number of men present interested me; it showed how much money there is to be made out of women's hair.

At 8.45 by agreement rang up Leonard Lockhart, recently released from Broadmoor, at an address he gave me in Sutton. He sounded a new man, full of vigour & energy; has numerous engagements, is seeing Sir T. Harder, Ministry of Supply, etc., wh. sounds like an industrial welfare job. (I saw a newspaper paragraph recently on the shortage of industrial welfare medicals, and wondered if he would be released.) It must be strange to start life all over again at 43 in the middle of a Great War.

Saturday April 11th
Morning, started article for U.S.A. *Fellowship* on "The Ordeal of British Pacifism", 3,000 words.

Afternoon, sat on platform at grand meeting at Central Hall, Westminster, put on by Nat. Council of Civil Liberties on "The Freedom of the Press". Packed out. Speakers were Horabin, M.P., Coppock (a T.U. official), Rose Macaulay, who spoke of "Romantic Attitude to Facts" of the *Daily Worker* & was apparently regarded as a huge joke by the mainly Communist audience, Michael Foot of the *Evening Standard*, Joad, Edith Summerskill, D. N. Pritt and Aneurin Bevan. There was much criticism of Herbert Morrison & much commendation of Frank Owen (Editor of the *Evening Standard* who has been called up with sinister suddenness) who finally came to sit on the platform.

Failure of British Plan for India reported in evening papers. Cripps coming home.

Lovely letter from John, & a good drawing.

Sunday April 12th
Beautiful April day. All blossoms suddenly out in warm sunshine. Able to discard overcoat for first time. Spent day at Peaslake with William & Rosalind Seymour; took Philip a Hornby train, and saw the superb new baby, Gerald — who kicks and at 4 months tries to sit up just as Shirley did. Before tea & my bus we walked over to the Pethick Lawrences' charming house, designed by him 20 years ago when Peaslake was almost uninhabited. Mrs Pethick Lawrence welcomed me warmly, also her sister Miss Pethick and aged friend Mary Neale. Pethick took me over the house and garden, told me he was writing his autobiography "Fate Has Been Kind", and picked me a beautiful bunch of fresh young daffodils.

Monday April 13th
Miss Paine in bad temper bec. I can't afford to employ her any longer owing to failure of income tax appeal & increased American income tax.
    Started drafting Letter No. 81 on failure of the Indian plan. Then had late lunch at Paddington Hotel with Leonard Lockhart — who was quite his old self, full of vitality & eagerness. As he talked (particularly about Broadmoor's system) I saw a bigger sociological novel, bringing in facts about "criminal lunacy", than the one I originally meant to write about. He gave me a grand lunch & said I had had a "tough time" when I outlined the events of the past two years. Sent Amy Johnson's parents a copy of *Truth is Not Sober* wh. arrived from U.S.A. last week. Newspapers, espec. *Times*, filled with news & articles on India.

Tuesday April 14th
P.P.U. Executive this afternoon. After Committee over, talked to Stuart about my own suppressions by Home Secretary, & whether anything could be done to get travel ban removed. Stuart said he would talk to Lord Ponsonby & Reg. Sorensen.

Thursday April 16th
Spent most of day going to & returning from Birmingham (9 hours' travel altogether from door to door) to make a 40 minutes speech to the W.I.L. Annual Conference. Put realistic case for closer Anglo-American co-operation, including reciprocal citizenship, and made some impression on a group of women with vague predilections for "some form of world citizenship" not likely to be realisable for generations. Speech based on 2 paragraphs of a letter from Dorothy Detzer (W.I.L. of U.S.A.), the first deploring anything wh. might lead to a U.S.-British hegemony, & the second reporting American anxiety because only supporters of the British war effort were allowed to go to U.S.A. Developed the last point, quoting my own experience.

Friday April 17th
Muriel Lester came to tea. We conversed chiefly about her experiences

when she was interned in Trinidad, put in a Glasgow jail on arrival & then taken to Holloway. Despite the dangerous journey & the anxiety of her family, they were not notified of her arrival in this country until the Thursday though she landed on the Monday — & then only because the C. of E. chaplain at Holloway broke the rules.

We talked also of the frustration of the young in Pacifist Service Units & the comparative acquiescence of the peace movement in the repression of its members.

G. persuaded me to go to the new Disney film *Dumbo* but it depressed me very much by reminding me of the children.

Saturday April 18th
Letter from George Brett outlining the financial situation & suggesting summer plans for the children. He doesn't think it would be wise to try to get them home as things are at present. Financial situation may involve their transfer to ordinary U.S. high schools. (A good thing too in many ways.)

Another lovely day, but no time to get out into it. Went off after tea to spend the night with the Catchpools at Hampstead Heath & discuss Quakerism. Their whole family — 3 girls & a small boy — were home from school, so after long meal in kitchen, music, etc., we didn't get to discussing the main topic till nearly midnight. By then I was almost too tired to be coherent, but did manage to express the doubt whether the Society, which is collectivist, was a suitable religious affiliation for the artist (whether writer, musician or painter), who is by nature individualistic, egotistical & exhibitionist. No conclusion reached by late bedtime.

Evening papers reported first bombing of Tokyo & other Jap. cities by American 'planes.

Sunday April 19th
Went to Hampstead Quaker meeting with the Catchpools, walking there & back across Hampstead Heath in beautiful sunshine. I felt quite happy & at peace during the hour of silent worship. On the way back to the Catchpools' house we saw a sweet wire-haired terrier killed by a tough beefy motor-cyclist (army) going much too fast down the hill. The man tried to avoid the dog, but ran over it; he was thrown over but was unhurt, but the poor dog lying in the middle of the road died just as we reached it. The group of passers-by coming from various churches took much more interest in the dog than the man, but nothing could be done for it.

Monday April 20th
Working at home. Pleasant sunny day, making the newspaper accounts of the devastation done to Lübeck and other places by our bombings of Germany an incongruous nightmare.

Tuesday April 21st
Fuel & light rationing announced for June 1st. Amy & Burnett came in afternoon. Burnett had much to say about the attitude of his squadron towards the fiasco of the *Scharnhorst* & *Gneisenau* going through the Channel. According to him the Admiralty & Air Ministry had information a *week* beforehand that the ships were leaving Brest, yet failed to take adequate measures. The Swordfish aircraft were sent to Burnett's squadron in readiness, and the men on them knew they were going to certain death, as these aircraft are only meant for reconnaissance flights from aircraft carriers & are too slow to be protected by fighters. There was high feeling in the squadron after the affair was over; the men were openly saying that it was just cold murder to send those obsolete craft to attack German battleships. Burnett is soon leaving the squadron to join a mobile unit in England.

Wednesday April 22nd
Had "Liberty Cut" done for Ministry of Health's benefit (very nice, though; all hair gets thoroughly cut, & only two pins are needed). As "perm" was necessary for back, had to sit there from 1.30 till nearly 5.0 and after that be photographed for M. of I. distribution. Got back home in time to have dinner before taking the chair at a Richmond Food Relief meeting at a café in the Kew Rd, organised by the local P.P.U.

Thursday April 23rd
Corrected & sent off "Ordeal of British Pacifism" article for Nevin Sayre. After tea sat in sun in Buccleuch Garden & drafted one for *Peace News* called "Betraying Time's Trust", on the bombing of Lübeck.
   Mrs H. dropped the alarm clock on the curb in my bedroom, but a shop here think they can mend it. No more to be bought.

Saturday April 25th
Daily papers filled with more grim details of the Lübeck raid, including a photograph of the town & bombed areas ("the dead heart of a city of 150,000 people", said the *D. Herald*). Also equally gruesome details of Rostock, bombed this week. Added some paragraphs to my article. What will all this ghoulish gloating do to our psychology as a nation?
   Went to Friends' House for the P.P.U. Annual General Meeting. Early in the proceedings James Norbury attacked me for saying that "a pacifist could support this war" — a complete misreading of my letter to *Peace News* on Sorensen. Replied with vigour. The evening session was to have been opened by Canon Raven on "The Individual, the Area & the Group", but he never turned up, so Lord Ponsonby, who was to have closed the discussion, opened it — commenting on the present evil of widespread "acquiescence". Debate rather poor owing to lack of prepared opening speech.

Sunday April 26th
Opened morning session of A.G.M. with 15-minute speech on "Immediate Policy". Made 5 points (registration of youth, food relief campaign, wider protests against bombing, anti-Vansittart counter-move, and practical methods of serving truth) emphasising that the pacifist is now & always to change the thinking of this country &, beyond that, of mankind. Much better debate followed than last evening. Met Corder Catchpool & T. C. Foley for a few moments after session, & joined T. C. Foley for lunch in the tea-room at Euston to discuss his emergency resolution on bombing.

Second session opened by J. Middleton Murry on pacifist long range policy (the usual penetrating analysis). Then came the reports on the three sessions by Alan Eden-Green, Winifred Rawlings & Stuart Morris — and finally Foley's emergency resolution on bombing which I seconded & Albert Belden supported; passed easily.

Monday April 27th
Inevitable Nazi reprisals for destruction of historic buildings in Lübeck have begun; Bath was heavily raided on Saturday night and again (more lightly) on Sunday. Miss Paine said Stuart M. tried in vain to get through to Bath P.P.U. last night. Wondered whether our furniture, Mother's & the Burnetts', all at Powell's, has been destroyed. Don't mind furniture, which can be replaced, but Edward's portrait & all his letters & other war letters, as well as Winifred's letters, are there; also all her MSS except *South Riding*, & copies of all the articles I have ever written. Also, in black box, all G.'s & my letters, & his mother's diaries. Luckily took all my own diaries & MS. of *South Riding* to Cornwall; also G.'s diaries. Mother's letter reported wide raids on Devon — several Alerts 3 nights running; one [bomb] dropped only 2 miles away. Exeter & Exminster were badly bombed; also Newton Abbot.

Worked most of day on Letter 82, on effects of atrocities & other war propaganda, espec. the war sadism of the newspapers abt. our "area bombing".

Tuesday April 28th
More grim details in *Evening News* abt. the Rostock raid, wh. has left tens of thousands homeless & the town a heap of ruins. Germans have now announced reprisals on "works of art, monuments & residential districts — everything with 3 stars in *Baedeker*". Last night they attacked Norwich in sharp raid, with heavy casualties. This fulfilled my own prophecy as I wrote yesterday that our new method of bombing meant a new peril for our loveliest cities — "Winchester, Norwich, Lincoln, York & a dozen others". Papers have many pictures of bombed churches & houses in Bath — but no news of furniture yet.

Wednesday April 29th
Another prophecy of mine fulfilled — Nazis raided York last night. The

Minster was unharmed, but a girls' school got a direct hit, and the headmistress & five teachers were killed.

A telegram came from Mother first thing to say that she had heard from Powell's about the furniture — "safe, slight blast, roof damaged, doing our best."

Evening papers reported that Rhys Davies has already asked the question sent him by our night-bombing committee on whether we had changed our bombing policy. Sinclair blandly and fallaciously said: "No."

Thursday April 30th
Norwich raided again last night. Papers this morning (*Times* & *D. Herald*) have leaders on bombing wh. are obviously Govt. inspired, shrill & defensive. *D. Herald* in particular had abandoned all attempts at morality. Sent in a short letter over the telephone which they tentatively accepted; then had various conversations on the immorality of the present bombing policy with Stuart Morris, Tom Foley, Humphrey Moore. Finally went in this afternoon to Tom Foley's office to discuss how to get the anti-bombing committee on a broader basis. Corder Catchpool there too. We decided to ask Reg. Sorensen to help us get a meeting with M.P.s before taking any further step.

Friday May 1st
Terrific day of correspondence for Miss Paine's final visit — 27 letters in all, on a great diversity of subject. All my money goes in stamps. I did get an hour of lovely sunshine, despite the still cold wind, sitting beside the golden and orange wallflowers in the Buccleuch Garden with their scent like a benediction all round me.

Government defeated by Independents in the two by-elections at Rugby (W. J. Brown) & Wallasey.

Saturday May 2nd
Worked all day on "Humiliation with Honour"; went through chapters, found Fortnightly Letters that bore on them, & tried to get myself into a writing mood again.

Afternoon sun lovely again, but weather still very cold. All leaves out now & the chestnuts in bud. Bluebells coming out in the Buccleuch wood. Garden now superb.

Monday May 4th
Had another postcard from Ruth, sent March 9th; she told me that Shirley now bicycles alone for miles. I only hope the small venturesome girl takes sufficient care of herself, and asked Ruth in a return p.c. to beg her to show caution for my sake. William Kean Seymour reported results of sale of my

Ford shares (now partly armaments, so I mustn't keep them) wh. realised approx. £95 as against £124 — i.e., a loss of roughly £30.

Evening papers reported Exeter severely bombed again; I fear Mother must have had another bad night at Dawlish. Wrote letter to *Evening News* about their leader "The Vandals", wh. stated that Exeter, Bath & York had no military objectives!

Tuesday May 5th
Letter from Mother described bombing of Exeter on Sunday night; the hotel at Dawlish shook for hours, & she couldn't get in at all for a hair appointment she had. She says the Cathedral is damaged, though repairable, & most of the shopping centre down.

Wednesday May 6th   Cambridge
Got up late as incipient cold of yesterday & late return made me feel wretched. Got up at last & tackled correspondence, but left a loaded desk when I had to leave for Cambridge.

At 7.30 spoke at a Food Relief meeting under the usual auspices of a "neutral" Committee. Master of Selwyn in the Chair; other speaker a young scientist, Dr Neil Jenkins, who dealt with the medical effects of starvation. I took the general political background & answered most of the question with what Dr Wood called great success. Hall of the Baptist Church where meeting held was crowded with young men & women. They were critical & intelligent, but passed the resolution that I proposed *nem. con.*

Thursday May 7th   London
Returned early from Cambridge with Alex Wood; took 8.16 train & was back at flat by 11.30. Got on with correspondence till after lunch.

Went on to Friends' House & attended Council meeting of Nat. Peace Council to hear Maude Royden describe her recent visit to U.S.A. She took a somewhat "Ministry of Information" view; thought the exclusion of pacifists from U.S.A. reasonable on ground that they didn't help war effort. Sorensen asked v. pertinently if some of the people sent by the Govt. helped the war effort either, & she had to admit that they didn't. General discussion followed on exit permits for pacifists & the N.P.C. delegation, wh. is again refused facilities for America by Brendan Bracken. I urged maximum publicity.

Went on to the "Council of Seven" meeting arranged by Mrs William Paterson at the luxurious Lansdowne Club. Elizabeth Sprigge was there & warned me that it was "Fascist" — a conclusion to wh. I came after hearing the speeches. But decided to become an hon. member in order to watch it.

Friday May 8th
Amy came. Said she would gladly come back to us with Marian whenever

the children could return. After tea went to Conference organised by Geoffrey Pittock-Buss on Vansittartism. Victor Gollancz there; we shook hands & spoke to each other cordially for first time for 3 years. I thought he might go as there were so many pacifists at the Conference, but he stayed to the end & spoke in the discussion, saying that hatred was *not* a necessary ingredient in a successful war (a questionable paradox). Set speakers were Corder Catchpool, Dr Moisel (German), Karl Schneider (German), G. & myself. V. successful discussion ended in decision to form anti-Vansittart Committee. V.G. came along with G. and me to a meal at the Euston Hotel.

Saturday May 9th
Large naval battle still raging in Pacific. Norwich raided again last night, while the R.A.F. "did a Rostock" on Waremunde 5 miles away.

Large mail, chiefly consisting of requests to do things. W.I.L. want me to join their Executive, Dr Belden wants me to join the Council of "Christianity Calling", Mrs Paterson to lunch with her & discuss the "Council of Seven", Ronald Mallone to write an introdn. to his poems. He can't understand why I haven't read them after 2 months!

Worked all day on article for *Quiver* on "How War Changes Our Daily Lives", and got manuscript draft done by evening.

Another postcard from Ruth this morning. Wrote saying how much I wished J. & S. could return here by Clipper when it begins going to Ireland.

Sunday May 10th
Coldish day, weary & exhausting. Left Richmond early to speak at Northampton. Ten hours spent on a 25 minutes speech at a small meeting (shared by Stuart Morris) in a rather gloomy Baptist chapel. Thought what I might have done with the ten hours & decided to refuse all meetings for indefinite period & get on with writing.

Wednesday May 13th
German offensive against Russia in Caucausus (Kerch peninsula) seems to have begun.

Morning spent on telephone calls, mail, revision of Letter 83, wh. I sent off. Went to Westminster for a H. of Commons Committee at wh. several M.P.s (R. R. Stokes, Rhys Davies, Sorensen, Cove, Harvey, Wilson) met the bombing committee and reviewed the general situation re bombing & gas — but nothing very conclusive emerged. Three German pastors there gave evidence about the treasures in Lübeck.

Thursday May 14th
Rockery & blossom in the Terrace Garden so lovely now that the treasury

of scent & colour makes me want to dance. Even the Old English Garden in Battersea Park was not such a miracle as these beautifully planned rare shrubs & rock plants. Lilac (several colours), broom, cherry, a species of syringa, rhododendrons, prunus & chestnuts are all out together.

Friday May 15th

Letters from V. Gollancz explaining difficulties of reprinting *T. of Y.* owing to its length & from Macmillan passing on a Swedish translation offer for "Humiliation with Honour" which I forwarded to Dakers. Rache, on the telephone, told me that the new edition of *T. of Friendship* is now ready.

Lunched with Eliz. Sprigge at her charming small flat in a mews, 8 Rex Place, just opposite G.'s office in South Street. She has inquired about Clipper transport & has ascertained that Clippers *are* going to Ireland, and that the children could be got on to one by negotiations at the American end. I promised to try to help her 19-year-old daughter who joined the A.T.S. on a promise of further training in draughtsmanship wh. she has not received.

Saturday May 16th

Rained all last night; damp but very warm day. Terrace Garden and the view over the river & Surrey unbelievably lovely after the rain. There must be twenty different greens in the vivid young trees between Richmond & the horizon, and the rock garden heals my mind with its rich beauty like a superb concert or a noble poem. Flowers have always been a great comfort to me.

Huge battles on German–Russian front at Kharkov (Russian offensive) & Kerch in the Crimea (German offensive).

Sunday May 17th

Finished writing second chapter (first draft) of "Humiliation with Honour" — "Numbered with the Transgressors". Incredibly lovely morning, hot & sunny, but turned cloudy and blustery later. Between lunch and tea went for long walk with G. through remaining "corridor" of the Park (the rest being occupied with camouflaged military encampments, guns, allotments and fields of sown grass) to Roehampton Gate. Park scented with budding may, pink & white. Chestnuts in full bloom; young oaks bright green.

Fire-watching, 9.0–12.0.

Monday May 18th

Large correspondence. Kept me at work till tea-time, when I went to Daniel Street School in Bethnal Green to act as interviewer of newly registered girls of 16–18 as representative of Youth Groups for the L.C.C. Interviewed with Miss Peter, the headmistress of the school. She had founded a Girls' Training Corps for the Services, but invariably put the good of the girls first & I thought her very fair. Young women — machinists, factory workers, waitresses, clerical workers — very different from the girls of the 1920s. Elegant, painted, & on the whole clean. Only one little slut who was "keeping house" for her family. The girls who wanted to enter the Services or to do nothing were quite positive about their own views; the others we "directed" to Clubs, etc. Interviewed about 20. Bethnal Green Rd almost unrecognisable since the demolition of the blitzed buildings; gaps are so huge. Back to very late supper; journey took about 1½ hours.

Tuesday May 19th
Elizabeth Sprigge & I lunched with Mrs Paterson at the Lansdowne Club, & discovered her "Council of Seven" movement to contain a great deal of mystical nonsense akin to the Nazi attitude to women. I told her that (a) I would work for anything that would rehabilitate the disintegrated family & restore it to its place in the nation, (b) I would *not* take any part in a move to treat women as either super or sub human.

Wednesday May 20th
In Richmond all day. Struggled again with a mass of correspondence & *Quiver* proof to get on to Chap. 3 of "H. w. H.", but didn't even finish revising Ch. 2. Bright early day turned dull & heavy. Amy & Burnett came, & Burnett said goodbye in view of possible embarkation leave. I told him that whatever happened, we would always look after Amy & give her & Marian a home.

   G. exploring situation in S. Poplar, where the M.P. has just died. Put through various telephone calls. Stuart Morris said he thought of standing as an Independent Pacifist, but Patrick Figgis, whom I rang up later, said there was no pacifism in South Poplar, & he thought it would be only a gesture plus the loss of a large sum of money.

   Angry debate on war situation proceeding in H. of Commons. Much criticism of Churchill, who is not there & has left Attlee & Cripps to cope.

Thursday May 21st
G. in bed (except for brief visit to Labour Party headquarters) with a cold & temperature. Attempts to get on with my book considerably thwarted by ensuing domesticity & preparation of small meals.

   Hair shampooed after tea. Did manage late in evening to finish revising Ch. 2.

Friday May 22nd   Loughborough
After early lunch went to Loughborough to give a lecture for the Professional & Business Women's Club ("The Shape of the Future"). Met at Loughborough station by my hostess, Miss English, a local bookseller, P.P.U. member & reader of my Letter. Lecture was public & very well

attended; biggish hall in Town Hall was full. Audience very mixed including some Service people; some of them must have been critical, but there was no discussion at the end. Put a trunk call through to find if G. was all right. He was, but told me that British Council is trying to crab his Anglo-American two-ways Institute — want nothing to be done till after the war & then for the Govt. to do it! We seem already to have adopted the totalitarianism we are fighting!

Monday May 25th   London
To-day the workers' one holiday & of course it had to be wet. Everyone tramping miserably round Richmond in showers & standing in queues outside cinemas.

After tackling mail & revising Letter 84, went to Central Hall, Westminster, to Labour Party Annual Conference. Afternoon discussion not very interesting, but question of the party truce kept cropping up. Rhys Davies told us he had attacked it at the session this morning, & several delegates this afternoon mentioned diminution of local party membership & loss of members to Communist Party. Attlee, Herbert Morrison, Laski, Ellen, Barbara Gould, Arthur Greenwood, Philip Baker on platform.

When session ended took Freda White to tea at St Ermin's; she is now sub-editor of the *New Statesman*. She agreed with me that Kingsley Martin is feminist in theory but anti-feminist in practice. Gave terrifying description of civil service workings of M.o.I. where she was previously. She described Middleton Murry's mind as phosphorescent!

Wednesday May 27th   Winscombe
Went to Winscombe by 12.30 train from Paddington via Frome. Spoke at Food Relief meeting in Village Hall. Good crowd there of about 300 — of wh. about 50 were girls & boys from Sidcot School. Gave general talk & answered questions. Meeting passed resolution urging Govt. to extend relief to Belgium etc. with only one dissentient. Man who seconded it was an elderly doctor, who said he didn't altogether agree with my point of view, but my statement of case was so reasonable that he felt he could second. Collection v. good — amounted to about £8.

Thursday May 28th   Weston-super-Mare
Went on by afternoon bus to Wester-s.-Mare. Gave 7.30 address in local Methodist church on "Vansittartism", with C. of E. Vicar — a pleasant and intelligent young man — in chair. Church absolutely packed; people standing & many turned away. Subject obviously a "draw" — helped by large notice outside church & advts. in press. Crowd very miscellaneous; expected heckling but got none, only several v. intelligent questions.

Friday May 29th   Bath
Left Weston-s.-M. by 9.40 train for Bath. Day of gales & showers. Much

damage to small houses near railway on outskirts Bath. Town itself badly damaged in spots but not comparable to many other Blitzed places. Main shopping centres almost intact. Francis Hotel demolished; roof of St James's Church gone; also many houses near station. Abbey was closed; at East End stained glass all shattered in famous "Lantern Window", gargoyles lying in heaps on ground. Drove straight to Powell's & then with a member of the firm to the warehouse; hundreds of tiles gone from roof but damage nowhere near our furniture or Burnett's; a little nearer Mother's but everything quite all right.

Lunched with Mrs Husband of Malaya — a charming, dark, hazel-eyed girl of about 30. Her husband, a planter, had *not* agreed with her views — wh. she held alone in Johore. When she last heard of her husband he had been trying to escape from Singapore. She came home via the Cape on a 7-weeks voyage expecting to be torpedoed all the time, with 13 people in a 2-berth cabin; they were on a troop ship wh. took 2,000 people home. They were attacked outside harbour but got away.

Sunday May 31st
Got out "Humiliation with Honour" and spent wretched day over it. As I was arranging notes for Ch. 3, realised that the thing was dead, read like a tract, must be re-written in accordance with some new technique that would make it live. Suddenly got inspiration of doing it as a series of letters to John — based on Ruth's information of his criticising and questioning my pacifist ideas while Shirley loyally champions them. Began drafting first short letter but felt tired, depressed & bad-tempered after wrestling with it all day.

Monday June 1st
Morning papers reported a mammoth air-raid on Saturday night on Cologne. Over 1,000 aeroplanes took part. Terrible damage done. Last night Canterbury was raided as a reprisal. There were a large number of casualties and many people made homeless. Pictures in papers showed extensive damage to Exeter Cathedral. The world has gone quite mad. The worst peace would not have caused one hundredth part of the suffering which this war has caused — and those who suffer are never the ones who made it.

'Planes going over again round midnight — some unhappy German city raided again.

Tuesday June 2nd
News of huge raid on Cologne yesterday followed by news of another similar one last night on Essen & district. 1,036 bombers went out, 1,001 returned. 44 lost yesterday.

Evening paper to-day reported news from a "private source" via New

York of 20,000 killed in Cologne & 54,000 injured. Cathedral not damaged but city such a shambles that outbreaks of disease are feared in this hot weather. Three-quarters of Cologne's population said to be transported to Munich. Churchill spoke in the House to-night — vulgarly jubilant as usual over the suffering caused to Germany. Why can't he at least be dignified & regretful as Abraham Lincoln was over the South? At lunch-time people said to be leaving London area again for fear raids return.

Spent day re-writing Chap. 2. Beautiful warm day, magnificent evening, but felt too bitterly ashamed of our raids to feel anything but its incongruity. Ipswich raided last night.

Wednesday June 3rd
The Glasgow girl, Margaret Hammes, who was interned for 8½ months in 1940–41 because she was born in Hamburg of German parents and lived there for 8 weeks as a baby, came to tea, with her MS. on her experiences in an I. of Man internment camp. From a glance I fear it will need a good deal of alteration to be published.

There was an Alert at 2.45 a.m. to-day; waking up & seeing miles of London, flooded with moonlight, I thought we were for it & wasn't surprised. However, the All Clear went ½ an hour later & nothing apparently happened, but to-night's paper reports hundreds of incendiaries dropped in a London park.

Thursday June 4th   Sheffield
Went to Sheffield to speak at a Food Relief meeting (by midday train). Sweltering heat in carriage; pinned to seat for about 3 of the 4½ hours by the crowd — mainly soldiers & their equipment. The meeting was in the small hall of the big City Hall; Stuart Morris was the other speaker. It was not full, probably owing to the very hot evening. Stuart & I divided the subject as at Northampton, but on account of the heat the audience seemed much more apathetic. At the end an elderly man, fairly obviously from the Min. of Information, defended the Government in a series of questions. He said we made the Govt.'s case seem "very puerile". After answering the questions I said I thought it *was* rather puerile — & was applauded by the audience.

Friday June 5th   London
Got to London at 6.0, double summer time (really 4.0). Sun rising redly as we left St Pancras. Went to the P.P.U. office with Stuart for a cup of coffee; then home by an early & dilatory 73 bus. Sorted 2 days' letters, left replies till evening & spent most of day writing book under a fir tree in a secluded corner of the Terrace Gardens. Finished Ch. 3 & started 4. Reluctant to put it aside for letters in evening, tho' tired in afternoon & kept falling asleep. Very hot night but slept like a log.

Saturday June 6th
Evening papers said a raid on the Ruhr last night completed "a week of
hell" for Germany, & a Cologne newspaper reported that "The Cologne
we knew is gone forever".

Monday June 8th
Strange day, full of minor pleasing events — tho' it started sadly with
reading of the details of the tragic delayed bomb explosion at the Elephant
& Castle on Saturday night — 13 months after the bomb fell. Wrote a
sonnet this morning called "Lament for Cologne (May 31st 1942)".

At 2.0 arrived at Paddington, to meet Mother; on station ran into
Dorothy Plowman. She had been talking abt. food relief to Pethick
Lawrence, who told her that "anyhow the war will soon be over".

Tuesday June 9th
W.E.G. came & we did about 20 letters between us. Also I completed
Letter 85 & she typed it. Rather a rush to get to the Abolition of Night
Bombing Committee at Friends' House. This was attended by a new &
eminent adherent — Professor Jevons of London Univ. who got assuran-
ces from Archibald Sinclair at beginning of war that we shd. only bomb
military objectives — & now has written him a 4-page letter pointing out
various consequences of the Cologne raid. Tom Foley reported that
according to an informant of his who accompanies the King to various
functions, the King was upset about the raids. He sent a recent letter of
congratulations to the Commander in Libya, but none to Air Comm.
Harris on the big raid. Committee decided to broaden its base & become a
Bombing Vigilance Committee. Went on to Regent Palace & had dinner
with Mother, who looked much better than yesterday.

Thursday June 11th
Letters from Shirley, one to me alone, one for G. & me jointly. Mine
contained an excellent impressionistic sketch of a thunderstorm. She begs
for a dog when she comes home. I had a letter from Ruth also, mainly to
enclose a sketch for an oil painting which John has done called "Arsenal of
Democracy", some rough drawings of a girl he met at Stillwater, a word-
impression of early morning in Chelsea, & a really brilliant study of his life
at the Community Centre at Stillwater called "The Hypocrites" (tho'
Ruth says he enjoyed it all!). She herself comments on his brilliance,
extravagance & egotism. He certainly isn't an easy boy to handle — never
was in a way, yet always I have felt in tune with him, never irritated.

Friday June 12th
Went with G. to the "Flag Day" party given at Gunter's by the American
Outpost — Prof. Newall made a perfect speech, to a crowded room eating
a so-called "Austerity Tea" — several kinds of sandwiches, iced chocolate
cake, strawberry ices. Brendan Bracken followed; not good, strange

impediment (inherited from Churchill?), tactlessly said America's entry into war was happiest day of his life.

Saturday June 13th
Went to P.P.U. Council; Patrick Figgis, there for first time, said he hoped G. would not misunderstand his standing for S. Poplar himself as a Christian Socialist. Session before tea was fairly interesting, dealing with matters arising from the Annual General Meeting, but after tea, *3* hours was spent on discussing John Barclay's position as Development Officer, for which consideration of bombing, Vansittartism, a technique of non-violence, youth registration, etc. was shelved! The P.P.U. is terrible when it gets on to personalities — as it so often does. John Middleton Murry suddenly emerged as Barclay's champion — with what secret sinister design I can't guess, unless it is to make J.B. one more person in his debt. Discussion went on so late & I became so bored that I left before the vote; I didn't anyhow care whether J.B. was kept on or not. Dropped in at Regent Palace to see Mother; then came back to find Amy here with Burnett, who really thinks he is going this time.

Sunday June 14th
Spent all day drafting synopsis of next book — the novel on the Lockhart trial, "Day of Judgment".

Monday June 15th
Twenty-fourth anniversary of Edward's death on the Asiago Plateau; our notices in *The Times* as usual. Richmond having a Poison Gas week; notices everywhere saying: "Have you brought your Gas Mask?", "There has to be a First Time", "Don't be a Gasualty" — etc.
   Took synopsis to town & lunched at the Viking Rest. in the Mayfair Hotel with Rache & Mr Bergh of Esselte Aktiebolag, my Swedish publishers; young smallish fair man who recognised me as soon as I entered the Rest. He & Rache both pleased with the synopsis; Rache going to send it to the Paramount Film people that evening. Mr Bergh said that *England's Hour* did v. well in Sweden & got some excellent reviews. His firm was anxious for me to come over for a four weeks' lecture tour; it is now possible to get to Stockholm in $4\frac{1}{2}$ hours by air from Aberdeen. I said I would go if they could overcome the snags, & he & Rache promised to see the British Council, in whose hands all such arrangements apparently lie.
   Got an introduction from Mrs McCready to Miss Jackson of Cook's, & went along to see her & Mrs Rogers about what could be done to get the children home. Found that Clipper is going direct to Ireland & that there is a connecting 'plane here. Though the waiting list is long Miss J. seems to think it not impossible that J. & S. might get home before September — so I registered them & put in for a Treasury permit. But G. was very damping

when he came home, having as usual apprehensions abt. the general sitn. & wanting J. & S. to stay longer.

Tuesday June 16th

Discussed question of children further with G. & we compromised on trying to book them definitely for next May if this was possible. Cabled George to this effect & said we could make all arrangements from here, including payment. Felt flat & tired all day owing to fading of sudden hope of getting them home soon.

Dropped into Regent Palace on way home for a late tea with Mother, who has taken a little room in the Onslow Court Hotel.

Wednesday June 17th

Sent George, Ruth, & Miss Elliott of the Macmillan Co. of Toronto copies of synopsis of "Day of Judgment". These letters & a few others took all day as I had bad backache & stiff arm. Neuritis, lumbago, or whatever it is, was much in evidence & made me tired & slow.

Libya Battle seems to be going badly for us. Tobruk now threatened by Rommel. Naval battle in Mediterranean wh. followed our attempt to get supplies through was only a "limited success".

Thursday June 18th

Times reported John Masefield's son killed in action "far away from home". The similar death of Sir Ernest Graham-Little's only surviving child — a pilot officer of 27 — was reported yesterday. So they go — "down, down, down into the grave" — & like Edna St Vincent Millay, "I know, but I do not approve, and I am not resigned."

News bad in general — shipping losses & Libya both grim. According to a note to G. from J.M.M., Molotov at time of his visit here demanded not only the post-war control of the Baltic and Balkans, but the economic control of Germany!

Friday June 19th

Saw Mother off at Paddington — of course she insisted on being there more than an hour before the time — wh. meant much complication with luggage & porters.

On the way to pick her up at the Regent Palace, when changing at Hammersmith station I saw a young man with a haversack get the entire contents of chocolate out of an automatic sweet machine & go off with it. I remembered the little girl at Dawlish who looked for sweets at the station machine in vain, & felt very angry.

War going badly for us again — reverses in Libya, Germans almost in Sebastapol, huge shipping losses.

Saturday June 20th   Langham

Libya news getting steadily worse. Talk of Tobruk being threatened, after months of resistance.

After clearing up week's correspondence, went down to Langham for week-end to give a talk on the Sunday. Weather growing hot; train very crowded. Walked round garden with Joe Watson & had a long talk on the general Langham situation. It appears that the aerodrome actually is coming, in the fields opposite the front of the house, that work will begin in July, & that the Centre will probably have to move by next spring. Joe is already looking for a new property. He talked at length abt. John M.M.'s relations with his wife — whom he has left & is now trying to divorce for cruelty! — and with Mary Gamble, with whom he is living at a cottage in Langham. But he has bought a farm in Suffolk and is going to take her & Ruth Baker there in October. Joe remarked that Ruth is having to confront all the problems "without getting any of the fun", that she is in fact acting as a kind of unpaid servant to John & Mary, & has often consulted him whether she should leave them (after living with Mary ever since the last war). Joe is much disillusioned abt. J.M.M. He told me that he left his last wife to die while carrying on with the present one, that Max took her in, & that she died at his house. The whole community seems to be now critical of John bec. he turns up once a fortnight to give an unintelligible lecture wh. is part of his next book but never has a meal in the place or talks to anyone. Had coffee with J.M.M., Mary & Ruth after supper. J.'s charming 17-year-old daughter was there. Felt the sense of strain. They seemed glad when I only stayed an hour, & J.M.M. walked back to the gate with me.

Sunday June 21st
Beautiful day, hot & sunny. Lanes filled with campions and wild roses. Walked in morning to Max's grave in Langham churchyard. Birds singing & lovely smell of hay exactly as on the day of his funeral over a year ago.

Sat in garden all afternoon reading *The Screwtape Letters* & starting to review it. Gave talk on "Vansittartism" after supper (now 5.30!). Good discussion, lasting over an hour.

Monday June 22nd   London
Returned to London by 9.37; Joe saw me off. J.M.M. & Mary on station, but I avoided them just as they were certainly avoiding me.

Realised from a *Daily Herald* lent me in the train that we have celebrated the anniversary of Hitler's attack on Russia by being driven out of Libya & losing Tobruk. The garrison with quantities of material is captured. This grave disaster will certainly lengthen the War and its heartbreak. Churchill is still in America; he seems to have made a habit of going there when England is faced with a major crisis. He will find it hard to explain away his optimistic pronouncements about Libya — not only on our second launching of the campaign, but recently. Poor families whose sons have fallen there!

Tuesday June 23rd
In middle of morning Cook's rang up to say that the Treasury had given permission for the export of money to buy the children's tickets on the Clipper, & asking for instructions. I said (after G. had consulted them too) that I would pay the money, & then if a vacancy occurred on a Clipper we would decide whether it was in the children's best interests to take it or to pass it up till next spring. That is what G. is hoping we will do — but I feel that to pass up a chance and perhaps not get it again will be more than I can bear. Cook's thought it unlikely that any vacancy would be available for at least 2 months. Perhaps the international situation will be clearer then — perhaps! The visit to Lyndhurst next week-end should at least make it clear how far the cottage is affected by Southampton raids & whether it is desirable to take it back.

Dictated about 15 letters & finished Letter 86. Another hot sunny day.

Wednesday June 24th
Letter from Cook's came asking for £400 deposit for the Clipper fares. Sent it to Mother asking if she would deposit half. Newspapers as usual full of criticisms of the Government and Churchill, & Sir J. Wardlaw-Milne has tabled a resolution of "No Confidence" in the House which this time about 20 others are going to support. But none of these things ever succeed in getting Churchill out — which is the one thing we need to bring this senseless war to a sane end.

Thursday June 25th
At 2 a.m. just as I was going to sleep I heard a heavy bomber coming up, & thought it sounded slow & ponderous like a Nazi one. It had just droned heavily over or near this flat when half London's A.A. guns opened up. I got up and looked out of the window — from the side of the hill I had a grandstand view of South London and the flashes bursting up as the bomber passed over the city, just like a firework display. One flash from somewhere in the Kew-Brentford area was so terrific that I thought a bomb had been dropped, but the papers this morning said it was all guns. There was however a raid on Nuneaton — the first in the Midlands for 12 months — and ten people were killed. There were also some more in a town in East Anglia.

Fire drill this evening, wh. we attended. Abt. 45 turned up out of 300.

Friday June 26th
Rommel's troops have advanced 100 miles into Egypt already. Government had a better Press to-day without any reason for it. Current joke is as follows: "Some good news at last! Five of our generals were captured at Tobruk."

Mother sent the £200 cheque for Cook's and I sent mine & posted them, without any great hope of seeing the children soon, but at least with the feeling that *something* is in train. By a strange coincidence this is the second

anniversary of their departure for America. I pray that before the third
anniversary they will both be with me.

Mail as usual took till lunch-time. Paid rent for this flat & for Cheyne
Walk; account now pretty low. From 5.0 onwards finished first draft of Ch.
7, "Their Name is Legion", of "H. w. H." Only three more.

Another huge raid on Germany last night — chiefly Bremen.

Saturday June 27th
No further developments in Egypt. Churchill back from U.S.A.

G. came home bringing me a lovely nightdress (for wh. he had given 6 of
his own coupons!) as a 17th wedding gift. I gave him a silver-backed
clothes-brush as he lost his own in the *Western Prince*. We went to see the film
of *How Green Was My Valley*, which is here in Richmond. Some beautiful
scenes & excellent Welsh singing. Very moving altogether, though not put
together very well.

Monday June 29th   Lyndhurst
Morning papers show Rommel far advanced into Egypt; cautious but
pessimistic dispatches seem to show that owing to loss of material at Tobruk
our chances of holding Egypt are not great.

Very hot morning. Walked to cottage with large suitcase; little change
except for increasing evidence on road & in Forest of military occupation
throughout the area. Place made me feel sad with strangers in possession &
the children who loved it so far away, & G. was evidently similarly affected
as he was in a bad temper all morning through being unable to find a ms. wh.
he evidently left at Cheyne Walk, & argued all day about where we were to
live, what do, etc. To my great astonishment found *all* Margaret's letters wh.
I thought were at Bath; can now send them on. Brought away a quantity of
clothes & a few stores. Sat in garden & walked in Forest for rest of day as it
was very hot. Lovely dragon-flies & new butterflies in Forest. Orchids still
out.

Tuesday June 30th   London
Back to London with belongings by 9.48 train. Morning papers reported fall
of Mersa Matruh wh. puts a first-class war supply in Rommel's hands. A
quip I saw in one of the papers said that if Rommel had been an Englishman
he wld. still be a sergeant. Communiqués more pessimistic than ever.

Went to P.P.U. Exec. where endless discussion centred round John
Barclay, leaving little time even for judgment on John Middleton Murry's
mistaken adverse leader on food relief or for more important matters still.
James Hudson as Treasurer did just have time to report on serious financial
(cash) situation.

Evening papers report that Auchinleck has taken over from Ritchie in
Egypt. Charming letter from Shirley — very comforting. Reaffirms her love
of the cottage.

Wednesday July 1st
W.E.G. here; morning as usual occupied by correspondence. She typed a good deal of the first draft of "H. w. H.". Went into town at 5.0 for a Bombing Policy Committee; Corder Catchpool, T. C. Foley, Dr Stanley Jevons, Dr Belden, Stuart Morris. Discussed a long letter wh. Dr Jevons has written for *The Times*, for wh. he intends to canvass many important signatures.

Went on to dine at the Mactaggarts' flat. Sat next W. S. Morrison, who told me various stories of the way the Post Office functioned during the Blitz under himself as P.M. General. He had every post-office basement strengthened, even in the most unlikely places, including Exeter. In the Exeter Blitz the entire P.O. collapsed on top of the basement, wh. held. The 8 telegraphists (girls), who had taken refuge there, first gave their names & addresses of next of kin to the P.O. in the nearest town, & then went on sending out telegrams etc. all through the night, not knowing if they would be dug out of the ruins or not. They were.

News from Egypt getting worse.

Thursday July 2nd
At 6.15 took a 37 bus to Dulwich, where I was speaking on Food Relief for the Bermondsey & Camberwell Committee in a charming Friary garden where the head of the Friary (a home for delinquent boys) took the chair. Lovely serene atmosphere — tho' the local Vicar (not a pacifist) annoyed me rather by misrepresenting part of my speech in a so-called vote of thanks.

Friday July 3rd
Long accounts in all the papers of yesterday's long debate on the "No Confidence" vote, & of Churchill's speech. Aneurin Bevan was the most effective opposition speaker — but though Churchill spoke of "the gravest recession of our hopes since the fall of France", the vote for him was 475 to 25. Another purely Parliamentary triumph. This makes me feel we *shall* lose the war — what Bevan called the "Maginot mind" is in control, & *can't* be got out, thinking in terms of 1914–18, and using obsolete tactics & weapons. Churchill regards this war as his private contest, and thousands of fine young lives are sacrificed to his obstinacy. Why the country puts up with it was partly explained by a working woman with a heavy basket whom I overtook in Patten Alley coming up from the train. Putting it down she complained of its weight, but went on: "Mustn't grumble, must we? One day we shall wake up & hear all the bells pealing, and we shall have a lovely victory! That's the way to look at life, ain't it?" And Rommel is 50 miles from Alexandria!

Saturday July 4th   Bournemouth
Went to Bournemouth to speak at a garden meeting for local P.P.U. group,

which I finally addressed in a small crowded room on "The Shape of the Future", as it was raining. Back, by two more long bus rides to Ida Hillman's house after waiting nearly half-an-hour in cold wind & rain. Stayed the night with her & her husband in small but comfortable worker's home. He works in a ice-cream factory wh. has to stop making it in October, & she is a typist in the Bd. of Trade office in B'mouth. She told me that all Govt. offices are returning from B'mouth to London shortly as the "second front" area & barge concentration is the whole coast from Portsmouth to B'mouth, & they get Alerts & some bombs nearly every night. This & the rumour that all B'mouth is to be evacuated seems to rule out the cottage as a possible place for the children.

Sunday July 5th   London
Travelled in a.m. from B'mouth to Portsmouth. Small audience but good & appreciative in a new T.U. hall.

Got 5.0 train from Portsmouth Town going through some badly Blitzed areas. The young man who escorted me to the station said a persistent rumour credited Portsmouth with 8,000 air-raid deaths, but everything about casualties was kept very quiet.

Day much warmer & train crowded. Rommel apparently held in Egypt for a time; dispatches more encouraging.

Yesterday was celebrated here as U.S. Independence Day, & the Duchess of Kent produced a second son.

Monday July 6th
Wrote long & careful letter to Jon Creech Jones about a possible Civil Service job for G.

After lunch went into town, dropped off at S. Kensington to leave Mother a kettle. Then kept appointment with Dr Nina Kellgren at Eliz. Garrett Anderson Hospital and had radio treatment & massage (very strenuous for neck & shoulder. Trouble described as "fibrositis with secondary neuritis"). Dr K. said fibrositis is very common now largely owing to lack of eggs & meat in diet.

Tuesday July 7th
W.E.G. here; usual day replying to accumulation of letters. Had also to finish Letter 87 in time for her to type it. After supper went through M.S.J.'s letters & decided to have them copied before returning them. Quite apart from my personal interest in the contents, they are far too valuable in themselves to be destroyed. When I send them back & she has used them for her autobiography she will certainly destroy them, & this is the kind of literary massacre from which the perpetrator should be prevented. They couldn't be published in her or my lifetime any more than mine to her could, but the correspondence (extending for nearly ten years

— longer if the first two letters, wh. I am not going to return, are counted) could be left among my literary "remains" & published eventually by John & Shirley as my literary executors.

News still indecisive except that the Germans seem to have crossed the Don. Rommel in Egypt apparently in a mood of "reculer pour mieux sentir". Neck & shoulder v. painful after yesterday's treatment.

Wednesday July 8th
Mother came to tea, & very usefully ironed & darned for me. Discussed with her the possibility of bringing Shirley home.

G. out all day. From 6.0 onwards, after seeing Mother to the station, wrote Chapter 8 — "Youth & the War" — of "Humiliation with Honour".

Dull day, windy, little sun. No further determinate news of the war. Mother told me that Teignmouth — only $2\frac{1}{2}$ miles from Dawlish — was raided recently; God knows why, unless Hitler knows how hideous it is.

Friday July 10th
Worried about the children, to whom I wrote long letters to-day explaining about the necessity for their return. This was made very clear (though indirectly & politely) in a letter from George Brett to-day, saying that Miss Hockaday probably wouldn't relish the charge of Shirley now, as all private schools were feeling the wind in U.S.A. and many were "folding up". Wrote him & Ruth about return plans, indicating that each child could come back separately if necessary, Shirley first.

Sunday July 12th
News very bad. Germans advancing very fast in Russia. If war ends soon, bound now to end badly for us.

Difficult to concentrate on work, but somehow managed to get down (very badly) [to] first draft Chap. 9 ("They That Mourn") of "H. w. H.".

Early bed because fire-watching 3.0–6 a.m. Unidentified high plane, chased by searchlights, going over just when we got up. In sudden mood of determination that G.'s Institute *shall* succeed, promised to sell £500 of securities & give him the money if this would induce Dreyfus & others to give. He thought it would, as it removes necessity of spending £500 of Sir John Mactaggart, who puts the Jewish givers off bec. he is an anti-Semite.

Tuesday July 14th
Russians on the run. Germans flinging in huge reserves. On other fronts a comparative lull which seems sinister. What is really happening in Egypt, & why are the Japanese so quiet?

Drafted Chapter 10 of "H. w. H.", on moral deterioration in war — "The Descent of Society". At 7.0 spoke to a new London group of the Women's International League at the new offices of the National Peace Council at 144 Southampton Row. A considerable audience crowded a small room round a *very* large table — a regular museum piece. Talked on

"Today's Challenge to Women — the Answer of the W.I.L.". At 8.30 Mr Paul Gliddon of the A.P.F. picked me up there & took me to see their "Hungerford Club", run under the arches beneath Charing X Station for the dirty, lousy, abandoned "down-&-outs" whom no other shelters will take. A remarkable experiment run by five young C.O.s. Their leader, Bernard Nichols, who described everything to me, reminded me of a junior edition of Patrick Figgis — tall, thin, sandy-haired. Saw some of the "lodgers" in their bunks, & the baths, canteen, etc. all supplied by the Westminster City Council. One young man described how he was thrown on the floor by a methylated spirit drinker; another, at the medical aid post, how a drunken sailor came in cut to pieces because he had been fighting his own reflection in a plate glass window. Dropped in at St Martin's; then home very late.

Wednesday July 15th
Review of Ellis Roberts' biography of Dick Sheppard, by Hannan Swaffer in the *D. Herald*, sent me to Smith's to get the book — which is fascinating & remarkable, & will surely be a great seller. Decided to review it, with *Christocracy* & *The Right to Live* in my next Letter.
   Russians still being driven back East.

Friday July 17th
Got the 5.12 to Reading, had some supper with the P.P.U. & F.o.R. secretaries, & then spoke at Friends' Meeting House on "Vansittartism" to a crowded room. There were many questions & I was standing about two hours, then autographed a number of books. Had also to stand in corridors of the return train to London in which everyone was jammed like sardines.

Saturday July 18th
Read an excellent chapter "The Analysis of War" in typescript from G.'s new book "The Union of the West".
   Russians now "outnumbered" by the Germans, which really means there is not enough equipment for her superior manpower. J.M.M. in *Peace News* sees compromise peace made with Germany by the City, using Egypt (which still holds) as a bargain piece, but the *Evening News* prophesies 5 more years of war. Well, J.M.M. was right on Libya; let us hope he is right again.

Monday July 20th
Letters fortunately few, so finished "Shape of the Future" chapter & the Epilogue by tea-time. This completes first draft of "Humiliation with Honour".
   Russian & Egyptian news still indecisive. G. tired & depressed about equal indecisiveness of his prospects, as I about the uncertainty of the children's return.

Tuesday July 21st
We actually got half a ton of coal in to-day. By the time I had bought 5 sacks to keep it in the garage (costing 10/–), tipped each porter 2/6 & the cabman 1/–, that half-ton cost me nearly £2.10.0 — to say nothing of a morning's work chasing the coal man & then the porter. Still, the coal is there — nearly enough for the winter if we stay here!

Wednesday July 22nd
After lunch the telephone rang — it was Minturn Sedgwick, now in London as a U.S. Army Captain! I arranged to dine with him to-night at the Café Royal Grill.

Went in to town for tea with Jon Creech Jones at the House; talked G.'s affairs & discussed how to get the better of Frank Darvall at the M. of I.; also possible sources of jobs if the Institute fails. After tea Jon showed me the bombed Chamber (looking so much smaller in its clear open-air state) & the remnants of the Cloisters.

Took a taxi to Park Lane, had a quick drink & told all the news to G. who had been having tea with Dame Edith Lyttelton. He came to the Café Royal to give a drink to Minturn — looking huge & impressive in uniform. He is doing secret work & is not even allowed to give his address. Seeing an isolationist friend of his in uniform made him join up. He tells us he is a friend of John G. Winant & may be able to make a contact for G.

Thursday July 23rd
Spent all day revising the first typescript of "Humiliation with Honour". (Yesterday Arthur Wragg's design for the cover arrived — a gyved figure with head thrown back, surrounded by light — & I sent it on to Dakers.)

G. went off for a week, for speeches at Cambridge, Buxton, & to the troops at Catterick, Yorks. Late in the evening rang me up saying he must see Archibald MacLeish, the U.S. counterpart of the Minister of Information — so my evening was spent in telephone calls to Minturn, etc., endeavouring to arrange it.

Friday July 24th
Letter from George asking for definite instructions on the children. G. rang me up on his return from Cambridge, on way to Buxton, to say he had already got an appointment with Archibald MacLeish — so I agreed with him on the cable, which asked [George] to send Shirley back first if chance occurred & leave John till later.

Saturday July 25th
Had hair washed at midday; partly answered mail; then went along to Endsleigh Gardens to see Food Relief procession begin. Decided I needn't

walk in it as day had turned very hot, so went on to Trafalgar Square for Food Relief Mass Demonstration. Other speakers were Patrick Figgis (v. good), Stuart Morris, Reg. Sorensen, Mrs Duncan-Harris, Sybil Morrison & Geoffrey Pittock-Buss. Donald Soper wound up, proposing resolution. Carried nearly unanimously; only 3 voted against. Large crowd was very orderly; little heckling; police had nothing to do & looked v. good tempered. Managed first speech all right but it was a bigger effort than Hyde Park (no microphone), & I was almost voiceless by the time I had to make a second speech on another side of the plinth. One is v. high above the audience & the buses are very near.

As I was going towards Charing X young L/Cpl Berry, a distant cousin of Winifred's, who had written me a "fan" letter, came up & spoke to me. Charming young man of 21 — with a distant look of Winifred. He is in a bomb-disposal squad at Acton — compromise bet. being a C.O. & being in the Army. On an impulse I brought him back to supper with me & he stayed till after 10.

Monday July 27th

Shirley's 12th birthday, dear little heart. The consciousness of having been parted from her for yet a third birthday gave me a feeling of heaviness all day.

News much the same; Germans advancing towards Stalingrad in Russia, held in Egypt. Two short Alerts, almost on the top of each other, woke me from sleep between 6.0 & 7.0 this morning. Accord. to evening paper, single raiders dropped bombs in 21 districts, though none in London.

Spent all day revising "H. w. H.". Did 2½ chapters, a tiring job.

Tuesday July 28th

Wakened at 3 a.m. by loud guns & sound of German bombers going over. Alert went after a few minutes. Guns all over London. Got up & looked out of window; regular firework display of bursting shells in Chelsea direction. Put on warm dressing gown in case of bombs & got back to bed. I was glad when All Clear went in about an hour, after subsidence of noise. Have been through too many raids all alone to find the experience enjoyable. *Evening Standard* said only incendiaries were dropped in the London area (in fields on outskirts), but an unexploded A.A. shell fell in Chelsea Bridge Rd & made a crater. Birmingham had a heavy raid. London's "secret" guns were supposed to be in action & those who were used to raids noticed a different sound — but it seemed like the old familiar noise to me.

Wednesday July 29th

Worked all day at "H. w. H." & got all but the last chapter & Epilogue off to W.E.G. for typing. At 4 p.m. went to Bow to make a speech for Patrick Figgis, who is standing as Christian Socialist candidate in the South Poplar by-election. I took the story from the last war to this & Patrick spoke on his election programme.

Got home again just after black-out. Warm still night. Watched moon rising behind trees & felt sure there would be another raid. Russian news getting worse & worse.

Thursday July 30th

I was quite right about another raid. I was just dropping off to sleep when the Alert went. I heard it strike 2.0 & then distant guns. Long silence except for noise of fighters; then guns suddenly broke out loudly & fireballs of new shells appeared above trees over S. London. Got dressed this time & lay on bed. Was dozing when the All-Clear went at 4 a.m. Later learnt that some bombs were dropped in N. London & a load of incendiaries in another place, but little damage was done & there were apparently no casualties. Main raid again on Birmingham. Our bombers attacked Saarbrücken last night; what will the reprisal be for that?

Germans now within 300 miles of Caucasus.

Strangely didn't feel v. tired this morning. Saw a notice on estate board asking for "housewife" volunteers for care of casualties. Went to V. Post, said who I was, offered on request to be a "mobile" volunteer — i.e., one who goes out to casualties. Felt after lonely raids that I'd rather do anything than be in bed listening to guns & bombs. Came away complete with tin helmet, whistle & badge.

Friday July 31st

Another disturbed night — two Alerts between 2.0 & 4.0 & very loud gunfire which rocked the flat during the second.

Cabled Ruth by G.'s wish asking if by cutting expenses they could keep both children till spring — fairer to J. & S.

Saturday August 1st

Quiet night. Got up feeling much better after a decent sleep following two broken nights. G. rather more cheerful too. A letter from Darvall conveyed a message that the Institute should be run & financed by a University Committee — wh. is at least decisive & gives G. an objective in forming the committee. We decided we would give our enemies the go-by & both go to some country hotel for two or three weeks to get a change & start our books — prob. in September.

Started revising final typescript of "Humiliation with Honour" but didn't get v. far owing to various interruptions. The first was pleasant: Amy & Burnett both turned up for tea & did various bits of washing & ironing for me. It seems Burnett's squadron was ordered to South Russia!

but they didn't go because information "leaked" about their destination. He is now back at Ramsgate, & home on 7 days' leave. The second interruption was a lecture (on the tennis court) to the Richmond Hill Court fireguards by the little man who organises it, abt. 3 new types of incendiary bombs — one with an explosive nose instead of tail, another wh. exudes phosphorus & rubber, & a third wh. is combined with high explosive. The bourgeois audience, benevolent, tennis-dominated, totally ineffective (one highly rouged lady with a yapping pekingese in her arms) listened agreeably to the worried little man. What a comedy for an Aristophanes. I pictured them trying, quite unpractised, to identify these different sinister bombs in the dark — myself included — & prayed that we don't ever get a real fire-raid here.

Sunday August 2nd

Another quiet night — though a loud clap of thunder (followed all morning by heavy rain) which woke me at 8 a.m. made me think for a moment that the guns were off again.

Seven years to-day since poor Father's tragic death — well, if his invalid life would have dragged on, as it well might, he was wise to end it and avoid surviving into this terrible age. I suppose I shall never know just where & how he died & to which part of the river he went.

Mother came to tea, & we went to the cemetery to put fresh flowers on Father's grave. Revised typescript all evening.

Monday August 3rd

Brief Alert at 3.30 a.m., followed in about 10 mins. by the All Clear.

News still bad. Germans getting into N. Caucasus. G. gives the Russians another month.

Tuesday August 4th

W.E.G. came. She finished typing "H. W. H." while I revised it. Got revision finished by 5.0 & sent the MS. by the last post to Andrew Dakers. Funny to finish such a book on the 28th anniversary of the first Great War.

Felt thankful & relieved to have finished this exacting little book, till G. returned very late from dining with Ifor Evans, who had told him that he should never have left Cornell & got into the "free-lance" crowd out of a University post — and that even if an academic committee to run the Institute was formed he would be dropped from it at an early stage. I knew he was as always holding me wholly responsible, & forgetting his own eagerness to go into British politics. Certainly neither of us made friends with the Mammon of unrighteousness in relation to this war.

Wednesday August 5th

G. went off early to get train for Bangor in order to spend two nights at the

I.L.P. Summer School. Went to a "refresher" course in First Aid at W Defence Post at 8.30 & was ashamed to find I had forgotten how to tie reef knots & put on slings — though it soon came back.

Germans still driving into Caucasus.

Thursday August 6th
Tremendous noise of 'planes overhead soon after midnight last night, & sky brilliant with searchlights. I thought a raid was developing & waited about for some time before going to bed. But evening papers say that this was an "exercise" on the part of our own aeroplanes.

At home all day writing No. 89 of the Letter to Peace-Lovers. Got it typed & posted just before the last post at 7 p.m.

This morning Miss Bell of the Nat. Council of Civil Liberties rang up & asked me to speak at a demonstration on the Freedom of the Press in the Potteries (a Hanley cinema) on Oct. 25th. At first said I couldn't on account of "Day of Judgment" but later agreed as it is rather a special occasion & I have to go to the Potteries for my book anyhow.

Friday August 7th
Fire-watching 3 a.m.–6 a.m. Only got odd snatches of sleep before it as I was wakened first by a searchlight streaming into the room & later by distant guns. But no Alert went and I spent the watch writing to John & Shirley.

Got up to find several letters, among them one from Andrew Dakers, which said of "H. w. H.": "I started reading it after going through my mail this morning & everything had to wait until I had finished it. It is a shining thing in a dark world; better & lovelier than I had dared to expect. Your restraint gives it power, & it will shake the complacency of many who have not bothered to think out a conclusion for themselves. There is such reasonableness and tolerance in your presentation of your viewpoint that a great deal of criticism will be disarmed & withheld. The book moved me deeply, & is the best statement of pacifism for non-pacifists that I have come across . . . There is nothing in the book to offend any Christian citizen." This at any rate is cheering. He agrees that we send out review copies very discriminately in order to avoid the *England's Hour* situation in which M. of I. members attacked the book under the guise of impartial criticism. The American & Swedish reviews were in amazing contrast — the best since *T. of Y.* I noticed the other day that the National Book Council — wh. works in collaboration with the M. of I. — had omitted *England's Hour* from its list of books on the war — though all the other books on the Blitz were there.

This evening went down to S. Poplar to speak for Patrick Figgis. Found I had to do the job wh. I haven't done since about 1922, of collecting a crowd at a street corner. However, I *did* collect it, & talked for half an hour till I was hoarse.

Sunday August 9th

According to the one o'clock radio, the impasse in India has culminated in a raid on Congress, & the arrest of Gandhi, Nehru, Mrs Naidu, Azad, & others. "Whom the Gods destroy, they first make mad." The British Government deserve that the Japanese should now march in & bring them down in India's fall if the fall of Russia does not do it first.

Warm morning, but turned in afternoon to heavy thundery showers of rain. Strange incongruity of young people playing sets of tennis all day against background of practising guns.

Monday August 10th

Morning papers announce rioting in India following the arrests, & the fall of Maikop (oil town) on the Russian front.

G. was so much moved by the Indian situation & the Labour Party's flaccid acceptance of it that he went down to S. Poplar to speak for Patrick Figgis, rivalling a meeting held by the Communists at which Harry Pollitt was speaking.

Tuesday August 11th

More rioting in India. Germans right into Caucasus.

Went to P.P.U. Executive. Managed gradually to get the Committee on to the India situation, Armistice, etc.; told them they were rooted & bogged in personalities. Picked up following pieces of information: (1) Rumour has it that Churchill is in Moscow trying to dissuade Stalin from making a separate peace. (2) The plan of the Govt. to raid Congress & imprison the Indian leaders was made 6 weeks ago, to take effect whatever Congress did. (3) Cripps has now hardened against India, wh. has caused him a personal failure, & (according to Salter) is hand in glove with Churchill. Stuart had a story according to wh. Lloyd George is supposed to have said that the time to suggest an Armistice is immediately the Russians go down — not earlier & not later. He gives the time as about the end of September.

Evening papers announce that (accord. to Germans) Colchester & Hastings were bombed last night & the Mental Hospital at Colchester hit, causing many casualties. Langham must have had a bad night. Incendiaries were also dropped among the cornfields there.

Thursday August 13th

Alert at 3 a.m. Some gunfire; saw first searchlights & then guns firing across the river somewhere in the Ealing direction. Later papers reported 7 killed by a bomb somewhere in the London area. All Clear about 3.30.

Caught up on correspondence during morning. G. went off after lunch. Felt much depressed at having to spend the night so often alone in this flat, be wakened by the Alerts & lie thinking about the children. But G. regards this as just tiresome & unreasonable on my part. But it is so long since I heard from them. Sometimes I can't believe that this endless period without them is not a dreadful nightmare, from which I *must* soon wake up. From Winifred's death onwards they were all of my life that matters. If I could only see & talk to my darlings just for half an hour. How long — oh, how long?

Went to Fleet Street for a meeting of the Bombing Policy Committee. Had tea & dinner with Mother & brought home the electric iron which she had had mended for me.

South Poplar By-election result — Guy, 3,375; Figgis, 541. Patrick just saves his deposit. Less than 10% of the electorate voted.

Friday August 14th
No Alert last night. As I had gone to bed at midnight expecting to be roused by one, I had an extra long sleep & woke feeling much less depressed.

Went with Mother in the afternoon to see the film of *Mrs Miniver*. Noted with rueful amusement that though most of it was a study of the 1940 Blitz, not only Jan Struther herself but the script writers (e.g. James Hilton) had written the whole thing from the comfortable safety of America. The Blitz was realistic enough & parts (e.g. the Dunkirk episode) moved one despite the propagandist intention of the whole thing. But oh! the class conscious-ness (similar to *Cavalcade*; the griefs of the employers are tragic, but those of their servants comic) and the sweet sentimentality! And the people in the film are so *silly*; e.g. they leave their small children in an area of maximum danger, while Mrs M. fails to give even elementary first-aid to her dying daughter-in-law. By far the best actress, in my view, was old Dame May Whitty as the Lady of the Manor — a mixture of Queen Mary & Mrs Holtby — who really *would* be like that. As for the Vicar's final sermon, about the war being a people's war (wh., as the *N. Statesman* critic said, it wasn't, but only the best people's war) & our fighting it in our hearts — well!

Saturday August 15th
Fire-watching midnight–3 a.m. Was on reserve, but called because someone had only just left hospital. Took it rather than G. as he was so tired from travelling. Uneventful. Got to bed about 3.30.

In afternoon went to see Nancy Price and Maurice Browne (as the English chaplain) in *Nurse Cavell* by C. S. Forester & Bechofer Roberts. Scanty audience, but a fine play, in which Nancy Price uses the very prayer book in which Edith Cavell entered the hour & day of her own death. The final scene between her & Maurice Browne was almost unbearably moving — the more so because of the calm & restraint of the play. Nancy Price showed me the prayer book for a moment afterwards, & I had a cup of tea & 10 minutes' talk with Maurice Browne.

Sunday August 16th

News still dominated by India and Russia. Very little news coming through from India; fears grow among some of us that the silence may conceal a score of Amritsars. Riots reported in Calcutta, and many casualties. Gandhi's secretary had died in prison. In Russia the Germans are approaching Stalingrad and sweeping down the Caucusus towards Astrakhan.

Very warm sunny day followed a night of pouring rain. Spent it revising galley proofs of *H. w. H.* & got the first dozen off by the 3.0 post. G. starting work on his autobiography again, & consequently much more cheerful.

Monday August 17th

Letter from Agatha Harrison on India, asking if I could write a poem to appear in some general newspaper; also whether I could make any approach to America. Rang her up this evening and said I would write to Mrs Roosevelt. A letter from Gollancz said he has already collected 6,000 orders for a new edition of *Testament of Youth*; that the new setting is half completed & he *hopes* to publish about October.

Tuesday August 18th

Again very hot. Worked all day at correcting proofs, & despite Mother coming to do her ironing & to tea, got them finished & off by the 7 o'clock post. Ominous lack of news about India, but papers both morning & evening reported Churchill's visit to Moscow — showing information picked up at the P.P.U. Executive last week to have been correct. Reading between the lines of the Press reports & of Churchill's telegram to Stalin, relations do not sound too cordial.

A letter from Izetta Robb posted as recently as Aug. 5th spoke of seeing the children on her holiday in Minnesota. She commented on how much they had grown since she saw them in 1940; described Shirley as brilliant & popular, with a "flair" for telling anecdotes; John as harder to know but very good at painting — & most reluctant to go to camp.

Wednesday August 19th

Wireless, & later evening papers, reported a large Commando raid on Dieppe in the early hours of daylight, supported by a "ceiling" of aircrafts which people on the South Coast heard going over all night.

Went into town early, met Corder Catchpool & was introduced to the two young men who are planning the Friends' Post-War work. I suggested being associated with it as a kind of "Special Correspondent", to which they eagerly agreed. Went on to the Piccadilly Hotel & had tea with Andrew Dakers to discuss methods of publicity for my book.

Back in time for dinner & the third First Aid lecture — on stopping haemorrhages etc.

Thursday August 20th

Odd bits of news keep coming in about the Dieppe Raid. It seems to have been more for psychological purposes than anything else — to give Stalin the impression we are doing something. No one knows where Churchill is now. The German radio, quoted in *The Times*, says he went to Moscow because on July 22nd Stalin gave him an ultimatum to put down a second front within 12 days!

Friday August 21st

Letter came from Llandudno Hotel saying they would keep us a double room for a week of September. Just a week's holiday from work — reading & walking — seems quite attractive all of a sudden.

News much the same. India seems virtually cut off. Promised to sit on the platform at the big Central Hall demonstration next Tuesday.

Saturday August 22nd

Into town early for P.P.U. Council Meeting. Council opened with interesting & profitable sessions on India & an Armistice campaign. During the latter Dr Salter said that, according to Lloyd George, the Russians had lost quantities of raw material & wheat as well as 60 million of their 190 million in the territories occupied by Germany; that their bread ration was now 3 oz. a day & the problem was that of feeding them wh. would probably make another winter campaign impossible for Russia; that the Anglo-Russian Treaty said nothing about "victory" but only that Stalin would not make peace with any German Govt. that "had not abandoned its aggressive intentions"; that probably he would be prepared to make peace on the Brest-Litovsk lines with Germany returning to the 1919 frontiers. Ll. G. thinks Stalingrad will fall in Sept. & Russia be negotiating peace by November. He advised the Parliamentary Peace Group to have an Armistice motion ready for tabling by then. Rumour is that Churchill went to Moscow to persuade Stalin to carry on the war from behind the Urals & did not succeed.

After tea, we had a long & stormy session on John Barclay. J.M.M. ended by losing his temper so completely that I proposed a motion that whole discussion be postponed till morning.

Sunday August 23rd

Got to the Council meeting by ten. My suggested postponement was wise as the John Barclay discussion ended amicably in a mandate to the *Peace News* Directors to find him a job. Left at midday & got back in time for lunch. In afternoon sent a personal letter to Mrs Roosevelt urging her to use her influence in favour of a return to the principle of negotiation. Sent copies to Amery at India office; also to Stuart, Gerald Bailey & Krishna Menon.

Tuesday August 25th

Letter from Gerald Bailey outlining a new policy of repressive measures v. pacifists apparently being pursued in U.S.A. under the so-called Voorhis Law. We discussed it as emergency business of the P.P.U. Executive this afternoon. G. didn't think it need be taken too seriously as a similar act had been on the statute book before. But at the P.P.U. we agreed to ask Bailey to call a small conference. Learnt also that thanks to an approach to Sumner Welles in U.S.A., the visit of the N.P.C. delegation may be possible. Gerald Bailey & Barbara Duncan-Harris have been asked to go. (? Could I ask her to bring back the children?)

Went on to a somewhat stormy & much packed (by Communists) meeting on India addressed by Dean of Canterbury, Pollitt, Pritt etc., at Central Hall, Westminster. Learnt later that an Alert was sounded about 5.0 & All Clear in half an hour. Never heard either.

Wednesday August 26th

First Aid Class after dinner was on fractures.

News told of Russian advance still getting to Stalingrad; also of the death of the Duke of Kent yesterday in an air crash (apparently an accident) in the North of Scotland on his way to Iceland. All the 15 passengers & crew were killed except a rear gunner who was thrown clear.

Heavy humid evening; full moon obscured.

Friday August 28th

Had early lunch & then went to look at 2 Cheyne Walk where I met G. House quite dry though very dirty; some ceilings peeling; Burnett's room on top floor has ceiling down, obviously from one of the raids. Front garden quite tidy though back a riot of weeds; decided we must have it cleared. Front rooms looked bright despite dirty windows & patches mending breaks from blast, but the whole depresses me with its memories of the children.

Had tea at Friends' House with Mr Gangulee, Tagore's son-in-law, who gave us copy of a memorandum he had prepared for Sir Stafford Cripps. It contains some excellent suggestions for compromise in India wh. he wanted us to put forward as our own. A vital, intelligent man.

Dined with G. at the small Indian restaurant in Richmond.

Saturday August 29th

Page proofs of *H. w. H.* arrived by afternoon post. Evening papers contained news of non-stop Blitz on Stalingrad; also descriptions of the funeral of the Duke of Kent (almost a family affair, semi-private) at Windsor.

G. spent evening packing for his lecture trip at Catterick followed by his two or three days as observer on a mine-sweeper. Heat broke after black-out in thunderstorm (prolonged but not loud) & heavy rain.

Sunday August 30th
Spent quiet morning catching up on mail & diary. Sent message to Stuart
Morris for the P.P.U. India meeting, wh. I shall miss, urging (on lines of
Mr Gangulee) that India be treated as a world problem, not a narrow issue
between the British authorities and the Indian people; also hoping that the
speakers do what they could to inform the public about the real work &
philosophy of Gandhi, who has been so much maligned & misrepresented
by the Press. (Sent J.M.M. two extracts from the Bombay correspondent
of *The Times*, who in successive paragraphs said that Gandhi's "vanity"
must be mortified by lack of world support for him, and that he had not
been allowed to see any newspapers!!)

Monday August 31st
Fire-watching 12–3 a.m. Corrected proofs all through period. Got up late
& went on with them most of day. Amy came, & we talked a good deal
about the children. She reminded me how she last saw Shirley at
Brockenhurst when Burnett was bringing her up to London to get the boat
at Liverpool, & how she cried afterwards.

Tuesday September 1st
Lunched Elizabeth Sprigge at the White Tower Restaurant (Greek) in
Percy St. & talked abt. Sweden. She was v. agreeable & asked me to let her
have a letter outlining my invitation tho' she didn't think I should be
allowed to go. Went on to Helen Mayo who decided to remove my top back
tooth on Thursday; then she told me that her friend "Tanks" (Capt.
Reddish) who had been missing since Nov. was killed fighting beside his
tank; the news came from a private who was a prisoner in Italy. She only
heard about a week ago — & said it was almost a relief to stop mentally
"listening" as she has for months.
    Went back & did some shopping rather in a daze, thinking of my own
casualties in the last war. It seemed incongruous to be buying (at Peter
Jones, where I had picked up some material for G.) a new grey cloth hat to
go with the re-made tweed dress. At Richmond on the way home I had a
curious accident; as I was walking through the short cut between the shops
a shutter fell off one & knocked me down flat. My head was unhurt thanks
to my straw hat but I fell bang on my side & had a huge bruise just below
my hip.

Thursday September 3rd
Third anniversary of the Second War to End War!!
    Worked all morning at Letter 91 so as to have first draft finished before
visit to dentist in afternoon. At 3.30 went to Helen Mayo to have double
back top tooth out; on way bought her a dozen scarlet roses in memory of
"Tanks". This morning I wrote her a short note about him with the sound
of the broadcast War Anniversary Service coming through the windows.

In the last War I used to attend Victory services. Now I don't; that isn't the way we shall end war & create lasting peace.

Took a taxi to S. Kensington & had tea with Mother; then went back to Richmond & started to type Letter when a telegram was 'phoned from G. to say that he was back from the minesweeper already & wanted to dine with me late. He finally arrived too late for us to dine out anywhere & I had to get the meal in the end! Fell finally into bed too tired for words! Bruised hip still very black.

Friday September 4th
German drive on Stalingrad appears to be checked for the moment, but so little news comes through about either the Russian or Egyptian fronts (to say nothing of the Atlantic, where we know nothing whatever about the fate of any ship) that we seem to be living in a world of swift news & vast communications which tell us less than absolute silence.

Saturday September 5th   Llandudno
G. & I caught 10.35 train from Euston to Llandudno. Euston very crowded but train not bad; got corner seats tho' travelling third. After we passed Chester & were travelling past the sands of Dee I realised that I had not been on that bit of line for over 30 years though it was familiar in my childhood when we went to Conway & Colwyn Bay.

Hotel not as bad as G. had suggested; family commercial type much like many where I have stayed when lecturing in the North. Food good, sufficient, well-cooked & swiftly served. Bedroom bare & bed very hard — typical of the North — but bath-water hot. Walked round with G. after supper (early, served at 6.30); I had quite forgotten the magnificent position of the place — the two Ormes, Penmaenmawr at the back & beyond it the mountains of Snowdonia. All the major hotels are taken over by the Govt., the chief one — the Grand — being used as the Supertax headquarters!

Sunday September 6th
After breakfast walked with G. over Great Orme to St Tudno's Church (Celtic, older than Llandudno itself). The Vicar held a most memorable open-air service — wh. has apparently become the custom as the church is so tiny. Several hundred people sat or stood among the tombs of the large churchyard on this Welsh hillside, with the shining blue sea below them and the creeping gorse bright yellow on the green summit of the mountain which reflected the shadows of passing clouds. Three aeroplanes circled round the headland as we sang "Thy Kingdom Come, O Lord" and "Onward, Christian Soldiers", and listened to the Vicar's quite good & tolerant little sermon (against sin, not against the Nazis). I couldn't make out whether the aeroplanes were being reverent or irreverent — especially as one skimmed just over our heads, and three times during the sermon

made the Vicar inaudible with his engine. Except that the church was not bombed it reminded me of the last scene in *Mrs Miniver* — but was much more moving because genuine.

We walked back through the Happy Valley, pleasantly laid out with rock plants, called in at old Mr Catlin's church — Christ Church, a quite impressive Congregational Church where G.'s father as a young man had his most successful ministry before becoming an Anglican. A photograph of him preaching stands on the vestry mantelpiece.

Monday September 7th
Grey day, wind mounting to gale. Too cold to sit outdoors, so wrote long letters to both children in morning — to John about the faith in his abilities that I always have had, to Shirley about Mrs Catlin cf. with myself, & that a mother who can pass on a good heritage of abilities is better worth having than one assiduous at "chores".

Tuesday September 8th
Hot sunny day, unexpected in Wales. Spent nearly all of it sitting in sun in the Haulfre Gardens, looking over the mountains & the sea, & reading Ellis Roberts' biography of Dick Sheppard. Lovely scent of flowers and pines; purple shrub beside me covered with Red Admiral & tortoiseshell butterflies. One tortoiseshell alighted quite placidly on my arm & sat there for some time.

Too much of the human race here & too little accommodation for it — this the one disadvantage. Queues for everything — teashops, buses, cinemas. Otherwise all is quite pleasant.

Had another appreciative letter about *T. of Y.* & my views on War from the forces — this time a young airman stationed in Wiltshire.

Wednesday September 9th
A second beautiful brilliant day, even hotter than yesterday. Walked all round the Great Orme. The evening was so lovely that we went across to the estuary by tram after supper & walked on the sands with the sun setting & flaming clouds over the Penmaenmawr. Pretty tired & very sunburnt at end of day; must have walked 8 miles.

Friday September 11th
Still fine & warm though rather more cloudy. Walked with G. on pier & over the hills before lunch; read in Happy Valley in afternoon, & had tea at Pink Farm near St Tudno's. Then at 6.0 accompanied G. to film of *Mrs Miniver* which he hadn't seen. Despite its sentimentality, the fact that I had seen it twice before, & that Jan Struther seems to me a charlatan posing as a patriot from the safety of America, I found myself weeping as before over Dunkirk and the Blitz scenes — so reminiscent, as was the service in the bombed church. Again, as last time, I found myself envying those whose

simple patriotic reactions & desire to serve the war machine (like mine at the beginning of the last war) give them the inspiration of feeling that they are fighting the powers of evil, & save them from the complexities of us who are critical of ourselves & our country, recognising the evil of war.

Saturday September 12th   London
G., who has to spend the week-end in Manchester, helped me to the station with my luggage & saw me off. I told him what a lovely holiday it had been, with its wonderful weather in a place of which I had never previously realised the beauty.

Journey back peaceful; never a great crush.

Evening paper reported fighting in the streets of Stalingrad.

Sunday September 13th
Boring day spent on dull correspondence; wrote about 17 letters — mixture of routine business & fan-mail. Mother came to tea. Grey windy day; sudden change to autumn.

G. turned up in the evening & we dined at the Indian Restaurant. In Manchester he saw Rhys Davies M.P., who gave him the following pieces of private information: (1) (via Bevin) 1,000,000 casualties are expected to result from our campaigns next year. (These old men at their desks calmly propose to slaughter another generation of young Englishman rather than negotiate — though no peace imaginable could produce such suffering.) (2) (via Samuel Hoare) The European countries see no victory in sight whatever happens & want the war to end. (3) The Brit. Min. in Hungary denounced our Balance of Power policy in Europe. (4) Chiang of China says we under-estimate our enemies just as the Chinese always *over-estimate* theirs.

No new information about Stalingrad.

Monday September 14th
Tiresome day of shopping, etc. Much depressed by the dirt in the house & the weeds in the garden shown up by the bright autumn sunlight. Though the house even now feels warm, dry & serene, I always feel when in it as if I were walking among the ruins of the gracious life I created there — as indeed I am, though I always pray that one day that life will be restored there.

News in general much the same; Stalingrad being reduced to ruins. Its fall & Russia's collapse can hardly be long delayed.

Tuesday September 15th
Long telephone conversation with Andrew Dakers about some belated alterations required in my book by the Censorship. These merely relate to the mention of the Charing Cross railway arches as the *locale* of the A.P.F. Hungerford Club. Dakers got on to the relevant department, which

reported that in the edition sent to U.S. they had merely altered the arches to "a deep basement" & sent the proofs forward!

Wednesday September 16th Sheffield
7.45 a.m. Long cable from Ruth reporting children starting school this week & confirming receipt of my cables.

Strenuous morning getting work done in time to go to Sheffield. Managed to get Letter No. 92 revised & typed & sent off to Brock. G. very pleased with his sunny room over the chemist's shop. Felt rather unworthily peeved because he always seems to get ideal working conditions (as at Cheyne Walk) while I both make & spend the money but have to put up with second-best circumstances for doing so. But this is probably simply my own mismanagement — due to always being over-worked & in a rush.

Sun just setting when I reached Sheffield at 7.30; queer, rather spectacular effect of red glow over cleared ruins near the station. Spoke to a small gathering at the Educational Settlement on "The Shape of the Future".

Evening Standard reported non-stop Blitz on Stalingrad & capture of main railway station by the Nazis.

Thursday September 17th Leeds
Had free morning for work & letters before going on to Leeds.

Met there at station by Mr Vincent Long. He told me of the difficulties of starting lecture courses in Leeds in connection with his big settlement, Belgrave. After that I didn't expect much; nor did he as he was using a small hall for my lecture on "America" — but it was crowded with a large audience of over 300, & extra benches had to be brought in. I got a great ovation at the end.

Friday September 18th London
Tired & stiff on arrival at King's X, espec. as day had turned very warm. Flat empty as G. is at B'm for to-night & at Oxford to-morrow. Usual distasteful pile of letters. One certainly was a Macmillan royalty cheque for £190, but another was a supertax demand for £133 which if correct nearly cancels it out.

Saturday September 19th
Worked all day at letters, & an article for *Peace News* called "The Family Front" which has been in my mind for some time, but was crystallised by Sir S. Hoare's speech yesterday to his Chelsea constituents (of which I am one!). In the course of this speech he said that Europe believed the Allies would win, but that the victory might take so long that European civilisation would crash in the interval. This reminded me of the Pope's

speech on the family, & seemed a clear hint to the United Nations to find some way out less humanly costly than "ultimate victory".

Sunday September 20th
Stalingrad still holding; same report of fighting in streets as we have had for days. Germans said to have lost 1,300,000 men in this battle alone, but the report comes from the chief Soviet publicity officer!

Flogged away all day at letters & got practically all of them done. Wrote John, Shirley & Ruth this evening.

Monday September 21st
Charming letter this morning from George Brett, who had just been on holiday in the mountains. Sounded so much better & more cheerful than he has been since his operation last November. He urged me not to worry about finance or the children. I replied by air, pointing out the difficulties of repayment in dollars, & asking him to make some sort of provisional arrangement for me with Colston Leigh for a long lecture tour when the travel ban on my movements is lifted.

Fighting of incredible ferocity still going on in Stalingrad. In *D. Herald* this morning a slashing & timely article by Alistair Cooke embodying forthright American criticisms of Churchill's policy on India. Last weekend's *New Statesman* & *Peace News* were largely given to that too.

Tuesday September 22nd
Letter from John this morning (dated Aug. 29th) disturbed us a good deal as it said that his school had been changed from the St Paul Academy to a smaller one called Pillsbury where they specialise in music & art appreciation. This is the first that either of us have heard of it.

P.P.U. Exec. at 2.0. Possibility of an India campaign discussed. Stuart told us (a) Cabinet had a cable (wh. he had seen) from Chiang-Kai-shek giving truth about Burma; (b) Govt. here had resolved to let Gandhi fast to death & had considered deporting him to Uganda but now weakening; (c) Viceroy had agreed to carry out repression policy only if no interference from China, Russia & America were guaranteed.

Wednesday September 23rd
At 5.30 driven over to the Ordnance Depot at Greenford, Mddx., to take part in a "Brains Trust" debate. Pleasant hospitality & entertainment by the Colonel & staff (many A.T.S.). Great fun despite my husky voice.

Friday September 25th
Sent letter to bank to be attached to my Will, urging formation of a general "Trust" from the Brittain estate for helping those in need of help, & that J. & S. should take for their personal use only enough to keep them from want, depending on their earnings for the rest. This cannot, of course, be

decided till Shirley is 21, as both children would have to be of age. Also made some suggestions for the welfare of the Burnetts & Marian.

Replies came to us both from Mrs Roosevelt for our letters urging American intervention on India (for wh. Amery scolded G. in a severe note!). Her answer was *very* cordial, was personally signed, & she said she would show our letters to the President, which he had not asked her to do! These little notes say volumes about the feeling in U.S. (& espec. Mrs Roosevelt's own feelings) with regard to the Brit. Govt.'s treatment of India.

Saturday September 26th
Large mail; also read up for Letter 93 on connection between cruelty to animals and cruelty in war. Began writing it after tea and finished after dinner.

Fight at Stalingrad still going on. Usual wish-fulfilment rumours circulating about Hitler's programme being thrown out, German morale cracking up etc. etc.

Sunday September 27th
Packed for Cheddar. Mother came to tea looking very poorly; said she fell from the steps of her hotel yesterday as they had been too much polished, & was feeling very shaken. But she insisted on doing some ironing & cheered up a little over tea. G. also depressed — (a) about money as usual, (b) because the Vice-Chancellors' group met yesterday, & as he has had no message from the chairman, he fears they have turned down his Institute scheme.

Cabled Ruth yesterday in reply to hers of Sept. 16th, again urging her to work for the children's return in May; also telling her of my visit to Cheddar & the publication of *H. w. H.* next month.

Monday September 28th   Cheddar
G. kindly helped me with luggage to Paddington & saw me off. Pleasant easy journey; no great crowd to-day. Arrived to find the Cliff Hotel really charming. Before unpacking walked up "Jacob's Ladder", a cliff staircase nearly opposite the hotel, to the top of the cliffs & had a wonderful view of Cheddar & Somerset & of part of the Gorge. Feel I shall be able to write here, & had already ideas for "D. of J." in the train.

Tuesday September 29th
Seven years to-day since Winifred died.

An Alert at breakfast-time, & guns. Later 6 people reported killed by one bomb somewhere in this area.

Settled down in earnest to start "Day of Judgment". Went thro' all the notes I made at the time of Leonard Lockhart's trial & since, the letters I received from him & others, etc., & divided them out into the 4 "Parts" of which the 100,000-word book will consist. Much going-through of news-papers, & collection & invention of incidents & conversations, will have to be done before I start the actual writing. But thanks to all the preliminary work already done, this should not take so long as with most books. No temptation to go out as it poured with rain all morning. Cleared up at lunch & I went for short walks to the village & then back up the Gorge — but wind was cold & sky still stormy. Went on with book after tea. Got hold of a *Daily Express* but fight for Stalingrad continues, & there is no other special news.

Wednesday September 30th
By first post came a report (from T. C. Foley's Public Affairs News Service) about the death of children in Greece & the refusal of our Min. of Econ. Warfare to allow Navicerts for dried milk to be taken to Greece from the Argentine — so horrifying that I sat down then & there and by lunch-time had written another Letter asking the subscribers to make the facts as given to them known. (They are vouched for by the *News Chron.*, *Man. Guardian*, Gilbert Murray, Wickham Steed, & Dr Carvadias, Chairman of the Greek Red Cross.) Sent it express after lunch from the P.O. in Cheddar to W.E.G. & also telegraphed her to substitute it for the animals one & postpone that for a fortnight. The rest of day went on with book, & answered letters at night.

Thursday October 1st
Beautiful day for a change. Found an excellent sheltered yet sunny seat in upper part of garden behind clumps of goldenrod & Michaelmas daisies. Lovely insects of all kinds flitting actively in sunshine — bees, dragonflies & several varieties of butterfly (Red Admirals, tortoiseshell, Painted Lady, swallow-tailed fritillaries, pale yellow sulphurs). Walked up the Gorge after tea but sinister effect of huge rock chimneys almost closing above my head gave me a kind of claustrophobia & a feeling with Jacob of "how dreadful is this place!".

Hitler made a speech yesterday wh. was reported fully in the *D. Mail*. He seems at any rate to have taken the measure of Churchill, who he described as a "military idiot". Has now changed Blitzkrieg for "a war of exhaustion"! (Whose?)

Friday October 2nd
Letters this morning included one from G. Wrote him at length, saying I may stay 3 weeks if weather holds. Do get freedom from interruption (except such as I want) & the invention of "incidents" for a novel cannot be hurried, any more than the *selection* of incidents for an autobiography or biography. They are largely based on small things happening to one's self.

Another lovely day. Got many notes made for book; have now started going through the Nottingham newspapers. When the sun left the garden I climbed the Jacob's Ladder again, walked along the top of the cliffs & then waited to see one of the loveliest sunsets I ever beheld, spreading right across sky from the last glimpse of the sun above Axbridge reservoir. A vast herring-bone of cloud turned first crimson & then pure flame; from bones it became ribs & then feathers of deepening flamingo.

Saturday October 3rd

Again worked on book in garden. Have now invented quite a few incidents.

One pathetic characteristic of this place is its derelict "tourismus" — little tea-rooms, restaurants, guest houses, "souvenir" shops, caves, etc. — all closed for the duration. A few troops here & there now take the place of the hundreds of week-end trippers who came here in peace-time. Empty shops still advertise cheese-straws, farmhouse cheese, etc. etc. — tho' cheese all taken over by Min. of Food. Many of the closed shops & restaurants now seem to be used as billets for soldiers.

Sunday October 4th

Began to read *The Neuroses in War* & found it fascinating. Got many ideas from it for my book. Continued it till bedtime. It is illuminating about our own family history & my own temperament — neurotic both by heredity & childhood environment. How well I know the "anxiety" conflict between standards of decent conduct & the instinct of self-preservation. It is because I know fear & despise myself for it that I get a "guilt" complex when out of dangers that others have to endure — and therefore tend (as in the Blitz) to go into them deliberately, for no purpose but the maintenance of my self-respect! G. doesn't understand this; having less fear than most people he has no guilt & therefore doesn't mind doing things that *look* cowardly. If I had gone with the children to U.S.A. I should have felt guilty, been querulous with them & might even have broken down. This is something M.S.J. never got near understanding.

Tuesday October 6th

Cold day. Worked in long coat & mittens, mostly in bedroom reading & making notes from *The Neuroses in War*. Very useful. Wrote one long scene for Part 2.

In *D. Express* to-day are references to a "scoop" of yesterday in which a letter from Stalin was printed calling on the United Nations to fulfil their obligations. From this I deduce that he may be intending to denounce his treaty with us & make a separate peace with Germany, and is holding Stalingrad so hard to get better terms. Significant things happening elsewhere. Chinese Generals all summoned to meet Wendell Willkie; & American Ambassador in Moscow going home to "report" to Roosevelt.

Wednesday October 7th

Received a whack of letters, among them one from Mother full of criticisms of G., his lack of regular work, despondency, etc., etc. Decided once for all that this must stop, so wrote her a long letter explaining: (1) That when I refused to live in U.S.A. in 1926 I sacrificed G. to my own work (though with some justification because of its nature, wh. was not self-regarding) and that my separation from the children now is a judgment on me for not settling down to the family life there wh. could have been carried on unbroken by the war. (2) That his inability to get a responsible administrative job now was due to *my* pacifism (which he has too much integrity to want me to give up or keep quiet about) making him "suspect". I told her of our crossed-out names on Wendell Willkie's list of people invited to meals, & the failure of Henry & Rebecca to ask us to their literary dinner tho' G. introduced Henry to Willkie. I ended by saying that the least we could do was to see that G. didn't lack money, & certainly could not expect humiliating expressions of gratitude from him. I told her to keep the letter in case the children ever misjudged their father.

Thursday October 8th
Still fascinated by *The Neuroses in War*. Gave me various ideas for conversations etc. Just before tea when I was working in the garden a cloud came over the sun and there was a sharp shower, which later became a downpour & then a thunderstorm, with two beautiful rainbows over the Gorge. When it stopped about 6.0 I went for a walk up Birch Hill to the Quarry & looked over Axbridge Reservoir from another side. Thought as I walked over the bits of *Testament of Youth* which I re-read this afternoon, & which bears out so much of the psychology as clinically defined in *The Neuroses in War*. Thought how all my life had really been a battle against fear, both inherited & environmental. Sometimes a lost battle, sometimes (as for most of the last war) *just* victorious.

Friday October 9th
Worked all day on "Day of Judgment" and finished reading *The Neuroses in War*.
    Letter from Stephen Hobhouse enclosed a new pamphlet of his — "Retribution & the Christian". Said he found some confusion in my own hurried little one, "The Higher Retribution", wh. is doubtless too true! Glanced at his after writing him — very late, just before getting into bed — & found I had to finish it. It was about the Christian obligation to forgive an enemy &, still further, help him to overcome his sin — and had an extraordinary cathartic effect, making me see the deeper aspects of my own novel & the connection between curative reform (e.g. in prisons) & internat. peace.

Saturday October 10th
After lunch caught bus to Winscombe, met at Sidcot Corner by Mr Harman, found all the Food Relief Committee gathered at Lanacre. Rather late, Mr Orr-Ewing, M.P., turned up — a youngish rather foolish-

looking typical Conservative lacking front teeth. He proceeded to explain his objection to the Food Relief resolution passed after my meeting in May; then Mr Harman stated our position & a general discussion began. But it was a case of "East is East etc. & never the twain shall meet"! [Orr-Ewing] tried to dodge or turn all our questions, & when I kept pinning him back & back to the point (espec. re Navicerts for milk for children in Greece), he slithered like an eel & took refuge when really cornered in attacking a young C.O. who was there & saying that Joad wasn't helping the war! Dingle Foot was much more enlightened. He left (Mr Orr-E.) promising to convey our concern to the Min. of Economic Warfare, but he spoke vaguely of "rabid" & untruthful propaganda (where again I tried to pin him to chapter & verse) & I doubt if we made any impression except on each other!

Sunday October 11th
Wrote long letter to G.; corrected Letter 94; also wrote to Stephen Hobhouse about his beautiful pamphlet. Wrote more scenes for book & made more notes. After tea walked along hillside for two miles to the nearest village. Walk took me high enough up hill to see one of the barrage balloons above Weston-super-Mare — wh. I gathered doesn't show very many signs of its recent little Blitz. Autumn lovely here now — sumac-like bush beside water in front of my bedroom window seems really on fire; on walls of cottages ampelopsis is vivid. All such a contrast [with] the controversy going on about chaining of prisoners; British & German politicians behaving like uncontrolled children.

Monday October 12th
Spent most of day recovering memories of first Great War by reading R. C. Sherriff & Siegfried Sassoon.
Controversy about manacled prisoners still going on. Germans still unable to take Stalingrad are announcing new defensive tactics. Everyone inquiring whether this is a bluff.

Tuesday October 13th
Letter from Andrew Dakers saying that book will be ready at least for autographed copies on Dick Sheppard House Celebration Day (Oct. 31). Also in press-cuttings one from the *News Chronicle* which to its credit did put in, & without any cuts, my letter protesting about the Korda film of Tolstoy's *War and Peace* on ground that Tolstoy was a pacifist, & this would inevitably be made a war propaganda film if done now.
Again warm enough to work in garden in afternoon. Continued to make notes on 1918 conditions on Western front.
Yesterday Churchill made a speech in Edinburgh talking again about Hitler as "that bad man" — as though he himself was an angel of light & had never referred appreciatively to Hitler in his own *Great Contemporaries*. Bombs yesterday on South Coast & Sunderland.

Wednesday October 14th
Finished the partial re-reading of *T. of Youth* & *Honourable Estate* to get the atmosphere of France in the last war & shall start Part 1 properly to-morrow. Only hope I shan't be swamped with letters.

No special news. *D. Express* contains gloomy paragraph prophesying bigger Blitz than ever as reprisals, & talks about re-constitution of Civil Defence.

Thursday October 15th
Lovely day till tea-time, when it went windy. Worked in garden till then; did 6 pp. altogether. After tea walked up the hill at the back & made a few notes on the view of Somerset (for Bk. 2) as best I could in the wind.

Felt cheered by getting book started. Were I able to remain here three months I could finish it; it is all bubbling & surging out of my mind. Oh, for 20 years freed from war & the threat of war, in which to write 20 more books now that I know how to do my job!

Friday October 16th
Smallish mail, so was able to finish Chapter 1 of book & do whole of Chap. 2 in rough draft. Couldn't get on as fast as normally after dinner, as three teachers (real school-marms) who appear to have come for the week-end destroyed the peace of the lounge by loud self-conscious conversation.

Saturday October 17th
Large whacking mail. Some interesting ones from Letter correspondents (e.g. Lady Wedgwood) reporting results of letters written about Greek children to the M.E.W., M.P.s etc. Lady W. enclosed a letter wh. she had received from Lord Selborne — saying all relief to Greece must be "co-ordinated" (which apparently means that Greek money must not be spent nor Greek sailors' lives risked to save Greece's own children!). As Lady W. says, what politician ever lacked plausible excuses for action or inaction! This week I have heard of two others, equally plausible but quite different — Dingle Foot & Mr Orr-Ewing M.P. at Winscombe! People with values of "the fashion of this world" will go their own way & invent ingenious excuses, so long as they think the opposing public will stand it — hence the need for constant protest.

Wrote more than half of Chapter 2, mostly in garden, despite wet morning. Guns sounding from Weston-Super-Mare.

Monday October 19th
Most encouraging letter from Andrew Dakers reporting excellent start to *Humiliation with Honour*. Well over 3,000 subscription sales already before the London booksellers have subscribed at all.

Pollard's *Short History of the Great War* arrived from the London Library to-day so I was able to check the facts for Part 1.

Tuesday October 20th

Wrote half of Ch. 3 of Part 1. (Very wet day.) Met G. at 3.10, & walked up to hotel. Still very rainy, but managed to get short walk up hills at back after tea.

Wednesday October 21st

Lovely morning after so much rain. Went first to village to get money & blackberries for jam; then climbed Jacob's Ladder & walked over top of cliff till we reached the peak & could see a long way across the open country towards Bath. Glastonbury Tor, the Quantocks & Brent Knoll all quite clear in the distance. Talked about G.'s work & our joint money arrangements. After lunch walked to the grass lane with the ripe elder trees which I found on Sunday & picked two or three pounds for jelly. Got back just in time to hear record of greater part of Smuts' speech to the H. of Commons this afternoon. He discussed peace aims, did not mention "retribution", & paid more attention to the "wickedness" of Japan than of Germany. Also acknowledged that the war was partly due to mistakes of Allied statesmen.

Thursday October 22nd   London

Returned to London; glad to get back; had reached stage when unbroken work on book must have become monotonous if continued much longer. Got early train [to Bristol], but could get nothing earlier than the noon train back to town — so went & looked at the beautiful church of St Mary Redcliffe — standing (except for some broken stained glass windows) almost undamaged by the extensive Blitz all round it. Walked from there over Bristol Bridge to the Grand Hotel for a drink, & realised (as I did not when speaking there) how very badly the city is damaged.

Friday October 23rd

After lunch met Andrew Dakers at Putnam's in Great Russell Street and signed about 50 copies of *Humiliation with Honour*, which looks a striking little book with Arthur Wragg's remarkable cover. Dakers said that Smith's ordered 500 & subscription sales are now over 4,000. Sent copies to various pacifist stalwarts & to personal friends.

Arranged with Amy to come daily (except Sundays) for half day for 25/– weekly (out of which she has to pay bus fares & cost of someone to look after Marian while she is absent).

Evening papers reported arrival of Mrs Roosevelt by air from U.S.A. Must think carefully if any method of contact exists. Suggested to G. that she be asked to A.B.C.A. party on Oct. 29th.

Saturday October 24th

Troubled again by vile dermatitis; wonder what can have agitated me this time! Worst of going away the vast accumulation of secretarial work that has to be dealt with on return.

Bed 3.30 a.m. Perfect moonlight night, clear, cold, everything as light as day. Nazis evidently don't intend to raid as nothing could have been easier for them.

Sunday October 25th

Long article by Raymond Gram Swing on Mrs F.D.R. pointing out how she has acquired a unique position as probably greatest woman in American history by disregarding, but without pushful aggressiveness, the self-effacement required of her by convention as the President's wife. Mrs F.D.R. said in a Press Conference yesterday that she hoped things would not be made too official for her, as she wanted to go about informally & see England & English people for herself. This was also echoed yesterday in her mouthpiece the *Washington Post*.

Monday October 26th

Sent Mrs Roosevelt a bouquet — 12 carnations & 12 roses in same shade of strawberry pink as her boudoir was decorated — at cost of nearly £3! Sent them to Buckingham Palace but saw later that she had left there — so don't know whether they will reach her or not.

On returning found a note from Dr Gangulee asking whether there was any hope of Mrs F.D.R. attending a private meeting at wh. the actual character of the deadlock in India could be placed before her. Wrote explaining that it would be more difficult for me to get hold of Mrs F.D.R. here owing to official supervision of her programme, & official reactions against me!

Dined at 55 Park Lane with Sir J. Mactaggart & family. He showed us plans of flats (the less costly ones) wh. [would] be available in the block. We talked largely about the big A.B.C.A. party on Thursday. General Smuts is coming, also the Mountbattens, & Mrs F.D.R. may come. Sir Harry Brittain apparently wanted to exclude the handful of women Founder Members, and Cyril Asquith (who is *much* too much impressed by the adverse reactions of the conservative American colony here against Mrs F.D.R.) was inclined to agree, but G. overruled both of them!

Tuesday October 27th

Morning disturbed by influx of letters about my Letter 93 on Greece. Three were critical, but a statement by Dingle Foot in a letter to Jennie Adamson, M.P., reported in to-night's *Evening Standard*, fully bore out the truth of my contention that the M.E.W. are not prepared to help in getting milk to the Greek children.

Worked all day on Letter 95 — about Retribution again, quoting Stephen Hobhouse's pamphlet "Retribution and the Christian", and Max Plowman's essay "Lighten Our Darkness" from *The Right to Live*.

Wednesday October 28th
Humiliation with Honour published to-day. Dakers rang up when I was out to say that "subscription sales" were over 5,900 — i.e. the whole 6,000 first edition is sold, since we gave away about 100 as review & presentation copies. Neither Dakers nor I expected this & he has telegraphed for a reprint, but wishes now that he had done a larger first edition.

W.E.G. came for letters; also typing of Letter 95. At lunch-time went to Friends' House to hear Eleanor Hinder speak at the W.I.L. Luncheon on her work at Shanghai, carried on after Dec. 8th '41 under the Japanese. Apparently they were none of them badly treated, though the food queues & deaths from starvation among the Chinese were terrible until food was rationed.

Went on from the luncheon with G. to call at Redfern Galleries (where Rothenstein's portrait of me is).

Thursday October 29th
Large attack by 8th Army in Egypt continuing. So strange in this war to know no one on these fronts, when in the last I was in anguish over every battle till 4 months before the end — when they had all gone.

Despite rain & general inconvenience of getting to 6 Stanhope Gate from Richmond, managed to get to A.B.C.A. party by 6.0. Distinguished enough gathering at which the charming & shy American Ambassador, John G. Winant, made a short speech — otherwise the hoped-for great (Smuts, Mrs Roosevelt, Mountbattens) behaved characteristically in not turning up. At party talked to Lord Gorell, Sir H. Brittain (who doesn't like having a namesake), Caroline Haslett, etc. Stayed on to dinner at 55 Park Lane but do *not* like this wealthy conservative crowd of capitalists.

Friday October 30th
Still raining. In new *Peace News* two large notices of Max's book apart from Dakers' advt. but not a mention of mine! Typical J.M.M. reaction. However . . . such is human nature!

Saturday October 31st
Pleasant letters from Lord Ponsonby, Canon Raven and James Maxton about *H. w. H.* This afternoon went to Friends' House for celebration by the P.P.U. of the 5th anniversary of Dick Sheppard's death. Proceedings began with beautiful concert by Peter Pears & Benjamin Britten; Pears sang first Schubert & then some of Britten's compositions, including the Michelangelo sequence. Large hall of Friends' House was packed. I took chair for Laurence Housman. He read a most moving play called *The*

Instrument, an imaginary conversation between ex-President Wilson & Tumulty about the League of Nations, written in 1922; its prophetic quality was extraordinary. J.M.M., his daughter Katherine, & Mary Gamble were among those listening to it; John said he had not known of the play any more than I did.

Sunday November 1st
Amy still away, so flat takes till nearly mid-day to straighten. Spent much of morning writing to Stephen Hobhouse (and sending photograph) in response to the strange "love letter" he wrote me two days ago. Wrote John last night, giving him some reasons for *not* staying in U.S.A. & "graduating" in 1944 — i.e., hurrying through his education — which he had suggested in his letter.

Went to bed directly after dinner owing to fire-watching 3–6. No Alert during night.

Monday November 2nd
Letter from an Eton master, Mr Tait, with whom I have been corresponding, about milk for the Greek children, informed me confidentially that a considerable supply is now being shipped with the necessary licence! It really looks as if Letter 93 & the efforts of my correspondents have achieved something! Mr Tait in his letter mentioned anti-British propaganda in the Middle West of U.S.A., & I told him that in my view nothing would better restore our popularity there than a really courageous attempt to feed the starving peoples of Europe on Hoover's lines.

Daily Herald gave headlines to a German communiqué indicating failure of our 8th Army in Libya. Hannan Swaffer foaming at the mouth about the Duke of Bedford's *Peace News* article: "If I were a Pacifist Premier". Do we grovel, typically asks H.S.

Tuesday November 3rd
Went to the P.P.U. Executive & heard two items of special interest: (1) The Govt. realises that it over-reached itself over the chaining of prisoners "reprisals", having had protests from most of the Bishops & many other people, & all parties put on a "whip" asking that no questions be asked about it either for or against — so Parlt. is muzzled & no one knows what is happening. (2) The *respectable* Food Relief Committee (Chairman the Bp. of Chichester & the two Archbishops among the supporters) is shortly taking a deputn. to Churchill to urge a humane policy of food relief — & if this move fails will come out against the Govt. themselves!

Found at the P.P.U. bookshop that the 36 copies of my book sold almost immediately, 21 at the party. They have many more orders & now regret not getting more.

Wednesday November 4th
Went into town early & dictated letters to W.E.G. in rest room at Marshall's. We lunched there & I got a pretty gold braid collar to renovate my old black silk & velvet dress. Then went on to Truefitt & Hill & had my hair "permed" — a thoroughly suburban matron's day except for dictating the letters! Had tea at Stewart's & got back to find letters from Lady Mayer & a very nice, almost ecstatic one from Mrs Pethick Lawrence about *H. with H.*

Thursday November 5th
Very wet again; except for part of yesterday it has now rained steadily for ten days. Morning papers jubilant over what is described as a "great victory" in Egypt; Rommel's army said to be "rolled up". Less attention paid to the result of the Congressional elections in U.S.A., wh. leave a Democratic majority of only 9 in the H. of Representatives. This will prevent Roosevelt from taking any new initiative, &, unless some preliminary undertaking is made, looks as if peace will come just in time to find another Republican isolationist majority, with a President less friendly to Britain than Roosevelt, wanting to cut America's responsibility for the peace.

Papers report Curtice Hitchcock, the U.S. publisher, over here, & an official party given for him to meet "leading authors" — from wh. I was of course omitted. Wrote Rache to inquire why George Brett, as head of a great firm, couldn't come over instead of a small publisher.

Friday November 6th
Newspapers still jubilant about our victory in Egypt.

Went along to Cook's with G. & saw Miss Jackson & Mrs Rogers, who had just arranged for a party of children & adults to come back on a Portuguese boat & got them safely to Lisbon & some are in London already. They offered us a place for John in the next party, also saying that air passages for children were less & less likely as "priority" passengers increased. Faced with grim dilemma of again risking John's life or losing him for the duration & virtually altogether, we told Cook's at least to go ahead & get the necessary Portuguese visa, which does not commit us.

At tea G. decided he had 'flu & got a dose from the chemist. After I had attended the Bombing Restriction Committee & had my own dinner, he came in late & went to bed. Rest of evening occupied looking after him.

Saturday November 7th
Still miserable & worried about John, the more so because a letter from George Brett to G. written Oct. 5th speaks of the importance of the children getting "continuity in education in the schools in wh. they have started over here", thereby showing that he, J.'s guardian & payer of the bills, did not know of the change of school at that date; while John writes

jubilantly (in a letter last night) of the easiness of his lessons at the new school, & the fact that he is not studying French or Latin, but only Geometry, English, Biology & Spanish (apparently no History). This doesn't seem like education to us!

G. in bed this morning & in a very bad temper, because of usual obsession that everyone else is getting on well & he isn't! Never got to P.P.U. Council.

Sunday November 8th
Again unable to get to P.P.U. Council (where I should have been yesterday) owing to numerous morning chores — including typing a letter for G. to Jon Creech Jones — partly apropos of the Ministry of Labour's written request to G. to volunteer for munitions work — some job for a Professor of Political Science of 20 years' study & experience! Could not get to lunch with Mother but dropped in to Hotel for a cup of tea on my way to Bow — where I had promised to substitute for G. in lecturing on "America & the Future" so that he could get to Northampton before black-out. He is going there for most of a week (& then to Cardiff, Pontypool & Birmingham) for lectures to troops.

Monday November 9th
Papers full of American landings (assisted by British) in N. Africa. Oran, Casablanca, Agadir, etc. etc. What price now are respect for other people's countries? Vichy-France seems to be putting up some resistance but not much. Meanwhile the Germans are in process of being pushed from Egypt back into Libya — the fourth swing of the pendulum.

Tuesday November 10th
More American landings reported. Algeria submits. "Second front" now in full operation in N. Africa. Italy beginning to be threatened from both ends of the Mediterranean.

Went into town early so that I could attend the "Women for Westminster" lunch-time Conference, with Mrs Sieff in the Chair & Dorothy Evans as Secretary. I became much more enthusiastic when I realised the hope (shared by Chairman and Secretary) that this movement to get more women into public life might end as an "avalanche" movement to eliminate war by women (rather as Mrs Roosevelt suggested in her excellent B.B.C. Postscript on Sunday night).

From meeting went to Cheyne Walk & met a representative of Gregg's, the builders, to discuss repairs to damage done by bombs & weather. Despite dirt & falling plaster, the house seemed so bright & sunny that I longed to get back to it — even though it is surrounded on all sides by big areas of ruin.

Wednesday November 11th
Strange Armistice Day. Thick fog, poppy sellers half choked. General

feeling of excitement everywhere owing to opening of the "Second Front" in N. Africa. Americans now in possession of Casablanca, Oran, Algiers. Rumours that Admiral Darlan is going to join the Allies, that Hitler will occupy all France & Italians Corsica etc. Radio competition for allegiance of France & especially the French Fleet, which is at Toulon.

Thursday November 12th
Major theatre of war now the Mediterranean. Churchill's speech to the House yesterday, given in full in this morning's newspapers, explained our victory in Egypt as first part of a "grand strategy" of which the U.S. landings in N. Africa are the second. The "Second Front" wh. could not be opened straight across the Channel owing to shortage of landing craft is now threatening Italy & the S. of France. Hitler, evidently taken by surprise, has occupied the whole of France in contravention of the Armistice terms, & has sent paratroops to Tunis. Anglo-American force racing to meet him there — where we have about as much right as he has. His violations are described as "invasion"; ours as "landings" or "rescue-parties".

Still anxious about John. Letter from Mr Hilary Taylor said several boys had entered Eton that half who had been 2 years in Canada or U.S.A., & had settled down well. He undertook to remove J.'s "prejudice"! But how get him there? After dinner attended lecture for fire-guards, chiefly on the new "anti-personnel" incendiary bomb from which there is apparently nothing to be done but run away!

Friday November 13th
Letters from Lord Gorell & W. K. Seymour both advised me to leave John in U.S.A. at present rather than risk a journey via Portugal where anything might happen with the whole Mediterranean ablaze. Have been gradually coming to this conclusion myself; and fear that there is nothing to do but wait until things "clarify" (as Lord Gorell puts it) in that part of the world.

Wrote Ruth & Shirley asking for a cable if and when there was any hope of passages on Pan-American Airways. Letter from Geoffrey Mander (Air Ministry) yesterday indicated that nothing is to be hoped for from British lines.

Saturday November 14th
Two charming and encouraging letters about *H. with Honour* from the Catchpools and from Stephen Hobhouse cheered me up considerably after yesterday's black depression. Stephen writes of the little book "How splendid . . . it will surely do a lot of good!" and C.C. calls it "one of the most lofty and inspiring appeals to all that is best in human kind that I have for a long time read." After clearing off all outstanding letters,

actually got back to my novel in the evening. Alas! a month next Tuesday since I last wrote it.

News still seems incredible after the long story of defeat; our forces actually took Tobruk back last night, and press reports say they may reach Benghazi within a few days. Rommel apparently putting up no fight — not yet anyway. Anglo–U.S. forces said to have reached Tunisian border & to be looking for Axis troops. French in response to Darlan are collaborating with the Allies. Genoa raided; German troops have occupied all France except Toulon, where the Fleet is. An *Evening Standard* article about the probable increased activity of U-boats in the Atlantic off the Mediterranean confirms yesterday's judgment about leaving John alone.

Sunday November 15th

11.30 a.m. Church bells have been ringing all over London — the first time we have heard them for $2\frac{1}{2}$ years — to celebrate the victory in the Battle of Egypt. I suppose it was by Churchill's order that this rather childish premature rejoicing was performed. Most people — with sons lost, children evacuated, homes broken up — will only feel, as I have felt, the more heartache on hearing the bells. Their ringing should have been postponed till the end of the War. That is the only thing which most of us want to celebrate. All morning, a gun — or fog signal — has kept on going off somewhere nearby, mingling oddly with the bells. Newspapers report Allied forces over the Tunisian border, advancing towards Tunis & Bizerta. From the other end of N. Africa, Rommel is retreating still at great speed towards Benghazi, leaving quantities of "booty" in our hands. Genoa — alas! — raided again yesterday for the third time in 8 days; "great fires" left blazing.

Lunched with Mother, & then went on to Friends' Meeting House at Muswell Hill, where I gave a "Reading" from my own books (*T. of Y.*, *England's Hour*, *H. with H.* & two poems) in aid of Dick Sheppard House Fund. Collection (counting sales of books) brought in near £6. Vile cold coming on — I suppose caught from G.

Monday November 16th

Wretched influenza cold. Could hardly breathe; had semi-nightmares all night. Stayed in bed till Amy came. Got up at 10.0 & she got me some breakfast.

Long letter from Harold Latham, explaining regretfully why — as I expected — the Macmillan company of New York could not publish *Humiliation with Honour*. They are, as I realise, too much tied up with official policies, like Macmillan here; but they evidently debated the matter much longer than I expected before deciding to turn the book down. H.S.L. suggested that after the war they might publish the book, perhaps with some additions, & I spent most of day drafting a reply to him which I thought might appropriately be one of those additions. This reply justified both his line from his point of view *and* mine from my own.

Tuesday November 17th
News of a large American victory over the Japanese navy last Friday, near the Solomons. Lost force said to equal size of a large invasion fleet. Nobody mentions the lost *men*. In N. Africa battle is concentrating on Tunisia; a force of about 30,000 Germans said to have been landed there.

Cold still obstreperous but felt rather better. Not able to do much else but answer large mail. Pleasant letter from Laurence Housman saying he had sent his review of *H. w. H.* to *P.N.*, but telling nothing about it — tho' he said I had paid John (my John) a compliment by treating him as an open-minded rational person, & he wondered how he wld. react. Dakers reports Murry evasive abt. my book & saying it was "difficult" to publicise my book & Max's together.

Wednesday November 18th
Cold still abominable, but went into town, met W.E.G. at Friends' House, did "Letter" business, & then at W.I.L. took Chair for Prof. N. Gangulee, who gave a beautiful address on "India To-day". This dealt mainly with the aspirations behind the Congress movement — their "Three Freedoms" — wh. Gandhi has defined as Freedom from Ignorance, Freedom from Fear, & Freedom from Conflict. The whole speech so much impressed me as a contribution to understanding & an illustration of how much *we*, the active, aggressive West, have to learn from the East, that I asked him to write it as an article & I would undertake to get it published somewhere. One of Tagore's poems was also recited (rather too dramatically, I thought) by a dark good-looking Austrian woman, Mme Lily Freud-Marle, who is a niece of the late Sigmund Freud. Very tired; put on fire-watching clothes & lay down at once.

Thursday November 19th
Fire-watching 12–3, but according to new regulations one is now allowed to rest in bed & sign off in the morning provided one stays dressed so as to be ready immediately if there is an Alert.

Cold v. bad all day. Letter from J. Middleton Murry saying that Laurence Housman's review of my book will be in next week's *P. News*, & will I do an article for the special Christmas number.

Mother came to tea; it is her 74th birthday to-day. She had hardly come & was helping me to wrap up presents for John & Shirley, when the telephone rang from someone who wanted me to speak at Golders Green on Monday evening, wh. I refused; in the middle arrived Miss Schofield, editor of *Parents*, with 50 photographs of babies for me to judge! I had arranged this, but forgotten she was coming. However, she & Mother had tea while I chose & marked 10 out of the 50 photographs of mostly lovely babies, & finished them (getting what tea I could) in time for her to take away at 5.0. G. went to Manchester till Sunday for more Army lectures.

Saturday November 21st

Hints of political row brewing between us & U.S.A bec. General Eisenhower appointed Admiral Darlan to the N. African Command.

After morning on mail and an afternoon of fire-fighting practice, I managed at last to do 5 pages of my book. Too tired after the exercise to do more — especially as I fell over the feet of a too-large boiler suit & came flat down on my knees. One of the odd incongruities of this war to think that John — who must now be a fairly vigorous boy on the verge of 15 — is safely in America while his middle-aged mother scrambles round in trousers fighting fires (or learning to).

Nice letter from Sybil Morrison about my book. *Evening Standard* reports British now in Benghazi.

Sunday November 22nd

Sunday papers report very heavy raid on Turin on Friday night, almost equivalent to the one on Cologne. *Sunday Express* exulting as usual, saying that there *were* 50,000 workmen at the Fiat Works in Turin, & this was only the beginning of what we are going to do to Italy, etc. etc.

Monday November 23rd

Estimate arrived from Gregg's for repairs & partial redecoration of 2 Cheyne Walk — £78 for repairs, £32 for War damage. Claimed for this yesterday (ceilings down, broken windows and panes, etc.).

Cripps out of War Cabinet — demoted to Minister of Aircraft Production by Churchill instead. Herbert Morrison — "the industrious apprentice" — in the Cabinet instead. Query: Why didn't Cripps resign?

Tuesday November 24th

Cold & foggy again — a dreary November.

Allies now in occupation of Jedabaya. Russians conducted a successful offensive at Stalingrad, Germans pressed on all sides for first time in war.

Spent all day doing Letter 97 — on various kinds of post-war planning and the lack of preparation for a cultural revival.

Wednesday November 25th

G. & I dined with R. R. Stokes after dropping in to see Mother at the hotel for a few moments. But he was tired after making a long & tiring "opposition" speech in the House yesterday — largely about the negotiations with Darlan — and we got the impression of a rather isolated if vigorous & courageous person. He is a bachelor living alone, looked after by a housekeeper; his Parliamentary policy is moved entirely by opposition to Churchill, whom he regards (not incorrectly) as a bumptious self-seeker with no real honesty of purpose, but merely a wish to go down to history as Marlborough's illustrious warlike descendant.

Thursday November 26th

We both attended this morning a wonderful Thanksgiving Service in Westminster Abbey for the American troops and their friends; came up from Westminster Station to see the Stars & Stripes flying from the Abbey Tower. It is the first time in the 900 years of the Abbey's history that it has been handed over to the representatives of a foreign power. Inside packed, both chairs & aisles, with American troops — waves of khaki broken only by an occasional navy-uniformed sailor or nurse. We stood near the Unknown Warrior's grave. Four American Chaplains, Winant, & the Dean of Westminster took the service. It concluded with the hymns "America the Beautiful", "Lead on, O Father" & the song "God Bless America". Afterwards the bus conductress inquired: "What's this — Independence Day?"

Friday November 27th

Firewatching 3 a.m.–6.a.m., but now able to stay in bed & sleep, though dressed. Large morning mail from people who want to consult me on their problems; then wrote to George Brett, John & Shirley. Cable from Ruth said: "Had beautiful Thanksgiving, John home four days grown two inches looks wonderful still interpret your instructions Cook's for May much love." John must certainly be a grand-looking boy now; I shall hardly know him again. By my reckoning, he is now 5 foot 7 inches tall. Trying not to feel too grieved because he is growing so tall and handsome and I am missing it all. But the years pass & the war gets nearer to him without my having his attractive youth at all.

Saturday November 28th

News in this morning's papers that the French Fleet had scuttled itself at Toulon, just as Hitler's men were about to occupy the town. The whole Greek tragedy of France in this war might be entitled "The Futility of Power". What sacrifices the French people made to build the Maginot Line which proved useless, & this fleet now burned & destroyed.

G. lecturing to Federal Union groups at Clapham, & Alliance Hall, Westminster. Bright morning; v. cold this afternoon.

Sunday November 29th

Sick & miserable half of night; evidently upset or poisoned by one of the peculiar synthetic foodstuffs one eats nowadays. Would have been tempted to stay in bed but for my P.P.U. Reading. Got up just before lunch, to which I went; then betook myself to the Labour Club in Church Rd for the smallest of the three Readings for the Dick Sheppard Fund. It was a pleasant & friendly little group, and afterwards bought several books. Though tired felt better, & returned to work on my novel. Managed, to my surprise, to complete Part 1 by bedtime.

Monday November 30th
Sick, tired & wobbly again; obviously didn't give myself a chance to recover yesterday. Stayed in bed all day & more or less starved. Thankful of Amy. She told me how reluctant Burnett had been to go to the war — always meant to wait till he was fetched & rather despised those who didn't. They both regarded volunteers as "the men who make war". Cf. last war attitude — an astonishing contrast. The disillusion of its soldiers has lasted on even among those who were only children at the time.

Review of M.S.J.'s latest novel by Philip Toynbee in the *New Statesman* suggests that it is completely sterile (another of her obsessive studies of Nazi frightfulness).

Tuesday December 1st
Beveridge Report on Social Security published. Corrected proofs of Letter 97.

Wednesday December 2nd
Very busy day with accumulated correspondence. W.E.G. here. Dictated & got off 23 letters altogether, most of them long, & left for her for that reason. She is a wonderfully quick and methodical worker.

G.'s little (edited) pamphlet on American Aims out, but Major Simnett the pamphlet man on A.B.C.A. never sent him a proof & calmly left his name off the cover. A pettifogging sort of meanness, this. W.E.G. brought the completed Christmas "token" for my Letter (Beryl Chapman's woodcut with the words quoted on the back from Johan Bojer that I used in the Introductory Issue of my Letter: "I went & sowed corn in mine enemy's field that God might exist"). All W.E.G.'s idea except the quotation.

Vile, tedious but necessary evening filing all the letters that have accumulated since I came back from Cheddar.

Columns about the Beveridge Report in all the papers & people talking abt. it as if it were a *fait accompli* instead of a scheme. Beveridge is to marry Mrs Mair this month.

Thursday December 3rd
After tiresome morning & afternoon of interruption, managed to get to my book. Put the Notes for Part 2 into shape, planned the chapters & chose their titles.

Foggy, cold.

Saturday December 5th
Correspondence even more massive than usual; must have received about 30 letters & written nearly 20. Amy at last had one from Burnett — an

airmail letter & most discreet, but it seems quite obvious that he was in the big N. African Convoy. By a pleasant coincidence Shirley's present for Burnett — a pine-cone freak bird called a "Yard Bird" — arrived to-day; Amy undid it to see if Shirley had sent a letter which she could forward, & found a card & note inside. She was naturally in the seventh heaven all day & bought a 14/11 doll for Marian. She also told me that I virtually took the place of her mother & I was the person she missed when she went to Woking.

War now going less favourably for us; Axis has superior air power in the bit of Tunis which it holds & will be hard to dislodge. We made a daylight raid [on] Naples yesterday — that lovely city. The Pope has apparently announced that if we raid Rome he will move from the Vatican & live right in the middle of it.

Sunday December 6th

Was actually able to spend most of day on book — reading the various writings Dr Lockhart gave me on industrial medicine, & making notes for the "Progress Comes to Halkin's" chapter of "Day of Judgment".

Went for short walk in the Park after lunch. Pleasant pale sunshine.

Sir A. Sinclair nominated for next Viceroy of India.

Tuesday December 8th

Still mild; more like October. Back to book; went through the Hobhouse prison material sent me by Stephen. Journey into town to go over 2 Cheyne Walk with the Surveyor. Large sunk Anderson Shelter put into the back garden by Council workmen over the weekend looks a very good job.

Wednesday December 9th

W.E.G. here. Usual rather tedious day of letter dictation & correction. Got off about 20–25 letters all told. Revised Letter 98 & she typed it. She has had up to date 52 orders for the "token" card & subscription.

The news seems to have retired in the usual rather sinister fashion behind small headlines. Advantage of the N. African invasion becoming more dubious now that the Germans hold both Toulon & Bizerta. Further indications of this in an *Evening Standard* article suggesting that the Germans may well be able to salvage & *use* the French fleet within a matter of months.

How tired I am of this country fighting the Germans (who are so efficient & thorough) — I am sure that the future peace of Europe depends on our ability to be friends with them — & upon little else.

Thursday December 10th

Amy received two more letters from Burnett to-day — written at sea before the airmail one. Asks "Have you heard from Algy lately?" As we know no Algy, he has obviously gone to Algiers.

Worked all day on "D. of J." & began to draft Chap. 5 (the beginning of Part 2). Filled with admiration for Leonard Lockhart's medical writings wh. I have been reading.

Another heavy raid on Turin last night — poor amiable Italians!

Friday December 11th

Terribly grim stories of Nazi treatment of Jews filling all the available space in the papers. Degree to which Jewish suffering has been extended by war is immeasurable; the worst peace would not have caused one-tenth of it.

Went to tea with Mother in her room. She really does seem to be having some heart trouble wh. concerns me & we altered our Xmas arrangements on her account. She showed me an article by Lord Ponsonby in this week's *Peace News* which most warmly commends *H. w. H.* as "clothing profound thoughts in the simplest language."

Sunday December 13th

Drafted a reply to Rebecca Sieff's invitation to the protest meeting about the terrible Nazi policy of exterminating the Jews on which all the papers have comments.

Uninterrupted Sunday at last spent on my book.

Monday December 14th

Spent much of day getting off Christmas cards and a few parcels — which I am resolutely sending despite "austerity".

Went into town after lunch to hear Dr Gautier, the Swiss member of the Health Section of the League of Nations, talk on present conditions in Europe to the Friends' Post War Section at Friends' House. Edith Pye who was in the Chair made the interesting statement that, according to the International Red Cross, the Germans have scrupulously kept whatever undertakings they have made about relief sent to starving peoples. In the case of Belgium we will not give the Navicerts for the food to come from America, & unless we give Navicerts the Germans will not give undertakings — the usual vicious circle. Dr Gautier gave some grim facts about Europe, saying that 200,000,000 people are waiting & longing for one thing only — the day when they can have a square meal again. Immediately war ends (unless it ends gradually) 1 million tons of concentrated food will be required. He strongly backed what I have so often urged — the giving of "token" relief if only to give the starving peoples the sense of support & to save some children.

Tuesday December 15th

At 3.45 G. & I went to the Beveridge–Mair wedding reception at the Dorchester — really a touching occasion, especially when Sir William referred to her as "my Janet". She had on a dark red frock & two white gardenias — no hat, white hair beautifully waved as usual. Party was more select than I had thought — not more than 200 people at most, though filling the Dorchester's "Park Suite" — so it was all the more of a pleasure to be asked. Speeches were made by Philip Mair (Mrs Mair's only son) who had evidently learnt it by heart & forgot his words in the middle — by Brendan Bracken, & by Clement Davies M.P. Both Beveridge & his wife replied; both hoped that the war would be over soon & they wold be able to see all their friends at the Master's Lodge at Univ. Talked to F. W. & Mary Ogilvie (who wants to put me up for Somerville Council), David & Mrs Low, Caroline Haslett, Lord & Lady Addison, Mrs Tawney, Roy Harrod etc. Introduced for second time to American Ambassador. M. Maisky also there. Party seemed to be divided between Oxford, politics & the Embassies. Had pleasant word or two with the bride and bridegroom; then went to Kensington to tell Mother about it while G. attended a committee. Don't know where ceremony was but Archbishop of Canterbury married them.

Mild, spring-like day after rain; bright half-moon.

Wednesday December 16th

Most depressing — in fact devastating — letter at last arrived from George Brett about John. As I suspected, his change of school was due to a falling off of work at the St Paul Academy. He has obviously been wrongly handled and made recalcitrant (partly, no doubt, because Shirley seems very obviously the favourite at St Paul). George thinks John should come home in May & *so do I*; he appears to believe that transport will be available. Alas & alas! I have gone without the children for 2½ years, only to produce this situation. I knew all along that they shouldn't have gone, & if G. & Margaret S.J. had not overruled me, they wouldn't have.

Went to a P.P.U. Conference at Friends' House on the forthcoming Armistice Campaign, held with the object of getting support from other organisations. Took part, but could think of nothing but John all day.

Thursday December 17th

Felt better about John to-day; realised that he is just being the same old John who, so far as a boy can be of a girl, is a replica of my 15-year-old self reacting adversely to affectionate friends who have treated him with a little less than complete wisdom. Wrote a long letter to George about him of wh. I asked him to send a copy to Ruth.

At tea-time, after two days of inward agitation following weeks of suspense about poor John, I got on to Chapter 6 of my book.

Another Rommel retreat going on in N. Africa. Amy heard again from Burnett, who said he was in a land where you could buy oranges *ad. lib.*

Saturday December 19th

Air raid yesterday on a place in Sussex which is alternately described as a "town" and a "picturesque village". It sounds like Rye — especially as other bombs were dropped in Kent. A young C.O. called Benttler who lives in Dolphin Square & is a full-time A.R.P. worker sent me a summary of a novel he has written on the Blitz called "Only Slight Damage", which seems rather promising.

Worked all day on Chap. 6, going out only for a short walk with G. to the library. The Christmas number of *Peace News* contains not only my article "The Spirit of Mr Scrooge" (on generosity & the war) but a good advt. by Dakers explaining that the first edn. of my book sold out & a new large one will soon be ready.

G. & I sent a cable to John for his 15th birthday on Monday. I still feel bad about him, & could kick myself for not having both children back last summer. 40 children & 12 adults have arrived in Lisbon from another Portuguese ship, but after a very bad voyage.

Sunday December 20th

All the papers are so full of horrors about the Nazi behaviour to the Jews in Poland, & all of them get more & more fantastic. G. has a theory that all this material about atrocities being so widely publicised just now is a method of making people subdued over Christmas and therefore being discouraged from spending much money.

Monday December 21st

My darling John's fifteenth birthday.

Devastated by letter from Alex Wood by (late) morning mail announcing that Stuart Morris had been arrested & summoning an emergency Executive meeting for to-morrow. Later, newspaper paragraphs in all papers announced that this was done under the Official Secrets Act, & the hearing would be held in camera. Decided it was best to keep off the telephone — but various committed people rang up about various things — Howard Fox, who thought the trouble was due to the Armistice Campaign; Corder Catchpool, who wanted to know where he could still get *H. with H.*; & Mother who doesn't grasp the meaning of "Official Secrets", & said (over the public 'phone!) that she hoped I wouldn't be arrested too!

Wrote Letter No. 99 on the promised subject of an Armistice, but being somewhat disturbed was rather slow.

Tuesday December 22nd

Item about Stuart repeated in morning papers. Spent morning writing the *next* Letter (on whether children should be taught pacifist principles) in case the Armistice one had to be abandoned. Then went into town & attended the emergency Executive (held at Maurice Rowntree's house in a room without a telephone & all the doors & windows shut till I felt as if we

too were living under the Gestapo). It was clear that Alex Wood &
Maurice Rowntree, having seen Stuart, knew much more than anyone
else & that several members of the Executive knew, or suspected, more
than I did. But the following items emerged: (1) the actual hearing is on
Dec. 31st & chances of the charge being dropped are slight; (2) the
charge is a personal charge & doesn't involve — so far — the P.P.U. as
such & probably won't unless someone has made public use of informn.
improperly acquired — though the whole thing can hardly do us any
good; (3) it has nothing to do with the Armistice campaign. Executive
urged that whole meeting was Confidential, so couldn't tell G. about it.

Wednesday December 23rd
Crowded & exhausting day trying to finish off existing letters & Christmas obligations.

In the afternoon Amy's sister Sheila brought Marian & we had an
uproarious time giving her her presents — including two frocks, 3 pairs of
socks & a bottle of sweets from Ruth & Shirley. We also opened our own
gifts from Shirley & Ruth; china sweet jar for G. (unhappily smashed
except for the lid), cigarette box & pill box in white & gold for me, also
two "Worry Birds" made out of pine cones (a symbolic comment by my
affirmative daughter on me?)

Friday December 25th
Fourth Christmas of the war — an appropriately grey, cold, foggy day.
In morning went to join Mother at St Martin-in-the-Fields. Church
completely filled as usual. When I sat down by Mother she said: "Have
you heard any more about Darlan?" I said: "No, what?" & she told me it
was announced on the morning radio that he had been assassinated at
Algiers.

Took Mother back to lunch in the Dorchester Grill-room, wh. was
crowded, noisy & expensive. She went back to her hotel to hear the
King's Speech & I had tea alone with G., who had been in a bad temper
all day, wondering how to overcome the general line-up against him of
the jealous, self-interested & suspicious. Finally he threw off his depression & managed to be quite charming to Mother over dinner, which we
had with her at the Onslow Court Hotel.

Sunday December 27th
Papers issued at last, giving news about Darlan and fact that his assailant
was a young Frenchman with an Italian mother living in Italy, whose
name is being kept secret. Goebbels is publishing it abroad that Roosevelt was responsible for Darlan's appointment, & Churchill had arranged
to have D. assassinated to stop complications here. Another war
mystery which only time is likely to solve.

Worked all day at mail, cheques & writing up diary. Wrote to Stephen

Hobhouse — & to Maurice Rowntree asking if there was anything I could do for Stuart in addition to the books which I sent to Brixton Prison last Wednesday.

Dull grey day again, slightly less cold. Got to book at last and wrote 3 pages after supper.

Monday December 28th

Rung up on telephone while it was still dark by long Christmas cable from Ruth. The first part contained Christmas & birthday messages; the remainder said: "Pan-American friend advises plane earliest possible midsummer all children's exits regarded unpatriotic now, wish you could come instead." Felt very depressed about this all day. It won't be so bad if a 'plane *is* available at midsummer, but more likely then we shall be told that nothing can be done for another 3 months etc. In consequence G. kept talking about Portuguese boats.

Tuesday December 29th

My 49th birthday. How little I should mind about the march of time if only I could get the children back! G. gave me a pretty blue-handled umbrella, Mother a cheque for my new coat & skirt & Amy an inkstand. W.E.G. came & I dictated an accumulation of Christmas letters. She sold 120 tokens altogether.

Wednesday December 30th

Up late; kept going with mail till lunch-time. Very cold — as yesterday; bitter wind laden with sleet & snow flurries. Didn't go out much; spent greater part of day writing first half of Chapter 8 over fire in sitting-room.

Russians doing another winter push. Giraud elected in Darlan's place in N. Africa.

Long telephone call from Mrs Clarke (Fräulein) to say she is in town; tried to find me at Cheyne Walk, then got my number from the P.O. Said she was terribly lonely in Sherbourne where she & her boy were evacuated in the Blitz; nobody will speak to her bec. she is German though her husband is fighting in Egypt. She would like to come back to London but doesn't know how. Said I would try to help, & suddenly thought she might be a solution for Mother.

Thursday December 31st

Final day of a year which I am not sorry to see the last of. Papers announced appointment of Harold Macmillan to be Minister in N. Africa, to collaborate with America's Mr Murphy. Darlan assassination plot apparently threatened Murphy & Gen. Giraud as well; it is now said to be a purely French affair, & about 12 people are involved.

After lunch there was some lovely sunshine & I went for a walk along the towing path. Came back to go on with book.

1943

Friday January 1st

New Year started out badly, if typically, with a morning of so much mail & so many telephone calls that I never got down to my book till after tea. One call was from Maurice Rowntree, suggesting that I see Stuart next Friday.

Everybody in letters & messages expressing the now customary hope that the next New Year's Day will see the war over. But the news does not look much like it, with stalemate in Tunis & the situation swinging to & fro in Russia despite immediate Russian victories. When will some statesman of vision realise that overwhelming victory is both difficult & disadvantageous?

If only, only, I could get the children back! Life without them gets more, not less, like a double amputation, & every achievement is dust & ashes.

Sunday January 3rd

Cold & windy, with pale streaks of sunlight but no heat. Spent day drafting out Chap. 10 of book ("Crisis in Prague").

Wretchedly depressed this morning wondering if ever I'd get John home. Mother came to tea while G. attended a conference on India at Conway Hall.

Monday January 4th

Very cold & frosty. Went early to London Library to look up *Times* of March & Sept. 1939 for Chapters 10 & 11 of "Day of Judgment" — & was taken by an apologetic woman librarian into the basement. She apologised for the basement being cold — which it certainly was — & for the dirtiness of the bound volumes of *The Times* "as we have no dusters on Monday". I read & took notes for 2 hours & certainly did become very cold & stiff.

G. had a brilliant idea of an anthology collecting instances of human charity & co-operation (like the two letters between a British pilot & a German mother in the last war reproduced in this week's *Peace News*). I thought of a title "Above All Nations" from the quotation above one of the Cornell University buildings — "Above all nations is humanity". Drafted out a scheme for the book, & urged G. to write Victor Gollancz to see if he will agree to publish it.

Tuesday January 5th
Telephone call from Dakers to say 2nd edition of *H. with H.* out on Friday.
W.E.G. here, spent morning dictating letters & finishing Letter 100.

At P.P.U. Executive long discussion took place over Stuart Morris.
Mention of fact that it was the *India Office* who were adamant against
granting Stuart bail threw a flood of light on the whole situation. It
suddenly occurred to me that it was just too, too convenient for the Govt.
for a leading pacifist to have acquired, & used, secret information on wh.
he could be arrested, & I suddenly saw the "document" presented to him
in Hyde Park as a deliberate official "plant" to make him incriminate
himself. Began to see Alex Wood & Maurice Rowntree as having cold feet,
& the whole organn. as taking the wrong line — espec. as Alan Staniland
mentioned that the *News Chronicle*, anxious to splash the whole story as a
sinister Gestapo-like proceeding, had sent one of its leading editors to
P.P.U. headquarters.

Wednesday January 6th
Long letter from George Brett about putting the children on a *British* boat
made us decide to go to Cook's & discuss possibilities. But first rang up
J. M. Murry & met him at L'pl. St. Station to discuss yesterday's
impression of the Executive's attitude towards Stuart, the "frame-up"
idea, etc. He listened sympathetically & said he would think carefully
about it over the week-end. G. & I met & lunched at Athenaeum Court,
then went on to Cook's. They confirmed impression about 'plane & we
made provisional arrangements to put John on a Portuguese boat. Had tea
with Mother & came home very depressed by the grim alternative between
leaving my dear boy in U.S. for the duration, perhaps to be called up, &
bringing him home through the dangers of wartime travel. G. came home
in a vile temper & we had the usual quarrelsome argument abt. whether J.
should come home or not which left me completely pulverised.

Friday January 8th
Left flat early, bought sour apples and (at Fortnum & Mason's of all
places) a head of celery — the last one left, price 1/–, *very* dirty & I could
take it or leave it! Took it, as my object was to procure some vitamins for
Stuart.

Lunched at the Westway Hotel with Howard Kershner (Director of
Relief in Europe for the American Friends' Service Committee) who told
me many interesting facts about the food situation (including the fact that
Churchill & Roosevelt are the persons really responsible & nothing but a
large public agitation will move them). He also said that 6,000 Jews
escaped to Spain from France, & are now in danger of being sent back to
Germany by starving Spain, yet our Govt. despite all its talk of atrocities
will do nothing for them!!

Went on to Brixton Prison (a grim-looking building in a dreary street) to see Stuart Morris. Waited for nearly an hour in quite a cheerful cream-distempered waiting room with poster-pictures on the walls & a good fire. Finally, I was taken over to the remand side & found Stuart waiting in a little glass-pannelled waiting room. Was surprised to see him as I expected to be taken to a cell. Strangely pathetic to see an ex-Canon of B'm Cathedral a prisoner, in his old shabby coat, tho' he was quite cheerful. We talked about his family most of the time. To encourage him I said goodbye so warmly that the warder who took me to the gate was quite sympathetic!

Saturday January 9th
Bitterly cold. Large mail wh. took me all morning to answer. At 5.0 went to the City Literary Institute and lectured on "Vansittartism: its cause & cure". (This was not an attack on Vansittart apart from a showing up of his inaccurate history, but a general picture of Guilty Nationism & its consequences.) Audience was divided in the usual way between my "fans" who would have agreed with me anyhow, & people who came to criticise, listened to what I had to say without taking it in, & then made exactly the comment they came to make however irrelevant to the lecture it may be. Came more than ever to the conclusion that lecturing is a waste of time. It was quite dark when I came out & I had forgotten to bring my torch, so it took me ages to get from Drury Lane to Holborn & again up Richmond Hill.

Sunday January 10th
Wrote Victor Gollancz about his very moving pamphlet on the Jewish persecutions, *Let My People Go*, which he sent me yesterday. Said I would do a Fortnightly Letter on the subject.

Mother came to tea, v. early. Took her to station, got back just in time to see Nancy Morris, Stuart's sister — a pleasant white-haired woman of about 58, rather deaf. We discussed my suggestion about giving a home & education to the elder girl, Anne; then she went on to tell me about Stuart's arrest; how they last saw him at 9 p.m. on the Friday night & despite various calls to Scotland Yard never discovered where he was till Sunday night when Maurice Rowntree discovered him in Brixton Prison. She agreed with me abt. the "plant" idea; also that the P.P.U. was making a great mistake in keeping everything so "hush-hush" & allowing rumours to spread.

Monday January 11th
Took G. to dinner with Howard Kershner at the Westway Hotel. Before it saw Howard Whitten & discussed possibility of a pamphlet on "Europe's Children". Cold & damp with strong wind. Shirley talks of fuel rationing in U.S.A.

Tuesday January 12th
Reply to our cable received from George Brett, saying that he was in touch with Cook's & John would probably leave towards the end of Feb. Whole business gives me a pain in the neck & everywhere else.

Dictated letters to W.E.G.; after lunch went to Westway Hotel, letting G. go rather before me, to discuss Stuart's affairs with J.M.M. Got there to find not only G. & J.M.M. but Alex Wood & Mary Gamble. Learnt from Alex Wood the following facts wh. I hadn't known before: (a) Stuart not only got one lot of documents re India from the man at his Hyde Park meeting, but went on getting them. Man has lost his job & is likely to get a heavier sentence than S. (b) S. told the whole story to Roy Walker in prison in front of a warder who had to report it after saying to Roy: "He didn't ought to have told you that!" Govt. had no choice but to prosecute. (c) Stuart now realises what he has done, sees it is the grave polit. indiscretion it is, & has offered his resign. from the P.P.U. G. said (& I agree) that he was now convinced no publicity useful to the P.P.U. could be given to the case, but he thought we ought to keep S.'s job & reaffirm our belief in him — otherwise he will be suspected of far worse than he has done, & we shall be "panned" for disloyalty.

Very wet. Fire-watching 12.0–3 a.m.

Thursday January 14th
Tried to work all day without much success. Felt absolutely exhausted; seemed to have been through whole gamut of emotions re John in 24 hours.

Most favourable letter from V. Gollancz about our "Above All Nations" Anthology idea.

Friday January 15th
Soon after breakfast Mr Hinshelwood rang up, having got on to Min. of War Transport. He said: (1) There have been some polit. sinkings of Portuguese boats (i.e. when Hitler wants to bring Portl. to heel) but this unlikely for 2 months at any rate; (2) Port. boats definitely much better than British & M. of W.T. man would regard them as "safe as houses" if coming himself; (3) no connecting passenger plane w' Lisbon has been brought down by enemy action or attacked. This all seemed reassuring enough to decide us to let the arrangement stand though the decision is one of the most awful we have ever made, comparable only with the one to let the children go. How I wish to God I'd followed my own "hunch" & kept them here; in that case my maternal instinct was surer than G.'s political intuitions. Poor John — pushed perilously across the Atlantic, horribly mismanaged, & now to be pushed perilously back! I can't write or work for thinking of it & him.

Sunday January 17th
Had dinner latish & not till then did G. show me a cable received during

the afternoon from the Colbys, saying John was fearing badly prospect of sea voyage, did we insist? British Consulate was objecting, & coming now would mean forfeiting re-entry permit. (Could not understand these two last statements at all.) G. & I were discussing this when a large raid started in retaliation for our raid on Berlin last night. Much noise & heavy gunfire round here but we hardly heard it as problem of deciding whether to call off plans for John & perhaps not see him for duration was so grim. Went to bed very tired by exhausting problem & was woken again at 5.0 by another raid. Terrific gunfire & huge shells bursting into smaller ones — some over this flat.

Monday January 8th
Second raid on Berlin last night. Usual horrid exuberance.

Strange day devoted to Stuart Morris's affairs. Nancy Morris rang up early to say Kathleen Rutherford was in town. Met her after getting my hair washed early & missed breakfast to do so. Kathleen & I discussed Stuart's affairs; K. confirmed all the facts I had already heard, was scornful of the P.P.U.'s "cold feet" over the case — also about the way most of the more eminent had failed to visit Stuart; the little typists etc. had gone but not J.M.M. etc.

Alert abt. 8.0 just as we returned from dinner; All Clear in half an hour.

Tuesday January 19th
Agitating & exhausting day. Late morning a cable came from George Brett saying John unlikely to leave before mid-March. Wondered all day while engaged on Stuart's affairs whether I wanted John to travel against his will — & finally decided that I didn't yet, however much it was George's advice.

Got to the P.P.U. Exec. just in time to see Kathleen Rutherford tell Alex Wood that the result of Stuart's trial was much better than we had expected, & that Travers (defending Counsel) had been excellent. Neither J.M.M. nor Maurice Rowntree were at the Exec. but I still had a struggle against Alex Wood's conviction that Stuart (whose defence he has not heard) was guilty of a grave moral delinquency for continuing to receive secret documents in the interests of the Indian people. Managed in the end to get over a resolution that he should be re-appointed, which was passed with only two dissentients. But whether he is to be Gen. Sec. again or to have his place filled cannot be decided till an emergency Exec. before the Council on Sat. as the length of his sentence & the charge are not yet officially known. At 4.30 left Exec. & had tea at King's Cross Hotel with Kathleen Rutherford, whose courage & energy I admire more & more. She told me confidentially: (1) Stuart's sentence is 9 months, wh. means six. (2) A public statement is to be put in the press abt. the case; it was originally to be put in by the Judge (Mr Justice [Hallett], who wanted an open trial), but the India Office insisted on drawing it up themselves &

letting the Judge merely vet it! The Judge's view was obviously shown in the short sentence; there is an obvious conflict between the legislature & the judiciary here. K. said the India Office had abt. 12 solicitors in court.

Had violent headache by the time I got home. Decided send cables postponing John's booking; then had to go to bed.

Wednesday January 20th
No less than 3 Alerts to-day. The morning one, about midday, brought a good deal of gunfire. One loud crack sounding just over the roof made Amy & me jump out of our skins; 'plane must have been just above. All Clear at 1.15. Other two were after dark & both short; one about 8.30, the other soon after ten.

Spent most of day writing Letter 101, about V. Gollancz's pamphlet & persecution of the Jews.

Thursday January 21st
Arrival of Famine Relief material notifying that great effort is now to be made since the Foreign Secretary turned down the scheme for very moderate relief for Greece & Belgium recently put before him by the Archbp. of Canterbury & Card. Archbp. of Westminster. The Archbp. is to address both Houses of Parlt. on this on Feb. 17th. Suddenly it came over me that I could probably reach a large, non-pacifist public of novel-readers with a personal pamphlet on this. Felt a real call to write it. Wrote Edith Pye, & Andrew Dakers to ask if he would publish it; said I'd give the royalties of *H. with H.* to it if these would help. Then started to write the pamphlet, wh. is to be abt. 10,000 words. Made a scheme & collected relief material together. Felt I *must* make this effort before going on with my novel.

8th Army advancing towards Tripoli.

In yesterday's daylight raid a London L.C.C. school was bombed & so far over 30 children are known to be killed.

Friday January 22nd
Worked all day writing Food Relief pamphlet. Got as far as the last section, leaving all the long quotations to be put in in the typing.

In evening telephone call from Andrew Dakers not only willing but *eager* to do the pamphlet. Seems as concerned abt. this famine relief question as I am, & not minding about profit. Says he can do 50,000 copies & thinks he could sell them all, in wh. case I should not lose any of the money wh. I am guaranteeing him against loss.

Saturday January 23rd
Lovely review of *H. with H.* by Laurence Housman in *Peace News*.

Couldn't get any more pamphlet done owing to P.P.U. Council & Exec.

Saw Alex Wood before the Emergency Exec. abt. what Kathleen told me but it made no difference as he was determined to take a highly moral line (I mean non-Christian moral) about Stuart. James Hudson & I stuck out for non-condemnation (on ground, for myself, that "dissociation" was (1) non-Christian, (2) politically naive — as it means we condemn Stuart for being found out more than we condemn the Govt. for what it is doing on India). J. Middleton Murry on both Council & Exec. completely intolerant, but there was unexpected support on Council for my view & vote for "dissociation" was ult. 17–13. Got whole question of Stuart position postponed to an Emergency Council on Feb. 20th.

Sunday January 24th

Spent all day on Food Relief pamphlet — "One of These Little Ones". Finished writing it by lunchtime, then started to type it. It made 28 pp. of typescript. I started doing it at 3.0 & finished at 1 a.m. (it wasn't straightforward typing but constant looking up & reproduction of quotations) having had only two small breaks for tea & dinner. Felt tired but not nearly so bad as I had expected. I hadn't known I could type 10,000 words in the time; had thought I should be up all night. In $2\frac{1}{4}$ days have written & then typed the whole.

Fall of Tripoli to 8th Army officially announced.

Wrote about yesterday's Council to Kathleen, Mrs Morris & Nancy Morris — also to James Hudson saying that I was disturbed that a grave injustice was likely to be done to Stuart (whom the P.P.U. appears to be making its scapegoat now he has been found out).

Beautiful day, like early spring. Snowdrops & one or two crocuses coming out in Terrace Gdns.

Monday January 25th

G. gone to Aldershot for a week to lecture to the troops there.

Got up feeling pretty tired but again not as bad as I had expected. Made final small typings of pamphlet, then went off to hear Howard Kershner give his talk on France to an R.I.I.A. audience at Chatham House wh. was less critical than I had expected. Edith Pye there, astonished to hear I had done the pamphlet; said the Famine Relief Committee *might* back it. I promised to send her the spare copy. Lady Barlow & Cornelia Sorabji tried to intimidate me abt. my India speech to-morrow & said Congress was backed by the Axis etc. etc. but I stood my ground.

Tuesday January 26th

Last Wed. W.E.G. was walking across Blackheath when two or three Nazi planes flew across the heath roof-top level. She could see the black crosses & the pilots. Ten mins. later the bombs fell.

In another talk with Dakers on 'phone in morning he told me that the

2nd edition of *H. with H.* is going out quite quickly, & he has ordered a
third, which will make 10,000. Says his printer can have the pamphlet
ready by Feb. 10th.

After lunch sat in sunshine in shelter in Terrace Garden (blowing a bit
cold but sun lovely) reading *Free India*. Then had early tea & went off to
dine with Dennis & Diana Stoll at the Waldorf Hotel before my India
meeting. Charming young couple; he is the youngest (third) son of the late
Sir Oswald Stoll, has been in prison for 6 months as a C.O., has written a
novel wh. is now "going the rounds", & is specially interested in Indian
music. They gave me an excellent dinner at the Waldorf, & then we all
went on to the meeting, held by the Society of Indian Congressmen at the
Kingsway Hall. Speakers included Fenner Brockway, W. G. Cove M.P.,
Silverman M.P., Fred Messer M.P., & a number of Indians. Far too many
speakers as usual. I only spoke for abt. 10 mins. Most of the speeches were
very fiery; Fenner referred to Amery as "that little dwarf who has had the
power to put giants like Gandhi in prison".

Wednesday January 27th
Went to the Trades' Union Club in Great Newport St. & took the Chair for
Edward Thompson, who gave a brilliant & most illuminating address on
"Bankrupt Statesmanship in India". Talked after it to Howard Whitten &
Roy Walker — who looks surprisingly well after 6 months in prison. Roy
said he believed in "inner commands" such as I had to write the pamphlet.

Papers full of a long melodramatic confab. between Churchill &
Roosevelt at Casablanca; apparently nothing but strategy & no mention of
post-war aims. Long description in *Evening Standard* of the mass funeral at
Hither Green cemetery at wh. most of the children from the Lewisham
School were buried.

Thursday January 28th
John Fletcher told me yesterday that one way by which the leakage of
information was discovered was through a question Reg. Sorensen asked
in the House; Amery sent for him afterwards & asked where he got the
information, wh. was presumably from S.M. This seems to prove that
S.M. was actuated by far more than just the "vanity" wh. J.M.M.
attributes to him. He was undoubtedly wrong & indiscreet, but he was
trying to make a normal democratic use of the information.

Had a letter from Edith Pye in which she expressed warm approval of
my pamphlet, wh. she has sent to the Bp. of Chichester. She also gave me
some small suggested alterations. I rang up Dakers & found I could put
them in as I am getting a proof after all.

A German Army encircled this side of Stalingrad.

Friday January 29th
Amy much excited to-day owing to 3 letters from Burnett. In one he said

she would be interested in *The Times* of Nov. 24th; we looked it up & found a picture of a place called Gafsa — in N. Africa — where presumably he is. By second post came a letter from John, enclosing a typed poem by himself called "Morning", surrounded by a really remarkable design of figures showing great strength & movement. The poem was *very* good — full of imagination & derivative only up to a point. I begin to wonder if my son is a genius! Certainly his maturity, & achievements, are greatly in advance of mine at his age. I sent him an airmail p.c. at once, telling him that his promise filled me with joy & thankfulness.

Wrote an article for *Peace News* called "What Does Europe Really Think of Us?" Then turned to my novel & wrote the last chapter of Part 2 called "The First of September". Went on writing till I finished it at nearly 2 a.m.

Saturday January 30th

Had early lunch & went long windy journey to Poplar to open the fête of the Relief Service Unit at Trinity Hall, right in the midst of that much Blitzed area. They had recently had a visit from the police resulting from an anonymous letter trying to denounce them as avoiding military service when they are fully established C.O.s. Returned to find G. home from Aldershot — bored with his week of lecturing to troops & worrying about the Red Cross job he put in for. I *do* wish he wld. remain in his own field, do his own kind of scholarly work, & I told him so.

Sunday January 31st

Very wet blustery day. We bombed Berlin *twice* yesterday, interrupting Goering's speech at 11.0 & Goebbels' proclamation of Hitler's announcement about 5.0 The retaliation which will undoubtedly come is evidently postponed by the weather.

Started work on Part 3 of my novel; got the 6 or 7 chapters planned out & several pages written of the first one (Ch. 12).

Huge German armies getting defeated at Stalingrad & in the Caucasus. Are the Russians going to win the war? And if so, what?

Tuesday February 2nd

Long talk & lunch with J. H. Hudson & John Fletcher about the Stuart Morris case. Followed by *most* exhausting Executive in which J.H., Sybil Morrison & I were in a minority of three which had no chance against the Chairman's conviction that everyone who disagreed with him belonged to a lower order of morality.

Wednesday February 3rd

Lunched with Rache Lovat Dickson at Pastoria's in Leicester Square & discussed methods of bringing the children home. He told me that Charles Morgan's boy Roger had come home by a British boat, on his own, just after his 15th birthday last July, & is now back at Eton. Neither he nor Charles (both ways) saw a sign of a 'plane or submarine! However I told Rache I wouldn't submit my one & only boy to the chances of the U-boat campaign. We also discussed my novel & his eagerness to get hold of it.

Went on, mostly walking, to Knightsbridge, & tea at the Rembrandt Hotel, with Baroness von Reitzenstein, a German refugee author to whom Corder Catchpool introduced me & in whom Gollancz is interested. She has a son here & a daughter left in Germany, to whom she has written a set of literary "letters" not unlike *H. with H.*. I promised to write an introduction for it if this would help publication.

Thursday February 4th

W.E.G. here. Terrific day of letter dictation; got 25 off, tho' this didn't finish them. After supper wrote Letter 102 (on Famine Relief, to accompany my pamphlet).

Andrew Dakers rang up this morning to say that the Bp. of Chichester sent my pamphlet on to the Archbp. of Canterbury, who doesn't want it publicly associated with his address to the members of both Houses of Parlt. on Feb. 17th because of its mild & vague criticism of the Govt.! So Dakers, to his disgust with the Church, cannot mention the Archbp.'s address in his advts. to booksellers. He wanted to go ahead & do it just the same, saying what a "separatist" & official attitude the Archbp.'s was — but though agreeing, I said that both the Archbp. & I had the same object, & if *his* type of approach failed, it would never do for him to think this was due to my pamphlet. But this dreadful willingness of the official Church to let the Govt. get away with anti-Christian evil without ecclesiastical protest!

Saturday February 6th

Strenuous day of slogging on small but necessary jobs. Very large correspondence kept me going till lunch-time. Then went for a brief walk, finished the difficult correction of the shorthand version of my Vansittart lecture for James Avery Joyce, wrote some more letters, prepared "Lament for Cologne" & Paul Hildebrandt's translation for Brock to print, & wrote the 600-word supplement to the F.o.R. monthly Letter which Leslie Artingstall asked me for last Tuesday. Pray Heaven I get to my novel to-morrow!

Mild pleasant day. To-night, the brilliant new moon above the river was vividly holding the old moon in its arms.

Monday February 8th

Fifty copies of my pamphlet *One of These Little Ones*, came from the printer in Edinburgh. Cover not very striking owing to the white letters on the red cover being too small — but not bad for a rush job. Got copies off to 6 of the papers (*News Chron.*, *D. Herald*, *M.G.*, *Catholic Herald*, the *Friend*, *Peace News*) & to one or two key people.

Drafted out Ch. 13 of "Day of Judgment".

Tuesday February 9th
W.E.G. came & we had a tremendous day at letters. We sent off about 40 copies of the pamphlet, she typing the short personal notes to go with each.

An Alert early this morning as I was getting the tea, about 8.30; evening papers report bombs dropped on the S. Eastern outskirts & several people killed. They got another school but luckily it was too early for the children to be there. Extensive retreat of Nazis along the Russian front goes on.

Wednesday February 10th
Met John Fletcher at National Gallery & had a talk about S.M. — who now thinks there will be *no* public announcement, & sees himself only as a cog in a vast official intrigue. Went on to lunch with Arthur Ponsonby in the H. of Lords on the same subject. Old man rather deaf & a little feeble but fully mentally alert; told me the Bp. of B'm is getting uneasy about S.M. & wants a question in the H. of Lords. He said he was only given 3 mins. to testify for Stuart & Counsel asked him no questions giving opportunity to enlarge.

Went home to find *lovely* photographs of Shirley arrived — looking almost a young woman, one with a dog & the other with two Siamese cats. She is still absolutely blonde & looks beautifully fit — but these pictures make me miss her worse than ever, dear little thing. Found also letter from Miss Pye saying the Famine Relief Comm. wld. back my pamphlet to extent of ordering it for their groups.

Friday February 12th
Worked all day on Ch. 13 of "Day of Judgment" — "The Crown v. Heyworth". Very excited myself by story. These trial scenes are terribly slow & intricate; every bit of evidence has to tally with what went before in the story.

Germans still retreating in Russia. All newspapers filled with Churchill's speech in the House yesterday, about the Casablanca Conference and "making the enemy bleed & burn". Wonder how many years it will take this country to recover from having an Al Capone at its head.

Saturday February 13th
Spent morning on correspondence & then went to Sutton for the last of the three A.P.F. readings. Local Friends' Meeting House (a new pleasant room) absolutely packed; some people standing & one or two others on floor. Read from *T. of Y.* & *H. with H.*, also the Cologne poem. Bernard Nichols thanked me in a v. graceful little speech for giving the Club my "time and genius" — the last being a word I don't often hear or ever think

of in connection w' myself. It had a queer encouraging effect, somehow. There was an Alert as we were walking there & guns in distance, but All Clear went in ½ hr. Hurried back for fire-watching at 7.0 but found the reserves had taken over for us both. G. away lecturing at Downside Abbey. Sat up late reading Steinbeck's *The Moon is Down*.

Sunday February 14th

This has been the most wonderful winter, for wh. at least one can thank God. No snow, very little frost; weather mild & even sunny most of the time. The buds are all coming out & the birds singing; some of the shrubs in the Terrace Gardens are even in flower on this Valentine's day (for wh. G. left me a charming Valentine). The lawns there are spangled with gold crocuses & one bank is thick with patches of snowdrops. Even the magnolia is budding & one can see the daffodil heads in their sheaths. I even found a ladybird on the stone steps of the Rockery the other day. The country's stocks of coal must have been remarkably conserved by the weather. I can't help remembering, in the illogical way one does, how mild was the last war winter of 1918–19. An omen? Even the weeping willows by the river have begun to wear their spring green.

Monday February 15th

Very strenuous day getting off dozens of copies of my pamphlet — which is published to-day — chiefly to a list of addresses supplied by Stephen Hobhouse. Don't know when I have felt so tired, but managed to get to my book & write a bit of Ch. 14 after dinner. Found it difficult to get to sleep after, however — especially as the sky was filled with noisy aeroplanes (ours) half the night.

The mail to-day was really *most* encouraging — not only a pleasant understanding letter from Harold Latham about *H. with H.* but also a delightful letter from John Nevin Sayre, telling me that the F.o.R. is going to publish it in U.S.A. — starting off with 2,000 copies & binding 1,000 to begin with. This is really good news as it means I *shall* be able to publish in U.S.A. what I think of the war while it is on.

Fighting in Tunisia getting near to Gafsa where Burnett is. The Americans seem to be having a bad time there. Dr Sayre says that the War is *not* popular in U.S.A.

V. excited about my novel — really interesting to write.

Wednesday February 17th

Longish notices (both rather grim) in *Times* & *Herald* re Stuart's case this morning. The *Herald* headed its last section "Shocking Conduct". It was also on the wireless last night — shorter. I am afraid this will upset Alex Wood, & if he can't get his moral indignation expressed in one way he will manage it in some other. I fear that when the P.P.U. is put to the test it may accept the judgment of the world, for very few people as yet understand what a Christian attitude to "delinquents" really involves.

Wrote (or rather compiled) Letter 103, consisting of extracts from the letters I received about the education of children in Christian values. Then wrote a long letter to Shirley, about her photographs, her horses &dogs, *H. with H.*, and my pamphlet.

Papers filled with debate on Beveridge report showing obvious intention of Govt. to do nothing.

Thursday February 18th

Amy said her sister Sheila met a *little girl* in the street yesterday who said: "Did you hear about those two men being jailed? Those Peace Pledge Union people are all traitors." Poor Stuart — he *has* brought down an avalanche on himself & us!

Went to tea with Kathleen Rutherford & discussed Stuart's predicament for about 2 hours. She spoke of his being always "driven" & overtired — & I told her to write the Chairman abt. this as I don't think it is realised. I myself am giving up speaking for a time bec. I am too hard-worked at the moment to be able to get up speeches with responsible attention, let alone answer questions.

Friday February 19th

Gandhi's fast beginning to look serious. Grave medical reports are coming in. The Government appears to be as unconscious of the incalculable repercussions which will follow his death if he dies as the Roman officials who thought they were merely getting rid of a Jewish agitator when they crucified Christ.

Howard Whitten tells me on the telephone that the Archbp.'s talk to the Members of both Houses on Famine Relief on Wed. was a "flop" because everyone was listening to the debate on the Beveridge Report.

Saturday February 20th

Woke up feeling very limp & tired; decided to stay in bed till nearly lunch-time so as to be able to cope with the Council this afternoon. G. consulted the chemist, who thought I had a touch of the gastric 'flu that is going round & gave me an excellent medicine which made me feel much better in a few hours. Was able to go to the Council & sit all through it. This time Alex Wood was a much fairer Chairman — thanks to the criticisms of J.H. & I. He even offered to vacate the Chair, but we asked him to stay. He read several letters all supporting his point of view (chiefly from people in Cambridge, tho' Donald Soper contemptibly said he must resign to maintain his own integrity!) but allowed me to read one from Arthur Ponsonby & all to read the minority statement that J.H. & I prepared. We had excellent support from Wilfrid Wellock, who made a very wise political speech. But those who want to accept Stuart's resignation were very vocal — partic. John Middleton Murry, who was completely uncharitable & first said he would resign if Stuart was kept & then appeared to take that back but was as intolerant of other people's opinions as always. Right until the end I had the impression that J.H., W.W. & I were in the minority until the votes were taken, when we astonishingly turned out to be the majority, thus showing that the Exec. does not really represent the Council, & that the younger & more obscure members of the movement have more courage than some of its distinguished leaders. The voting was: Against accepting S.'s resignation, 16, for, 11; for reappointing him now, 11 for, 12 against; for letting his resignation lie on the table till he can meet with the Council — a large majority about same as first vote.

Sunday February 21st
Went to bed relatively early last night and woke up feeling much better. Worked all day on the "Heyworth v. the Crown" chapter, which seems interminable, but is of course the longest, most dramatic & central chapter in the book.

Mother came to tea, & was in a bad mood — huffy as always bec. we were both so preoccupied with our work & irritated bec. G. was here. He doesn't of course conceal his boredom nearly enough. I wish we could get her settled in her own flat with more to occupy her.

The Sunday papers say that Gandhi may die in 48 hrs!

Tuesday February 23rd
Paper this morning full of resounding tributes to Red Army on 25th anniversary; Russian victories still going on, & Stalin seems likely now to be the chief victor of the war. In Tunisia the American retreat has been almost a rout. Recently too, two American transports were sunk in mid-Atlantic & about 700 men lost.

Letter from James Hudson says we may have some "consequences" to face in the defeat of the Chairman's policy at the Council on Sat. He may resign, so may Salter & Middleton Murry. I should be sorry abt. Alex Wood & Salter, but feel that if J.M.M. would only depart, the movement might recover some of the spiritual power that it lost with Dick Sheppard. G. & I went to a private meeting called by Reg. Sorensen to discuss the Indian deadlock & Gandhi, who has rallied a little.

Wednesday February 24th
G. & I sent a telegram to Bernard Shaw asking if he could possibly be at the India service to-morrow as I learnt privately from Howard Whitten that he might be at the Tagore Society meeting. Got on to chapter "Galaxy of Experts" in "D. of J." & did the preliminary planning. Beautiful day; walked in Park & Gardens; daffodils coming out.

Thursday February 25th
Went into town to attend India Intercession service at St Martin's; saw

Fielden, Gangulee, Agatha Harrison, etc. etc. — all the "usuals". Floor of the Church, however, was quite full, & the Service, taken by 3 clerics & the Bp. of Southwark, was really beautiful. One prayer was for Gandhi. Mother came too, & wanted to do some shopping after — so I went to Fortnum & Mason's & bought a black angora blouse for my new black skirt from Baird Lewis. Then attended the meeting of the Tagore Society at the Dorchester & promised to join; Bernard Shaw sent a message & Hannan Swaffer was there for a few minutes.

Friday February 26th
Had to go into town in afternoon to sign nearly 50 copies of *H. w. H.* at the P.P.U. for their "Social" to-morrow, as the 20 I signed at the Council last Sat. have all been sold. Noticed excellent display of *One of These Little Ones* in window of Friends' House bookshop. My article on what Europe thinks of us on front page of *P.N.* this week tho' with my name as small as J.M.M. could well make it. He has printed the Council's verdict on S.M. as published in the Group letter.

Sunday February 28th
Mild day; less sun than the rest of this brilliant week. Worked all day at Chap. 15 of my book, "Galaxy of Experts", & finished it by 10 p.m. G. very nobly went to a "Tribute to Gandhi" meeting at Holborn Hall on behalf of us both; I sent a message by him which was read. Gandhi's fast is nearly over & the general impression now seems to be that he will survive.

Went for longish walk in the Park; mild & pleasant.

Monday March 1st
Worked all day at book. Definitely decided to be "strategically absent" from town all this week.

Most wonderful day yet of so many. For about the first time in my life, Wordsworth's description of "the first mild day of March" was true. Brilliant sun all day; daffodils in Buccleuch Garden all came out amongst the vivid pink prunus. Magnificent sunset like a flamingo's feathers.

Tuesday March 2nd
Long letter from Alex Wood giving his reasons for resignation from Chairmanship. Decided that strategic absence from the Executive was more than ever advisable. One letter about my pamphlet was from the Women's National Peace Council of Wales, saying it had created great interest & sympathy there & asking if it could be translated into Welsh — to which I agreed if Dakers did.

W.E.G. came; not so many letters as usual as I had done most of them as I went along — so she was able to read through the MS. Two invitations to speak at Food Relief Committees, one at Lancaster; rejected both.

Evening papers reported biggest bombing of Berlin yet attempted; I suppose we shall get it back. Gandhi still alive and "cheerful"; his fast ends at dawn to-morrow.

Wednesday March 3rd
Large mail this morning including card from Lord Ponsonby saying he had wired to Alex Wood yesterday and "can't we all forget about S.M. for a bit" — which I endorse *ex immo corde*. Had a real red-blooded letter of abuse from Canada. One of the most encouraging factors in life is the mental & spiritual status of one's opponents.

Darkness came early to-night (accompanied by a cold March gale) & I had only just got back from dinner when the retaliation raid for Berlin started with an Alert at 8.20. All fireguards had this time to gather at the Assembly points with tin hats, buckets, stirrup-pumps etc. Very noisy beginning, with flares & much flickering of guns in the sky. One terrific crash quite close to us was quite like old times; it didn't however sound like a bomb exactly & most people thought it was probably a dud A.A. shell. All Clear went at 10 p.m. Before the raid was over G. rang me from Park Lane where he was & I rang him again when it was over; also tried to get Mother but line was down somewhere between here & Kensington; however G. got her for me & then 'phoned that she was all right.

Thursday March 4th
Large mail, especially in connection with pamphlet. Howard Whitten rang up & asked me if I would be Chairman of the P.P.U.'s reconstituted Food Committee & campaign, & I agreed if I didn't have to attend all the meetings.

In spite of all this managed to get down to my novel & to finish Chap. 16 ("Before the Verdict") before going to bed.

Strange & terrible accident (reported to me by Mother from wireless) in relation to last night's raid; nearly 200 people killed by suffocation in a crowd jam getting down to one of London's largest shelters. Beautiful day though colder.

Friday March 5th
Minutes etc. of P.P.U. Exec. revealed that my strategic absence plus letter has done what I suggested & hoped for; consideration of Alex Wood's resignation has been referred back to the Council (which really defeated his policy as I indicated, & not the Exec.) in mid-April. By that time, please Heaven, I shall have finished my book, & feel more able to cope with the controversy. *But* the Exec. has decided to put A.W.'s letter of resignation into *P.N.*, thus advertising to the world his view of S.M. & also of the Council! Wrote to Ponsonby & James Hudson about this.

Mother came to tea. Took her to the Buccleuch Gardens on the way back to see the daffodils & pink prunus out together.

Meant to write to-day but owing to mail & various interruptions never really got to my book.

Saturday March 6th
Cabled George Brett about Shirley coming home soon after John.

The mail for once was mercifully small so I was able to get to my book in the morning. By tea-time had written the last chapter of Part 3 ("Judgment is Given", a shortish chapter of 11 pp.) & with it finished $\frac{3}{4}$ of the story.

Sunday March 7th
Cutting from last night's *Evening Standard* seems to show that the publication of A.W.'s letter in *P.N.* has done the P.P.U. more damage than any act of Stuart's.

Worked most of day on book. Planned the last Section (5 chapters), & then revised first half of Part 2 for W.E.G.

Monday March 8th
Did some reading for book, on prisons, but had little time owing to letters. Heard from John Nevin Sayre that Harry Emerson Fosdick is going to write the preface for the Amer. Edition of *Humiliation with Honour* — a most pleasing arrangement which shd. greatly help both its sales & its status.

Wednesday March 10th
In town most of day. Called at U.S. Embassy at midday to make affidavit for application for re-entry permit. Lunched at Greek House with Andreas Michalopoulos & G. Kingsley Martin at another table. From there dropped in for $\frac{1}{2}$ an hour at 3.0 to talk to Mr Hamilton, an *Evening News* writer, at his flat in Half Moon Street abt. my pamphlet. From there went on to an American Outpost tea at Claridge's, where Sir William & Lady Beveridge were guests of honour. Both made good speeches; her Scotch voice is especially pleasing. They are just off for a lecture tour of U.S.A. & will certainly be mobbed there.

Papers full of the big raid on Munich.

Friday March 12th
More letter-writing. Never got to book. Papers all full of Sir A. Sinclair's speech on the "successful" results of our bombing of Germany — centre of old Nuremberg destroyed, 3 Art Galleries in Munich demolished, etc. etc. The whole world seems to have gone mad. Last night when something of this was in the evening papers, G. said: "And not one voice raised in protest." This morning we found that one voice was — that of R. R. Stokes, who said that the bombing of Nuremberg sickened him, & that mothers & children were mothers & children just the same even if they belong to the enemy. *The Times* recorded the remark, reporting a speech by Harold

Balfour, that if German civilians get killed in these raids it is their own fault! (Does this apply to babies?) Wrote a letter supporting Stokes to the *D. Herald*, wh. certainly won't publish it; also wrote Stokes himself, sending a copy of my Cologne poem & telling him abt. the Bombing Restriction Committee; also wrote Corder Catchpool & said that Stokes shd. be associated with this in some way. I feel more than ever (with Stokes) like Athanasius *contra mundum* — tho' I know in their hearts that people don't *like* this bombing.

An Alert about 8 a.m. Papers later reported damage & casualties in one London suburb — presumably in the East as we heard no gun-fire.

Saturday March 13th

Very appropriately, the Bombing Restriction Committee's pamphlet "Stop Bombing Civilians!" arrived from Corder Catchpool this morning. Letter writing, as usual now, occupied the whole morning.

Lovely day but very cold wind. Daffodils & a thick carpet of purple, mauve, yellow & white crocuses are all out *together* on the lower lawn of the Terrace Garden, & even the magnolia is coming out into pink buds. The warmest winter & spring for 30 years.

Mother came to tea, & did some ironing. In the midst of her conversation came a card from Lord Ponsonby, begging me *not* to resign from the P.P.U. Exec. & saying "No. Don't do that. It will only add fuel to the flames. You are one of the few who really count & will eventually lead them back to sanity." After that I couldn't, so I rewrote my letter to Maurice Rowntree.

Evening papers reported "Biggest ever" raid on Essen; felt sick at thought of the civilian suffering behind the gleeful communiqués. World has gone mad.

Monday March 15th

Beautiful day. For nearly the whole of it sat out on the tennis court reading prison reform material & the Broadmoor book for last section of my novel.

In afternoon Sybil Morrison caught me on the telephone & tried to argue me into attending P.P.U. Committees & joining in the Stuart v. Chairman controversy again — but I firmly maintained that I was going to follow Lord Ponsonby's advice & keep out of the controversy now that I couldn't further help S.M. within the movement.

Tuesday March 16th

W.E.G. here. Got off many letters, including rather delayed ones to Ruth & the children. Dictated some out of doors, as it was such a marvellous day, more like June than March. Sat out till 6 p.m., writing Letter 105 (on Famine Relief again).

Telephone call from Mr Hamilton whom I saw last week, who told me that he had prepared three interesting paragraphs on my pamphlet, which were passed till they reached the Chief Editor, who stopped them on the ground that I was a member of the P.P.U. & "notorious"! Wrote Dakers asking him to take this up & mentioned all the other things I belonged to (R.I.I.A., Society of Authors etc.) & that I was much better known as a writer of books.

Friday March 19th
Went to town for meeting of Famine Relief Comm. at Waldorf Hotel abt. conditions in Belgium. Took form of Press Conference addressed by M. Pierlot, the Belgian Prime Minister, & Dr Bigwood. I gathered from T. C. Foley, who sent me the invitation, that at the previous Conference on France, addressed by Howard Kershner, no pacifist was permitted at all! My pamphlet has created a breach in that wall — shown in the mixture of enthusiasm & embarrassment with wh. the Famine Relief Committee regard me.

Picked up a sandwich or two at the Waldorf; went on to London Library in the lunch-hour & looked up the Trial of Lunatics Act 1883. Then down to Cheyne Walk, where I found the men working & top floor done. Went across to look at Cheyne Court flats & didn't like them, but was shown one at Rossetti Gardens Mansions wh. I thought would do beautifully for Mother — 4 small bedrooms looking south over back gardens of Cheyne Walk houses, & two sitting-rooms looking west. Continued Chapter 18. Charming letter from Shirley w' sketch about the New Forest.

Saturday March 20th
This week's copy of *The Week* contains a lengthy attack on the P.P.U. (on usual grounds — Fascist, playing Germany's game etc.!) in a long section entitled "Peace Offensive" — from wh. I infer the P.P.U. is really becoming more effective than I think it, and is actually beginning to alarm Mr Claude Cockburn! He makes the expected kind of nefarious attempt to identify S.M.'s imprisonment with the German "Peace Offensive".

Mother rang up just before dinner to say she had taken the flat.

Sunday March 21st
Large offensive said to be preparing in Tunisia. Weather said to have prevented the continuation of our big bombing raids (thank Heaven). Sense of lull & waiting in the rather empty papers.

Monday March 22nd
Long letter from Laurence Housman about the S.M. controversy wh. I had to answer bec. it was Laurence. Long conversation with Humphrey Moore abt. the attack on *P. News* in *The Week*. He said W. Wellock didn't want to stand as Chairman & would I write to him — which I did. So we go on — everything done but my book. I hardly got out, had just abt. one hour of revising the trial section for W.E.G.

At 6.30 went to dine (at 7.30) with Eliz. Sprigge to meet Dr Greta Hedin a Swedish Educationist. Both Eliz. Sprigge & Phyllis Bentley find that the Min. of I. gives them no time to write; Elizabeth even seemed to envy my pacifist pariah position as I get through some permanent work while their office years are consumed by the locust.

Tuesday March 23rd
Terrific day of letter-writing. Must have dictated 30–40 letters & wrote quite a few as well. This business of being swamped gets worse & worse. When W.E.G. left she had still 17 letters to do. Never got to book at all.

Letters from George Brett this morning. Said that present plan is to send John home by the June or July boat, & Shirley back with Miss Boston in August. Wrote Cook's asking them to get John on the June boat if possible so that he can make some contact with Eton before it breaks up.

Cheque from Capt. Larke of the Canadian Army came to-day for distribn. of *H. with H.* to 50 people — a few his friends.

Wednesday March 24th
Big battle going on in Tunisia — 8th Army again. Mareth line reported pierced this morning, but the bridgehead lost again to a German counter-attack this evening.

Wrote various sections this morning for the concluding chapters. This evening wrote 5pp. of Ch. 19 — "Tea on the Terrace".

Thursday March 25th
Cheque from Dakers to end of last year for royalties on *Humiliation with Honour* — £52.10.10, making about £100 in all (minus nearly £10 for "extra corrections" which seems a large amount for so small a book). I shall give the Famine Relief Committee half the profits on the pamphlet, which are already £30; Dakers tells me it cost £270 & has now brought in £290, & there is another £10 from my Letter readers after the circulation has been paid for with the money they sent.

Mild cloudy day, started with soft rain. Trees & flowers just racing out, more like May. Battle in Tunisia going none too well. A Werth broadcast from Russia indicated depression there over Churchill's cheerful assumption in his radio speech that the war must last another two years.

Saturday March 27th
Still concentrating on book. Re-wrote air-raid section & nearly finished the chapter.

Remarkable sunset; sun went down into a bank of deep cloud — like the sun over Axbridge Reservoir last autumn. Began as a glowing Chinese lantern & ended as a bright orange tiddly-wink.

Sunday March 28th
Finished last three pp. of Chapter 20, and wrote the first $9\frac{1}{2}$ pp. of Chap. 21. Too tired to do any more; rather hard writing.

In last night's heavy raid on Berlin, twice the amount of bombs is reported to have been dropped as in the heaviest raid on London (April 16th–17th, 1941). Communiqués gleeful as usual. Wonder when we shall get it back. Large geometrical pattern of searchlights bisecting the sky to-night.

Monday March 29th

Daily Herald this morning described burning Berlin on Saturday night as having looked "like an oven". I wonder who really gets satisfaction out of this terrible deterioration in human values.

Tuesday March 30th

The R.A.F. bombed Berlin again last night. Very windy to-day; dark evening. Daffodils all blown down; blossoms falling off trees. Magnolia in full bloom.

Mareth Line "turned" in Tunisia; supposed to be a great victory.

Wednesday March 31st

Bad night last night. Only about 4½ hours' sleep, and that mostly nightmares — chiefly of trying to sleep with large barking dog in the room the size of a bear. Expected raid after second attack on Berlin but it did not come.

Small mail luckily, so spent day on Letter 106 (wh. being on prison reform indirectly gives my views on Stuart Morris) & got it done by dinner-time. After dinner there was a big fire-guard exercise lasting till 10.0. Mostly consisted of standing about in the cold wind & carrying buckets of water. Large "pretence" fires all over the place. Real March night; heavy clouds & small gale.

Fire-guard exercises really very funny. Major Hyde-Roberts racing about like a small boy with a box of matches starting fires (magnesium) all over Richmond Hill, lighting up the flats like a beacon for the bombers if there had been any about. When we had waited in the cold for about 1½ hours somebody inquired: "Where's Major Hyde-Roberts?" and somebody else said: "He's crept round to Cardigan Rd to start another fire." A girl said: "Can't we creep into the bushes & douse him with water?"

Thursday April 1st

Went out for a while this afternoon & saw the war-time (15th) edition of *Testament of Youth* in a pile at Smith's. Horrid paper, small print, quotations & chapter headings all run together, but I suppose V.G. had no alternative if it was to be published at all. The edition is 15,000, at 6/–, and the whole of it has already been taken by the book-shops. Smith's chief woman assistant had as much to say about the book's appearance & the iniquities of the Ministry of Supply, as I had.

Friday April 2nd
Small mail so was able to work hard all day at my book. Finished Chapter 21, and started the last one, "The End of the Beginning".

Knocked off only to go for a short walk into the town & back by the towing path. Found myself thinking deeply & with a queer kind of obsession about Leonard Lockhart (the trial part of whose story the book is based on, though the rest of my story is invented and the central character is not really like him).

The book really is very exciting — I only hope it will be as exciting to read as it is to write! — so I wrote on & on till I was really worn out, and went to bed feeling exhausted & bad-tempered. The drive to get this book done has meant three wretched nights.

Saturday April 3rd
 Finished "Day of Judgment" this morning. Actually it was done about 1.30; Amy gave me some lunch here so that I did not have to break off. Oddly enough I started this book on the seventh anniversary of Winifred's death on Sept. 29th last year, at Cheddar. Of course it isn't strictly finished, because there is still all the verbal revision to do, but the really agitating part of a book is getting the ideas out of one's vulnerable head on to rather less vulnerable paper. Once that is done, the rest becomes relatively pleasurable.

I couldn't have finished my book on a lovelier day; it was more like June than April & after I had stopped writing I went out for 1½ hours along the towing path towards Teddington. The day was quite hot, & the Terrace Garden (where my book ends) almost singing with blossom. Mother came to tea; she was inclined to grumble about all the work involved by the flat (hers) but is really pleased with it, I think.

While I was writing in the garden after tea a woman who lives in these flats came up to me & said she had always loved my books but only learnt last week who I was. She & her husband had thought what a devoted wife I was, always working so hard at my husband's lecture notes! Queer how the assumption persists that when a woman is working it must be for a man, and never for herself!!

Monday April 5th
Discovered by *D. Herald* this morning that all women with nursing experience (including V.A.D. experience) between 17 & 60 must register on Saturday — so at last I become involved directly in the totalitarian state. This is in readiness for the "impending offensive".

Went on revising book. This afternoon I had a letter from, of all people, Leonard Lockhart, written on, of all days, April 3rd, and telling me that he is going, of all places, to Carbis Bay — as a country G.P.! It looks as if life is too much for him again — & raises possible difficulties about the English publication of my book. I fear he isn't as tough as my "Dion Heyworth". Went for a walk after tea with G. In Kew Gardens — which is perfect.

Tuesday April 6th
Father's 79th birthday. Went to his grave this afternoon in Richmond Cemetery and found it covered with daffodils & scyllas. Put a few more into the iron vase. The whole cemetery was filled with blossom & looking quite beautiful despite the strong cold wind. On a grave at the top opposite the military section I saw, in front of the memorials of his parents, a stone in "proud and loving memory" of an Air Raid Warden named Fanshawe, aged 35, killed while on duty in the raid of May 10th–11th, 1941.

Thought all day about Leonard Lockhart while revising my book. Answered his letter. He *would* go to Carbis Bay of all the possible villages in England — i.e., to a place where I am well known & each book I write likely to be read with interest. It does seem to make the English publication of my book difficult unless he consents as he did before — though I can hardly believe he will. I don't really think it is wise to go to a village with a past like his — & I don't want to add to the difficulties of one who has suffered so much.

Wednesday April 7th
Immense mail-writing — 20 letters this morning, mostly sending of this week's Fortnightly Letter to various people interested in both Stuart & penal reform. Went into town this afternoon, & had a look at 2 Cheyne Walk which is now practically finished & really looking very nice. Gardeners have been & cleared up well.

New attack by 8th Army in Tunisia.

Thursday April 8th
Revising novel all day. Much depressed by growing certainty that I cannot publish "D. of J." in this country for I believe that much of it has real beauty. In a way I suppose it was foolish to spend so much time on the book when I found I couldn't fulfil all L.P.L.'s conditions; but if I had waited any longer I shd. have forgotten all the atmosphere of the trial etc. And it really is a marvellous story — of which my version will surely achieve publication here someday. Only hope nothing interferes with its issue in U.S.A., Canada & Sweden.

Chill blowy day wh. added to my feeling of depression.

Friday April 9th
Finished revising the MS. of "Day of Judgment" to-day — so that even if it is no more than a "literary legacy" for my family, the book at least is done except for the light job of going through the typescript. I can't be thankful

enough that Leonard's letter did not arrive till I had finished the first draft and the "inventing" part. Don't think I should ever have had the heart to finish it if I had known of his Carbis Bay plans first.

21 bombers lost over the Ruhr last night. One very short Alert this morning; All Clear in about ten minutes. Note in *New Statesman* suggests that the Americans are wildly bombing Continental towns like Rouen & Antwerp & causing huge civilian casualty lists.

A.P. (presumably Ponsonby) in *P. News* suggests that some mysterious fate *has* happened to Hitler.

Saturday April 10th
Directly after breakfast went to Richmond Labour Exchange and registered as a "nurse" (those with Red Cross experience — last War or this — being required to do so).

P.P.U. Council at 2.0. After long & tiring discussion Council's decision was again reversed & Stuart thrown out. I made my protest & plea on the usual grounds but this time it was useless; several people had thrown up the sponge. Though on principle I voted for his retention I think it would have been difficult for him to come back to such a divided Council.

When I came back, very tired, at 9 p.m., I found a letter from Rache (amid a large mail) asking me for a "blurb" for "Day of Judgment". This faces me with the grim necessity of explaining the Lockhart situation to him — which would have to be done soon in any case, only I should have liked to get the book completely revised & off my hands first.

Monday April 12th
One of the most trying days I have ever experienced. Last week I promised the C.B.C.O. to appear (as Chairman of the Food Relief Campaign) for Howard Whitten at Clerkenwell Police Court as a witness to his sincerity, & to-day had to go there. I gave him lunch first at a little café opposite King's Cross. He was admirably calm in his behaviour since he thought he might be facing anything from six to twelve months' imprisonment for non-compliance with his Tribunal condition. After lunch we were joined by Roy Walker & Sybil Morrison & sat talking in a pub opposite the Police Court till it was time for the case to begin. The Ministry of Labour in the Police Court (wh. seemed to be crowded with policemen) was represented by a solicitor who had got the facts & dates of Howard's various appearances quite wrong. Howard very calmly made his admirable statement & then I was summoned to the witness box by the magistrate. Here he literally heckled me about the Food Relief Campaign, calling it "mere propaganda" etc. etc.; in fact I was much more "on trial" than Howard. I brought in the Archbp. of Canterbury's views w' some effect; but discovered that I am not a good witness if bullied as the effort of keeping my temper puts all my ideas out of my head (as it does on Committees). In fact I can only really think properly with a pen in my

hand. The Magistrate first sentenced Howard to 7 days on remand in order to get the inaccuracies made straight; but Sybil M. protested vehemently that this was unfair as the mistakes were the Ministry's fault. Finally the Magistrate sent for Howard back again & sentenced him to only 2 months to everyone's joy. Whether I helped at all I don't know; probably the mistakes of the M. of L. helped more.

When I got home I found a charming note from Leonard Lockhart who obviously has no idea or suspicion of the book problem. Went on revising it after dinner. V. tired.

Wednesday April 14th
Another warm & lovely day. Continued solidly to revise book except for a trip into Chelsea which occupied five hours of a very precious day, to help Mother decide where she wanted to put the refrigerator in her kitchen! When I got there, of course I found that she had decided everything already. 2 Cheyne Walk full of sunshine and gardens at the back looking beautiful despite neglect. Got back as quickly as I could and continued revision.

An Alert about midnight. No noise, but could see shells from distant guns (direction of docks) & one bright light like a moving fire in the sky. Was it a hit 'plane or a fire from an incendiary, we wondered. "All Clear" came in about an hour.

Thursday April 15th
A third superb day — more like July this time, the sun was so hot. The Terrace Garden was a riot of beauty & everything smelt as warm & scented as it does at mid-summer. Woke with a headache & never thought I would get through the day's work, but I did, & washed my hair into the bargain. This afternoon resolutely stayed in & did Letter 107 (on adolescent & adult values) mostly straight on to the typewriter. Got it posted by 5.15 tho' it was as long as usual — & then at last was able to take my revision into the Terrace Garden & have a deck chair on the lawn. Sat out again after dinner till the sun set. By missing a fire exercise (which G. this time attended) I managed to get the revision done to the end of Part 3, ready for Helen Mayo to-morrow.

Letter from Cook's about pocket money for John, saying they had cabled about him being on the June boat. A night or two ago the *Eve. Standard* reported that the *Serpo Pinto* had picked up 3 lots of torpedoed people.

No news of the raid to speak of — no incidents in London, but bombs & damage at a Thames Estuary town. Three raiders brought down, so perhaps we saw one.

Friday April 16th
Yet another July day. This incredible spring gets more & more amazing.

Mrs Rowlands told me that it was 86° here yesterday. The chestnut trees beside the river are in full flower; the prunus japonica is as lovely as if it were indeed in Japan, & the view along the Thames valley with its vivid green & the blossom from the Terrace Gdn. in the foreground is so beautiful that it takes my breath away.

Saturday April 17th

Very hot again. Spent much of day in Terrace Garden again reading MS. of Baroness Reitzenstein's book of "Letters" to her daughter in Germany. I thought them very good, and drafted the Introduction I promised to write for them. They reminded me all the time of Shirley.

G. very unhappy all day — and justifiably — because after Frank Darvall at the M. of I. sedulously discouraged his Institute idea & sent him racing after Vice-Chancellors etc., the English-Speaking Union (of which he is ex-Secretary) has stolen the idea and set up an Institute with Prof. Newall as Secretary. In other words, Darvall used knowledge obtained through his official position in M. of I. of G.'s plans to slow them up while his own show was putting them on! Told G. I doubted whether anyone so independent & unorthodox as he could get institutional positions in wartime & would only court set-backs if he tried.

Firewatching 3 a.m.–6 a.m.

Tuesday April 20th

W.E.G. came just before lunch-time bringing the finished typescript of "Day of Judgment". It was another lovely day (though the wind was colder than it has been) so I sat out correcting one copy of the typescript of Part 4. Came in after dinner & went on with it as it became too chilly to stay out.

We hadn't done the black-out very long and I was still correcting when I heard the guns, then almost on top of them the sirens here — and then (a sound not heard since 1941) the once-familiar long descending scream followed by a "wonk" which shook the whole Court. Major Hyde Roberts, getting too excited for words at really having an "incident" in his sector, blew the whistle & we all had to go out in tin hats etc. The guns were making a terrific noise and I was only too conscious that all the typescript copies of Part 4 and the MSS. were in the flat! However the raider didn't come back and the All Clear went in about ½ an hour, at 11 p.m.

Wednesday April 21st

Learnt from the porters etc. that last night's bomb fell just on the other side of the river. When we went to breakfast, found dozens of windows on the Hill smashed. One A.T.S. girl had been injured by blast at the hotel.

Thursday April 22nd

Meant to spend most of day clearing up flat but had such a large mail (involving the sending out also of various change of address p.c.s) that I only began the sorting of papers after tea. Cooler day with less sun. G. finished reading my novel & seemed to think it good. We discussed possibilities of (a) changing it & making the central character something other than a doctor — which I think would only spoil the book without effecting any sort of disguise, (b) persuading L.L. to let me publish it abroad.

Friday April 23rd
Whole day spent in clearing up papers etc. Dirty & dreary job. Took G. to the Indian Restaurant in the evening as an antidote.

A short Alert about 10 p.m. — followed by three separate All Clears — presumably from different districts, the person responsible perhaps being in a pub having a Good Friday binge. It was later reported that one 'plane went over & no bombs were dropped. After so many sirens, kept on hearing the noise till I fell asleep.

Saturday April 24th
Still clearing up; went through large letter file (1941) & threw masses of it away. Dreary job. By afternoon post came one long and one short letter from Shirley (in the same envelope), the former taking me to task for a letter in which I apparently suggested that she did too much running round and growing popular, and not enough application! Did I really think brains more important than friendliness, she inquired? with a true touch of old Mr Catlin's moral indignation. She then proceeded with a quite well-written "theme" on England which she concluded by describing as the home of "a great nation". Darling Poppy! And how she disapproves of John, with his self-centred creative egoism & lack of the small-town social virtues!

Sent in letter of resignation from P.P.U. Exec. Shall now gradually ease myself out of it.

Sunday April 25th
All the bells sounding this morning, the rule forbidding them now being permanently abrogated after 3 years of silence (broken only at the time of the N. African landings). But I don't feel like celebrating Easter. "Christ is risen!" What a mockery, when the world has buried him more completely than ever before in history. I'll celebrate Easter (I hope) when the War is over.

Spent morning writing Letter 108 to get it out of the way before moving home. G. & I went to the cemetery for an Easter Day visit to Father's grave — which looked very well cared for with the flame-coloured tulips Mother took yesterday and a few scarlet ones blooming. Went on packing when we came in from the sunny windy day. At 6.15 gave a small farewell cocktail party for the people we know in Richmond.

Monday April 26th

Day of clearing up & packing. About the ninth pack-up since 1940.

V. tired; back bad as always when packing.

Tuesday April 27th

Russians have broken off diplomatic relations with Poles thanks to German discovery (said to be a "frame-up" & a "wicked lie") of the bodies of 10,000 Polish officers murdered near Smolensk.

Removers (with Amy) came from Hounslow & picked up our things from Richmond Hill Court about 11.0. Amy & I rode to Chelsea in the van, & everything was deposited in our empty house before lunch — wh. we had at the British Restaurant at No. 8. Spent rest of dirty & tiring day getting the things out of the dining-room to other parts of the house.

Staying for nights till furniture comes at Sloane Court Hotel. Walks to the hotel & to the Food Office revealed Chelsea as very empty & even more Blitzed than I remembered. View from our house back & front about the only unchanged part of Chelsea. It is rather like living amid the ruins of Pompeii. I feel like a revenant — with all the past in fragments around me.

Cable from Ruth welcoming our return — says John "reconciled" to coming via Portugal.

Wednesday April 28th

Furniture still not arrived but was kept busy all day clearing up the Richmond things. Amy came late & tearful to announce that her sister Lily's husband was killed in N. Africa on April 6th and the news came by letter from the War Office yesterday. Her fellow-workers at the factory collected abt. £10 for her so that she could have a few days away from work. She asked if I would draft a letter of thanks for her, which I did. She & the young man only had abt. 3 weeks together all told after they were married — & never a home of their own at all. Such is war for the "little people" whom the politicians indifferently sacrifice to satisfy their own swollen egos. I only hope Burnett comes through.

Russian–Polish row featured in all the papers. Russians haughtily refusing an investigation (why, if the Germans did it?); Churchill intervening; said to have "no differences" with Roosevelt (which means he has them!). Poles will presumably be made to climb down & cease annoying the dear Russians — such is wartime diplomacy!

Thursday April 29th

Tiring day of waiting about for furniture which did not come. Amy & I finally mopped over most of the rooms. Whole place now clean & ready, but self v. tired & dirty. Lunch as usual at the British Restaurant 3 doors away & supper with G. at Caletta's.

Friday April 30th
Got to Cheyne WAlk at 9 a.m. to let in the gas men & Rawling's fitter. Found letter from Rache calling "D. of J." a "fine novel" & saying that I made the central figure "a most heroic character", but saying he thought there was no alternative to getting L.P.L.'s agreement before I publish, even abroad. Rang up Rache & said I would do this in a week or ten days — i.e., as soon as Leonard is settled in Carbis Bay & I am straighter in Cheyne Walk.

Part of the furniture arrived at last, at 2 p.m. Was pleasantly surprised to see that very little of the china & glass is missing (though I had a catastrophe myself & broke 7 of the 12 green & white cocktail glasses Lady R. gave W. & me years ago). The silver will be the test; that has not yet come. The furniture looks terrible but will doubtless clean up. No carpets yet & only two pairs of curtains so far — but even a few of our things made the house begin to look itself again. Amy worked like a Trojan & we got all the more valuable things put away.

Sunday May 2nd
Knocked off housework for the day. Prepared & gave a speech on Famine Relief & India at the P.P.U. Annual General Meeting — the only time I was able to appear there. This was the Open concluding meeting. Alex Wood (who has been re-elected Chairman) was in the Chair, & the other two speakers were James Hudson (who made a v. good speech) and Wilfred Wellock.

Monday May 3rd
In midst of general uproar (2 handymen from Walter Nash, Amy & Lily, a gasman, & the daily woman's first morning) two unexpected visitors descended on us — Stephen Hobhouse & Captain Larke — the Canadian Methodist chaplain who distributed 50 copies of *H. with H.* Both of them, particularly Stephen, wanted private conversation with me at a moment when there was no privacy in the house, & I was in my overall & very dirty! The Canadian liked the informality, but Stephen (looking like an elderly pelican who had wandered into the wrong suburb — he was actually on his way to the cremation of Mrs Sidney Webb) seemed rather perturbed by it. We all had lunch together at the British Restaurant a few doors away, & the total situation was so funny that I kept on finding it difficult to keep my face straight.

Thursday May 13th
Morning papers reported war over in Africa; German prisoners amount to 150,000; Von Arnim captured. What next?

At lunch-time gave lunch-hour address on Famine Relief to Society of Women Journalists at Stationers' Hall. It is almost the only thing standing in that part of the City and I picked my way to it along a narrow path through debris where men were working. In spite of one or two critical questions the audience was favourable to my address, & at the end one member of their Council pledged them all to do their best to get a 500-word summary of my speech into abt. 200 magazines where they have access if I could provide cyclostyled copies.

Friday May 14th
We had an Alert at 2 a.m. to-day. Much noise of what I thought was heavy gunfire, with flashes in the sky. Got the children into the shelter without much fuss & were there for 45 mins. before the All Clear went. Later the removal men told us that what we took for guns was a heavy thunderstorm! Raid was on Chelmsford. To-day evening papers reported non-stop 40-hr. Blitz on Germany & Italy; including Berlin.

Saturday May 15th
Grim description in *Herald* of "encirclement" of Germany by aerial bombardment.

Spoke this afternoon at Conway Hall at the Famine Relief meeting arranged for the London area. Other speakers were Emile Cammaerts, Doctor Helene Lambridis (Greek) and John Hadham (in the Chair). Audience entirely of sympathisers who passed the resolution *nem. con.* Meeting followed by a private meeting of the London Group to discuss relations with the Famine Relief Committee & the part to be played by pacifists and "respectables".

Sunday May 16th
Sunday papers full of news of our non-stop bombing raids on the Continent; also of jitters in Italy & riots in Germany. Sounds like wishful-thinking to me, though our raids sound grim enough in all conscience. 1,000 were reported killed in the last raid on Palermo. Raid last night on Berlin.

Cleaned & cleared all day, first Mother's flat, then our own house.

Lovely day though wind cold. After supper G. & I walked across the bridge into the Old English Garden. Queer to see the gap where the Old Church used to be, and the sun which used to be hidden by it sinking like a huge red globe. Lovely sunset, moon nearly full. Bombers going out in large numbers; asked G. to put Beethoven's Concerto which Edward used to play on the gramophone to drown the noise.

Press reported ten boys killed at Downside Abbey & others injured when an R.A.F. plane flying too low crashed yesterday on the school playing field.

Monday May 17th
Bad night last night; 3 Alerts. The first went about midnight; sound of heavy bomb (or gun) came before siren. Place later reported as Ealing. Got everybody into shelter, when All Clear went, followed almost at once by another siren. Long Alert this time; much gunfire; sound of 'plane overhead. Went upstairs half way through; was asleep when All Clear went. Amy very worried bec. Marian had gone to Isleworth for the night with Sheila. Third Alert about 4 a.m. just as Amy, Agnes & the boy had got upstairs again. All v. tired this morning so I got up & made tea for Amy & Agnes. Had to be at Rosetti Gdn. Mansions at 8.30 a.m. to "let the men in", but they didn't turn up till 11.0. In the meantime I had breakfast, sorted large mail, took Mgt. Lewis to the Food Office to register for herself & Mother, registered at the shops & laid in a stock of provisions. Corrected my Letter & answered the day's mail after lunch; sat in the sun for a while over tea; back to the flat & unpacked a trunk for Mother. *Very* tired; went to bed early.

On July 18th, John Brittain-Catlin reached England after sailing from New York in a Portuguese ship and flying on from Lisbon. "At first . . . I did not recognise him," Vera Brittain wrote later — "it would take time to get to know him again".

Monday July 26th
Fall of Mussolini!
   Dear Josiah Wedgwood died — just too soon to know that the dictators were beginning to fall.

Tuesday July 27th
Shirley's 13th birthday.

Friday July 30th
Very hot again. Somewhere near the 90°s. Record crowds at all the railway stations.

Saturday July 31st
Letter from Florence Wedgwood enclosed one written to Lord Wedgwood by some Austrian refugees in California named Kraus; they had been trying for 3 years to get their children from England to U.S.A. F.W. asked if I could help. I replied that I would try & tentatively asked how she would feel about my attempting a memoir of Josiah. I reminded her how he had once said to me at the H. of Commons: "Well, I unveiled the memorial to Arnold Bennett at Hanley, and I look forward to the day when you'll unveil mine at Stoke-on-Trent."
   Two thunderstorms — one at 9 p.m. & one late at night, sounding like an air-raid — broke the heat wave.

G. struggled through terrifically crowded trains to give 2 lectures at Reading.

Sunday August 1st
Spent day at Eton seeing the Taylors, Mr Herbert & the Art Master Wilfred Blunt.

Terrible account in *Sunday Express* of our week of raids on Hamburg, which have virtually obliterated Germany's fine second city, blown corpses into tree-tops and caused 10,000 deaths. Terror beginning in Berlin. God what a world. I hope they include Sir Arthur Harris (who planned all these heavy raids) among the War criminals.

Eton wants to fit John into its system & make him specialise in Latin, instead of finding out what he wants to & can do, & helping him to do it. This day explained to me why Mr Amery expects India to adapt itself to the British Empire & why no civil servant can ever change a damnfool regulation.

Tuesday August 3rd
A card from Florence Wedgwood said that "nothing would please her better" than a book of mine about her husband.

G., Mother and I went to his Memorial service at 2 p.m. at St Margaret's, Westminster. It was a warm day but the sun was never bright though it went in & out. St Margaret's was quite badly damaged on May 10th, 1941, & the once lovely rose window is mended & plain. On the left of the aisle was the large & miscellaneous family, mostly not in mourning. On the right, where we were, were mostly members of the H. of Lords & Commons quite orthodoxly clad; I saw Lords Cecil & Listowel, Attlee, Arthur Greenwood, Jon Creech Jones, Eleanor Rathbone, Cunningham-Reid, etc. etc. The service was most intelligently chosen, starting off with "He who would valiant be".

Wednesday September 8th
Italy's surrender announced.

Tuesday September 14th
Stuart started work on the Anthology. Looks older & more worn after his prison experience — & even more by the disillusioning conduct of his colleagues.

Had an interesting talk with him at tea-time about the origin of the Official Secrets Act & the public part of his trial, at which (as I suspected at the time) the Judge — Mr Justice Hallett — *was* in conflict with the Govt. He wanted a public trial, referring to the secret documents only by letter; and he gave S. a short sentence to indicate his disapproval of the Government's methods.

Papers full of stories of rescue of Mussolini by Nazis. 10,000 Americans killed in the landing near Salerno (country familiar to us from staying in Capri).

Wednesday September 15th
Early lunch; went again to Clerkenwell Police Court to support Howard Whitten's appeal against his second summons for non-compliance with his condition. This time the Magistrate did not even put me in the witness-box, but sentenced Howard to 6 months, & threatened him with a longer sentence still if he appeared in the Court again on the same charge. Wrote a long letter to Creech Jones abt. this Cat & Mouse business when I got home.

An Alert at 10.10 p.m.; a good deal of gunfire followed, & one reverberating crash which sounded like a bomb about a mile away. All Clear about 11.0.

Sybil Morrison told me that J.M.M. & Pat Figgis had a row at the Executive yesterday about Patrick's idea of not employing persons having unorthodox marital relations at the P.P.U.!

No news of Shirley yet.

Thursday September 16th
Attempted landings round Salerno are causing "tremendous losses" among American Fifth Army troops.

Discussed possible holiday in Cornwall with Cook's. No more news of Shirley.

Amy with us 13 years to-day.

Had a long talk with Stuart before he left about the possibility of his writing a book on his prison experiences.

Sunday September 19th
Expected news of Shirley all day but it never came. Began work on my Introduction, "The Forgotten Prisoner", for the Prison Medical Reform pamphlet.

Made list of books in my study useful for the Anthology, for S.M. to look through.

Monday September 20th
G. rang up Cook's & learned that Shirley's boat has not even arrived at Lisbon yet. It may get in to-morrow.

G. and I went to a U.D.C. tea to meet Norman Angell & have a discussion on his return from U.S.A. Expected a crush, but found it a small eclectic tea-party at Queen Anne's Gate, well worth attending. Kingsley Martin took the chair; others there included Strabolgi & Lady Marley.

Fighting in Italy is all round the area we visited in 1936 — Amalfi, Ravello, Salerno, Sorrento. Amalfi has just been captured, with other heights round Naples. Russians nearing Smolensk & Churchill back.

Tuesday September 21st
Cook's rang up to say that Shirley's boat had been held up for some time in the Canaries. (?Why did it go there? John didn't.)

Long talk with S.M. who said Middleton Murry had always been jealous of me bec. he regarded me as his only serious rival in the P.P.U. Apparently there was once an attempt to get him out of the Editorship of *Peace News* & I was the only possible other choice. I told Stuart J.M.M. needn't have worried; I didn't regard *him* as a rival since the P.P.U. didn't represent so much as a quarter of all my work, & I would never narrow down my influence & contacts in U.S.A., Sweden, India, the Dominions etc. by becoming editor of *P.N.* I was more interested in getting my ideas & that of the movement into non-pacifist spheres than in writing for pacifists.

Applied for my re-entry permit extension (now given at the U.S. Consulate here) & bought J.'s shirts & socks. J. showed me a huge pagan picture he had painted — wild & remarkable.

Wednesday September 22nd
Great battle going on for Naples; total Mediterranean situation affects Shirley's return. Cook's rang up this afternoon to say that the *Serpo Pinto* has arrived safely in Lisbon — but as all the big air transports have gone to the Mediterranean & only little ones are doing the Lisbon–England route, 200 children are still there from the last Lisbon boat & the *Serpo Pinto* has brought 170 more. Cook's said that 370 children will take a good while to clear, though Shirley, as unaccompanied, may expect to come early. We were lucky to get her on this boat as the Air Ministry is closing down the route for children for the present owing to shortage of transport.

Went to a tea party this afternoon where the India Liaison Committee & the Women's International Alliance met Lady Wavell to send goodwill wishes to India. Lady Layton & Mrs Corbett Ashby made speeches & Lady Wavell replied; then we were all introduced for two minutes' conversation & inevitably said the wrong thing.

Saturday October 2nd
P.P.U. Council, which I attended as I had no further news of Shirley. First part spent in discussing the moral issue & Patrick Figgis's ultimatum, which he defended with a somewhat fanatical speech. After tea Stuart made a statement on his own case; it was characteristically generous & courageous, but Alex Wood obviously did not accept his account of his motives. After he had ended & one or two others had spoken I said that the P.P.U. had failed over Stuart in 3 ways wh. had nothing to do with the details of what he or Alex Wood did: (1) as a Christian community, which

should surely be ready for vicarious suffering and vicarious penalisation; (2) from the point of view of justice, in accordance with wh. we shd. not have condemned a man in his absence but protected him; (3) by failing to go "all out" against the Official Secrets Act & the whole paraphernalia of totalitarian secrecy. George Davies came to me afterwards & said he now realised that the P.P.U. had been wrong to disown Stuart.

Sunday October 3rd
P.P.U. Council in morning. Carried the Famine Relief fast proposal through the Council by 20–5 (6 abstentions). J.M.M. insultingly opposed ("middle class mentality" behind the proposal, according to him), & later we had an altercation about his habit of putting his own "election address" in *P.N.* at a time of crucial decision.

Immediately following lunch went to Harrow to spend the afternoon with John. He met me at the top of the hill in his Gilbert & Sullivan Harrow tails (looking very nice); I was glad to learn he seemed far more happily settled than his letters suggested, and is doing a good deal of music. We walked about the playing fields together & then had tea at the School Stores, where J. most uncharacteristically ate three large cakes.

Monday October 4th   Leicester
Spoke Leicester on Famine Relief. Crowded meeting; Martin Parr, formerly Governor of Equatorial Africa, was the other speaker.

Wednesday October 6th   Swindon
Spoke Swindon (Famine Relief). Pouring wet day but quite good meeting.

Thursday October 7th   London
Hard work catching up on letters. Evening, spoke Walthamstow (Famine Relief) with Émile Cammaerts, in a pavilion in the middle of a local Park. Just as Cammaerts finished speaking the Alert sounded. A few people left the meeting but we went on answering questions to the sound of distant gunfire (later I learnt it was noisy then in Chelsea and that an A.A. shell — later reported to have killed & injured several people in Battersea — fell with a rushing noise quite close). I left the meeting about 9 p.m. to go home. The Mayor's car carried me to Manor House Station two or three miles away, & during the drive it was quiet though I could see shells bursting far to the right & the searchlights were vivid. I quite thought the All Clear would go during the half hr. Tube run, but the raid was still on when I got out at Knightsbridge Stn. to get the 19 bus. Several people were waiting at the bus stop, but I had hardly got into the bus when pandemonium began; our own 'planes going to Germany (which quietened our guns) had now stopped going over. The noise of the guns increased as we went down Sloane St. & just beyond Sloane Sq. the bus stopped. Several passengers pulled down the windows to stop any shattering of

glass & we could see A.A. shells bursting just above our heads (S.M. said later that 3 enemy planes were caught in the searchlight but I didn't actually see them). Couldn't decide whether to stay in the bus or get out & risk the shell splinters ("What goes up has to come down," said the woman bus conductor) when the bus went on. I got out at Flood Street & dashed for home with the battle still overhead & the sky like a Fifth of November pageant. Had to take refuge in a Rossetti Gdns. doorway on the way; then made a dash for our house & got in to find everyone in the shelter & thankful to see me. All Clear about ½ hr. later.

Friday October 8th
Newspapers reported German announcement that last night's raid was "the heaviest on the capital for many months". Actually, 60 bombers crossed the coast, 15 got to London, three were brought down, & bombs were dropped at scattered points with several casualties.

Attended a Bombing Restriction Committee at T. C. Foley's office at 3 p.m.; at the end Corder Catchpool & I raised the possibility of Stuart working for it. Jevons demurred & seemed nervous, but I mentioned S.'s work for us, & Jevons rather reluctantly agreed if S. would undertake donkey work anonymously.

Another Alert about 8.30 to-night but planes did not actually get to London.

Saturday October 9th
No further news of Poppy's return.

Foggy evening; no Alert.

Sunday October 10th
Very tired, so spent morning in bed. Mild & foggy. Took Marian into the Park this afternoon. The leaves were falling fast & it was all rather melancholic — too sadly reminiscent of the days ten years ago when Winifred & I used to go the same walk with John & Shirley (who was then just Marian's age). But now Battersea Park looks shabby & rather neglected, though its flowers are still quite good.

Sunday October 17th
SHIRLEY RETURNED!
Came back on a very cold wet day from lecturing at Nottingham to find a tiny fair-haired creature in red jumper & plaid skirt — so pretty! — waiting for me behind the drawing-room curtains!

Air raid.

In November, Vera Brittain began to write her "final appeal, through a companion booklet to One of These Little Ones, *against the policy of 'area bombing'". Its title,* Seed of Chaos, *was taken from Pope's* Dunciad: *"Then rose the seed of Chaos, and of Night, /To blot out order and extinguish light."*

1944

Saturday January 1st

Extra pleasant New Year's Day owing to presence of both children & a double party — 5–7 with "rum-punch" and conversation, & afterwards a dinner for the Arthur Greenwoods who came about 6.0. I had about 20 mins.' talk with Arthur Greenwood before dinner; he said that this will be a fearful year in terms of casualties for the Allies; that the Second Front will start in a matter of weeks & make many homes desolate. He also predicted renewed heavy bombing of London & the Eastern Counties as soon as the attack starts.

Sunday January 2nd

Peaceful Sunday. Rewrote Chap. 10 of "Day of Judgment" (now "Account Rendered"). Children uproarious over tea; Mother blames their manners on America!

Shirley continually pressing for a dog; wants to cable about her Labrador retriever "Middie".

Altered the Arthur Harris section of my bombing booklet which Corder Catchpool's solicitor alleged to be libellous.

Russians only 27 miles from the Polish frontier. R.A.F. out in force yesterday (accord. to *Sunday Express*) attacking unspecified targets on the French coast (? rocket guns).

Ninth heavy raid on Berlin early this morning. Alert here just before midnight; one raider flew low over us but there was very little gunfire.

Monday January 3rd

Started revision of Chap. 11 of novel this morning. Spent afternoon 3–5.30 at a Famine Relief Committee Conference at Caxton Hall to hear report of delegation wh. had gone to meet Minister of Economic Warfare. Discussion of American situation followed; Roy Walker & I brought forward Howard Kershner's suggestions wh. have now been put before the State Dept. & asked whether the Committee shd. not consider substituting something like this for its minimum proposals. F.R. Committee rather floored by this, espec. as Conference delegates were sympathetic. Delegation finally turned up having achieved next to nothing; Hugh Lyon reported (it was led by Bp. of Wakefield).

Tenth heavy raid on Berlin — another 1,000 tons, last night.

Tuesday January 4th

W.E.G. came. Huge collection of post-Xmas letters. Spent all day dictating and signing them.

Young Indian called at 3.0 (Mr Afsal, only in this country one month) to discuss the 600-word talk which I am writing for broadcast to India by the B.B.C.

Wednesday January 5th

Shirley invited to stay with the Roughtons at Cambridge. After much turmoil, got her off at Liverpool St. by the 2.20. Went on to a *Peace News* Directors' meeting to discuss the establishment of that much-needed institution, the Sheppard Press.

Alert at 2.30 this morning, followed by very noisy gunfire quite close. Shelter very cold.

Wrote a letter on Famine Relief policy to the *M. Guardian* at Roy Walker's request.

Thursday January 6th

Wrote Letter 126 — again on Famine Relief — for most of day; just got it posted in time.

R.A.F. raided Stettin in moonlight last night. London is announced as Eisenhower's "invasion H.Q.".

Corder Catchpool reported that Brock's are printing 2,000 copies of *Seed of Chaos*.

Monday January 10th

Revised novel all day. Now more than half way through.

Accord. to *D. Herald*, Americans have set the "invasion date" for Europe but still have 20,000 more landing craft to build.

Turning very cold.

Russians 35 miles into Poland.

Tuesday January 11th

Lunched early at Brit. Restaurant & went to Zwemmer's to order a book on Leonardo da Vinci for John. On to Food Relief Campaign Committee at Endsleigh St. — we discussed the whole U.S.A. situation re food relief, & the possibility of bringing Howard Kershner over. Later at tea at the Express Dairy met Wilfred Wellock, who is v. worried about (1) the Second Front & probable casualties, (2) the way in which a "mass mind" is being created by propaganda. No time for book revision to-day owing to huge size of mail.

Wednesday January 12th

Most interesting memorandum received from Dorothy Detzer of the

American W.I.L., showing how her group was behind the Food Relief discussions in the Senate, & giving a detailed account of the negotiations. Sent it on to Roy Walker.

Went on revising Chap. 14 in the intervals of a long visit from Corder Catchpool to discuss further small changes in *Seed of Chaos* & its publication, a long evening telephone call from Prof. Jevons for the same purpose, and a visit to Mother to talk about her investments.

Huge air battles yesterday over Germany between Germans & Americans. Germans say Americans lost abt. 130 aeroplanes.

Thursday January 13th
Worked all day revising book. Replied to Victor Gollancz's letter saying I would try to get the Anthology to him by the end of Feb. Asked Stuart, who is back in town, to give me two more weeks' work on it. Washed John's & G.'s hair after an Alert had sounded just at the end of supper (about 7.45 p.m.). No noise or gunfire.

Friday January 14th
Revised all day. Got within a page or two of the last 4 chapters of book. Perfectly lovely day; walked in Battersea Park this afternoon. Beautiful weather of course meant the sound of heavy bombers going out again to-night. We don't seem able to have lovely weather now without it meaning more death and destruction.

Good Group letter from Patrick Figgis mentioned the forthcoming publication of *Seed of Chaos* at 2/6.

Saturday January 15th
Foggy day. Shirley returned from Cambridge. John went to Liverpool St. to meet her, but missed her, & she came home alone by the Underground! Helped her unpack before lunch. Went out with G. & the children to buy their sweet ration after lunch; then revised until 6.0 when we took them to Chelsea Palace to see the Chelsea pantomime, *Jack & the Beanstalk*. Amusing lowbrow inanity. At the end the manager announced that an Alert had been sounded & we were to leave without showing our torches — which was difficult as it was pitch dark through the fog. The guns started up as we passed Swan Court so we took refuge there for a few minutes; then came home & got supper as Amy, Sheila & Marian were in the shelter. All Clear sounded in about half an hour. We raided Berlin last night & there was a huge 2,000-ton raid on Brunswick.

Sunday January 16th
Grim account of the Brunswick raid in *Sunday Express*; the town (same size as Coventry) described as "saturated"; 450 tons of bombs (more than in any London raid) dropped on the wretched place & people in 3 minutes.

Sofia yesterday was described as "wiped off the map" as a city. Retribution — the kind inherent in universal law — will come to us one day for all these outrages.

John rude at breakfast as so often — apologised after. Worked at "Account Rendered" till after tea which we had with Mother. Finished revising (& largely rewriting) it between 5.0 & 7.0. Even now it has only taken from end of Sept. 1943 till to-day. The son of the present Prime Minister of Poland, M. Michaloczyc, came to lunch, as he is to be J.'s room-mate at Harrow next term.

Tuesday January 18th

John returned to Harrow this afternoon. Shirley & I went with him to Baker Street; then I took her to Harrods where we bought a fox-terrier pup (a little 2-months-old bitch, not beautiful, but very awake-looking) for £4. I hadn't meant to buy it, at least till Friday, but only to see what was there, but the moment the little creature was put into Shirley's arms it licked her face affectionately, & we couldn't resist it. She tucked it inside her coat & we brought it home on the bus. Immediately she had it she became quite a different child, & spent the evening looking after it & reading up about it.

Wednesday January 19th

Russo-Polish row still boiling up. Seems odd, when we entered the war to "save" Poland.

Activities of everyone demanded by lavatorial activities of pup. In spite of this, managed to get Letter 127 (on post-war reaction) written & typed by supper-time.

Thursday January 20th

At 11.30 went to see Harold Nicolson on Food Relief with Roy Walker and Patrick Figgis. He spoke of Selborne & Dingle Foot as "humane" in themselves, but it seemed to me that if humane men could take their job, they must have split personalities. H.N. said that, having been a Civil Servant, he had resolved never to ask a question in the House, but he advised us to arrange one & to go on pressing, despite Govt. obstinacy on Belgium & their dislike of the U.S. Senate.

D.H. published a map showing proposal for Poles to take Pomerania & Silesia (wholly German) in return for districts ceded to Russia. What a first instalment of the Peace!

Friday January 21st

Another 2,000 ton raid on Berlin last night. I knew from my unhappy feeling & the noise of the bombers beneath the clear stars that we were up to it again. Revised book all day & got it finally finished, but very late because the expected Alert sounded at 9 p.m. followed by a very noisy raid which lasted till nearly 10.30.

Lovely day; had a longish walk in Battersea Park this afternoon. But one can't enjoy lovely weather any more than one could in the last War. Then it meant huge infantry offensives; to-day it means the annihilation of great cities by ourselves.

Saturday January 22nd

Another very noisy raid — the heaviest for about a year & noisier than the one I was caught in on Oct. 7th. This one occurred in the early morning, at 4.30 a.m. At the height of the gunfire came three loud crashes, so close that we didn't hear the scream of the bomb. Shirley & Marian were very good; the latter is a miracle at her age.

This morning we learnt that 3 time-bombs had fallen in Radnor Walk off Flood St. & are lying there unexploded! 90 planes tried to get into London but only 30 got through the barrage, in the 2 raids. The last equally large attack, accord. to to-night's *Evening Standard*, was a daylight attack last Jan. 20th when only 10 planes reached London.

P.P.U. Council this afternoon; quite peaceful for a change.

Friday January 28th

Twelfth raid on Berlin last night.

Dog poorly all day, looked starved & wouldn't eat. Finally sent for vet who said it was rickety, had a skin disease & would never be strong. She advised me to let her destroy it painlessly. I agreed, & let it go with her straight away, knowing that I could never bear it otherwise, & also that Poppy would try to hold on to it & let it drag on a miserable sick existence. She wept bitterly by herself after I told her, but said, as usual, very little to me.

Saturday January 29th

Thirteenth heavy raid on Berlin last night; day raid to-day on Frankfurt. What is left of that attractive old town?

Worked all day on Anthology, expecting retaliation — which came just before 10 p.m. Noisiest barrage so far, & we could hear the German bombers above manoeuvring to avoid the flak. Shell splinters tinkled down all round like hail. Terrifying & so head-cracking that I had to cover my ears. It was the 701st raid on London! I must have been through about 600. What craziness!

Sunday January 30th

Quiet lovely day — so far not too many bombers about. Nowadays one prays for bad weather. Finished sorting of press-cuttings for Anthology. Rather a headache all day owing to last night's noise.

Shirley found four largish shell splinters in garden & on roof.

Monday January 31st

R.A.F. made their 14th heavy raid on Berlin last night. Another 1,500 tons. *Evening Standard* exults in fact that we have now dropped 21,000 tons on Berlin since the heavy raids began. The people who invented "saturation raids" are nothing but homicidal maniacs who ought to be shut up in a criminal lunatic asylum. Berlin was cut off for 15 hours from the outside world. The papers don't give much detail now of what happens to the population — probably ashamed.

Worked all day at Anthology. Stuart came in in the afternoon; stayed till nearly 10 p.m. G. had a Polish Count to discuss writing of his pamphlets. The Pole is convinced that the Katyn murders were done by the Russians.

Friday February 18th

Noisy night raid; heard great rush of incendiaries. Many fires; one from Kensington direction; biggish one in distance towards Clapham. S. & I went to the top of the house to look after the All Clear.

Saturday February 19th

Went to Harrow to see John; in the tuckshop over tea we had a long talk about different generations & their outlook. He said that last night's raid was the noisiest they had had in Harrow; phosphorus bombs were dropped somewhere near.

Learned that the fire in Clapham direction last night was Tate & Lyle's sugar factory, & the one to the north of us was in Kensington High Street. A bomb fell on the Mews at the back of Ponting's, killing about ten people.

Sunday February 20th

Very bad fire-raid at about 10 p.m.; bombs all over S.W. London & afterwards we were ringed with fires. Shirley dashed off to Chelsea Bridge to watch a tobacco factory burning down opposite Dolphin Square, & from Battersea Bridge I saw the whole horizon to the S.W. red from fires in Hammersmith and Fulham.

Monday February 21st

Shirley had half-term holiday; cycled over to her friends & found Fulham in state of devastation.

Amy decided to take Marian out of London, & I fixed up for them to go to the Kean Seymours till the cottage is available. Means closing the house, & probably removing Shirley from St Paul's & sending her to boarding school. Wrote Mrs Roughton to ask if she could go to them till the cottage is ready. Decided to find a tiny flat for ourselves.

Tuesday February 22nd

Bad raid just as S. & I had got to sleep (about midnight). Terrific noise & gunfire.

Couldn't sleep properly all night after the raid; felt unusually troubled & apprehensive.

Wednesday February 23rd
Learned that Harrow was bombed by incendiaries last night; J.'s House set on fire, also the School tuck-shop, but no casualties. Much abt. it in evening papers, including a large picture of the Harrow boys standing round the bomb canister.

I suppose J.'s danger was the reason for my sleeplessness.

Herbert Morrison at dinner with the Mactaggarts — recognised me immediately — asked me to dance before anyone — referred delicately to our differences of outlook. Took a great fancy to S. & asked her to lunch. Early heavy raid — spent w' Morrison in the doctor's flat.

Thursday February 24th
Learned that raid last night did great damage in Chelsea & Battersea — one bomb on the Guinness Trust Buildings caused hundreds of casualties, & four others destroyed two streets in Battersea. Went to the Albert Bridge Rd to see if I could find & help Mrs Millard. Great wreckage behind the road & some in front; long line of ambulances & rescue lorries all down the street. Eventually found Mrs Millard's daughter sweeping up glass in a partly-wrecked house — suggested that Mrs M. came to see me & they could sleep at our house if they wished. Went on to the Harrisons & found them almost in the same state; Ruth Harrison had been sweeping up glass for hours.

Another early evening raid — not so bad yesterday — again spent in doctor's flat.

Friday February 25th
John rang up this morning in response to a letter from me, to say that he was all right & had been in the shelter during the raid. (We purposely had not rung up as we knew they would have more than enough to do.)

Tuesday March 7th
Shirley up in town for day; met her at King's Cross & took her to the Home Office for her lunch with Herbert Morrison (who said later that he hoped he hadn't spoilt S. but she did so attract him!). S. said she didn't like "wire-pulling", but I assured her that it wasn't wire-pulling if she met a Cabinet Minister unexpectedly & he took a fancy to her! She was anyhow more interested in her little collie puppy which I purchased for her from the Chelsea pet shop immediately after the luncheon.

Friday March 10th
Press-cuttings from *M. Guardian* & *News Chronicle* indicated that a so-called

"article" of mine in the U.S.A. *Fellowship* entitled "Massacre by Bombing" had caused a real furore in U.S.A. as it was accompanied by a signed statement by 28 Protestant Clergymen & Oswald Garrison Villard condemning "saturation bombing". Apparently $3\frac{1}{2}$ columns of the *N.Y. Times* were given up to it & produced much abuse of me — from which I deduced much bad conscience in U.S.A.; I suspect that this is actually the MS. of *Seed of Chaos* wh. Felix Greene has now received & turned over as I suggested to John Nevin Sayre.

Good work!

Saturday March 11th

Spent afternoon with John at Harrow. Good deal of evidence of the fire-raid in the village; one shop on the hill burnt out. Only the roof of the tuck-shop was damaged, & only one room in the Headmaster's house. J. said he heard the raid all right but didn't see much of the fires as the younger boys were kept in the shelters. We had a long talk about poetry, poets & the drama, sitting mostly in the War Memorial building wh. was warm, as the tuck-shop heating had failed & the restaurant was very cold.

Tuesday March 14th

Wrote Rache, Soc. of Authors & Rubinstein re my book. Visited Helen Mayo to have a tooth stopped; she said I needed to "build up", having lost far too much weight & showing a calcium deficiency. Had tea at Marshall's, bought tonic, returned home & wrote Letter 131 in $1\frac{1}{2}$ hours.

Horrid air raid started at 10.30 p.m. & went on till nearly midnight. Neil from roof reported flares & incendiaries falling all round. We went down to 3rd floor & one bomb fell so close that it shook the flats. After All Clear we saw at least 10 large fires; one big blaze looked like Kensington, another the East End. Thought of John & G. Fires ringed whole city.

Wednesday March 15th

In morning, found Hyde Park peppered with incendiaries all among the crocuses.

Learned that the dramatic Kensington blaze (with the Albert Memorial outlined against the red glow) was, alas! St Mary Abbott's; the steeple is saved but the roof burned out & fell among the pews, gutting the interior. When we went to Sloane Avenue to take possession of our one-room 9th floor flat we discovered that a large bomb had fallen in Sloane Ave. abt. 30 yards from the block, wrecking dozens of small houses on either side & breaking 300 windows in Sloane Ave. Mansions. Stepped through blasted door & found our flat full of broken glass, dust & crockery. Bathroom & kitchen windows broken but sitting-room intact. Mrs Millard tidied it up & we moved our things in.

Thursday March 16th
Said goodbye to Ella & others at 55 Park Lane & moved in to the Sloane Ave. Mansions flat late in day. Felt rotten in day with bad 'flu chill. At 4.30 had interview with Harold Rubinstein about my novel; took some of Leonard Lockhart's letters. Talked for an hour; partly encouraging, partly inconclusive.

Also received letter from Gollancz to say the Anthology was not exactly what he wanted; he had thought in terms of press-cuttings about compassionate *action* in this War only, & less general material re mercy, etc. Decided to leave a day or two before replying.

Went to bed v. depressed in cold flat with broken windows & no central heating. Symbol of this war is a broken window. Sick to death of seeing destruction.

Friday March 17th
Still feeling 'flu-ish after bad night; no Alert but kept on coughing & couldn't sleep. In spite of pains in limbs had to pack; in midst rushed off to Helen Mayo for renewal of stopping to a tooth done Tuesday. She told me again to rest, & no bunkum.

Managed to get most of packing done. Back to Sloane Ave. to find bathroom window mended; dust settling after bomb & block getting to look itself again. Flat quite a cheerful little place wh. faces due south. Felt better. An Alert about 9.30; only brief gunfire in Central London; went down to reinforced room on third floor as top floor very blitzed & draughty. All Clear in abt. ½ hour.

Saturday March 18th
Spent all day doing odd jobs. Corrected Letter 131 proofs & finished packing. Letter from Harold Rubinstein to say he felt "reasonably sure" he wld. be able to advise Macm. to publish book but wants to see me again to discuss L.L. letters. Wrote Rache, & sent C. Catchpool the article by Dorothy Thompson in *Sunday Dispatch* saying that my "Massacre by Bombing" article in *Fellowship* has roused America to fury!

Sunday March 19th
Final jobs at 2 Cheyne Walk. Wrote Victor Gollancz saying I would revise the Anthology, but gently pointing out that he could have been more precise at earlier stage on basis of various "examples" submitted for preliminary judgment.

Monday March 20th   Lyndhurst
Came to Lyndhurst with Amy, Sheila, Marian & G. & Shirley after returning from Cambridge, & took back cottage. Place clean but garden like a rough field.

Tuesday June 6th   Grimsby
Invasion of Europe started early this morning. Heard first rumours from
porter at flats; then G. rang up about 11.0 & confirmed it. No excitement
or demonstrations anywhere. Streets seemed quieter than usual, & almost
hushed, & no one was talking about the invasion even on the bus. Didn't
discuss it with anyone till we had Christina Foyle to lunch at 55 Park Lane
& all listened to the 1 o'clock news. Had to catch 4.5 train from King's
Cross to Grimsby for my Luncheon Club lecture. Station quiet & almost
deserted; blitz ruins more Pompeii-like than ever. Very few trains running
or people travelling. At Grimsby taken for a Famine Relief talk by the
Vicar, who expected Alerts all over the country. One did end our meeting
just before 11.0, but nothing happened, & I talked to the local M.U. in the
lounge of the Yarborough Hotel till it was over.

Wednesday June 7th   Lincoln
Spoke at 10.30 to Grimsby Women's Luncheon Club on "Famous Women
I have Known" (Mrs Roosevelt, Dame Ethel Smyth, W.H.); at 12.45 to
the Rotary Club on "How I Would Shape the Future"; then was taken
home & given tea by a local doctor & his wife, & driven over (since the
train I was going by had been cancelled) to Lincoln by a business friend of
theirs. Spoke in a picture gallery on "Famine Relief" to an audience wh.
Brian McCoulty, the organiser, said was the biggest gathering they had
had for a pacifist subject since the War. Papers selling wildly with news
that invasion is "going according to plan". Went to bed early but woke
about 2 a.m. to hear masses of 'planes going over.

Thursday June 8th   London
Returned to London. Read papers carefully, but truth is at present hard to
discover amid all the official optimism.
     Answered letters all afternoon & then had early supper with Mother
before going to speak at a Congregational Church in Junction Rd,
Highgate, on "The Shape of the Future".
     Papers all commenting on failure of the Luftwaffe to attack the huge
invasion fleets spread out between the I.o.W. & Cherbourg Peninsula wh.
at Lyndhurst we have seen gathering for so long.

Tuesday June 13th
Two Alerts during early hours of this morning. Some gunfire bursts near
flat; G. & I went down from the top the first time but not the second. Later
we heard that a Nazi plane was brought down in the East End of London,
& knocked over about a hundred houses in the process.
     Spoke to a lunch-hour meeting on Famine Relief at Friends' House &
went on to take the chair at our Food Relief Campaign Committee. Long
discussion on possible effects of the Second Front on Food Relief work.

Wednesday June 14th
Met Shirley, Mrs Roughton & Rosemary at the Haymarket Theatre to see
the Jooss Ballet — member of which stayed at the Roughton home while
rehearsing. Much impressed by the concluding Ballet, "The Green
Table", showing failure of talks by L. of N. statesmen & the outbreak of
war in which death — a sinister green figure — takes control, carrying
away soldiers, their women, & finally even the bowler-hatted profiteer. It
was much applauded despite its keen comment on the present situation.
Afterwards G. met us at the theatre door, & we all had tea at Stewart's
before putting Mrs Roughton & the children into a taxi for Liverpool St.
Baba though tousled looked pretty. I gave her 2/6 to get her hair cut.

Thursday June 15th   Lyndhurst
Most of day spent packing & shopping; returned to Lyndhurst by 5.30
train; no crowd.
    Night full of noise of distant guns, & far away horizon seemed to be
periodically illuminated as though by distant sheet lightning.

Friday June 16th
Raids by pilotless 'planes began last night over "Southern England" (no
further indication of location to be given for fear of helping Nazis).
Everyone talking about the appearance at last of this "Secret Weapon" —
which makes nonsense of John Gordon's statement in last Sunday's *Express*
that the majority of people in this country would probably never hear an
Alert again!!
    At 9.0 heard Herbert Morrison's explanation re 'planes given by B.B.C.
A good many casualties & some damage of a sporadic kind have been
caused by the attacks.
    Wireless said nearly 4,000 Americans killed in France since Invasion
day.

Saturday June 17th
Letter from Mother said Alerts started at 11.45 p.m. Thursday night &
went on all night & next morning! She had gone shopping directly after the
All Clear but the Alert began again before she got back. She did not report
any damage in or near Chelsea. German commentary gloated over
keeping Londoners in shelters for "16 hours" ("the longest raid of the
War").
    Most of working time spent on galley-proofs of *Account Rendered*.

Sunday June 18th
Three Alerts here last night, at 11.30 p.m., about 1.30 a.m., & at 5 a.m.
Final All Clear in broad daylight. Beginning raid was noisy; in fact the
night seemed to be full of strange noises before it was dark. The 9 a.m.
news said last night "P-planes" were again over "Southern England", &

that scientists were going to confer on methods of shooting them down before they reach "built-up" areas. On European news Germans stated to have described crowds going to Wembley & the Derby as a "mass evacuation of London"!

When the papers came they stated that the P-plane raids actually started on "Tuesday morning", which explains the two short Alerts.

Monday June 19th

Large German army cut off in Cherbourg Peninsula, & battle for Cherbourg beginning. Three sirens here during night; last about 7.0, followed by a huge distant bump which various villagers later told us was a P-plane crashing near Wellow, north of S'ampton. Paris radio, reported in to-day's papers, said that the robot 'planes were directed specially against Portsmouth, S'ampton & Bristol as well as London. Letter from Corder C. remarked on the "distressing experiences" we must be having in Hampshire. One robot crashed on a church during morning service yesterday & killed many people. (Later, known to be the Guards' Chapel, Wellington Barracks.) Another short Alert at about 9 this evening. Corrected proofs of novel most of day, but G. & I went for a walk after tea.

Tuesday June 20th

Letters from Mother saying robot 'planes still very active over London, though nothing actually in Chelsea yet. Evening wireless announced that Nazis had said they had enough P-planes for 14 days & would then try something else. According to them, London is in ruins & the whole South Coast covered by a pall of smoke. It was a hot sunny day though very windy & we walked up to the highest point of the Forest at Emery Down to see the Isle of Wight basking serenely in evening sunshine, & looking clearer & more peaceful than usual! Wrote Letter 138, on the invasion, to the thumping of distant guns or bombs — perhaps our bombs on P-plane installations south of the Pas de Calais which the 9 p.m. wireless reported. Actually no Alert last night. Fight for Cherbourg still going on.

Wednesday June 21st

Cherbourg Peninsula nearly encircled by the Americans; thousands of German troops hemmed into Cherbourg itself. Robot 'plane attacks going on & causing many casualties despite attempts to shoot them into sea or country by fast fighters. Large number of "by enemy action" casualties in The Times wh. is usually only abt. 1 per cent of the total.

Thursday June 22nd

Lovely day — almost as beautiful, except for wind, as the one when Germany actually attacked Russia. I was staying with the Rothensteins, & we actually believed our raids were over — as, for a time, they were. More "enemy action" casualties in Times, including one at Kenton, wh. is near

Harrow & increases my anxiety about John. Not a line from him since I got off his drawings to him last Friday. Letter from Corder C. decribes life in London as "unpleasant", which seems an understatement cf. with descriptions in other letters. Papers report another 2,000-ton raid on Berlin yesterday; war has become a complete insanity; both sides now are committed to retaliation, endless & idiotic.

4 sirens during night & early morning.

Friday June 23rd   London
Came to London, arriving Waterloo just after 12.0 — two hours after part of the station, York Rd & the County Hall got a direct hit from a crashing robot 'plane. Saw no signs of this but soon heard the robots, as it was an ideal day for them, with heavy clouds. They sound like a mixture of an angry bee & a broken-down tug on the Thames, wh. keeps you in suspense as it gradually nears. The engine stops — a light flashes, & someone is "for" it; the explosion follows immediately, causing its own cloud of smoke — but there is no smoke-pall over London. Again not much sleep amid the intermittent explosions.

Saturday June 24th
John rang up this morning, but was very reticent in reply to my questions. A letter to G. picked up later from Mother's flat said that they are spending the nights in the shelter & diving under desks by day when the robots come over. J. told G. not to tell me — wh. knowing me better he promptly did. I wrote later to tell John that it was suspense about those I loved, rather than danger for them, which got me down — & to Shirley explaining that the War had settled that she must go to boarding school, as work is impossible in town. Robots actually kept off all day as bright sun & cloudless sky must have made them easy to detect. Managed to get all my proofs finished, & sent off the final English & third bundle [of] American sets. An Alert soon after midnight lasted till after 6.0; explosions rather worse than night before.

Sunday June 25th   Doncaster
One robot said to have fallen on Victoria Stn.; this must have been the nearest of the three near crashes. Went to King's Cross to get the 11.0 train for my three lectures at Doncaster — to find it jammed full, mostly with families of small children. I was there an hour beforehand but couldn't get a seat & was turned back — so had to telegraph to cancel this evening's lecture & make up my mind to get the evening train. Used interval to revise my pamphlet for the Bombing Restriction Committee, bringing in the robots. Finally got a corner seat in the 6 p.m. train by being there $2\frac{1}{4}$ hours beforehand. It was almost as crowded as the morning one.

Monday June 26th
Spoke to Doncaster Rotary Club in morning (small luncheon group) &

Famine Relief meeting in evening. Should have had a third meeting at Friends' House last night but a substitute speaker was found.

Much enjoyed the pleasant rest of having breakfast in bed & reading Charles Morgan's *The House of Macmillan*.

Tuesday June 27th　　*London*

Returned to Euston to find pouring rain & London in the throes of its sixth Alert since dawn. Went to the flats & changed; got to Whitefield's Tabernacle where I was taking the Chair, without an Alert, but one went just after I arrived. (The second of the F.o.R. meetings on "Towards a Christian Peace".) Both the German speakers (a Pastor & a Quaker relief worker) turned up & I opened the meeting. The Alert continued for an hour or more & occasional doodlebug sounds & distant crashes made me hope I didn't appear as scared as I felt. All Clear came just before the questions; second Alert went just at end of meeting. Got safely to Dorchester to sound of bomb chasing me across Park, & dined there with G. to celebrate our 19th wedding anniversary.

Wednesday June 28th

Went on to Lincoln's Inn to see Mr Cash about the Codicil to my Will leaving £750 to Ruth & £250 to George Brett in return for their care of the children.

Doodlebugs aggressive again; Alert sounded just as I had fininshed & two went noisily over.

Friday June 30th

One of the worst flying bomb days we have yet had, & of course we had chosen to have John over from Harrow as it was the Training Corps day from which he is free. When we had lunched & took the train to Piccadilly we emerged from the Tube to find the bottom of Regent St. all over glass from a bomb wh. had just fallen on the Regent Palace. We joined G. at the Academy with bombs buzzing over us all the time; I didn't feel at all happy under the glass-roofed rooms at Burlington House, which was not unnaturally very empty. Dropped in at the Indian Exhibition & then had tea at the Dorchester, where a huge crash from a bomb on Victoria shook the Hotel. After tea took a taxi to Mother's flat so that she could see John; we had only been there a few minutes when we heard a doodlebug making straight for us; the engine cut out just above us & we rushed into the passage as the bomb screamed down. It shook the whole place & gave us all a shock but nothing was broken in the flat. We went out to see whether our house was still there & found everything covered with smoke & dust & crowds rushing down to the Embankment. Bomb had fallen just opposite on the other side of the river by the Hovis building but house seemed all right. Hurried John back to S. Ken. & put him on the train for Harrow.

Saturday July 1st   Lyndhurst
Returned to Lyndhurst by 3.30 train. Huge crowd in the subway at Waterloo, & we were near the back of it. Managed to get on to the train but carriage & corridors were already full. Someone offered me a square inch of space but G. had to stand all the way down.

28th anniversary of the Battle of the Somme & Edward getting wounded.

Friday August 4th
Thirtieth anniversary of Aug. 4th, 1914 (the Second Thirty Years' War).

Wednesday August 9th   London
Up to town with G. to pack up best antiques & papers for removers to-morrow. In afternoon met Bombing Restriction Committee at Maurice Rowntree's house; only Corder Catchpool & Jevons there. V. hot; Maurice R. sitting [at] tea in shirt sleeves with his daughter when we left; cordial & friendly as usual. Helped G. at house sort & arrange furniture. Found large crack had developed in front of nursery wall, & the two window frames (one of which was blown out in April 1941) were both loose again.

Quiet night; short Alert abt. 4 a.m.

Thursday August 10th   Lyndhurst
Spent morning on furniture; Southampton removers duly turned up, & as day was unusually free from flying bombs we made good progress. Left G. to finish up with men, & went to 6 Endsleigh St. to take chair for Food Relief Campaign.

Tuesday August 22nd   London
Got through letters in morning & went up to town by 1.56 to see Mother off to Wales. Evening papers reported Americans racing beyond Paris. Alert went at 4.35. Three loud flying bombs came zooming over in quick succession; put pillow over head & bolster over rest of me, but they went over & I only heard one of them crash in the distance.

Wednesday August 23rd
Breakfasted at 6.0; All Clear went during breakfast. Got to Paddington 7.30 to find train didn't come in till 8.30. Another Alert, followed by immediate danger signal & zooming doodlebug; second danger signal shortly after. Finally with help of a foreman porter got Mother on to train for Carmarthen. Had second breakfast at Paddington Hotel & heard third danger signal. Took Underground to Bond St.; All Clear went while in Tube. Bought grey dress & red & blue woollen coat at Marshall's.

Returned to flat & put through several telephone calls. Learned from Roy Walker that at the P.P.U. Summer School at Spicelands Maurice Rowntree fell from flight of steps in black-out, fractured his skull & died soon after; bitter irony after being in London throughout the wartime raids. Roy also told me that Canon Raven's wife had just died suddenly too.

Went up to my study at Cheyne Walk to get a book & found half the ceiling down on the top of my books & furniture; chair knocked over & door almost unopenable. One of to-day's early bombs must have brought it down.

Thursday August 24th   Lyndhurst

French patriots have driven out Germans & liberated Paris. Romania has quit the War & accepted an Armistice with the Allies; Bulgaria is suing for terms. In France the forward American divisions are only 125 miles from the German frontier; in the North they are surging towards Rouen & the Pas de Calais. To-day's papers like last night's evening paper said that the air yesterday was "alive" with flying bombs, presumably sent before Germans vacate sites. Except for this, it is like 1918 again. G., indifferent to bombs, went up to town till Saturday. Page-proofs of *Account Rendered* began to arrive.

Friday August 25th

News much the same as yesterday; general progress. Some fighting by Germans in Paris. News of continued heavy fly-bomb attacks makes me anxious about G.

In afternoon took J. & S. to Southampton to buy shoes & other school clothes. I still find it difficult to find my way about the grass-grown ruins of Above Bar, covered with willow herb & other weeds. The wreckage of Plummer's store carries the notice "Plummer's Fashion Centre"!

Long talk with children at sunset under the trees opposite the cottage, about people & character.

Sunday August 27th

Hillmans over from B'mouth for the day; Pamela now quite a young woman, with painted lips, very mature for her age & an utter contrast with Shirley — who was on the defensive as usual. Very hot; between lunch & tea we sat mostly in the shade under the forest trees. Rather heavy going, as doing nothing always is.

Sunday papers speculating why V2 weapon has not been used yet. Surmise that the Nazis may be thinking better of it as apparently some examples were ready a week ago.

Monday August 28th

Took J. & S. as far as Reading for their fortnight at Moreton-in-Marsh.

S.'s bag fell from the rack on to my head at the outset of the journey nearly stunning me for a moment — which made the children annoyed with themselves & hence unresponsive to me. Papers which I read on journey full of accounts of the Paris shooting which accompanied de Gaulle's visit.

Tuesday August 29th
Comparative lull for moment in war after spectacular advance of British & Canadians towards the Seine N.E. of Paris — towards the "rocket coast". Some V1 & a few (unfinished) V2 sites already captured.

Poured with rain all day, which will further hold up the advance; not a 'plane in the sky.

Wednesday August 30th
Dispute between Anglo-Americans & Russians over supplies to Warsaw.

Large spate of letters — many abusive — followed mine in *Sunday Express* last Sunday on being willing to continue rations if this would save Europe's children.

Thursday August 31st
Rouen given up by Germans, who are now slowly being encircled on fly-bomb coast. (Brit. newspapers predict no respite; say that "V2 can be operated from inside Germany".) Battle moving into area of old familiar names — Amiens, Abbeville, Rheims. *Evening Standard* military correspondent (Oliver Stewart) discussing still more massive bombing of Germany from nearer bases.

Friday September 1st
Corrected page proofs of book most of day. British & Americans racing towards Belgium & Germany. Dieppe taken without a fight; Amiens occupied.

G. returned from London this evening to say he had hardly an Alert & no bombs of which he was conscious while in town.

Letters from a Belgian lady & a German girl who said she was one of the starved children of the last War, thanking me for the *Sunday Express* letter.

Weather cold & showery. Noise of aeroplanes over this area much diminished.

Saturday September 2nd
Very large mail, including one from Gollancz who says that the Anthology still is not quite what he wants to publish. Gives various reasons & in the end suggests that he & his "associates" should work on it themselves. G. & I thought this a good idea, as I really don't want to spend any more time & money on it, & to do it effectively is too big an undertaking for one person.

Corrected proofs of Letter 143. *Peace News* filled with tributes to Maurice Rowntree; also announces the death of Dorothy Evans (who apparently had cancer). I wrote & sent in a tribute to her; also replied to a letter yesterday from John Nevin Sayre, & mentioned the value of an invitation to lecture from America. Allies still swiftly advancing closer to Belgian & German frontiers.

Sunday September 3rd

The fifth anniversary of the outbreak of this War — & the first time we have been at the cottage for it since 1939. I wished the children were here, as they were then (though G. wasn't, but in Manchester). Sunday papers reported that American troops are said to have crossed the German frontier; also announced American estimates of the War in Europe as only lasting 3 or 4 more weeks.

Monday September 4th

Evening papers reported Brussels entered by British Second Army at 2 p.m. yesterday afternoon. Patton's (American) Army approaching German frontier by way of Nancy & Metz. *News Chronicle* reports "Battle of flying bomb won". "V2" probably too unfinished to be used, & the pick-a-back 'planes (2 of which crashed on Britain on Saturday) unlikely to be used on any large scale, being too clumsy.

Letter from John saying Shirley likes being at Compton Scorpion Manor but doesn't mention himself so I suspect he is bored. It is anyhow wretched weather for farming; it poured in torrents all to-day.

Tuesday September 5th

Wireless & also morning papers report the Allies 12 miles over the Dutch frontier, as far as Breda. *News Chronicle* reporter says that flying-bomb sites between the Somme & the Scheldt can be "written off" & A. J. Cummings, in an article on "Wonderful London", says that London has been "liberated" by the British & Canadian immobilisation of these sites. (His comment that London has been the most "viciously" attacked of all great cities is hardly true when I think of what we have done to Berlin etc., though it has been attacked most frequently.) I just can't get used to the idea of the Germans being no longer on our doorstep, or believe that I have reached the end of sleeping in the many odd basements, shelters, corridors etc. where I have spent nights during the War. Was the Lyndhurst siren when I got back from London on Aug. 23rd (that bad day of bombs) the last I shall hear?

Wednesday September 6th

Further advances into Holland, almost as far as Rotterdam. Papers report that, owing to a mistaken report from a doubtless over-excited Brussels radio station, London was yesterday filled with rumours that the Germans had capitulated. People stood each other drinks in pubs, restaurants etc. This recalls the so-called "false Armistice" — the premature announcement in U.S.A. on Nov. 7th 1918 which set all New York rejoicing. Certainly a remarkable silence prevails about what is happening in Germany & where the American armies are.

Corrected proofs all day — tho' it was difficult to concentrate on anything — & after tea went for walk in the Forest. Three squadrons of returning bombers went over the trees. There has been more air activity to-day than recently — obviously due to attacks on Channel ports still holding out. G. at Liverpool discussing possible candidature at St Helens, Lancs.

Thursday September 7th
Papers announce that the black-out will be partially lifted in most areas (more caution in London & the Southern Counties but some more light even here) when the daylight changes on Sept. 17th. Also the Home Guard is to be disbanded except for those who still wish to serve voluntarily. These two announcements certainly mean that the end of Germany's resistance is near. Herbert Morrison made a speech yesterday thanking London & the "Bomb Alleys" of Southern England for their endurance. I wrote Mother that she could come back from Wales on Sept. 18th as she wishes. The difficulty is going to be to learn how to relax at night again — after 4 years of listening & tension.

Friday September 8th   London
Came up to town; train very late. Went to Endsleigh St. for long Food Relief Committee at which on basis of a draft by Roy Walker we thrashed out future policy for ourselves & the Union as a whole owing to the swift changes in the military situation. Got home under lowering rainy clouds wh. looked like thunder, & was just up in the flat when two terrific explosions occurred, shaking the whole building. Sounded like a large gun or time bomb going over but I never got an explanation.

Sunday September 10th
Fighting still before German frontier. *Observer* predicts piecemeal end to War — not sudden as last time.

Long policy discussion at P.P.U. Council; very interesting, & satisfactorily equable. Roy's excellent Food Relief report, which I introduced, initiated it. P.P.U. Council preceded by moving little service for Maurice & Dorothy.

Wednesday October 4th   Coleford, Gloucestershire
Went to The Coombs, for a fortnight's rest & treatment.

Sunday October 8th
Wendell Willkie's death in New York this morning announced by lunch-

time wireless — another blow for G. He was only 52 & in full vigour of middle-age.

Monday October 9th
Mrs Elliot away & Mr Elliot gave me osteopathy. Irritating man who thinks no one's work is worth getting tired over.

After treatment walked across fields to a forest walk at the beginning of the road to Symonds Yat. The trees here are different from the New Forest. There are few beeches or birches, but many holm-oaks, Spanish chestnuts, sycamores, oaks, & planes.

One almost forgets the War here — but the evening wireless had news of the first "blueprint" for a new League of Nations — so-called!

Tuesday October 10th
Visited Tintern Abbey; bus to Chepstow (fine old castle on the Wye but otherwise an ugly town) & thence by same bus to Tintern. The Abbey & its surroundings are really exquisite; it is the first ruin that has not disappointed me. The Wye curves almost in a circle round the lovely valley village circled with wooded hills showing autumn tints, & as you turn away from it towards Chepstow you see the Abbey perfect against (to-day) a hazy rich background of wooded hill above the river. Just to the right of the Abbey was part of a wall covered with scarlet ampelopsis — a perfect touch. The Abbey — tall, grey, slender, the stone tracery of its East & rose windows still perfect, with a carpet of green grass & green plants springing from its high stones — is like a perfect anthem, an aspiring oratorio.

The final months of 1944 were depressing, however: Gordon Catlin lost his bid to stand as Labour candidate at St Helens in the coming General Election, and Vera Brittain's Account Rendered, *published in New York to "tendentious reviews" in November, sold badly.*

1945

Monday February 26th   London
Caught the 1.56 train to town. I was alone all evening & got my packing sorted out into the lecture clothes & others needed in town. No "incidents"; quiet night.

Tuesday February 27th
A domestic day; went to Marshall's & bought the blue & red plaid country coat which Mother saw, & took black silk dress to Baird Lewis to be renovated. Had a quick & early lunch at Marshall's & then went to Barker's to have hair permed. Got away about 5.30 & walked down High Street to see for the first time what I had dreaded seeing — the immense damage done by a flying bomb last summer to the Earl's Ct. Rd corner of the High Street, Troy Court, & the long-loved entrance to Holland Walk. It fell on the Lyons Restaurant at lunch-time & killed many people. The clearance had left in full view the ruins of Our Lady of Victories, bombed in 1940, making the whole scene peculiarly desolate.

Wednesday February 28th
Called at Foyle's lecture agency office & discussed the details of my little lecture tour with Maurice Frost. (He said that one or two engaging organisations which began by displaying great enthusiasm had found later "circumstances" which prevented them from having me — presumably [because of] my pacifist views.) Went on to 6 Endsleigh Street where I met Patrick Figgis who took me out to lunch — to discuss Stuart, as I had half expected. I tried hard to convince him that S.M. & his family *must* be saved by the P.P.U. giving Stuart a job again; that S.M. was suffering deterioration from under-employment.

Long talk on 'phone to Corder Catchpool, who has not been well; agreed to sign cables (with Jevons & Belden) to Roosevelt & Churchill protesting about the mass bombing of Berlin.

Thursday March 1st
In afternoon went to Harrow to see John. He seemed pleased with the 14 tubes of water-colours that I gave him. As always at school, his manners were better than they are at home. As I walked down the hill I

saw three large squadrons of bombers flying across the sunset — going out, I suppose, for more obliteration raids on Germany.

Friday March 2nd
Gave luncheon lecture at Kingsway Hall for National Peace Council on "Grounds for Hope" (analysis of present situation & hopeful factors, such as they are). Lunched first with Gerald Bailey at Holborn Restaurant. He told me that for the first time *The Times* had not put this lecture in their (quite short) list of the day's announcements, tho' they had advertised other less well-known speakers! Went on to American Embassy & started usual process for the renewal of my own & the children's re-entry permits. Used evening to catch up on correspondence. One very loud rocket so startled me just as I was making the cocoa that I nearly dropped the kettle; shook the flat.

Saturday March 3rd   Saffron Walden
Gollancz contract arrived for *Above All Nations*; generous & satisfactory. Took afternoon train to Saffron Walden for lecture at Friends' School. Hideous & depressing Blitz ruins half across Essex, showing different years, from the water-filled bomb holes covered with green scum of 1940, to the raw debris from flying bombs & rockets. (Several rockets last night; also an Alert & a flying bomb about 3 a.m.)

Sunday March 4th   Colchester
Returned to Liverpool St. for 4.0 train to Colchester. Damage between L'pl St. & Chelmsford even worse than that yesterday. At Colchester spoke at Service at a Congregational Church & answered questions in an upper room afterwards. The Alert went just before I finished. Piloted 'planes came in over the town, guns & searchlights on coast; wardens running round telling people to put up black-out. All Clear after about an hour.

Monday March 5th   London
Americans according to papers reaching banks of Rhine for many miles. Piloted plane raids reported over both South & North. Just after I got back Maurice Frost rang me up to say that Christy's chief assistant (the pleasant middle-aged woman who took me [to] Foyle's last Wednesday) was killed by a V2 rocket at her home on Saturday morning (I think I heard the bomb). The office is consequently in distress & chaos, & they don't know whether any further bookings will be made or not. Packed feeling much depressed by this & hating to leave G., Mother & John in the London area for so many nights.

Tuesday March 6th   Holt
Six or seven rockets during night — one very loud, with a huge flash due

south. No sirens during darkness. Got up at 7.0 & caught 10.0 train from Liverpool St. to Holt, Norfolk, for lecture at Gresham's School. Papers all full of descriptions of the American entry into Cologne, showing that the city we knew is a heap of ruins, tho' the Cathedral spires look unchanged & the Cathedral itself is repairable. The Cathedral Square, the museums & medieval buildings, the wide ring streets in the outskirts — all are gone . . .

Thursday March 22nd   Shrewsbury
Spoke Shrewsbury for N.P.C. in Council Chamber. Unexpectedly good meeting.

Saturday March 24th   Bangor
Spoke in a large chapel in Bangor; they said [I] had the biggest audience of the war (P.P.U. & F.o.R.).

Monday March 26th   Lyndhurst
Several rockets during night; two at 10.30 & 11.30, shortly after I got into the flat from Bangor. Also a flying bomb Alert.

Went down to Lyndhurst for Easter. Another rocket fell heavily (I was told by a naval man in the train that it was near Euston, where he had just been) as I was waiting at Waterloo. G. who came with me to help me with my luggage, said it was only an engine, but I knew better.

Tuesday April 3rd   London
No bombs. Strange sense of relief, like convalescence after an illness; found myself still listening, & not really believing that the British & Canadians turning the Germans out of Holland have cut the supply of V-bombs off.

Thursday April 5th
G. left to get a boat from Glasgow for the San Francisco Conference. Went as Special Correspondent of *Cavalcade* & a group of Indian papers. Whole trainload of Special Correspondents went off in very dirty train with no First-class carriages & no food. G. shared a compartment with Claude Cockburn of *The Week* & the *Daily Worker*.

Wednesday April 11th
Saw Peter Fraser, Prime Minister of New Zealand, on behalf of the C.B.C.O., about conscientious objectors in N.Z. Found him more interested apparently in my books than in C.O.s. I came to the conclusion after talking to him that he couldn't (given his agreeable temperament) do much more until opinion in N.Z. changed, & suggested to Joe Brayshaw, who met me outside, that they should try to work on that, by letters to the N.Z. Press & the Returned Servicemen's Association.

Friday April 13th   Lyndhurst
It was announced at midnight that yesterday afternoon President Roosevelt died at Warm Springs, Georgia, from cerebral haemorrhage. Thought all day of my talk with him at the White House in December 1937 &, despite the altercations over bombing, felt I had lost a personal friend. Above all I was stunned with dismay, wondering what would happen to the future organisation. Sent a cable to Eleanor Roosevelt. Seems an ironic end — like Lincoln's — when the victory he worked for is almost here & both armies are approaching Berlin.

Saturday April 14th
Huge notice of Roosevelt in *The Times* & other papers. Incongruously hot lovely day, like June. All the leaves & blossoms coming out. Wrote an article on Roosevelt for *P.N.* Couldn't stop thinking about him all day.

Friday April 20th
Went into Southampton. Had early lunch & hoped to see news-reel of Franklin Roosevelt's life which the children saw on Tuesday, but found it was already changed for pictures of the Memorial Service at St Paul's. But I did see the most terrible pictures of devastation in Germany — the Ruhr, & Hanover, like a vast spreading nightmare. How do the Germans endure?

Got home to find that G.'s cable saying "Arrived safely" & asking about a Yorkshire constituency had come just after we left. Great relief.

Both armies (East & West) approaching suburbs of Berlin.

Thursday April 26th   London
Up to town for last of J.'s holidays. On S'ampton bookstall saw *Cavalcade* with G.'s first dispatch from San Francisco; got several copies. At Waterloo, large pile of *Above All Nations* on bookstall.

Friday April 27th
Link-up of American & Russian armies at Torgau announced on 6 o'clock news. At San Francisco dispute going on about Chairmanship of Conference, but Polish question regarded as "not on the agenda", wh. is concerned solely with making of a world-peace organisation.

Dittmar, famous Berlin radio commentator, has given himself up to the Americans. Goering, with his family & valuables worth £5,000,000, has fled by air from Germany to an "unknown destination". Mussolini has been captured trying to cross the Swiss frontier. Amid these enormous events it seems almost extraordinary that ordinary daily life goes on! John returned to Harrow this afternoon.

Saturday April 28th
Letter from Sheila Hodges said that *Above All Nations* had had an advance

sale of 45,000 copies! Had Lady Mayer to lunch at Euston Hotel to discuss the record of pacifism that she wants to write. Took her to opening session of the P.P.U. Ann. Gen. Meeting. *Times* announced execution of Mussolini by Italian partisans. Very cold; sharp snow showers.

Sunday April 29th
Sunday papers appeared with huge headlines, "Germany Surrenders", meaning that Himmler through Count Bernadotte is said to have offered "unconditional surrender" to U.S. & Britain only. In afternoon spoke at P.P.U. A.G.M. on "Cease Fire — & Then" in packed Friends' House Great Hall, to about 1,000 people. Corder Catchpool in Chair. In late evening answered letters & then sat up till midnight news. No more about Germany's surrender but heard grisly details of Mussolini's execution & the exhibition of [his body] in Milan. My chief reaction was concern that — having worked to return sensitivity — I didn't react more.

Monday April 30th   Lyndhurst
Talked to Barbara Duncan-Harris about going to Europe to meet "opposite numbers". She thinks Sweden the only hope & will do what she can abt. it. Lunched at Friends' House [with] a group of key pacifists. Evening papers reported rumours of all kinds abt. Himmler, Bernadotte, & their reported exchanges; also a rumour that Hitler has died raving mad in Berlin, where the fighting between Nazis & Red Army continues.

Tuesday May 1st
This morning's papers contained horrible photographs of Mussolini and his young mistress hanging upside down from the top of a garage in a Milan Square. Had to write letters all day; in one to Alex Wood & others, suggested that pacifist groups shd. visit the concentration camps. A very nice letter abt. *Above All Nations* from Liddell Hart; sent copy to Gollancz.

   Went into Lyndhurst with letters to get *Evening Standard* but nothing new abt. negotiations. Churchill in House said he would announce end of war when it came. But at 10.30 Mrs Burdett rang me to say programme had been interrupted to announce death of Hitler & appointment of Admiral Doenitz as his successor. Heard this at midnight. Three world-figures gone in 3 weeks is too much to take in.

Wednesday May 2nd
Long obituary notices of Hitler in all the papers, including *The Times*, which evidently accepts his death as a fact. *Evening Standard* continues to suggest, as on Monday, that he probably died several days ago from a stroke due to injuries received in the bomb attack on his headquarters last July. General impression seems to be that split between Doenitz and

Himmler — the one wanting to fight on & the other to surrender — is likely to prolong a little the final stage of the War.

Cable this afternoon from G. in San Francisco saying he has hopes of a 'plane to get him back in time for the Blackpool L.P. Conference. The nine o'clock news (& before) reported the unconditional surrender of the German troops (1 million) in Italy & Western Austria to Field-Marshal Alexander (the end of Burnett's campaign; Amy & I listened in the kitchen to an eye-witness description of the surrender ceremony). Wireless also gave an interesting (& most friendly!) talk between the commentator Dittmar & his captors.

Thursday May 3rd
Fall of Berlin to the Russians yesterday afternoon announced on last night's midnight news. News, & also of surrender in Italy, confirmed in morning papers. Went in to S'ampton with Amy (amid pouring rain) to see news in cinema giving the atrocity pictures of the concentration camps. Saw also Roosevelt's burial. Pictures of camps (as horrible as I expected, largely pictures of living skeletons & disintegrating bodies) accompanied by a hate-arousing talk wh. omits to point out that half victims in camps (& all before 1939) were Germans; & that camps, & Gestapo, wouldn't have existed if opposition to Hitler had not been tremendous. Russians now in Wilhelmstrasse, the Whitehall of Berlin, say that Hitler & Goebbels probably committed suicide.

Friday May 4th
Still awaiting end of War — looks as if it may end by progressive disintegration. Nazis trying to escape to Denmark & Norway from Russians. No one knows where Doenitz is. Russians have still found no trace of Hitler or Goebbels in Berlin.

Wrote short article on Hitler for *P.N.* Shirley came back from school for weekend. Weather cold & dull.

On the midnight broadcast came the important news that all the Nazi forces in N.W. Germany, Denmark, & Holland have surrendered unconditionally to Montgomery.

Saturday May 5th   London
More details about the second German surrender to the British in the morning papers. Saw news-film at Waterloo (including the concentration camp atrocities twice over), then got to Mother by tea-time. Had early supper & went to Labour Party "Social" at Friends' House. Dropped in at Caxton Hall on way home for a meeting of the Dorothy Evans Memorial Committee & made a short speech. No special further news in evening papers except that Germans are continuing the fight only v. Russia.

Sunday May 6th

No further news of total German surrender but 9 o'clock news said that Churchill would broadcast on Thursday (5th anniversary as Premier) & probably would have announced "V.E. Day" before. This morning spoke at the Royal Cinema in Edgware Rd before a showing of the *South Riding* film by the D. Evans Memorial Committee; Sybil Morrison in Chair; Mrs Pethick Lawrence also spoke.

Monday May 7th

Morning papers made it clear that end of war was likely to come today so I decided to stay in town till the end of the "V" holidays. Lunched with Josefine von Reitzenstein at the Rembrandt & told her it was appropriate that she & I spend the day together. Previously cabled G. from Piccadilly saying I wished he was here. After lunch, owing to a persistent rumour that the announcement for wh. everyone was waiting wld. be made at 3 p.m., Josefine von R. & I drifted to Westminster where an expectant crowd was gathering. In early afternoon evening papers came out saying "Germany Surrenders", but nothing happened in Whitehall & finally a policeman said nothing wld. be said to-day. So J. von R. & I dined together at Sloane Ave. Mans. & went home. Later 9 o'clock news announced Germany's total surrender & said official announcement wld. be made to-morrow at 3 p.m. Flags now everywhere.

Tuesday May 8th

Felt disinclined to hear a "Victory" service so went to the little meeting of the London Mission at Kingsway Hall to hear Donald Soper give a really inspiring address on thanksgiving, penitence and dedication. After lunch again went back to Whitehall determined to end this War near Westminster as I ended the last. Flags now everywhere; 'planes flying over crowds; bells ringing; mounted policemen moving back a throng which grew immense between 2.0 & 3.0; yet sense of anti-climax persisted in contrast with spontaneity of Armistice Day 1918; it was all so formal & "arranged".

At 3.0 Churchill's voice duly announced the end of the War & after silence the crowds cheered. Typically he ended with the words "Advance Britannia!" & introduced no phrase of constructive hope for a better society which renounces war. Caught a glimpse of him standing in his car as he went from Downing St. to the H. of Commons surrounded by cheering crowds, waving his hat, with the usual cigar & self-satisfied expression.

Walked half the way home for tea with Mother, thinking how strange it was that, though this time I have kept (so far) all my private world which last time I had totally lost, not one of them is here, & again I experience the end of a European war half-exasperated & half-saddened by the triviality of her preoccupations in contrast to the immensity of world events.

Dined at Rembrandt with J. von R., talked to her till past 11 p.m., when we walked to Sloane Avenue & looked at partially flood-lit buildings & a display of searchlights half-obscured by a cloudy sky; saw it from the roof of the flat. Left her at S. Kensington station & walked home with the War officially (at 1 minute past midnight) as well as actually over in Europe. Bonfires in St Luke's Churchyard & elsewhere; Chelsea Town Hall floodlit; people in streets, but everything orderly & controlled.

Wednesday May 9th
Spent quiet day & was glad to do so. Wrote & sent off Letter 161. Then dusted dining-room in Cheyne Walk, & wrote more letters.

Thursday May 10th   Lyndhurst
No more sensational news for a change. German submarines starting to surrender, beginning in Weymouth Harbour. Quite an amicable inteview reported between Goering, who has been captured by the American 7th Army, with its General Stack.

Read Gollancz's remarkable & timely pamphlet on "What Buchenwald *Really* Means".

Friday May 11th
Got request for article from *Christian Pacifist* by May 14th, & spent most of day writing it. Very hot; Mrs Mills mowed lawn. Pictures in papers of Keitel signing surrender in Berlin.

Sunday May 13th
Thanksgiving Sunday. Listened in afternoon to the service broadcast from St Paul's Cathedral while out of the kitchen window I watched the intermittent sun on the trees & the shadows of clouds passing over the green, & thought how the European War had ended for me where it began, & on much the same kind of day, & a Sunday. In evening listened to Churchill's speech summing up 5 years of war. He mentioned the more powerful rockets & shells from "multiple long-range artillery" being prepared for London.

Monday May 14th
Quiet day. Much cooler. Letter from Friends' Aliens Council saying that War Office has passed *Above All Nations* for prisoners' camps — so I hope to be able to take advantage of Muriel Lester's offer of £50 to send a good many. Wrote letters & gardened.

Wednesday May 30th   London
Great peace-meeting at Central Hall — huge crowds — 2 overflow meetings & a third overflow in Hyde Park.

Spoke with Joad, Gollancz, Leslie Weatherhead.

As the War ended, Vera Brittain was overwhelmed by an "abysmal fatigue" which, she decided, was not merely war-weariness but the result of her "long struggle against hostility and suspicion . . . I felt as though I had just emerged from a serious illness". So for a second time she went to The Coombs at Coleford for rest and treatment, and there began to write her final novel, Born 1925.

Thursday July 26th
Results of General Election announced; by a silent revolution, Labour is overwhelmingly in power for the first time in History with a majority of approx. 200 over all other parties. *Evening Standard* announced above headline "SOCIALISTS IN", "Britain Swings to the Left & the National Government Goes Out in a Landslide." Listened all day on wireless to the incredible results coming in. Whole Churchill clique defeated except the old man himself. Amid surging feelings of excitement we both felt personally stricken because G. hadn't stood. Bilston where he lost the nomination by 2 votes was won with a majority of 16,000. In evening took Shirley to Transport House, where Herbert Morrison spoke to her; then on to the Central Hall & heard the newly elected London Labour Candidates make 2-minute speeches.

Tuesday August 7th   Lyndhurst
Newspapers announced earth-shaking discovery (equal in probable revolutionary consequences to discovery of steam) of the harnessing of atomic energy (to destruction, of course) & the dropping of the first atomic bomb on Hiroshima in Japan — a city of over 300,000 people who are now probably all killed. It was dropped early yesterday morning.

Wednesday August 15th
V.J. Day. Last night at midnight Attlee broadcast the news of Japan's surrender. One is thankful that the awful slaughter has stopped, but the manner of its ending leaves no such feeling of relief as the end of the War in Europe — because the atomic bomb means that far from terror being over, its possibilities have only just begun. Squarely upon this demoralised generation is laid the awful responsibility of deciding whether the human race is to continue or not.

For me personally, the War ends in the New Forest where it began — 6 years ago all but 19 days. And whereas the last War deprived me of everyone that mattered, this one leaves me with everyone that matters alive, in spite of the air raids & torpedoes that have threatened each one of us. Almost as if the "poor Catherine" fairy tale which I quoted at the beginning of *Testament of Youth* were prophetic — though there is time before that can be proved. The atom bomb is not exactly an encouraging guarantee of happiness or even survival for anyone. But John has just missed the War . . . only just.

Thursday August 16th
V.J. Day 2. Pictures in papers of colossal crowds in town, King & Queen

on balcony etc. etc. Only one cleric — the Dean of St Albans — refuses to allow the Abbey there for thanksgiving on the ground that the war has been ended "by a misuse of power". Maude Royden Shaw — of all people — writing in *The Times* trying to justify the Atom Bomb! I am glad to be out of London — one experience of people rejoicing over their defeated enemies is enough.

Friday August 17th
Lovely hot day. Went on with 3rd chapter of my novel, "Born 1925".
   J. & I went for an evening walk after supper, ending when the half-moon was becoming bright over the moor.

Saturday August 18th
Reassuring mail to-day, indicating Foreign Office support for my Denmark lectures, & much appreciation from the Help Holland Council of my willingness to go to Holland. Also came a statement from Macmillan showing that about $1,550 (approx. £390) is due to me in November from *Account Rendered*. Spent all day answering my big mail; wrote 21 letters.

Sunday August 19th
Wrote letters all morning to Denmark & Sweden, sent lecture list; notified various people about going to 3 countries. Finished chap. 3 of "Born 1925", & went for a walk with John through the Forest after tea. *Account Rendered* advertised in the book page of the *Observer* to come out next Friday.

Monday August 20th
Letter from Myrtle Wright said that invitation from Norway will soon follow those from Denmark & Sweden. Notified Cook's & Foreign Office. Letter from Patrick asked me to be a Director of the new P.P.U. Bookshop, Housmans Ltd. Contract for "Letters to Peace-Lovers" came from Dakers.

Friday August 24th
Account Rendered published. Pre-publication sale of 50,000 copies; edition exhausted.

Vera Brittain had recently received two invitations: from the Netherlands Government to visit Holland in September with a party of writers, to help publicise that country's desperate need for aid; and from Scandinavian branches of the Women's International League for Peace and Freedom, to give a series of lectures in October.

Thursday September 13th   Holland
Bus to Croydon, aeroplane from Croydon, left just before 10.0.

Drove from Eindhoven to Hague, arrived there about 6.30. Went through war-damaged area, saw many bridges down. Attended reception given for us at house of British Ambassador.

Total party consisted of John Marsh, Henrietta Leslie & Dr Schutze, M. Bowen, Godfrey Winn, Olaf Stapledon, & self.

Saturday September 15th

Stopped at Vucht at house of Mrs Timmenga, head of local Underground movement. Then taken to see Vucht Concentration Camp (the most famous in Holland), now full of Dutch collaborators. Saw young children.

Drove to Arnhem, got out & walked to edge of broken bridge & through remains of town.

Sunday September 16th

Saw collection in Rijks-museum of world-famous pictures (Rembrandts, Franz Hals, Vermeers, etc.) hidden during War. Huge crowds, long queues; taken round by Director.

Reception at wealthy household in Amsterdam, opposite canal where many "accidents" happened to Germans. Met many writers, editors, journalists. A Professor from Leiden told me that Prof. Leo Polak of Groningen is dead, & probably his family also.

Monday September 17th

Drove round Hague. Saw devastated area again (one quarter of Hague is damaged); the Festung (walled-in houses concealing ammunition which the R.A.F. were trying to get); houses almost demolished because evacuated, and stripped of all their wood last winter by desperate people in need of fuel; ceilings, floors, staircases etc. all gone; in one house half a staircase was hanging in mid-air; opposite, only the skeleton walls of the houses were left. (This happened espec. to houses of Jews, who were not expected to return.) Then drove to Scheveningen to see Atlantic Wall, a reinforced dyke with dug-outs inside it, guarded by young boys from Underground. Warned to be careful of mines, not yet collected.

On way back stopped outside Queen's present residence, a modest villa called "Sibilla"! Dr Schutze took a photograph & was almost arrested. Then we saw the Queen, a broad figure in voluminous white coat & skirt, informally riding home on a bicycle, followed at short distance by male retainer on another bicycle. Got off & went in; no fuss or ceremony.

After lunch drove to Rotterdam & saw warehouses where goods received from other countries for Holland. Gifts from U.S. & Britain mostly clothes, but saw pile of wooden packing cases containing gifts of food from Sweden & Denmark.

Wandered round shops with Marjorie Bowen. Noticed children again; feet coming out of shoes.

After dinner met two journalists; interviewed by one (all of us) for a National Press Association article. The other told me I was on a list, published a few days ago in the *News Chronicle*, of the first people whom the Gestapo intended to arrest when Nazis invaded England.

On way back from Rotterdam picked up a nurse in uniform who nearly wept when I gave her cocoa, silks, etc.

October
Notes from Sweden

Met two Polish women who had come to Sweden for a rest from Ravensbrück Camp. One, a small elderly woman, arms like sticks, was wife of former Polish Minister at The Hague (for 4 years) & was much interested in what I had to tell of Holland. She had just discovered that her husband is still alive, & was looking forward to going back to Poland; [she] had been arrested in Warsaw for being in the Resistance Movement. Had remarkably reasonable attitude towards the Germans; thought we should not try to repay them in kind — not, she said, out of pity for them, but because to kill was so terribly corrupting, so bad for the killer especially if he was young. She felt no special hatred for the German officials who had imprisoned her because, she said, they had their orders from above, & had no choice about fulfilling orders which damaged them in the fulfilment.

On speaking at the Nobel Institute

Small but attractive hall normally holding about 300 people, with dark furnishings & a raised platform with a tall reading desk. (They put a foot stool behind it for me so that I should be raised above it.)

Spoke on "The Shape of the Future". The hall was absolutely crowded; I don't think I have ever seen so many stand patiently all through a lecture, at the back of the hall stretching right into the vestibule, round the sides, & up the middle aisle. One person at the back even fainted! so great was the crowd.

When I mentioned the appeal for feeding the German children there was a great burst of applause.

Oslo, Norway: Memorial Service to a Woman Resister

Birgid Nisson was a woman of about 42, teacher and student of literature & a journalist. She was part-editor of an underground newspaper; was arrested & taken first to Gruni, the prison for women outside Oslo, & then sent to Ravensbrück. When she finally returned to Sweden she appeared quite well, but in 3 weeks she suddenly went down with a terrible headache, and developed spotted typhus & died. The body was cremated in Sweden & the ashes brought to Oslo.

Memorial service held in the smaller section of a double crematorium, a dome-shaped building with dark green walls painted with frescos. The

place was absolutely crowded with men & women. Just behind the lectern
with its little dark wooden cross stood the small urn covered by the
Norwegian flag. On either side of it were 2 rows of seven candlesticks each,
the only light in the place. Behind it, on a carved wooden chair, sat the
Lutheran priest with his black gown & pleated white ruff. High above the
urn stood a huge tall red standard, the standard of the Labour Party to
which the dead woman had belonged.

The service began with music & then the singing of a hymn, after the
priest had shaken hands with the dead woman's family. Then he read
prayers & gave a short address. Another hymn followed. By this time
many members of the congregation were crying, as it included people
who had been in prison with the dead woman & had previously worked
with her in Oslo. Next came quite a long procession of men & women,
each of whom made short speeches & laid magnificent wreaths one on
top of the other on the urn. They represented various organisations —
e.g. Labour Party, Women's International League & others — about 12
altogether. Myrtle Wright said that the flowers had an almost mystical
significance, & symbolise Norway's worship of nature & of beauty. When
the speeches were over, a funeral dirge was played on the organ, and the
man holding the Labour Party standard dipped it three times towards
the urn.

Sigrid Helliesen Lund told me that these services occur almost daily, as
so many who have been in prisons & concentration camps continue to die
from the after-effects.

Reflections on being a Prominent Name on the Gestapo's List
This list, of British people (approx. 3,000) to be shot [or] imprisoned by
the Gestapo when the Nazis landed in England, was discovered by the
Americans in Berlin & published in British newspapers in mid-September
when I was in Holland.

Finding my name on this list, together with G.'s & [those] of many
prominent pacifists who like myself were under a cloud & almost
"suspects" in 1940, gave me a remarkable experience of catharsis.

(1) It showed that the Nazis understood, far more clearly than those at
home who tried to identify pacifists with Fascists, anti-patriots and pro-
Nazis, the danger to themselves, & to their doctrines, of Christian
pacifists. They realised that those who were ready to resist them by
spiritual, non-violent means were at least as dangerous as those who were
prepared to fight them by military weapons; they understood that the faith
by which we lived was a power inimical to, because precisely the opposite
of, their own doctrines.

(2) It placed me, once & for all, above the further possibility of
suspicion, yet left me with the experience of knowing what being a
"suspect", & humiliated, had meant; of losing prestige & gaining kinship
with the outcasts.

(3) It filled me with an overwhelming sense of gratitude to the fate (or God) which had brought me right to the edge of the abyss, so that I could see what suffering & loss I might have known & then — with the rest of the 3,000 whose names were there for different reasons — drew me back.

Notes
& Index

NOTES

VB: Vera Brittain. The numbers refer to text pages. Notes on VB's text have been restricted generally to information considered to be of immediate relevance and interest. The information has been derived from writings by VB (notably *Testament of Experience*) and her contemporaries, from memoirs, diaries and histories of the Second World War, and from an array of standard reference works. In general, personal honours have not been noted.

INTRODUCTION

12 **"the trouble makers"**: See A. J. P. Taylor, *The Trouble Makers*.

12 **Indeed, the suggestion of a negotiated peace . . .**: Noel Fieldhouse, "The Anglo-German War of 1939–42: Some movements to end it by a negotiated peace", *Transactions of the Royal Society of Canada*, 1971, 9: 285–312. See also Fieldhouse, "Noel Buxton and A. J. P. Taylor's *The Trouble Makers*" in Martin Gilbert (ed.), *A Century of Conflict 1850–1950: Essays for A. J. P. Taylor* (London: Hamish Hamilton, 1966), 175–98.

12 **"When the history of this age . . ."**: VB, "Letter to Peace Lovers", 152, 11 January 1945. See also Brian Bond, *Liddell Hart, A Study of his Military Thought* (London: Cassell, 1977).

12 **"If the Nazis have really been guilty . . ."**: John Middleton Murry, *Peace News*, 22 September 1944, 3.

13 *Seed of Chaos*: VB, *Seed of Chaos* (London: New Vision, 1944). See also VB, *Stop Massacre Bombing: An Appeal to All Belligerents* (London: New Vision, n.d.). After reading *Seed of Chaos*, Basil Liddell Hart wrote to express "profound respect for your courage in upholding the claims for human decency in a time when war fever is raging. . . . Since you are likely to have had abundant evidence of the resentment you create, you may like to have some evidence of the respect you inspire" (Liddell Hart to VB, 25 July 1944, VB Papers, McMaster University, Hamilton, Ontario). *Seed of Chaos* was published in the US as *Massacre by Bombing*.

13 **savage criticism . . .**: George Orwell, *The Collected Essays, Journals and Letters of George Orwell*, vol. 3, 179–81 and 213–15.

13 **"As we now know, bombing . . ."**: Solly Zuckerman, *From Apes to Warlords: The autobiography (1904–1947) of Solly Zuckerman* (London: Hamish Hamilton, 1978), 148.

13 **"To walk through the ruined cities . . ."**: George Orwell in the *Observer*, 8 April 1945.

13 **the FRC sought to gain governmental permission . . .:** See Dingle Foot (Parliamentary Secretary to the Ministry of Economic Warfare) in "Food Relief for Occupied Europe", the Report of addresses given to a meeting of the Peace Aims Conference held in London on 9 March 1942, by Dingle Foot, Edith Pye, Roy Walker and Herbert Elvin. This document is marked "Private" and "Confidential" — and priced at fourpence! (VB Papers)

13 **Critics considered it of vital importance . . .:** Roy Walker, *Famine Over Europe: The Problem of Controlled Food Relief* (London: Andrew Bakers, n.d. [1941]), 22.

13 **In 1944, however . . .:** Richard Rempel, "The Dilemma of British Pacifists during World War II", *Journal of Modern History*, 50 (1978).

14 **"the struggle against war . . .":** VB, "Women and Pacifism", *Peace News*, 15 August 1941, 3.

14 **Vera Brittain's unstinting efforts . . .:** VB, *Testament of Experience*, 281.

14 **"the Congress Party . . .":** Leo Amery, Secretary of State for India, to VB: quoted in *Testament of Experience*, 281.

14 **"decision was unfortunate . . .":** Quoted in *Testament of Experience*, 281.

14 **Similarly, her ability to frequent restaurants . . .:** Yet it should be remembered that "eating out" warrants some consideration of perspective: the practice "had increased enormously as a result of the war to seventy-nine million meals a week in May 1941 and a hundred and seventy million in December 1944 . . ." (Angus Calder, *The People's War: Britain 1939–1945* (London: Panther, 1971), 446. Calder's study is a superb social history.

15 **"The young supporters . . .":** David Thomson, quoted in A. Sked and C. Cook, *Post-War Britain: A Political History* (Harmondsworth: Penguin, 1979), 223.

18 **"What Can We Do In Wartime?":** VB's article was published in *Forward* (a Scottish "weekly journal of Socialism and Democracy"), 9 September 1939.

18 **my only brother:** Edward Brittain, VB's younger brother, was wounded on the first day of the Battle of the Somme (1 July–18 November 1916), and afterwards awarded the Military Cross for his bravery. He was killed at Asiago in June 1918.

18 **long agony, Battle of Passchendaele:** The Third Battle of Ypres (31 July–10 November 1917): around the village of Passchendaele troops fought in mud. Casualties were very high (the Allies lost 300,000 men), and for the first time mustard gas was used. Passchendaele epitomises the horror of warfare.

19 **Battle of Cambrai:** On 28 November 1917, supported by nearly 400 tanks, the British advanced five miles, taking 10,000 German prisoners.

19 **emotional ferocity, Treaty of Versailles:** VB, with many left-wingers, argued that a French and British desire for vengeance at the end of the First World War had promoted the 1919 treaty's imposition of harsh, humiliating

conditions on the Germans; and that this in turn, by fuelling German anger, was leading to a second conflict.

20 **Lord Ponsonby:** Arthur Ponsonby, 1st Baron Ponsonby of Shulbrede (1871–1946), statesman, pacifist and writer; he had been a Liberal MP 1908–18, Labour MP 1922–30, Parliamentary Under-Secretary and Leader of the Opposition in the House of Lords 1931–35. VB admired his book *Falsehood in War-Time: Containing an assortment of lies circulated . . . during the Great War* (London: Allen and Unwin, 1928).

20 **Bertrand Russell, Laurence Housman:** The eminent philosopher (1872–1970), and the prolific writer and artist (1869–1959), were stalwart pacifists during the First World War. (During the Second, Russell recanted, but Housman remained an active pacifist.)

20 **Society of Friends:** A religious sect (its members are often called Quakers) founded in the mid-seventeenth century. One of its central tenets is its peace testimony, and in 1816 a Quaker, William Allen, founded the first organised peace group, the Society for the Promotion of Permanent and Universal Peace.

20 **Ruth Fry:** (Anna) Ruth Fry (1878–1962), a prominent social activist, had been Secretary of the Friends' Relief Committee 1914–24.

20 **battlefields, Spain, China:** A reference to the brutal fighting of the Spanish Civil War (1936–39), and the long Communist–Nationalist struggle in China together with the Japanese invasion in 1937.

1939

25 **Lyndhurst:** Near this Hampshire town in the New Forest (some four miles from the railway station at Brockenhurst), VB bought a small house, Allum Green Cottage, in April 1939, with money from her best-selling *Testament of Youth*. Here she escaped from London for weekends and longer periods, to write and relax.

25 **German–Russian Pact:** Signed by Nazi Germany and the Soviet Union on 23 August 1939, it bound both countries to neutrality in the event that either should be at war. A secret protocol divided Eastern and Central Europe and the Baltic States into German and Russian spheres of influence.

25 **children:** John and Shirley Brittain-Catlin were eleven and nine years old respectively.

25 **Ruth Colby:** An American friend of VB's (1899–1985), she was "a poet, an artist, and the Minneapolis Chairman of the Women's International League for Peace and Freedom". She and her husband Woodard, a specialist in children's diseases, lived in St Paul, capital of Minnesota.

25 **Chamberlain:** (Arthur) Neville Chamberlain (1869–1940), Conservative Prime Minister, May 1937–May 1940; much criticised for his policy of appeasement.

25   **Sir Edward Grey:** A Liberal statesman, 1st Viscount (1862–1933), he was Foreign Secretary 1905–1916. In August 1914 he told Parliament that the compact to defend Belgium must be honoured, thereby committing Britain to participation in the First World War.

25   **Danzig taken over:** Now called Gdansk, this industrial city with its strategic port at the mouth of the Vistula was Prussian from 1793 to 1919; it then became, under the terms of the Treaty of Versailles, a Free City, administered by a League of Nations Commissioner, and providing Poland with an outlet to the sea. In 1933, Danzig's elected senate fell under the control of the local Nazi Party, and on 1 September 1939 the Nazi Gauleiter pronounced the union of Danzig and Germany, whilst German troops poured over the German–Polish border although war had not been formally declared.

25   **G.:** VB's husband George Edward Gordon Catlin (1896–1979), a prominent socialist, political scientist and academic. In her diary he is always called "Gordon" or "G.".

25   **"Anglo-Saxon Traditions"** : Catlin's book, published as *Anglo-Saxony and its Tradition* (1939), was the first of several fervently advocating Anglo-American Federal Union.

25   **Ministry of Propaganda:** The Ministry of Information was a new wartime ministry established to channel news to the news-media and to sustain morale on the home front. It had a rapid turnover of ministers during its first nine months — Harold Macmillan, John Reith, Duff Cooper — before the appointment of Brendan Bracken in July 1941.

25   **French and British military missions returning:** The low-grade Anglo-French mission sent to Moscow to discuss military means of countering the German threat did not inspire Soviet confidence and the talks, which began on 12 August, broke down two days later over the refusal of the Poles to grant Soviet troops transit rights in the event of a German attack on Poland.

25   **W. N. Ewer:** A prominent journalist (b. 1885), he specialised in foreign affairs.

25   **Tannenberg Rally:** The First World War Battle of Tannenberg (26–30 August 1914) was a major victory of the German Army over the Russian; some 100,000 prisoners were taken.

25   **Nevile Henderson, "plan" from Hitler:** The British Ambassador in Berlin 1937–39, (Sir) Nevile Henderson (1882–1942), encouraged Chamberlain to appease Hitler, whose 25 August "last offer" to Britain (of various putative guarantees, conditional on compliance) was followed by secret exchanges in which Henderson continued to act as intermediary.

25   **Seymours:** William Kean Seymour (1887–1975), a poet, novelist and journalist, was also VB's bank manager; his second wife was the novelist Rosalind Wade (1910–89). They had been friends of VB's for some years, and their son Philip (now Professor in Cognitive Psychology at the University of Dundee) was her godson.

26 **children all being evacuated:** The official evacuation of children, mothers and the disabled from major urban centres began on 1 September 1939. Within three days almost one and a half million were moved to safer areas. Many, however, quickly returned to their homes, and a second evacuation, of over 200,000 children, took place between May and July 1940, after the collapse of France.

26 **Reichstag:** The German Parliament — a rubber-stamping agency after Hitler (1889–1945) became Chancellor in 1933 and the Enabling Act gave him the legislative means of establishing a totalitarian regime.

26 *Europa, Bremen:* Both these large transatlantic liners were German.

26 **Sept. 21st:** i.e., when the next school-year would begin.

26 *Pygmalion:* This admired 1938 film of Bernard Shaw's play was co-directed by Anthony Asquith and Leslie Howard, the latter also starring in it, with Wendy Hiller.

27 **Queen Wilhelmina:** Queen of the Netherlands 1890–1948, Wilhelmina (1880–1962) fled to London on 13 May 1940.

27 **King Leopold:** Leopold III (1901–1983), King of the Belgians 1934–50.

27 **personal Peace Letter:** VB composed a weekly, and then fortnightly, "Letter to Peace Lovers" throughout the War, its first issue appearing on 4 October 1939. Endorsed by the PPU, it reached 2,000 subscribers, and was judged by a Government memorandum on Anti-war Publications, in May 1940, to be one of the most important pacifist publications of its kind.

27 **black-outs:** black-out regulations came into force on 1 September, requiring concealment of all artificial light.

27 **anonymous letter from Glasgow:** VB quoted from this letter in the article "Lift Up your Hearts!", written on the day war was declared. (It appeared in *Peace News*, then the organ of the PPU, and has been reprinted in *Testament of a Generation: The Journalism of VB and Winifred Holtby*, ed. Paul Berry and Alan Bishop, 1985.)

27 **Canon Morris:** Stuart Morris (1890–1967) was a leading member of the PPU — he became General Secretary in 1939. He had served as Anglican chaplain to the Royal Flying Corps in the First World War, and as parish priest in Birmingham, but left the priesthood just before the Second World War began.

27 **Germany had attacked Poland:** The German invasion of Poland began at 4.30 a.m. on 1 September 1939. On 27 September Warsaw surrendered, after being subjected to a relentless aerial bombardment which destroyed an eighth of the city's buildings. In less than six weeks all of Poland was defeated, and in early October Hitler attended a victory parade in Warsaw. The Wehrmacht lost 45,596 killed, wounded or missing, against the Poles' 200,000.

27 **ARP:** Air Raid Precautions, which commenced on 1 September. Local government authorities had responsibility for protecting the population within their jurisdiction. This included the provision and control of public

air-raid shelters and trenches, air-raid wardens and ambulance drivers, rescue and first-aid parties.

27   **Rochdale Selection Conference:** Gordon Catlin hoped to be nominated as Labour candidate for an approaching by-election in this Lancashire manufacturing town near Manchester (it was a Labour stronghold, the co-operative movement having begun there in 1844).

28   **balloon barrage:** Barrage ballons, or "blimps", were designed to prevent low-level attacks and dive-bombing by enemy aircraft; they were attached to cables and winches, and operated by RAF Balloon Command.

28   **Arthur Greenwood:** A Labour statesman (1880–1954) who had been Minister of Health 1924 and 1929–31, he became Minister without Portfolio in Churchill's war cabinet 1940–42, and then, until the end of the War, *de facto* leader of the loyal Opposition.

28   **Mussolini:** The Italian Fascist dictator Benito Mussolini (1883–1945) proposed a five-power conference to discuss the European situation; but Britain made consideration of the proposal contingent on the withdrawal of German troops from Poland.

28   **PPU:** The Peace Pledge Union had been formed in May 1936 from the Sheppard Peace Movement founded by the Anglican priest Canon "Dick" Sheppard. At the outbreak of war, the PPU, with about 136,000 members, was Britain's premier anti-war organisation, and it remains in active existence today. VB joined in 1937, and throughout the War was a member of its governing Council.

28   **Poppy:** One of VB's pet-names for her daughter Shirley.

28   **Pacifist Service Corps:** Formed by the PPU shortly after the War began, to perform humanitarian work in the community.

28   **Morgan selected:** Dr Hyacinth Morgan (1885–1958) was Labour MP for Rochdale 1940–50.

28   *Athenia* **torpedoed:** This British liner, carrying 1,400 passengers en route to Canada, was torpedoed without warning by a U-boat off the west coast of Scotland; 118 were killed, including 28 Americans.

28   **RAF dropping pamphlets:** The first of several Royal Air Force "propaganda raids" over Northern Germany and the Ruhr.

28   **gas-masks:** In late August 1939, 38 million gas masks were issued.

29   **Sir S. Hoare:** Sir Samuel Hoare, later 1st Viscount Templewood (1880–1959); a Conservative MP 1910–44, he was Secretary for India 1931–35, Foreign Secretary June–December 1935, Home Secretary 1937–39, and Ambassador to Spain 1940–42.

29   **Margaret Storm Jameson:** A Yorkshire novelist, critic and social activist (1897–1986) who published as Storm Jameson, she was a pacifist in the 1930s, and from 1932 a close friend of VB's. Through the PEN Club (of which, from 1938, she was the first woman President), she worked indefatigably to help refugee European intellectuals.

29 **Bill:** Margaret Storm Jameson's son by her first marriage; in his mid-twenties, he was likely to be called up for military service.

29 **British bombed Kiel:** The first RAF offensive (4 September 1939). Directed at the Baltic port and industrial centre, this raid, by 29 Blenheim and Wellington bombers, was unsuccessful: seven were shot down, only eight found their target.

29 **rumours of an air raid:** A false alarm, but Spitfires downed two Hurricanes in the confusion.

29 **Siegfried Line:** On the eve of the War, Adolf Hitler adopted the name (of a line of defences on the Western Front in 1918) for new fortifications on Germany's western frontier.

29 **Max Plowman:** A poet and critic (1883–1941), he edited the *Adelphi* 1938–41 and had been Secretary of the PPU 1937–38. His book *The Faith Called Pacifism* (1936) was very influential.

29 **Edwardes Square:** VB's widowed mother Edith lived in a Kensington flat, 37 Edwardes Square, not far from VB's house in Chelsea, 2 Cheyne Walk.

30 **Spanish War:** Catlin had visited Madrid during the second year of the Spanish Civil War (1936–39).

30 **Oswald Garrison Villard:** An American journalist, social activist and pacifist (1872–1949), co-founder of the National Association for the Advancement of Colored People (1909). Although bitterly opposed to Fascism and Hitler, he struggled to keep the United States out of the War.

30 **H. N. Brailsford:** (Henry) Noel Brailsford (1873–1958) was an influential socialist, writer and editor; he was also a prominent worker for women's suffrage, pacifism and colonial emancipation.

30 **Percy Bartlett:** A well-known pacifist (b. 1888), he became a Quaker in 1911 and joined the FoR in 1915. He was imprisoned as a CO during the First World War, and was General Secretary of the British FoR 1924–38.

30 **Fellowship of Reconciliation:** A quietist Christian pacifist group founded in December 1914; it had developed into an international movement with particular strength in the United States.

30 ***Testament of Friendship*:** VB's biography of her close friend Winifred Holtby (who had died in September 1935) had been completed in July 1939 and was soon to be published.

30 **Rubinstein:** Harold Rubinstein (1891–1975). A London solicitor with literary interests (he wrote several plays), he handled VB's legal affairs.

30 **British troops now in France:** Advance units of the British Expeditionary Force had reached France on 4 September 1939; on 10 September the main body of British forces began to enter the country.

31 **Colston Leigh:** (William) Colston Leigh's very successful lecture and management agency in New York had organised VB's American lecture-tours in 1934 and 1937; a third tour was proposed for 1939.

31 **the Cornell job:** Gordon Catlin had been invited back to Cornell University, Ithaca, New York, where he had been Professor of Political Science 1924–35.

31 **Burnett:** Charles and Amy Burnett had been family servants of the Catlins since the early 1930s, she as housekeeper, he as handyman and chauffeur.

31 **Downs School:** Geoffrey Hoyland and his wife Dorothy, Quakers, ran this school (near Malvern, Worcestershire), at which John Brittain-Catlin had been a boarder since September 1938.

32 **WIL:** The Women's International League for Peace and Freedom, founded in April 1915.

32 **Phyllis:** Phyllis Bentley (1894–1977), prolific Yorkshire novelist and critic whose regional novels, especially *Inheritance* (1932), earned her international popularity. She had known Winifred Holtby well and, for a brief period in the early 1930s, had been a close friend of VB's.

32 **Creech Jones:** "Jon" (Arthur) Creech Jones (1891–1964), trade unionist and politician, socialist and pacifist. He was a Labour MP 1935–50 and 1954–64 whose main interest was in colonial affairs (he became Colonial Secretary 1945–46).

32 **Mrs Drury-Lowe:** VB's nearest neighbour: owner of Allum Green House, whose Cottage she had sold to VB.

32 **death of Freud:** Sigmund Freud (1856–1939), famous Jewish–Austrian neurologist and psychiatrist, had been arrested and held for ransom by the Nazis. Compelled, on his release, to sign a statement testifying that he had not been mistreated by the Gestapo, he is said to have written beneath his signature "I am recommending them to all my friends." After the Anschluss he fled to London, and died there from cancer of the jaw.

33 **Lloyd George:** David Lloyd George, 1st Earl Lloyd George of Dwyfor (1863–1945); Prime Minister December 1916–October 1922. Although Lloyd George did not support appeasement after Munich, he did advocate seeking a negotiated peace settlement in the early stages of the War.

33 **Garvin:** A well-known journalist and writer, James Garvin (1868–1947) was Editor of the *Observer* 1908–42.

33 **Dr Millais Culpin:** An eminent expert on psychoneurosis (1874–1952), he became Professor of Medical–Industrial Psychology at the University of London.

33 **Dr Lockhart's defence:** Leonard Lockhart, a doctor badly shell-shocked in the First World War, had become an acquaintance of VB's in 1937. He "killed his wife in a fit of amnesia at outbreak of the Second War".

33 **Dr Alfred Salter:** A distinguished doctor and pacifist (1873–1945), he was a Labour MP 1922–23 and 1924–45.

33 **UDC:** The Union of Democratic Control, founded in 1914, argued that open diplomacy, and democratic control of foreign policy, would keep nations from war and advance the cause of world peace.

33 **VC husband:** Robert Phillips (1895–1963) had been awarded the Victoria Cross in 1917 after rescuing his wounded Commanding Officer.

34 **Roger Eckersley:** A broadcaster (1885–1955), he was Assistant Controller of the BBC 1930–39 and Chief Censor of the BBC throughout the War.

34 **Edward Murrow:** An American journalist and broadcaster, Ed Murrow (1908–65) was European director of CBS 1937–46 and became famous as a war-correspondent for the CBS 1939–45.

34 **Duff Cooper:** The Conservative statesman Alfred Duff Cooper, 1st Viscount Norwich (1890–1954), Secretary of State for War 1935–37, First Lord of the Admiralty 1937–38, Minister of Information 1940–41. He was the only member of Chamberlain's cabinet to resign in protest over the Munich Agreement, and worked hard for American entry into the War.

34 **Mr Justice Singleton:** The Rt Hon. Sir John Singleton (1885–1957), Judge of the King's Bench Division 1934–48, and thereafter Lord Justice of Appeal.

34 **Mr Sandlands:** Paul Sandlands, QC (1878–1962), was Recorder of Leicester 1932–44.

35 **Leighton Park School:** A Quaker school founded in 1890, it is near Reading.

35 **Blockade:** The British blockade of Germany began on 3 September 1939. It was assumed (mistakenly) that the German economy was already near the point of collapse, so that a blockade could end the conflict without the carnage of the First World War.

35 **LNU:** The League of Nations Union, established in November 1918, had evolved into the most influential anti-war and internationalist organisation in Britain by the late 1920s. In the mid-1930s, however, its leadership espoused rearmament and the policy of collective security, alienating VB and many pacifist members.

36 **Guy Chapman:** A historian, writer and publisher (1899–1972), author of the fine First World War memoir *A Passionate Prodigality* (1933), and Margaret Storm Jameson's second husband. He served in the Army Bureau of Current Affairs from 1943, and was Professor of Modern History at Leeds 1945–53.

36 **to see Shirley:** Shirley Brittain-Catlin had just become a boarder at Oldfeld, a "progressive" school (endorsed by the Parents' National Education Union) near Swanage on the Dorset coast.

36 **Mrs Swanwick:** Helena Swanwick (1864–1939), a leading feminist, socialist, internationalist and journalist; she had been a British delegate to the League of Nations Assemblies of 1924 and 1929, and Editor of the influential *Foreign Affairs*, organ of the UDC.

36 **Howard Lewis:** This popular artist had recently painted (from photographs) the portrait of Winifred Holtby to be used as frontispiece for *Testament of Friendship*; his sketch of VB was for publicity associated with the book's publication.

36   **Lovat Dickson:** An Australian-born Canadian (1902–87) often called "Rache" by friends, he moved to England in 1928 and became a well-known writer, publisher and editor. He joined Macmillan of London in 1938, and became one of its directors in 1940.

37   **Soviet attack on Finland:** The "Winter War" of November 1939 to March 1940, a 15-week conflict which resulted in the deaths of nearly 25,000 Finnish defenders and the loss of some 16,000 square miles of Finnish territory to the Soviet Union. The Red Army lost 200,000 men.

37   **PPU Women's Crusade:** At the end of November 1939, the PPU established a Women's Committee, under the direction of Mary Gamble (later John Middleton Murry's fourth wife), and the Women's Peace Campaign commenced. Several marches and demonstrations were organised, with calls for a negotiated peace. The campaign ended in the summer of 1941.

37   **St Monica's:** A private school for girls, south of London, which VB had attended for four years and then taught at occasionally in the 1920s.

38   **Dr Kathleen Rutherford:** A Quaker and FoR member, she ran a medical practice in Harrogate.

1940

39   **Robert Lynd:** A writer and journalist of Irish extraction (1879–1949), he was a very influential reviewer.

39   **Clipper,** *Vulcania:* The Clipper was the first transatlantic passenger air-service, with 28-hour twice-weekly flights between New York and Lisbon (Portugal remained neutral throughout the War); but it was crowded, and subject to cancellation and delay in bad weather. The *Vulcania*, an Italian transatlantic liner, sailed from Lisbon on 10 January.

39   **"Battle of the Bulge":** On the night of 9–10 May, German forces invaded neutral Holland, Belgium and Luxembourg. Fierce fighting at the Sedan bridgehead ended in the rout of two French divisions; French attempts to counter-attack failed. On 14 May the Dutch Government fled to Britain and the centre of Rotterdam was obliterated in the first mass-bombing of the War; Dutch military resistance ended the next day. On 18 May Antwerp fell to the Germans, and they reached Amiens, punching a 50-mile gap in the Allied line defending France.

40   **Winston Churchill, speech:** Churchill (1874–1965) had become Prime Minister of a Coalition Government on 10 May 1940, after the famous debate in the House of Commons, on 7 May, when Leopold Amery had demanded Chamberlain's resignation in Cromwell's words to the Long Parliament, "In the name of God, go."

40   **Blitzkrieg:** Blitzkrieg or "lightning war" was the term used to describe the tactics perfected by General Heinz Guderian (1888–1954), of rapid penetration, in depth, by tanks and other armoured vehicles. These tactics

essentially won the Battle of France: by 20 May Guderian had reached the Channel coast at Abbeville.

40 **The Blitzkrieg, destroying . . .:** These three paragraphs, on a loose page dated "May 19th", have been added to the diary entry.

40 **Dorothy Evans:** A member of the PPU Council, she had been a suffragette and pacifist in the First World War.

40 **Gamelin, Weygand:** General Maurice Gamelin (1872–1958), Chief of Staff to Joffre in the First World War, French Chief of Staff 1938–39. In 1939–40 he was Generalissimo of Allied Forces in France before being displaced on 19 May by Marshal Weygand (1867–1965) when the former's cautious, defensive strategies proved ineffective against the German onslaught. But it was too late for Weygand (Chief of Staff to Foch in the First World War and Commander-in-Chief of the French Army 1930–35) to salvage the situation.

41 **Fifth Column:** Those who sympathise with the enemy and are ready to become collaborators if the opportunity arises.

41 **Vera Z.:** Mrs Brittain's foreign-born maid.

41 **bill to mobilise entire nation:** This was an extension of the Emergency Powers Act of August 1939, and enabled the Government to require individuals to place themselves, their services and their property at its disposal, for the more efficient prosecution of the War and the maintenance of supplies and services vital to the community. The original Act had empowered the Government, through the King, to formulate, by orders in council, defence regulations necessary for public safety, national defence and the efficient prosecution of the War.

41 **Attlee:** Clement Attlee, later 1st Earl Attlee, KG, OM (1883–1967). Labour MP 1922–55, he served in Churchill's Coalition Government 1940–45, and became Deputy Prime Minister 1942–45 and, after defeating Churchill in the 1945 General Election, Prime Minister 1945–51.

41 **Morrison:** Herbert Morrison, later Lord Morrison of Lambeth (1888–1965). A Labour MP for long periods 1923–59, he served as Home Secretary under Churchill during the War, and became Deputy Prime Minister in Attlee's Labour Government 1945–51.

41 **bill to punish spies and traitors:** The Treachery Act provided for the use of the death penalty in serious cases of espionage and sabotage.

41 **George Lansbury:** A prominent statesman, social activist, journalist (1889–1940), he was Labour MP 1910–12 and 1922–40, and Leader of the Labour Party 1931–35. As a leading pacifist, in 1937 he visited Hitler and Mussolini in a personal attempt to prevent the outbreak of war.

41 **Dr Wood:** Alex Wood (1879–1950), Physics don and Fellow of Emmanuel College, Cambridge; a Christian Socialist and pacifist, he became Chairman of the PPU in 1939.

41 **Maurice Rowntree:** A prominent Quaker (d. 1944), he was a PPU Sponsor and in 1939 became its Treasurer.

41   **tried for the poster:** Six members of the PPU (including its four chief officers, Wood, Morris, Rowntree and John Barclay) were tried at Bow Street for contravening Defence Regulation 39a(1) by inciting servicemen to disaffect. Central to the Prosecution's case was a poster which read "War will cease when men refuse to fight. What are you going to do about it?" The defendants were ultimately bound over for 12 months and forced to withdraw the poster.

41   **Gerald Bailey:** (Vernon) Gerald Bailey (1903–72) was Secretary of the NPC.

41   **Cyril Joad:** A popular philosopher, writer and broadcaster (1891–1953), C. E. M. Joad had also been an influential pacifist. His recantation, paralleling that of his fellow philosopher Bertrand Russell, heralded other defections.

41   **Sir Robert Dummett:** An eminent judge (1872–1941), he was Chief Metropolitan Magistrate from 1940.

41   **Brit. Union of Fascists:** The BUF had been founded by Sir Oswald Mosley as the New Party in 1931, and changed its name in 1932 following Mosley's visit to Italy — when it also adopted the style and ways of Continental fascist parties. In May 1940 the Government detained the BUF's leadership and subsequently banned the organisation.

41   **arrest of Captain Ramsay:** Archibald Ramsay (1894–1955), Conservative MP for Peebles and Midlothian South 1931–45; he remained imprisoned until the end of the War.

42   **Sir Oswald Mosley arrested:** Politician and 6th baronet (1896–1980), Mosley had been Conservative MP 1918–22, Independent 1922–24, Labour 1926–30, New Party 1930–31, before founding the BUF. He was arrested on 23 May under the provisions of Defence Regulation 18B, and not released until 1943.

42   **Maginot line system:** The line of fortifications, running along France's eastern frontier from the Swiss to the Belgian border; it ended at Sedan, since the Belgians objected to being cut off by it and it was believed that the Ardennes were impenetrable.

42   **Gollancz & Laski:** Victor Gollancz (1893–1967), publisher, writer, socialist and humanitarian. Harold Laski (1893–1950), socialist and writer, Professor of Political Science at the University of London, member of the Labour Party's Executive Council 1936–49. They were very influential left-wingers.

42   **Geoffrey Mander & Stephen K.H.:** (Sir) Geoffrey Mander (1882–1962), barrister and Liberal MP 1929–45. Stephen King-Hall (1893–1966), writer and Independent National MP 1939–44; he served in the Ministry of Aircraft Production and the Ministry of Fuel and Power during the War.

42   **Vansittart:** Sir Robert Vansittart, 1st Baron 1941 (1881–1957), Permanent Under-Secretary of State for Foreign Affairs 1930–38, was Chief Diplomatic Adviser to the Foreign Secretary 1938–41. He was an outspoken Germano-phobe.

42   **Cardinal Hinsley:** The Yorkshireman Arthur Hinsley (1865–1943) was Archbishop of Westminster 1935–43.

42   **Lord Lothian:** Philip Kerr, 11th Marquis of Lothian (1882–1940), British Ambassador in Washington 1939–40.

42   **Cordell Hull:** An American diplomat, statesman and judge (1871–1955), he was Secretary of State 1933–44. In 1945 he won the Nobel Peace Prize for helping to create the United Nations.

43   **M. Reynaud:** Paul Reynaud (1878–1966) was French Prime Minister from 20 March to 16 June 1940, when he resigned after refusing to issue an order to cease fire, and was succeeded by Marshal Pétain. He was imprisoned by the Vichy Regime and then interned in Austria by the Germans.

43   **Belgian King capitulated:** King Leopold III's capitulation order was repudiated by the Belgian Government-in-exile in France; it ordered him deposed, and Leopold was held prisoner by the Germans until the end of the War.

43   **"King Quisling":** Vidkun Quisling (1887–1945) was a Norwegian Staff Officer who served the Nazis as puppet leader of occupied Norway and was executed for high treason at the end of the War.

43   **the 700,000 BEF in France:** VB's figure is wrong, more than doubling the number of men involved.

43   **BEF being evacuated:** The BEF was evacuated from Dunkirk between 24 May and 4 June 1940. Some 225,000 British troops, and over 100,000 French, Belgian, Dutch and others, were lifted from the beaches by a fleet of 860 ships of various sizes, shapes and buoyancies. Most of the BEF was saved; only some 60,000 men — most of them French soldiers who fought a tenacious rearguard action — were taken prisoner by the Germans.

43   **Jean Monnet:** A French economist (1888–1979) who chaired the Anglo-French Co-ordination Committee seeking to promote economic collaboration. He became the principal architect of France's post-war industrial recovery, and first President of the European Coal and Steel Community.

43   **signposts being moved:** On 30 May 1940 the British Government ordered that "no person shall display or cause or permit to be displayed any sign which furnishes any indication of the name of, or the situation or the direction of, or the distance to any place." Signposts were accordingly taken down, milestones buried or mutilated, destination boards removed from buses, and, within 20 miles of the south and east coasts, railway stations became nameless. The resulting confusion was so great that in a short time some signs were restored, to provide a minimum of direction.

44   **Mrs Eden-Green:** Winifred Eden-Green, a secretary at the BBC before the War, was personal assistant to VB until 1964, and organised the "Letter to Peace Lovers" throughout the War. She also did relief work in SE London until the birth of her first child in 1944. With her husband Alan, she has edited a selection of the "Letters", published by Virago in 1988.

44 **NPC:** The National Peace Council was formed in 1908 to gather together representatives of organisations working for peace and disarmament and to provide opportunity for liaison and discussion.

44 **Defence Regulations:** The extraordinary powers assumed by the British Government on the eve of the outbreak of the War.

44 **G.L.'s Life:** VB was interested in writing a biography of George Lansbury.

44 **Victor Finney:** A Labour MP 1923–24, he was General Secretary of the Council of Action for Peace and Reconstruction.

44 **Harold Nicolson:** An eminent diplomat and writer (1886–1968), he was married to the poet and novelist Vita (Victoria) Sackville-West. After resigning from the Diplomatic Service in 1929, and working for the *Daily Express*, he was a National Labour MP 1935–45.

44 **Laurence Housman:** A prolific playwright, poet and artist (1865–1959), he had supported women's suffrage and was a leading socialist and pacifist.

44 **John Barclay:** A Christian pacifist since 1920, he resigned his job with the London Co-operative Society to become the PPU's National Group Organiser in November 1936; he became a Sponsor in 1938, and in 1939 a member of the National Council.

44 **Sybil Morrison:** A feminist, pacifist and social activist (1893–1984), she was a founding member of the PPU and was twice its Chairman after the War.

44 **John Middleton Murry:** Critic and writer, socialist and pacifist (1889–1957), he edited the *Adelphi* magazine 1923–38 and *Peace News* (then published by the PPU) 1940–46.

45 **in Valletta during the last War:** VB served as a VAD in Malta for several months in 1916–17.

46 **Hore-Belisha:** (Isaac) Leslie Hore-Belisha, 1st Baron (1893–1957), National Liberal MP 1923 and Independent 1942–45, Secretary of State for War 1937–40 and responsible for introducing the road safety device known as the "Belisha Beacon".

46 **Basil Mathews:** An educator and writer of British birth (1879–1951), he was Deputy Director of the Ministry of Information's American Division, 1939–40.

46 **Priestley:** J. B. Priestley OM (1894–1984), Yorkshireman, prolific and popular man of letters. He became a very important broadcaster during the War, rivalling Churchill in popularity. The BBC estimated that Priestley, who broadcast regularly to the United States, had "the biggest regular listening audience in the world".

46 **Vernon Bartlett:** A well-known journalist (1894–1983), he was London Director of the LNU 1922–32, and was an Independent MP 1938–50.

46 **Kingsley Martin:** Basil Kingsley Martin (1897–1969), an influential socialist, journalist, and lecturer in political science, was Editor of the *New Statesman* 1930–60. He was John Barclay's brother-in-law and until 1938 gave editorial advice for *Peace News*.

46 **Dan Macmillan:** Elder brother (1886–1965) of (Maurice) Harold Macmillan, he was Chairman and Managing Director 1936–63 of the family's publishing firm, Macmillan of London.

46 **Megan Lloyd George:** Daughter (1902–66) of David Lloyd George, she was a Welsh MP (Liberal 1929–51, then Labour 1957–66) for nearly four decades.

46 **Rhys Davies:** Trade unionist and Labour MP 1921–51, Davies (1877–1954) was a pacifist and an active critic of Churchill's Coalition Government.

46 ***The Admirable Crichton:*** A popular comedy (1902) by J. M. Barrie (1860–1937) in which a butler becomes master on a desert island.

47 **Italy entered the War:** The Italian declaration of war against France and Britain extended the conflict beyond northern and central Europe, into the Mediterranean and Africa.

47 **Edward killed fighting for Italy:** VB's brother, awarded the MC for bravery during the Battle of the Somme, had been killed during fighting in northern Italy, against the Austrians, on 15 June 1918.

48 **Roosevelt broadcast:** Franklin Delano Roosevelt (1882–1945), Democratic Party politician, US President 1933–45. He was highly critical of Nazi policies and gave massive assistance to the British prior to American entry into the War. His speech of 10 June has been seen as an important milestone on the way to that entry, although Roosevelt was careful to state that no plans existed to commit US troops to an overseas campaign.

48 **Italians bombed Malta:** Malta, the main base of the British Mediterranean fleet, was badly bombed between 1940 and 1942. In April 1942 King George VI awarded the George Cross (highest civilian award for valour) to the Maltese people.

48 **Princess Juliana and daughters in Canada:** Heir to the Dutch throne and later Queen; she and her family spent the war years in Canada.

48 **Viscount Elibank:** Gideon Murray (1877–1951), Unionist MP 1918–22 and prominent company director.

48 **Prof. Ogilvie:** F. W. Ogilvie (1893–1949) became Director-General of the BBC in 1938 after academic posts as Professor of Political Science at Edinburgh 1926–34 and Vice-Chancellor of Queen's University, Belfast, 1934–38. He was attacked for permitting religious broadcasts to be made by avowed pacifists.

49 **Church and chapel bells . . .:** Henceforth they were to be rung only by the military or the police, in the event of airborne invasion. (On 15 November 1942, however, Churchill ordered church bells to be rung in celebration of Montgomery's victory at El Alamein.)

49 **Raymond Postgate:** A prolific journalist and writer (1896–1971), he had a special interest in socialist history and was son-in-law of Lansbury. His *Life of George Lansbury* was published in 1951.

49   **Col. Wedgwood:** A senior politician, Col. the Rt Hon. Josiah (Baron) Wedgwood (1872–1943) was a friend of VB's. He had been a Liberal and Labour MP before becoming an Independent.

49   **"Look thy last . . .":** The quotation is a line from Walter de la Mare's "Fare Well".

50   **queues, Cook's:** CORB (the Children's Overseas Reception Board, charged with organising the evacuation) was established at the headquarters of Thomas Cook and Son, the travel agency.

50   **beginning of Blitzkrieg:** The Battle of Britain had begun on 10 July and was to continue until 31 October 1940. The Luftwaffe, with nearly 1,400 bombers and over 1,000 fighters, launched a series of attacks against shipping, airfields and finally cities, as a prelude to invasion. The highest German losses were on this day, 15 August, when the RAF shot down 75 aircraft for the loss of 34. During the whole period of twelve weeks 1,773 German planes were destroyed and 915 British.

50   ***Take Back Your Freedom:*** Winifred Holtby's play attacking fascism was written in 1934 and revised by Norman Ginsbury, but published and first performed in 1940.

50   **Desmond MacCarthy, Agate:** MacCarthy (1877–1952) and James Agate (1877–1947) were two of the most influential critics of the time.

51   **Mrs J. L. Hodson:** Wife of the well-known writer and journalist (1891–1956), then a War Correspondent.

51   **G. packing for U.S.A.:** He had been invited to lecture at Kansas City University, but was also on a semi-official "mission" to provide American politicians with information about British needs, particularly in the hope of securing the loan of 50 outdated destroyers. For three days he participated, as a temporary foreign-affairs adviser, in the losing Presidential campaign of the Republican candidate, Wendell Willkie, against Roosevelt.

52   **writing on book:** VB had now embarked on a popular study of the Blitz and its effects, *England's Hour*: it was published in 1941.

52   **45:** i.e., the forty-fifth air raid since 15 August.

52   **columns of smoke from docks:** This was, VB wrote later, "the first concentrated air attack" on London; apart from setting the docks on fire, it killed some 400 citizens.

53   **Bentley Carrs:** Edith Brittain's sister Lillie and her husband Arthur Bentley-Carr; their home was some 25 miles south-west of the centre of London.

53   **Fräulein:** She had been John and Shirley's governess before marrying an Englishman named Clarke, now away fighting.

54   **George Brett:** VB's American publisher (1893–1984), as President of Macmillan of New York. After an affair in the mid-1930s, he and VB had remained friends.

54   **Helen Mayo:** VB's dentist and friend; they met in the 1920s as members of the feminist Six Point Group, of which Mayo was Secretary.

55 **terrific battle overhead:** On this day, 15 September, "Battle of Britain Day", the RAF inflicted such severe damage on the Luftwaffe that the Germans subsequently abandoned their invasion plan: they had already resorted to night-bombing larger cities, especially London. (It was claimed originally that 185 German aircraft were destroyed on 15 September, but the figure was revised to 56.)

56 **Mortimer:** A village about five miles south-west of Reading.

56 **John Hoyland:** A writer, and social and political activist (1887–1957), he worked for Indian independence.

56 **Wells' fantasies:** The popular writer H. G. Wells (1866–1946); VB was probably thinking of *The War of the Worlds* (1898).

57 **Saturday booking:** VB had hoped to leave for America then, to see her husband and children.

57 **"And So — Farewell":** This chapter of *England's Hour* was painful to write because it described the departure of VB's children for the United States.

57 **ship torpedoed in Atlantic:** The *City of Benares*, carrying child evacuees, sank with the loss of 73 of the children.

58 **S. Riding:** *South Riding*, prepared by VB, as literary executor, for its posthumous publication in March 1936, is Winifred Holtby's most admired novel.

58 **CORB:** The Children's Overseas Reception Board, a Government-sponsored body of which VB's cousin Geoffrey Shakespeare (then Under-Secretary for the Dominions) was head. By early July 1940, it had received over 200,000 applications from the parents of school-age children, and in all it sent 2,664 children abroad, the majority to Canada (as many as 14,000 other children were privately sponsored). But, as a result of the *City of Benares* disaster, the Board was disbanded in the summer of 1940.

58 **Miss Darbishire:** Helen Darbishire, respected critic and editor (1881–1961), had been Tutor of English at Somerville College when VB was an undergraduate, and was now Principal.

58 **Miss Farnell:** Vera Farnell, Tutor in Modern Languages at Somerville.

58 **WVS:** The Women's Voluntary Service, an almost entirely voluntary organisation begun in 1938 by Stella, Marchioness of Reading, at the invitation of the Home Office. Primarily a middle-class body, its members carried out various tasks including the distribution of food and clothing.

59 **Alfred Haigh, Jessie:** Old friends of VB's parents; Alfred Haigh was Managing Director of Brittain's Ltd, the family paper mills near Stoke-on-Trent.

60 **Sybil Morrison, Holloway:** The women's prison in London. Sybil Morrison was imprisoned there for a month as a result of her pacifist activities (she was arrested at Hyde Park Corner for using "insulting words and behaviour likely to cause a breach of the peace" — the magistrate called her "a dangerous woman"). On requesting reading matter, she was given a book about the lives of British Field Marshals!

60 **Ellen:** Ellen Wilkinson (1891–1947): a cotton worker's daughter, union organiser, feminist, and — from 1924 — prominent Labour MP. In 1935 she helped to organise the Jarrow March of the unemployed, and was a member of the PPU 1936–37.

60 **PEN:** An international association of Poets, Playwrights, Editors, Essayists and Novelists, it was founded in 1921 to promote co operation, freedom of expression and international goodwill; and had helped many European writers and intellectuals to escape Nazi and Fascist persecution.

60 **Dawlish:** A seaside resort in south Devon.

61 **Dr Herbert Gray:** A Presbyterian minister and ex-Army chaplain, active in the FoR (1868–1956).

62 **Canon Raven:** The Revd Canon Raven, DD (1885–1964). He had become a pacifist in 1930 (he had been a chaplain in the First World War), then a leading member of the FoR and a founding member of the PPU. Raven was elected Dean of Emmanuel College, Cambridge, at the age of twenty-four, in 1932 Regius Professor of Divinity, in 1939 Master of Christ's College. At his instigation the PPU's "think tank", the Forethought Committee, was established in 1939 to provide clear directives for the PPU's membership.

62 **Laval & Pétain:** Marshal Henri Pétain (1856–1951), hero of Verdun (1916), Commander-in-Chief of the French Army (1917–19), became Prime Minister in June 1940 and negotiated an armistice with Germany. Pierre Laval (1883–1945) became Vice Premier under Pétain in 1940 and later Premier 1942–45 under German control — believing that collaboration was the only way to save France from destruction; at the end of the War he was executed as a traitor, after a trial of dubious legality.

62 **Vichy:** The name given to the regime headed by Petain which governed France (as far as permitted by the Nazis) for four years, following the French collapse of 1940.

62 ***Empress of Britain* sunk:** This transatlantic liner was sunk on 26 October 1940, 150 miles off the Irish coast.

62 **Italy invaded Greece:** On 7 April 1940, Italian forces invaded Albania, beginning an attempt to extend Italian influence in south-eastern Europe. The invasion of Greece in late October was a further step in this plan, but by mid-May 1941 the Greeks had successfully pushed the Italians back into Albania.

63 **Agatha Harrison:** A pacifist (1885–1954), she served on the Friends' Peace Committee; from 1931 she was Secretary of the India Conciliation Group, recognised as an "unofficial Quaker ambassador" to India.

63 **invitation to India:** VB had been invited to participate in a conference, organised by the All-India Women's Conference, at Mysore in late December 1940. Prevented from going by the Government's refusal of an exit permit, she was invited again, but was not able to visit India until after the War ended.

63 **Amery:** Leopold Amery (1873–1955), prominent anti-appeaser and im-

perialist, Conservative MP 1911–45; he was Secretary of State for India 1940–45.

64 **terrible raid on Coventry:** The attack lasted some ten hours and destroyed 100 acres of the city centre, as 449 German bombers dropped 30,000 incendiary bombs and 503 tons of high explosives on the city.

64 **Carbis Bay:** VB's mother went to live with her youngest sister in a cottage (called Idris) in Carbis Bay, about a mile south-east of St Ives, on the northern coast of Cornwall.

64 **Roy Walker:** A full-time worker for the PPU from 1937, he was the driving force behind several of its campaigns, such as the campaign against the Blockade (in which VB worked closely with him); later, after resigning, he became a critic and lecturer.

65 **Peake:** Osbert Peake, later 1st Viscount Ingleby (1897–1966), a Conservative MP 1929–55 and Parliamentary Under Secretary at the Home Office 1939–44.

65 **Harold Macmillan:** (Maurice) Harold Macmillan, Conservative statesman, later 1st Earl Stockton (1894–1987). An MP 1924–29, 1931–64, he held a number of important wartime posts, including Parliamentary Secretary to the Ministry of Supply 1942 and Minister Resident at Allied Headquarters in North-West Africa 1942–45, and became Prime Minister 1957–63. He had also been VB's publisher.

65 **town's own estimate:** Like so many such figures during the War, it was exaggerated: the actual toll at Coventry was 554 killed, 865 injured.

65 **Page-Croft's question:** Sir Henry Page-Croft (1881–1947) was a Conservative MP 1910–40 and Parliamentary Under Secretary of State for War 1940–45. His question in the House of Commons, about VB's lecturing in the United States, was asked on 21 February 1940.

1941

66 **Wendell Willkie:** A prominent American politician (1892–1944), he was Republican candidate in the 1940 U.S. Presidential election. Gordon Catlin admired him deeply.

66 **Reginald Sorensen:** A minister of the Free Christian Church and Labour MP 1929–31, 1935–64, Sorensen (1891–1971) was also a leading member of the FoR.

66 **Labour Pacifist Fellowship:** A small pacifist element of the Labour Party, it advocated, in the early stages of the War, a negotiated peace with Hitler. In November 1939, 20 Labour MPs signed a Memorandum on Peace Aims which included a call for negotiated peace at the earliest possible date.

66 **Roger Wilson:** A prominent Quaker and PPU member (b. 1906); actively pacifist since the 1920s, he was deeply involved in Quaker relief work in the post-war period.

66   **Friends' Ambulance Unit:** The FAU was founded by Philip Noel-Baker
     in 1914, and served in both World Wars.

66   **Kingsley Hall, Bow:** This well-known East End settlement was founded by
     Muriel Lester.

66   **Patrick Figgis:** A Nonconformist minister, he was forced, later in 1941, to
     leave his congregation because of his pacifist activities, and was to serve as
     PPU General Secretary 1943–46 during Stuart Morris's absence.

66   **Dorothy Hogg:** Apart from service at Kingsley Hall, she worked hard for
     pacifism and Indian independence, and in 1943 published *India: A Plea for
     Understanding*.

67   **Settlement:** The settlement movement arose from late nineteenth-century
     Christian Socialism. Members opted to live in poor working-class areas to
     advance the cause of social reform and to witness to Christian values.

67   **Fred Warburg, 30,000 word book:** Publisher, of Secker and Warburg;
     Catlin's book was eventually published in 1941 by Andrew Dakers, under
     the title *One Anglo-American Nation: The Foundation of Anglo-Saxony*.

67   **Fed. Union:** Federal Union; founded in 1938 to promote close political links
     between the US and Britain (and ultimately all democracies).

68   **"safe where all safety's lost":** From Rupert Brooke's sonnet "Safety"
     (*1914*, II).

68   **Corder Catchpool:** An influential Quaker (1883–1953), he had been
     imprisoned during the First World War as a conscientious objector. He
     founded the Committee for the Abolition of Night Bombing (precursor of the
     BRC) in the summer of 1941, and became Treasurer of the PPU in 1944.

69   **Mrs Leighton died:** Mother of Roland Leighton (VB's fiancé killed in the
     First World War) and Clare Leighton, Marie Connor Leighton had
     published over forty popular romantic novels.

69   **Clare:** An admired woodcut artist and writer, Clare Leighton (b. 1899) had
     moved permanently to the United States in 1939.

70   **cable from Phyllis:** On a lecture-tour in the United States, Phyllis Bentley
     visited John and Shirley Brittain-Catlin at the Colbys' in St Paul,
     Minnesota.

71   **Geoffrey Shakespeare:** Sir Geoffrey Shakespeare (1893–1980), a distant
     relation of VB's, was a Liberal MP who had been Parliamentary Secretary
     to the Ministry of Health 1932–36.

71   **Henry Cadbury, Robert Yarnall:** These two leading American Quakers
     were members of a commission sent to England in 1941 to survey relief needs
     caused by the War. Cadbury (1883–1974) lectured at various colleges on
     religion; Yarnall (1878–1975) was a mechanical engineer.

72   **Dick Sheppard Centre:** This name was frequently given to PPU local
     headquarters, in honour of the movement's founder.

72   **E. M. Delafield:** A prolific novelist, playwright and critic (1890–1943) best
     known for her witty *Diary of a Provincial Lady* (1931). She had been a VAD

nurse in the First World War, and contributed regularly to the feminist journal *Time and Tide* (of which she was a director).

72 **Hitler's troops have entered Bulgaria:** On 1 March 1941, under intense pressure, Bulgaria joined the Axis, and the next day the German Twelfth Army marched in to enforce control of the country.

73 **Swansea raided:** Between June 1940 and February 1943, Swansea, on the Welsh coast, experienced 44 air-raids, some severe; in all 387 people were killed and 851 injured.

73 **Lord and Lady Astor:** The Hon. Waldorf Astor, 2nd Viscount (1879–1952), Conservative MP for Plymouth 1910–19; his American-born wife Viscountess Nancy Astor (1919–45), the first woman elected to the House of Commons, Conservative MP for Plymouth Sutton 1919–45. (It was said that, on at least one occasion, she performed cartwheels in a public shelter to entertain its occupants.)

73 **Nancy Pearn:** VB's literary agent, from 1935 in the agency she established with Laurence Pollinger and David Higham.

74 **Edith de C.:** Edith de Coundouroff had lived with Winifred Holtby's family for many years after being widowed young; she and VB remained friends after Holtby's death in 1935.

75 **Wilfred Wellock:** A Christian Socialist and pacifist (1879–1972), he had been imprisoned during the First World War as a conscientious objector, and joined the PPU soon after its foundation.

76 **Max Plowman's place:** Plowman had warmly welcomed VB's offer, early in 1941, of occasional help in running the Adelphi Centre at Langham (a village near the Suffolk coast). He wanted his house there, The Oaks, to become "a meeting place for pacifists of all ages who believe there is a need for co-ordinated effort to realise pacifism as 'a way of life'". Langham Farm was already host to "a group of young COs, working roughly 70 acres . . . on a subsistence basis", and he had offered accommodation in The Oaks to "evacuees from the bombed areas, particularly old people who need young people to look after them".

76 **Sybil Thorndike:** The great actress (1882–1976) was also a prominent pacifist.

77 **fall of Salonika:** On 6 April 1941, German forces invaded Greece, and their capture of Salonika on 9 April was a severe setback for the Allies, with dangerous implications for the Mediterranean and the Middle East.

77 **Dorothy:** Max Plowman's wife. Their son, in his twenties, was called Piers (in honour of Langland's poem and its noble values).

78 **CO farm boys:** Young conscientious objectors were frequently given work on the land as a condition of exemption from military service; the Adelphi community at Langham provided them with support, work and accommodation.

78 **Virginia Woolf, Dame Ethel Smyth:** The famous writer (b. 1882) had committed suicide by drowning on 31 March 1941; Dame Ethel Smyth, prominent composer and feminist (1858–1944), was a close friend of Woolf's.

79 **Libyan campaign reversed:** By the end of April 1941, British troops had been evicted from Libya (except for the famous "Rats of Tobruk", who were besieged for 242 days), and the German Afrika Corps under General Rommel poured into Egypt.

79 **Prof. Allan Nevins:** An associate of Catlin's in the Federal Union movement, he was an American academic and writer (1890–1971), Professor of American History at Columbia University 1931–58, and during 1940–41 Harmsworth Professor of American History at Oxford.

80 **Richard Murry:** Younger brother of John Middleton Murry.

80 **Richard Ward:** An actor and writer (1910–69), he was the founder of The Adelphi Players, a travelling pacifist theatre company.

81 **Bishop of Chichester:** The Rt Revd George Bell (1883–1958) was a strong critic of area bombing and a staunch advocate of food relief for occupied Europe — though he was not a pacifist. His outspokenness eliminated him as a possible successor to Cosmo Lang, Archbishop of Canterbury, when the latter retired in 1942.

81 **Greek capitulation probable:** Greece had already been forced to concede defeat on that day, 20 April 1941, and formally surrendered three days later.

81 **George Canning:** Influential statesman (1770–1827); Foreign Secretary 1807–09 and 1822–27, Prime Minister 1827.

81 **Sir William Rothenstein:** A prominent artist (1872–1945), he had been Principal of the Royal College of Art 1920–35 and an official war artist in the First World War; during the Second World War he was artist to the RAF.

81 **Aberystwyth oration:** VB had been invited to give the annual Foundation Oration of University College, London; since the staff and students had been evacuated to Aberystwyth University College, her lecture was given there.

81 **view of Stour Valley:** Probably the famous "Dedham Vale" by John Constable (1776–1837).

82 **Lord Cecil, Dean Inge, Anthony Eden:** Lord Gascoyne-Cecil, 1st Viscount Cecil (1864–1952), President of the League of Nations 1923–45. Dean Inge of St Paul's Cathedral (1860–1954), popular Christian apologist. The Conservative statesman Sir Anthony Eden, 1st Earl of Avon (1897–1977), Foreign Secretary 1935–38, Secretary for the Dominions 1939–40, Secretary for War 1940, Foreign Secretary 1940–45 and 1951–55, Prime Minister 1955–57.

82 **Prof. John MacMurray:** An eminent philosopher (1891–1976), he was then Professor at London University.

84 **Gandhi:** Mahatma Gandhi (1869–1948), the great Indian leader, studied Law in England and practised as a barrister in Bombay before going to South Africa in 1907 and working among Indian settlers. In 1915 he returned to India and by the 1920s was the central figure in the movement for Indian independence. His advocacy of passive resistance and civil disobedience, as political weapons, was widely influential.

84 **King's Norton by-election:** Opposing Stuart Morris as independent pacifist candidate were Captain Basil Peto, for the National Government, and Dr Lumsden Smith, a "Bomb Berlin" candidate. Peto won by a majority of 19,877 votes; Morris, with 6.5 per cent of the poll, lost his deposit.

84 **Krishna Menon:** Born in Calicut, India, he (1896–1974) graduated from the London School of Economics with First Class Honours in 1927, was a borough councillor for St Pancras 1934–47, founded Penguin Books with Allen Lane in 1935, and was a member of the Labour Party until 1941. He became a close friend of Nehru, and after Indian Independence was named Indian High Commissioner to the United Kingdom.

84 **Donald Soper:** A Methodist minister, radical Christian and pacifist (b. 1903), Soper — later Lord Soper of Kingsway — was one of the original Sponsors of the PPU.

85 **Baba:** Another of VB's affectionate nicknames for her daughter Shirley, whose tonsils were removed on 5 April 1939.

85 **rising against us in Iraq:** Iraq's oil-fields were vitally important to the British war effort, especially for the Navy in the Mediterranean and the Army in the western desert. Iraq was then a British protectorate, but its pro-Axis Premier, Rashid Ali, used Rommel's victories to demand the withdrawal of British authority and troops. In response, the British Ambassador in Baghdad organised a coup, and a pro-British government was installed. On 1 June 1941, an Arab mob, angered by the British re-occupation of Baghdad, killed some 600 Jews and injured many more.

85 **Halifax:** Edward Wood, 1st Earl (1881–1959); he was a Conservative politician, Viceroy of India 1926–31, Foreign Secretary 1938–40, and Ambassador to the United States 1941–46.

85 **Mr Menzies:** (Sir) Robert Menzies (1894–1978), Australian Prime Minister 1939–1941 and 1949–66. Deeply preoccupied with the War, Menzies lost popularity at home and his English visit marked a rapid downturn in his political authority.

86 **Churchill's reception:** The Prime Minister had lost some popularity in 1941 as a result of Allied wartime misfortunes, and was increasingly criticised for his running of the war. However, he won a vote of confidence in the House of Commons on 7 May 1941 by a 447–3 margin.

86 **Winant:** John Winant (1889–1947), American diplomat and liberal Republican, was Ambassador to Britain 1941–46.

87 **Sir Stafford Cripps:** Sir Richard Stafford Cripps (1889–1952), Labour MP 1931–50; expelled from the Labour Party for a period for supporting the Popular Front, in 1942 he served as Lord Privy Seal and Leader of the House of Commons.

87 **John Rothenstein:** Sir William Rothenstein's son (b. 1901) was a prominent art critic and, 1938–64, Director and Keeper of the Tate Gallery.

89 **Rudolf Hess:** Subordinate only to Hitler and Goering, he was Deputy Leader of the Nazi Party from 1933. On 10 May 1941 Hess (1894–1987) flew

to Britain, on his own initiative, in the hope of arranging a negotiated peace. He was interned and at Nuremberg in 1945 was sentenced to life-imprisonment.

89 **Muriel Lester:** A prominent member of the FoR, she had been a pacifist during the First World War, protecting victims of anti-German riots. With the help of her father and sister, she founded Kingsley Hall, the East End settlement.

89 **Margaret S. J., Will:** VB's will had appointed Storm Jameson both literary executor and guardian of her children in the event of her and Catlin's deaths. Personal friction, exacerbated by Jameson's movement away from pacifism, led to increasing estrangement.

90 **Bill Grindlay, Alex Miller, Andrew Stewart:** Grindlay, later respected as a theologian and radio personality, worked at a London mission throughout the War. Miller, a New Zealander and charismatic Christian Socialist, conducted services in badly-bombed parts of East London. Stewart, a brilliant orator and journalist, had been leader of the Glasgow University Pacifist Society and largely responsible for Dick Sheppard's election as Rector (defeating Churchill) in 1937.

91 **Jennie Adamson, Sir Walter Wormsley:** She (1882–1962) was a prominent Labour MP 1938–46; he, 1st Bt (1878–1961), was a Conservative MP 1924–45 and Minister of Pensions 1939–45.

91 **Mary Adams:** First Director of the new wartime Department of Home Intelligence, established to monitor public response to the war. Her husband Vyvyan (1900–1951), a Conservative MP 1931 and 1935–45, had been Chairman of the British Commonwealth Peace Federation 1933–35, a member of the LNU Executive, and an advocate of disarmament.

92 **news from Crete sounded menacing:** Beginning on the morning of 20 May 1941, the Germans dropped some 23,000 airborne troops within 24 hours, on the island of Crete, which, after the British loss of Greece, was vital for the defence of Egypt and the Suez Canal, as well as an evacuation station for the BEF in Greece. Losses on both sides were extremely heavy.

92 **Jan Masaryk:** A Czechoslovak statesman (1886–1948), he spent most of the War in London as Foreign Minister and Deputy Prime Minister of the Czech Government-in-Exile. At the time of Munich (which provoked his resignation as Czech Foreign Minister), he commented to British delegates "If you have sacrificed my nation to preserve the peace of the world, I will be the first to applaud you. But if not, gentlemen, God help your souls."

92 *Little Plays of St Francis:* By Laurence Housman (1922).

92 **sinking of HMS *Hood*:** The German battleship *Bismarck* sank its British counterpart in the Denmark Strait on 24 May 1941; only three of the *Hood*'s 1,419 crew survived. The *Bismarck* was sunk by the Royal Navy three days later; only 110 of her 2,200 crew survived.

92 **Nancy Browne:** She had been Dick Sheppard's Secretary, and was now Secretary to the CBCO.

93 **Roosevelt speech, national emergency:** On 27 May Roosevelt stated that

"An unlimited national emergency confronts this country, which requires that its military, naval, air and civilian defences be put on the basis of readiness to repel any and all acts or threats of aggression directed toward any part of the Western hemisphere". He was not, however, granted any additional powers as a result of this appeal.

93 **Prof. Newall:** An astronomer (1857–1944), Hugh Newall had been Professor of Astrophysics at Cambridge.

93 **Mackay:** Ronald Mackay (1902–60), an Australian lecturer in Philosophy, History and Economics, held wartime positions in England with the Ministries of Labour and Aircraft Production. He wrote extensively in support of European Union, two of his books being *Federal Europe* (1940) and *Peace Aims and the New Order* (1942).

93 **Sir Wm Beveridge:** The prominent economist William Beveridge, 1st Baron Beveridge of Tuggal (1879–1963), then Master of University College, Oxford. A Liberal, he was author of "A Report on Social Insurance and Allied Services" — the Beveridge Report — which formed the basis for the welfare legislation of the 1945 Labour Government under Clement Attlee.

93 **Max Schmeling:** A German boxer (1905–41), he was world heavyweight champion 1930–32 — the first European in the twentieth century to win that title. His most famous bout was a twelve-round knock-out of Joe Louis in New York in June 1936.

93 **Andrew Dakers:** VB formed a productive partnership in 1940 with Dakers, who, from Pembury in Hertfordshire, set out to publish books promoting "the causes of peace, goodwill, social security, and sane domestic and international relationships".

93 **Zilliacus:** Konni Zilliacus (1894–1967), journalist, writer and Labour MP. He worked in the Information Section of the League of Nations Secretariat 1919–39 and in the Ministry of Information 1939–45.

93 **breaking the party truce:** The three main political parties had agreed at the outset of the War that vacancies in the House of Commons should be nominated by the Party in possession of the seat, without competition from the other two. By-elections, however, were still contested since independent and fringe-party candidates were not bound by the electoral truce.

94 **Ben Tillett:** Tillett (1886–1943) was a trade union leader and Labour MP 1917–24 and 1929–31, and a founder of the Independent Labour Party and the Labour Party.

94 **Richard Stokes MP:** A Major in the First World War, Stokes (1897–1957) had won the MC and Croix de Guerre. A Roman Catholic and Labour MP 1938–57, he was not a pacifist; but he was a staunch opponent of area bombing and of Winston Churchill's policies.

94 **Davies of Leek:** Harold Davies, Baron (b. 1904); Labour MP for Leek 1945–1970, and Joint Parliamentary Secretary to the Ministries of Pensions and Social Security 1965–67.

94 **Philip Noel-Baker:** A Labour politician (1889–1982), he was an MP

1929–31 and 1936–70, Parliamentary Secretary at the Ministry of War Transport 1942–45, and Minister of State in the Foreign Office 1945–6.

94   **Hugh Walpole:** (Sir) Hugh Walpole (1884–1941), prominent novelist and critic.

94   **death of ex-Kaiser:** Wilhelm II, German Emperor and King of Prussia 1888–1918; he had lived in exile in Holland. He despised Hitler and in 1940 Churchill offered him asylum in Britain.

94   **Mary:** VB had known Mary Macaulay before her marriage to F. W. Ogilvie, as a fellow student at Somerville College, Oxford. Widowed in 1949, Lady Ogilvie later became Principal of St Anne's College, Oxford, 1953–66.

95   **Frank Middleton:** A Certified Accountant as well as pacifist, he watched over the PPU's finances.

95   **Free French troops, Syria:** They were organised under the leadership of General Charles de Gaulle (1890–1970), who denounced the Vichy regime, and continued resistance to the Nazis. In June 1941, British and Free French troops invaded Syria to expel the 55,000-strong Vichy force (mostly soldiers from the African colonies) and to prevent the Germans from establishing air-bases in the Middle East. The fighting was bitter, but after a month the Allies prevailed.

96   **Idris:** The Cottage in which Edith Brittain was living at Carbis Bay, with her youngest sister.

96   **Lord Sankey & George Gibson:** Sankey (1866–1948) was Lord Chancellor 1929–35 and British Member of the Permanent Court of Arbitration at The Hague 1930–48; Gibson (1885–1953) was Chairman of the TUC 1940–41.

97   **"The Quick and the Dead":** VB abandoned this project.

97   **deeply in love with two men:** Presumably Roland Leighton and George Brett — although VB had offered to marry the wounded Victor Richardson shortly before his death in 1917, and had been attracted by Edward's friend Geoffrey Thurlow (who was also killed in 1917).

97   **Frank Pakenham:** 7th Earl of Longford (b. 1905), a socialist and writer often ridiculed for his extreme humanitarianism.

98   **Beaverbrook:** (Lord) William Aitken (1879–1964), Canadian-born newspaper magnate and Conservative politician, Minister of Aircraft Production 1940–41, Minister of Supply 1941–42, Lord Privy Seal 1943–45; a close friend and political ally of Churchill.

98   **Gilbert Murray:** Classical scholar and internationalist (1886–1957), Regius Professor of Greek at Oxford 1908–36; he was a Founder Member of the League of Nations Union and Chairman of its Executive Council 1923–38, and President of the UN Association 1945–49.

98   **Hardy:** The great novelist Thomas Hardy (1840–1928).

99   **William Longman:** Founder (1882–1967) of the prominent publishing firm.

99 **rations:** Food rationing was introduced on a restricted basis at the outbreak of war, but by mid-1941 the results of the sharp decline in the importation of foodstuffs were becoming noticeable, and by 1942 food imports were at less than half pre-war levels. In late 1941, points rationing was introduced to cover a wide range of foods. The general principle of rationing seems to have been almost universally popular (although the Ministry of Food did have to prosecute innumerable offenders): a survey conducted in summer 1942 revealed that 90 per cent of respondents approved of food-rationing, and over 60 per cent did so because they believed it ensured a fair distribution of food supplies.

100 **Hitler declared war on Russia:** Along a front of almost 2,000 miles Hitler threw more than three million troops (148 divisions). The Soviet Army was numerically superior but entirely unprepared for the Blitzkrieg; and in 18 days German forces had advanced within 200 miles of Moscow.

100 **Mme. Magda Yvois-Peters:** Now living in England with her artist-husband and daughter, she had been a member of the Antwerp City Council and the Belgian FoR.

100 **Cammaerts:** Emile Cammaerts (1876–1953), poet and Professor of Belgian Studies at the University of London 1931–47; he was an influential supporter of food relief for occupied Europe, and of Leopold III.

100 **Mrs Corbett Ashby:** Margery Corbett Ashby (1882–1981), prominent feminist, and Editor of *International Women's News*.

100 **Miss Solomon:** Daisy Solomon, of the British Commonwealth League, was an activist for Indian Independence.

102 **James Laver:** A prolific writer (1899–1975), he was Keeper of the Departments of Engraving, Illustration and Design, and of Paintings, at the Victoria and Albert Museum 1938–59.

102 **W. N. Hodgson:** The war poet William Noel Hodgson, MC (b. 1893), Lieutenant in the 9th Devons; his posthumously-published *Verse and Prose in Peace and War* was very popular.

102 **Eric Jellicoe; the Admiral:** Eric Jellicoe, a Lieutenant in the Sherwood Foresters, was killed at the age of twenty. His father John (1859–1935) became First Sea Lord in 1916 and Admiral of the Fleet in 1919, and then Governor-General of New Zealand 1920–24.

102 **Minsk & Lwow:** Minsk, the capital of Byelorussia, was captured on 28 June 1941, and Lwow (Lvov) fell two days later. By the end of June, the Germans had lost almost 9,000 men but by 10 July they were only 200 miles from Moscow.

102 **Lord Derby:** Edward Stanley (1865–1948), Director General of Recruiting 1915–16 (creator of the Derby Scheme), Secretary of State for War 1916–18 and 1922–24, Ambassador to France 1918–20.

103 **Caroline Haslett:** She was well known as a pioneer woman engineer (1895–1957).

103   **Owen Clover:** Warden of Friends' Hall, Walthamstow, a settlement run by Quakers.

103   **Dick Sheppard's** *Some of My Religion*: A collection (1935) of short essays originally published in the *Sunday Express*.

104   **Raymond Gram Swing:** An American broadcaster (1887–1968), he was the BBC's commentator on American affairs 1935–45.

104   **Jim Putnam:** A Macmillan executive in New York, he was an old friend of VB's.

106   **John Wheeler-Bennett:** An historian and biographer (1902–75), he worked in British information services in the United States 1940–44, and became Assistant Director General of the Foreign Office's Political Intelligence Department.

106   **treaty of alliance:** A treaty of mutual assistance was signed in Moscow between Britain and the USSR on 12 July 1941. The two countries also pledged that they would make no separate peace with Germany.

106   **John Gordon:** A prominent journalist (1890–1974), he was Editor-in-Chief of the *Sunday Express* from 1928.

106   **David Low:** A famous political cartoonist (1891–1963), best known for his "Colonel Blimp" cartoons; he was on the *Evening Standard* staff 1927–50.

106   **Christina Foyle:** As Managing Director of Foyle's, the famous London bookshop, she inaugurated, in 1930, Foyle's Literary Luncheons, so that "book lovers" could listen to "great personalities".

106   **Congress party:** The Indian National Congress was founded in 1885 and after 1920 was led by Gandhi. Congress leaders did not support the Imperial authorities over entry into the War since Indian opinion had not been consulted.

106   **Jennie Lee, Virginia Cowles, Polly Peabody, Mrs Sieff, Diana Wynyard, Lilian Braithwaite:** Women prominent in English life. Jennie Lee, later Baroness Lee of Asheridge (b. 1904), wife of Aneurin Bevan, was later a leading Labour MP, 1945–70. Virginia Cowles, an American-born writer and journalist (1912–1983), was Assistant to the American Embassy 1942–43. Polly Peabody, a writer, had published *Occupied Territory* in 1941. Rebecca Sieff (d. 1966) was wife of Israel (later Baron) Sieff, pillar of the British Jewish community and President of Marks and Spencer. Diana Wynyard (1916–64) and (Dame) Lilian Braithwaite (1873–1948) were eminent actresses.

107   **Mrs Tate, MP:** Mavis Tate (1893–1947) was a Conservative MP 1931–45.

107   **Prunella Stack:** founder, Women's League of Health and Beauty; her husband, 14th Duke of Hamilton (1903–44), had been a Unionist MP 1930–40.

107   **Frank Lea:** Later John Middleton Murry's biographer, Lea (b. 1915) was Editor of *Peace News* 1946–49, in succession to Murry.

109   **economic sanctions against Japan:** Japanese assets in Britain and the

United States were frozen in an attempt to curb a military build-up in Indochina; but Japanese troops began landings there only two days later.

110   **"She for God in him":** From Milton's *Paradise Lost*, Book I.

110   **Blake's theories:** John Middleton Murry had published a book on William Blake's poetry and ideas in 1933.

111   **possible book on Amy:** Unable to write a biography of George Lansbury, VB had now turned her attention to Amy Johnson, the famous aviator (1904–41) who had established many records for solo flights in the 1930s and had recently died flying, in mysterious circumstances.

112   **G.'s autobiography:** Catlin did not publish his autobiography until 1972; it was then revised extensively and entitled *For God's Sake, Go!*.

112   **Timoshenko's army:** Marshal Semyon Timoshenko (1895–1970), commander of the central army group on the Soviet western front. In October 1941, the Germans continued to make deep inroads into Russian territory, and on 10 October factories in Moscow began to be dismantled for transportation eastward.

112   **Anglican Pacifist Fellowship:** Founded in 1937, it had a membership of about 1,500 by the outbreak of the War.

113   **Dr Percy Hartill, C. Paul Gliddon:** Chairman and Secretary respectively of the APF. Among the books published by Hartill, who was Rector of Stoke-on-Trent 1935–55, is *Pacifism and Christian Commonsense* (1938). Gliddon was Editor of the *Christian Pacifist*.

113   **Atlantic Charter:** A statement of fundamental principles and democratic ideals drawn up and signed by Roosevelt and Churchill at their first wartime meeting in Placentia Bay, Newfoundland, 9–12 August 1941. The Charter was of immense propaganda value to Britain since it demonstrated the strength of the tie between the two countries, and the decline of isolationist sentiment in the United States. As a result, attitudes toward Washington hardened in both Berlin and Tokyo.

113   **Sir John and Lady Mactaggart:** They were wealthy friends (VB called them "near millionaires"). Mactaggart, later 1st Bt (1867–1956), had made his fortune as a builder, and was founder of the American and British Commonwealth Association.

114   **Derek Edwards:** A CO and member of the IVSP, of which he was later General Secretary; presently Vice-Chairman of the British Section of Amnesty International.

114   **Richmond, Father:** VB's father, deeply depressed, had drowned himself in the Thames in August 1935; his body had been found at Richmond.

114   **Cyril Asquith:** He (1902–67) was Secretary and Chief Organiser of the National Labour Organisation 1936–46.

114   **Ramsay Macdonald:** Labour statesman (1866–1937) and Prime Minister 1924, 1929–35.

114   **Plymouth Blitz:** Plymouth was badly bombed, especially in the March and

April 1941 series of blitzes. (On 20 March, 293 planes dropped 346 tons of bombs, destroying or damaging 18,000 houses, and the April bombings left 30,000 homeless.) In all, Plymouth's casualty figure stood at 1,172 dead.

116   **Andrew Marvell:** The Metaphysical poet and political writer (1620–78).

116   **Pearl Harbour:** The spectacular Japanese attack on the US Pacific Fleet near Hawaii brought the US into the War.

1942

117   **Hong Kong gone, Sarawak going:** The Hong Kong garrison surrendered to the Japanese on Christmas Day 1941; Sarawak was abandoned by the British on 1 January 1941, after Indian troops destroyed its oilfields to prevent them falling into Japanese hands.

117   **Penang gone, war in Malaya:** British troops were evacuated from Penang, the earliest British settlement (1786) on the Malay peninsula, on 19 December 1941. The peninsula's rich resources of tin and rubber made it very important to the British war effort.

117   **Rangoon, Singapore bombed:** Rangoon, capital of Burma, was bombed on 23 December 1941. Singapore was first bombed on 8 December, and further raids on 1 January 1942 caused extensive destruction.

117   **Manila burning, Americans outnumbered in Philippines:** Manila was repeatedly bombed in December 1941, declared an open city on 26 December but bombed further for two days, and occupied on 2 January 1942. Roosevelt and Churchill had agreed that the war in Europe was to have priority over the war in the Pacific, calculating that Japan could be defeated at leisure following Hitler's defeat.

117   **Russia, Nazis retreating:** By December 1941 the German army had advanced into the forests outside the western suburbs of Moscow, but the severity of the Russian winter and the tenacity of the Soviet defence halted its advance. This was the first severe German setback on land. There was no major retreat, since Hitler refused to accept any suggestion of a withdrawal, but the Soviets gained an incalculable psychological advantage: the knowledge that the Wehrmacht could be stopped.

117   **Libya, Nazis retreating:** In the first week of January the British 8th Army launched a successful offensive against Rommel's *Afrika Korps*, giving Britain her first victory over German troops since the War began.

117   **US, China as Allies:** Germany and Italy declared war on the United States, after the latter declared war against Japan on 8 December (although Hitler was not bound by treaty to do so). China had, since 1937, been fighting a full-scale, but undeclared, war against Japan, the aggressor; hence, following American and British declarations of war upon Japan, China became their ally.

117   **Whitman's *Leaves of Grass*:** The first, very influential book of poems by Walt Whitman (1819–92), published in 1855.

117   **Mrs Nehru, All-India Women's Congress:** Rameshuri Nehru was President of the Congress.

117   **fighting in Manila:** Japanese forces occupied Manila on 2 January 1942.

117   **Wavell:** Field Marshal Sir Archibald Wavell, later 1st Earl Wavell (1883–1950), Commander-in-Chief Middle East 1939–41, Supreme Commander in the Far East against Japan 1942, Viceroy of India 1943–47.

118   **Japs advancing on Singapore:** British troops were ordered on 9 January to pull back to Johore for a final stand in defence of Singapore.

118   **Roosevelt's budget:** US war expenditure in 1942 would be around £500-million per month, and it was expected that this would more than double in 1943.

119   **Sir Sefton Brancker, Lord Wakefield:** Both were aviation enthusiasts: Air Vice-Marshal Sir (William) Sefton Brancker (1877–1930), Director of Civil Aviation from 1922; Charles (1st Viscount) Wakefield (1859–1941), Alderman of the City of London, closely involved with aeronautical endeavour around the world.

120   **Jim Mollison:** Amy Johnson married her fellow-aviator in 1932, but divorced him in 1938; they had made several record-breaking flights together.

120   **Wilcox, Anna Neagle, Amy Johnson film:** *They Flew Alone* (American title: *Wings and the Woman*), directed by Herbert Wilcox, starring Anna Neagle as Amy Johnson and Robert Newton as Jim Mollison, was released in 1941.

121   **Australia getting alarmed:** Japanese advances in Malaya aroused great concern about the defence of the Australian continent. Between February and April 1942, Japanese aircraft attacked Darwin 14 times, and on the night of 31 May–1 June four Japanese midget submarines made an unsuccessful attempt to enter Sydney harbour.

122   **Churchill back:** He had left for the US on 12 December 1941, and remained there for five weeks. He went there to discuss with Roosevelt full Allied co-operation, and they established the Combined Chiefs of Staff to direct the war effort. The talks were held in Washington between 22 December and 7 January. Churchill also made a short visit to Canada, addressing the Canadian Parliament on 30 December.

122   **Major Braithwaite:** Albert Braithwaite (1893–1959), a Conservative MP 1926–45, was a member of a Military Mission to the US.

122   **ABCA:** The Army Bureau of Current Affairs, founded by Sir Ronald Adam, the Adjutant General, in August 1941, and directed by W. E. Williams. ABCA, under whose auspices Gordon Catlin often lectured, provided compulsory adult educxation for troops.

123   **Arthur Wragg:** An artist well known as a book-illustrator, he had been one of the PPU's original Sponsors and remained a firm pacifist throughout the War.

123   **Jap landings in New Guinea, agitation in Australia:** With these, Japanese forces moved to within a thousand miles of north-east Australia.

123   **Dr Nevin Sayre, *Fellowship*:** The eminent American pacifist was a leading member of the American FoR; and *Fellowship* its journal.

123   **Churchill, vote of confidence:** The debate took place from 27 to 29 January 1942, and Churchill won a resounding vote of confidence: 464–1.

123   **Hannan Swaffer:** A well-known journalist and critic (1879–1962), he wrote for many London newspapers, including the *Daily Mirror* and the *Daily Herald*.

124   **Admiral Kimmel, Lieut. Commander [Short]:** Rear Admiral Husband Kimmel and Lieutenant General Walter Short, the Navy and Army Commanders at Pearl Harbor, were found by a special court of inquiry to have ignored warnings of attack and to have taken inadequate defensive precautions.

124   **food for Greece:** The Government announced a relief shipment of wheat to Greece. On 13 March a British foodship, *Rabmanso*, left Haifa for Athens, carrying 7,000 tons of grain.

124   **George Shepherd:** He (1881–1954) was Labour Party National Agent 1929–46.

124   **Lords Denham and Moyne:** Senior Conservative politicians: George Bowyer, 1st Baron Denham (1886–1948) had been an MP 1918–37 and was in the War Office 1940–45; Walter Guinness, 1st Baron Moyne (1880–1944), was Colonial Secretary and Leader of the House of Lords 1941–42.

125   **Rev. Henry Carter:** General Secretary of the Methodist Social Welfare Department and a leading temperance reformer (1874–1951), he became a pacifist in 1933 and founded the Methodist Peace Fellowship.

125   **Singapore beleaguered:** British forces withdrew to Singapore island from the Malayan mainland 20–31 January; by 30 January, Japanese forces were within 20 miles, and systematic Japanese air attacks on Singapore began on 31 January.

126   **changes in Government:** Although Churchill won the 29 January vote of confidence, he conceded the main point made by his critics — the need for a Ministry of Production.

126   **Sir A. Duncan:** Sir Andrew Duncan (1884–1952), a Conservative MP 1940–50, was Minister of Supply 1942–45.

126   **PC:** Macmillan was appointed Privy Councillor in 1942.

126   **Ronald Kidd:** A former journalist (d. 1942), he founded the National Council for Civil Liberties in 1934 (primarily because of his concern about police handling of fascist marches in London) and was its first General Secretary.

127   **Ralph Ingersoll's *Report on England*:** This popular study of England during the War had been published by John Lane the year before, 1941.

127 **Singapore going:** On 11 February 1942 the Japanese issued an ultimatum demanding Singapore's surrender.

127 **Australia calling up 45's:** The decision to conscript men over 45 years old was another indication of Australian worry about the Japanese threat.

127 ***"Recessional":*** This well-known poem (1897) by Rudyard Kipling (1856–1936) warns of the disintegration of Empire.

128 **3 German capital ships:** The *Prinz Eugen* was a heavy cruiser armed with 8-inch guns; the *Gneisenau* and *Scharnhorst* were battleships armed with 11-inch guns. On 12 February they were sighted near Boulogne; six Swordfish were sent to attack them, and all were lost. Further British losses were incurred, but all three warships reached home port safely on 13 February.

128 **Compton Mackenzie:** The popular novelist (1883–1972).

128 **Alistair Cooke:** An English broadcaster and journalist domiciled in America (b. 1908), he is widely known for his radio reports, over several decades, on American–British affairs.

129 **fall of Singapore:** On 15 February 1942, the 85,000 British, Australian and Indian defending troops surrendered, after 70 days' resistance.

129 **Pethick Lawrence:** Frederick (Lord) Pethick Lawrence (1871–1961), prominent socialist, pacifist and campaigner for women's suffrage; he was a Labour MP 1923–31 and 1935–45, and Secretary of State for India and Burma 1945–47. VB wrote a biography of him (1963).

129 **Gallacher:** The Scotsman William Gallacher (1881–1965), Communist MP 1935–50, President of the British Communist Party 1956–63.

129 **Court of Inquiry:** The escape of the German ships was a signal victory for Germany since British oil reserves were very low and the submarine threat to the North Atlantic at its height (in March 1942, 95 ships were sunk in the North Atlantic).

129 **Bethel-bei-Bielefeld, Pastor von Bodelschwingh:** The Epileptic Hospital and Home there were bombed, with many casualties, in autumn 1940; VB admired the Pastor's subsequent plea for reconciliation.

129 **first air-raids on Australia:** The city of Darwin was bombed by some 150 carrier-based Japanese planes; 390 citizens were killed or injured.

130 **Cabinet changes:** Reaction to the reverses in the Far East, and the escape of the three German ships into the North Sea, forced Churchill to reform his War Cabinet.

130 **D. H. Lawrence idea:** The prolific writer (1885–1930), who had been a friend of Murry's, preached masculine dominance.

130 ***Sergeant York:*** Directed by Howard Hawks, this 1941 film about "a gentle hillbilly who became a hero of World War I" starred Gary Cooper.

130 **Margesson dropped:** David Margesson (1890–1965), later 1st Viscount, Conservative MP 1924–42, Secretary of State for War 1940–42.

130 **Lord Reith:** Sir John Reith, 1st Baron (1889–1972), Director General of the

BBC 1927–38, Minister of Information then Minister of Transport 1940, Minister of Works 1940–42.

130   **post-war planning:** Churchill was frequently criticised by his political opponents for his lack of attention to postwar reconstruction.

130   **"Day of Judgment":** The novel finally published in 1944 (New York) and 1945 (London) as *Account Rendered*. Because of legal problems relating to the protagonist's original, VB was prevented from publishing it as first written and, with the help of Dennis Stoll, rewrote it, with the protagonist transmuted into a musician to prevent identification.

131   **service at St Martin's :** VB's connection with St Martin-in-the-Fields, the Anglican church near Trafalgar Square, had begun in the mid-1930s, when Dick Sheppard was its Rector. She remained a member of its congregation to the end of her life.

131   **Mrs Pandit:** Vijaya Lakshmi Pandit, sister of Jawaharlal Nehru and prominent Indian politician; she was later Ambassador to the USSR 1947–49 and USA 1949–52, then High Commissioner in London 1954–61. VB was to write her biography, *Envoy Extraordinary* (1965).

131   **"The Higher Retribution":** VB's pamphlet was published by the PPU later in 1942. It argues against the Germanophobic views of Lord Vansittart and his supporters, recommending generosity towards the enemy ("We can safely leave the war's criminals . . . to the Almighty, who has claimed vengeance as his . . .").

132   ***Shall Our Children Live or Die?:*** This "Reply to Lord Vansittart on the German problem" by Victor Gollancz was published in 1942.

132   **heavy raid by RAF on Paris:** On 3 March 1942, Bomber Command attacked the Renault factory, killing 623 and injuring 1,500. These figures are, however, disputed.

132   **conditions worsening in Java:** The Dutch formally surrendered Java on 9 March, and the next day all Allied forces in the Dutch East Indies surrendered unconditionally to the Japanese.

133   **S. African war:** The Anglo-Boer War of 1899–1902.

133   **Mr Dingle Foot:** He (1905–78) was a Liberal MP 1931–45 and Parliamentary Secretary to the Ministry of Economic Warfare 1940–45.

133   **Edith Pye:** A Quaker, she was a prominent member of the Famine Relief Committee.

134   **Curtin:** John Curtin (1885–1945), Australian Labour Prime Minister 1941–45.

134   ***Exeter* and other ships disappeared:** HMS *Exeter*, a cruiser, was engaged in the Battle of Java Sea, which involved nine Allied destroyers and five Allied cruisers. *Exeter* was shelled early in the battle, and sank.

135   **MacArthur of the Philippines:** General Douglas MacArthur (1880–1964), Supreme Commander of the Allied Forces in the Far East 1941–42, then Supreme Commander in the South West Pacific 1942–45. He accepted Japan's surrender at Tokyo in September 1945.

137 **F. W. Ogilvie, BBC:** He had been forced to resign as Governor-General of the BBC in January 1942, as a result of allowing pacifist ministers freedom of speech in religious radio programmes. He became Principal of Jesus College, Oxford, in 1945.

137 **the growing Vansittart propaganda:** Lord Vansittart was openly German-ophobic and strongly in favour of unconditional Allied victory. In the autumn of 1940 he had made a series of BBC Overseas Service broadcasts, collectively entitled *The Black Record*, contending that the entire German people was criminal and deserving of punishment.

137 **dividend from Brittain's:** 3VB had inherited shares in the family paper mills near Stoke-on-Trent in Staffordshire.

137 **Herbert Morrison "watching"** *Peace News*: At the PPU's executive meeting of 31 March 1942, concern was expressed about the possibility that *Peace News* would be shut down by the Home Office, in the wake of a question asked about it in the House of Commons. Murry, as Editor, commented that he would be well advised to temper criticism of the Government, for the moment.

137 **J. B. S. Haldane:** A well-known writer, socialist and geneticist (1892–1964).

138 **Eden in Moscow:** In December 1941, Eden discussed with Stalin two treaties which the latter wished to make with Britain. To the one dealing with the postwar shape of Europe Stalin proposed adding a secret protocol which would have made a mockery of the Atlantic Charter's assertion of the right of peoples to choose their governments freely.

138 **Molotov:** Vyacheslav Molotov (1890–1986), staunch supporter of Stalin, Russian Foreign Minister 1939–49.

139 **V.G., meeting in Chelsea:** At that meeting of the Left Book Club in March 1939, Gollancz (who had published *Testament of Youth* in 1933) had spoken emotionally about the urgency of smashing German militarism, and their ensuing disagreement led to VB's publishing several of her later books with Macmillan. However, she found herself increasingly allied to Goll-ancz's political and social thought during the War, and sought reconcilia-tion.

139 **Emlyn Williams,** *The Morning Star*: This topical play by the Welsh actor and playwright (1905–87) was first produced in 1941.

139 **double summer-time:** By Government order, clocks were advanced two hours to gain maximum working advantage from daylight.

139 **collapse of India negotiations:** In late March 1942, Sir Stafford Cripps led a special delegation to India in the hope of winning Indian adherence to a scheme for self-government and dominion status. The Congress Party, however, demanded immediate independence. The failure of the talks was announced on 11 April 1942.

140 **Andreas Michalopoulos:** He was later Adviser to the Greek Embassy in New York.

140 **"Liberty cut":** A short, wavy hairstyle, easy to maintain, it was promoted by the Ministry of Health to combat lice-infestation during war conditions.

140 **Horabin, MP:** J. L. Horabin (1896–1956), Liberal MP 1939–47.

140 **Coppock:** Richard Coppock (b. 1885), formerly an alderman of the LCC, was General Secretary of the National Federation of Building Trades Operatives.

140 **Rose Macaulay:** An eminent writer (1881–1958), admired for her novels and travel-books; she had been a pacifist before the War.

140 **Michael Foot:** Labour politician and writer (b. 1913), he was on the staff of the *Evening Standard* 1938–42, becoming its Editor in 1942; he became Leader of the Opposition 1981–83.

140 **Edith Summerskill:** A prominent politician (1901–80) created Baroness in 1961, she was a Labour MP 1938–61, and became Parliamentary Secretary to the Ministry of Food 1945–50 and Chairman of the Labour Party 1954–55.

140 **D. N. Pritt:** A politician and QC (1887–1972), he was a Labour MP 1935–40, then (after being expelled from the Party because he supported the Soviet invasion of Finland in November 1940) an Independent MP 1940–50.

140 **Aneurin Bevan:** A leading Labour politician (1897–1960), MP 1929–60, Minister of Health 1945–51 and Deputy Leader of the Labour Party 1959–60. A Welsh ex-miner, on the left of the Party, he was a forceful critic of Churchill during the War.

140 **Frank Owen:** A journalist (1905–79), he was Editor of the *Evening Standard* 1938–42.

141 **Mrs Pethick Lawrence, "Fate Has Been Kind":** Emmeline Pethick Lawrence (1867–1943), like her husband a leading feminist, socialist and pacifist; his autobiography was published in the year she died.

141 ***Truth is Not Sober:*** Winifred Holtby's collection of short stories whose publication in America VB, as Literary Executor, had overseen.

142 **first bombing of Tokyo:** The attack did little physical damage, but in carrying the war to Japan helped to persuade its leaders to concentrate on territorial consolidation rather than further far Eastern expansion. Other Japanese cities were also raided.

142 **devastation, Lübeck and other places:** RAF Bomber Command's main offensive of the War against Germany opened on the night of 28–29 March with a raid on the medieval port city of Lübeck. On 10–11 April, the RAF dropped its first 8,000-lb bomb on Essen.

143 **fiasco, Swordfish:** Six of these RAF torpedo-bombers were sent to attack the German warships, and all were shot down.

143 **James Norbury:** A writer (b. 1904), he published two biographies and several books on crafts.

143 **letter on Sorensen:** In this letter ("Pacifists in Parliament", *Peace News*, 13

March 1943), VB defended Reginald Sorensen's right to support the Government on occasion, arguing that pacifists must be free to act as "leaven within the war-supporting lump".

144 **T C. Foley:** A Quaker member of the PPU and a free-lance journalist, he was also Secretary of the Pedestrians' Association.

144 **Alan Eden-Green:** A CO, he worked throughout the War for a voluntary organisation in SE London, providing emergency information and advice. Later he went into public relations and was co-founder 1977 of the Industry and Parliament Trust.

144 **Albert Belden:** Well-known as the Superintendent Minister of Whitefield's Tabernacle 1927–39, he (1883–1964) was the author of many books on religion.

144 **"area bombing":** Several terms were used for the policy of intensive bombing over a limited area. "Area bombing" and "strategic bombing", neutral or positive in connotation, were favoured by its supporters; other terms — "carpet bombing", "saturation bombing" and (favoured by opponents) "mass bombing" — quickly came into use.

144 **"everything with 3 stars in *Baedeker*":** The "Baedeker raids", referring to the well-known German tourist guidebooks, were attempts to destroy cities and towns known for their medieval architecture, and were ordered by Hitler in retaliation for the fire-raid on Lübeck. Exeter was bombed on 24–25 April, Bath on 25–26 and 26–27 April, Norwich on 27–28 and 29–30 April, and York on 28–29 April.

144 **Nazis raided York:** About twenty German bombers attacked the city; the Minster was not damaged, but a direct hit on a girls' school killed five teachers. The planes flew low in the moonlight, machine-gunning many streets, and five were shot down.

145 **Rhys Davies, question:** In the wake of the bombing of Lübeck and Rostock, Davies asked in the House of Commons, on 29 April, "whether the intensified bombing operations over Germany, including the attack on Lübeck, have involved a departure from the previously declared policy of His Majesty's Government that such operations would be confined to military objectives."

145 **Sinclair:** Sir Archibald Sinclair, later 1st Viscount Thurso (1890–1970), Liberal MP 1922–45, Leader of the Parliamentary Liberal Party 1935–45; he was Secretary of State for Air 1940–45.

145 **Humphrey Moore:** A journalist and early PPU member, he had founded *Peace News* and edited it until Murry took over in 1940.

145 **Government defeated in by-elections:** In Rugby and Wallasey, Unionist seats went to Independents after their incumbents were elevated to the peerage. Both winners (W. J. Brown and G. L. Roakes) supported the war effort and Churchill's government, and the result was widely attributed to reaction against undistinguished candidates nominated by party organisations under the truce.

146   **Master of Selwyn:** The Revd George Chase (1886–1971); a chaplain
awarded the MC in the First World War, he was Master of Selwyn College,
Cambridge, 1934–46, and subsequently Bishop of Ripon 1946–59.

146   **Maude Royden:** Later Maude Royden Shaw (1876–1956), she was well
known as a feminist, socialist, Christian activist and pioneering woman
preacher.

146   **Brendan Bracken:** Prominent during the War as Churchill's right-hand
man, the Irish-born Bracken (1901–58) was a Conservative MP 1929–45
and Minister of Information 1941–45.

146   **"Council of Seven", Mrs William Paterson:** Dorothy Paterson's group
seems to have been directed towards a "spiritual" response to war issues.

146   **Elizabeth Sprigge:** Well known as a biographer, translator and lecturer
(1900–74), she was a Swedish specialist in the Ministry of Information
1941–44.

147   **Geoffrey Pittock-Buss:** A socialist and journalist, he was Editor of a local
newspaper near London.

147   **Vansittartism:** In response to the wide dissemination of Vansittart's views,
this term implied for many the Germanophobia characteristic of "Bitter
Enders" (who insisted that the War must be fought until Germany
surrendered unconditionally).

147   **large naval battle:** The Battle of the Coral Sea, 4–8 May, was the first naval
engagement fought solely by aircraft flying from carriers. Although a
Japanese victory, losses were high enough to force cancellation of plans to
invade Australia. (The American Navy lost its aircraft-carrier *Lexington*, a
destroyer and a tanker; but at least 7 Japanese warships were sunk and 20
damaged.)

147   **Ronald Mallone, poems:** *Blood and Sweat and Tears: a selection of poems written
between November 18th, 1940 [and] May 31st, 1942*, by Ronald Mallone, was
published late in 1942. It has an Introduction by VB, and her copy is
inscribed with the author's "sincerest thanks for your encouragement and
all your kind advice". Mallone is today a prominent member of the PPU.

147   **German offensive against Russia:** This was launched on 8 May in an
attempt to capture the Caucasus oil fields.

147   **MPs Cove, Harvey, Wilson:** C. H. Wilson (1862–1945), Labour MP
1922–31 and 1935–44; T. E. Harvey (1875–1955), Independent Progressive
MP 1937–45; W. G. Cove (1888–1963), Labour MP 1929–59. All three
were pacifists.

148   **huge battles, Kharkov, Kerch:** The Russian offensive at Kharkov in the
Crimea, to counter the German offensive, was launched on 13 May; it was
halted on 23 May, and defeated five days later. German forces attacked the
Kerch peninsula on 11 May and took it on 15 May. The outcome was the
virtual expulsion of the Red Army from the Crimea; some 176,000 were
killed or wounded, and 100,000 taken prisoner.

149   **Miss English:** F. Winifred English, who lived in Loughborough, was an

ardent PPU member and subscriber to VB's "Letters to Peace Lovers"; they became friends.

150 **Communist Party:** The Communist Party of Great Britain was founded in July 1920. Official membership figures indicate a steady increase from 17,756 in mid-1939 to 22,738 in December 1941 and to about 56,000 in December 1942.

150 **Barbara Gould, Philip Baker:** Labour MPs: Gould 1880–1950 was also a NEC member; Philip Noel-Baker (1889–1982), was Parliamentary Secretary at the Ministry of War Transport 1942–45.

151 **mammoth air-raid on Cologne:** On 30–31 May, the RAF launched the first 1,000-bomber raid of the War. That night, 1,455 tons of bombs — most of them incendiaries — were dropped on Cologne by 1,130 aircraft (39 of which were lost), causing great fires and widespread destruction.

151 **raid on Essen:** This was the second 1,000–bomber raid. The target of 1,036 aircraft was the huge Krupp armaments works; 35 planes were lost.

152 **20,000 killed in Cologne, 54,000 injured:** These figures are greatly exaggerated. German records indicate that some 486 people were killed, 5,027 injured, and 59,100 made homeless by the raid; and that 18,432 buildings were destroyed.

153 **delayed bomb explosion at Elephant & Castle:** This famous public-house (in Southwark) had been at the centre of a huge fire after the last night of the London Blitz, 10 May 1941, when 1,436 people were killed and 1,792 seriously injured. The detonation of the undetected bomb killed 19 people and injured 59, destroying five big buildings and damaging some 200 houses.

153 **Professor Jevons:** H. S. Jevons (1875–1955) was, like his famous father W. S. Jevons, an economist. Although not a pacifist, he was co-opted as Chairman of the Bombing Restriction Committee in 1943 (his obituary in *The Times* made no mention of this).

153 **Air Comm. Harris:** Marshal of the RAF, (Sir) Arthur "Bomber" Harris (1892–1984) was Commander-in-Chief of Bomber Command 1942–45.

153 **Bracken, impediment inherited from Churchill?:** Because of their closeness and some physical resemblance, it was widely, but wrongly, rumoured that Brendan Bracken was Churchill's illegitimate son.

155 **Tobruk now threatened:** On 13 June, "Black Saturday", the British Eighth Army lost 230 out of a 300-strong task force in German ambush at El Adem: Rommel's way to Tobruk now lay open.

155 **deaths, John Masefield's son:** Masefield (1878–1967), Poet Laureate from 1930, was one of Britain's best-known writers.

155 **"down, down, down . . .", Edna St Vincent Millay:** The quotations are from "Dirge without Music" (1928) by the well-known American poet (1892–1950).

155 **shipping losses:** During 1942, the Allies lost approximately eight ships for

every U-boat sunk; the total British, Allied, and Neutral merchant-shipping losses in 1942 amounted to over six million tons in the Atlantic alone.

155   **Molotov, visit:** On 26 May 1942, Britain and the Soviet Union signed a 20-year mutual aid agreement. Molotov also requested the opening of a second front; Moscow's intentions in regard to eastern Europe and Germany were made clear during Eden's December 1941 meeting with Stalin.

156   **John M. M., wife, Mary Gamble:** Middleton Murry's second wife (after Katherine Mansfield), was Violet le Maistre (m. 1924); his third was Elizabeth Cockbayne; and in 1954 he was to marry Mary Gamble, his colleague in the PPU.

156   *The Screwtape Letters:* C. S. Lewis's popular religious book — it had some resemblance to VB's *Humiliation with Honour*, especially in form — was published in 1942.

156   **driven out of Libya:** Tobruk fell to the Germans on 21 June after a 33-week siege; some 30,000 Allied prisoners, and an invaluable store of supplies, were taken.

156   **Churchill still in America:** The second Washington Conference, 18–26 June 1942, decided on the establishment of a second front and a higher priority for atomic research.

157   **criticism, Sir J. Wardlaw-Milne:** A Conservative MP 1922–45, Wardlaw-Milne (1878–1967) was antagonistic towards Churchill's handling of the War; 25 MPs voted for his motion.

157   **Rommel's troops, advance:** On 22 June, Rommel's troops entered Egypt and by 25 June had advanced fifty miles. Rommel was promoted to Field Marshal on 26 June.

158   **Bremen, raid:** The third 1,000-bomber raid, it was carried out by more than 1,300 bombers. Bremen was an important military target since it was the second-largest German port and a U-boat manufacturing centre.

158   *How Green Was My Valley:* This sentimental 1941 film, based on Richard Llewellyn's novel about childhood in a Welsh mining-village, was directed by John Ford, and starred Walter Pidgeon and Maureen O'Hara.

158   **chances of holding Egypt:** On 28 June, British troops were ordered to withdraw to El Alamein, 70 miles from Alexandria. Rommel's success was so great that Hitler was advised to alter his military priorities and concentrate on the capture of Middle Eastern oilfields, rather than those of the Caucasus. Determined to prosecute the war in Russia, he resisted the advice, and so allowed the Eighth Army to regroup and re-arm.

158   **Mersa Matruh:** A town on the Egyptian frontier defended by the British Tenth Corps; 8,000 Allied soldiers were taken prisoner.

158   **adverse leader on food relief:** *Peace News*, under John Middleton Murry's editorship, adopted a destructive attitude towards the Food Relief Campaign, denying it publicity. In this leader, on 19 June, Murry had written: "It would seem an unwise use of the small forces of pacifism to concentrate them on a campaign which has no hope of success." Although the Food

Relief Campaign (unlike the campaign against area-bombing) was officially endorsed by the PPU, in January 1942 Murry had told the PPU's Executive that, as Editor of *Peace News*, he did not accept "the view that adoption by the National Council of any particular campaign carried with it *de jure* appropriation of space in *Peace News* in defiance of editorial judgement."

158 **James Hudson:** A committed pacifist, he was one of the first PPU Sponsors (1881–1962); a Labour MP 1923–31, and again after the War, 1945–55; Secretary of the National Temperance Federation.

158 **Auchinleck, taken over from Ritchie:** Sir Claude Auchinleck (1884–1981) took over personal command of the Eighth Army on 25 June 1942 and won the first Battle of Alamein (30 June–25 July), preventing Rommel from breaking through to the Nile delta. His predecessor Ritchie was held responsible for the disastrous ambush at El Adem.

159 **W. S. Morrison:** Later 1st Viscount Dunrossil (1893–1961), he was a Conservative MP 1929–59, Minister of Food 1939–40, Postmaster-General 1940–42, and Minister of Town and Country Planning 1942–45.

159 **news from Egypt worse:** On 30 June, German and Italian troops were only 15 miles from El Alamein. The Germans took Mersa Matruh (and some 6,000 prisoners). Alexandria was bombed. The Axis so confidently expected victory that Mussolini flew that day to Tripoli to prepare for a victory parade through Cairo.

159 **"No Confidence" vote:** This motion of censure was seconded by Aneurin Bevan, but Churchill won it by the high margin VB recorded.

159 **the "Maginot mind":** Blinkered optimism about military security.

160 **Duchess of Kent, second son:** Prince Michael was born on 4 July 1942 and christened by the Archbishop of Canterbury on 4 August.

160 **M.S.J. letters, copied:** Before returning them as requested, VB did have copies made of Storm Jameson's letters to her; they are among her Papers.

161 **news still indecisive:** By 4 July, German forces on the Eastern front had secured a base on the Don River, but on the desert front the Afrika Korps was suffering from exhaustion and ammunition shortages.

161 **Miss Hockaday:** It was possible that Shirley could attend the private girls' school, in Dallas, Texas, founded by Miss Hockaday, some of whose students had impressed VB early in 1939.

161 **Dreyfus:** Henry Dreyfus (1882–1944) was Chairman and Managing Director of British Celanese Ltd.

161 **happening in Egypt, Japanese so quiet:** In order to regroup and rest his force, Rommel began to use Italian units in frontline positions; Auchinleck, knowing this, successfully concentrated his troops against the less-hardened Italians, so forcing Rommel to replace them with his own men. In the Far East, the Japanese were preparing for their landing on the north coast of Papua.

162 **Hungerford Club:** This shelter, run under the aegis of the West London Mission, cared for a total of some 4,500 homeless Londoners.

162 **Ellis Roberts' biography:** *H. R. L. Sheppard: Life and Letters* by Richard Ellis Roberts was published by John Murray in 1942.

162 **Russians being driven back:** The German army, now routing the Red Army, especially at the southern end of the front, seemed on the brink of forcing a total Soviet collapse. But the Red Army's position was eased by the arrival of some T34 tanks, whose crudity made them less susceptible to the harsh conditions than the more sophisticated German machinery.

162 **G.'s new book:** "The Union of the West" was published later in 1942, retitled *Anglo-American Union as the Nucleus of World Federation.*

163 **Minturn Sedgwick:** VB had known this young American for several years, having met him during one of her lecture-tours.

163 **Dame Edith Lyttlelton:** Writer and administrator (d. 1948), she had been a substitute delegate to the League of Nations.

163 **Archibald MacLeish:** An eminent American poet and academic (1892–1982), he was Rede Lecturer at Cambridge in 1942.

164 **Paul Berry:** A writer and lecturer (b. 1919) distantly related to Winifred Holtby, he later succeeded VB as Holtby's literary executor, and is VB's senior literary executor. Author of *By Royal Assent* and co-author of *Daughters of Cain*, he is currently, with Mark Bostridge, completing a biography of VB.

164 **Germans advancing towards Stalingrad:** The city was an important communications and industrial centre; that it bore Stalin's name made it a vital target in Hitler's eyes.

164 **Germans held in Egypt:** The July fighting had prevented Rommel's advance, in what later became known as the First Battle of El Alamein.

164 **Birmingham, heavy raid:** Over fifty bombers attacked Birmingham, and only eight were destroyed. This raid was in apparent reprisal for the 26–27 July Allied raid on Hamburg.

164 **London's "secret" guns:** This seems to have been a rumour.

165 **Germans within 300 miles of Caucasus:** They were only 80 miles from Stalingrad; on 30 July, Stalin issued an order forbidding any Russian unit to retreat.

166 **Ifor Evans:** An economic historian and teacher (1897–1952), he was Principal of the University College of Wales at Aberystwyth from 1934.

168 **raid on Congress, arrest of Nehru, Mrs Naidu, Azad:** The leaders of the Congress Party were interned until the end of the War because of their opposition to the British war effort.

168 **rioting in India:** Serious disturbances occurred in Bombay and other major cities, following the Government's action against the Congress Party; troops were used to restore order.

168 **fall of Maikop:** It was taken on the same day, 9 August, as Krasnodor, the other important oil-producing centre of the Caucasus.

168 **Harry Pollitt:** He (1890–1960) was the founder and General Secretary 1929–56 of the British Communist Party.

168 **rumour, Churchill in Moscow:** On 7 August, Churchill visited the front in Egypt, then from 12 to 16 August was in Moscow to explain to Stalin that a Second Front was unlikely before 1944. Given Russian sensitivity on the matter, Churchill felt it best to convey the news himself. Churchill had earlier met in Cairo with King Farouk and General Smuts.

169 *Mrs Miniver,* **Jan Struther:** Directed by William Wyler and starring Greer Garson and Walter Pidgeon, this morale-boosting Hollywood film (1942) about an English housewife surviving the War, was based on the novel by Jan Struther (1901–53).

169 *Cavalcade:* The popular, patriotic, historical play by Noel Coward (1899–1973).

169 *Nurse Cavell:* A play (1933) by C. E. Bechofer (pseudonym of Bechofer Roberts) and C. S. Forester dramatising the story of Edith Cavell, the English nurse executed by a German firing squad in the First World War, for assisting wounded Allied soldiers to escape to neutral Holland.

170 **India and Russia:** While mounting anti-British feeling was expressed in riots and acts of sabotage in India, German forces appeared poised to seize Stalingrad.

170 **Amritsar:** When rioting broke out on 10 April 1919 in Amritsar, the local British commander, Major-General Dyer, ordered his soldiers to fire on angry but unarmed demonstrators supporting Indian self-government. Almost 400 died, and over 1,000 were injured, and the incident became notorious; Dyer resigned his commission after censure in an official enquiry.

170 **Izetta Robb:** An American friend of VB's (b. 1904) living near Duluth.

170 **Commando raid on Dieppe:** This large-scale raid on the Atlantic Wall (the German line of coastal defences) tested the feasibility of capturing a Channel port. It involved 6,000 troops, 4,961 of them Canadians, of whom 3,379 were killed, wounded or taken prisoner. It has been argued that the Dieppe Raid provided invaluable experience for the planning and execution of the North African and Normandy landings.

171 **peace on Brest–Litovsk lines:** The Treaty of Brest–Litovsk, signed in March 1918, ended the First World War on the Eastern Front between Bolshevik Russia and Imperial Germany. It was a victor's peace: Russia was forced to cede vast tracts and to pay reparations.

171 **Ll.G., Stalingrad will fall in Sept.:** Lloyd George's prognosis was a popular one: some units of the German Sixth Army reached the outskirts of Stalingrad on 20 August, and five days later Hitler gave his personal order for its capture.

172 **Voorhis Law:** Public Law 870, an anti-Communist measure introduced by the Democratic Congressman (and Chairman of the Committee on Un-American Activities) Jerry Voorhis (b. 1901), required that any organisation controlled by a foreign government should register with the Department of Justice.

172 **Sumner Welles:** An American statesman (1892–1961), he was Under-Secretary of State 1937–43, acting during that period as Roosevelt's special

representative in reporting on conditions in Europe 1940, and accompanying Roosevelt at a meeting with Churchill 1941.

172 **death of Duke of Kent:** Prince Edward (1902–42), younger brother of King George VI, was flying on active service to Iceland in a Sunderland flyingboat which crashed soon after takeoff on the night of 25 August.

172 **Gangulee:** Nagendranath Gangulee (1889–1954), agricultural scientist and writer, son-in-law of Rabindranath Tagore; while engaged in agricultural research in England, he lobbied for the appointment of a Royal Commission on Indian agriculture.

174 **Russian, Egyptian fronts:** The German Sixth Army and Fourth Panzer Army were engaged in the assault on Stalingrad; after failing to take the city by storm, the attackers were embroiled in street-fighting of extreme ferocity. In Egypt, heavy fighting was going on around El Alamein.

174 **the Atlantic:** In August and September 1942, over 200 Allied vessels were sunk, mainly by U-boat packs. Total Allied tonnage lost in 1942 was nearly eight million tons, mostly in the Atlantic.

175 **the last scene in *Mrs Miniver*:** The film ends with the Vicar preaching in his bombed church: "This is the people's war. It is our war. We are the fighters. Fight it, then. Fight it with all there is in us. And may God defend the right."

175 **old Mr Catlin:** Gordon Catlin's father, the Revd George Catlin (1858–1936).

175 **Mrs Catlin cf. myself:** Gordon Catlin's mother, a feminist like VB, had left her husband. VB sympathised with her desire to seek fulfilment, but not with her abandoning of her young son.

176 **Bevin:** Ernest Bevin (1881–1951); formerly a farm labourer and cart driver, he was Secretary of the Transport and General Workers' Union 1921–40, a Labour MP 1940–51, and Minister of Labour 1940–45.

176 **Chiang of China:** Chiang Kai-shek (1887–1975), Chinese nationalist and dictator President of the Chinese Republic 1928–49.

176 **the house:** 2 Cheyne Walk, Chelsea; VB returned there, after living for most of the War in a series of service-flats, shortly before the children returned from the United States in 1943.

177 **Pope:** Pius XII, Eugenio Pacelli (1876–1958).

178 **Stalingrad still holding, 1,300,000 Germans lost:** In the bitter hand-to-hand fighting, the Germans captured almost all of the city and held it, a smoking ruin, between 16 September and 18 November. The Soviet account of enemy losses was exaggerated but in all *c.* 247,000 German soldiers did die in the battle for Stalingrad.

178 **American criticisms:** The deep-rooted American antagonism towards British colonialism found a focus in news about the turmoil in India.

178 **Gandhi, fast to death:** In fact Gandhi was not fasting at this time. His arrest, with the other Congress leaders, on 9 August 1942, provoked

widespread unrest, and when the Government blamed Congress for this, Gandhi did fast in protest, from 29 January to 3 March 1943.

178 **"Brains Trust" debate:** One of the debates recorded in the series of enormously popular Forces Programmes in which celebrities answered questions from the audience.

179 **Cheddar:** Recalling her working-holiday at this famous resort, V B added, 13 years later, a note to the September 28th diary entry: "Visit to Cheddar instance of policy of escaping from London to write my books in country hotels or cottages pursued ever since College. London no place for a writer, but G.'s passion for urban living has compelled me always to base myself there except when travelling abroad."

180 **Min. of Econ. Warfare:** The Ministry of Economic Warfare was a new ministry formed by Chamberlain at the outbreak of war to manage the blockade, customs evasion, and wartime trading agreements with neutral powers.

180 **Navicerts:** Navicerts were an important administrative element in the machinery of the blockade, controlling cargoes from neutral sources, since all merchant shipping was forced to apply for navicerts or run the risk of interception by the Royal Navy. Non-possession of the navicerts (which were issued by the MEW) rendered ships and cargo liable to seizure.

180 **Wickham Steed:** A prominent journalist and lecturer (1871–1956), he was Foreign Editor of *The Times* 1914–19 and a broadcaster on overseas affairs for the BBC 1937–47.

180 **"how dreadful is this place":** Genesis 28:17.

181 **Min. of Food:** This was a new wartime ministry, one of whose main tasks was to organise wartime rationing.

181 *The Neuroses in War*: Edited by Emmanuel Miller and other members of the Tavistock Clinic, this collection of psychological studies had been published by Macmillan in 1940.

181 **letter from Stalin:** This made the pointed observation that Allied aid to the Soviets was of minimal military value when compared with the military contribution the Soviets were making to the Allied war effort by holding down the Germans on the Eastern Front.

181 **American Ambassador in Moscow:** Admiral William Shandley, Ambassador to the USSR 1942–43, had had no previous diplomatic experience.

182 **Henry & Rebecca:** The well-known journalist, novelist, critic and feminist (Dame) Rebecca West (1892–1983) and her husband Henry Andrews, a banker (d. 1968); they had been friends of V B's before the War.

182 **Stephen Hobhouse:** A firm pacifist, he had been imprisoned as an absolutist objector during the First World War (he was closely related to Beatrice Webb and Sir Stafford Cripps).

182 **Mr Orr-Ewing MP:** (Sir) Ian Orr-Ewing, Conservative MP for Weston-super-Mare 1934–58; in 1942–43 he was PPS to the Parliamentary Secretary, Ministry of Food.

183   **chaining of prisoners:** On 7 October, the Nazis threatened to manacle the soldiers captured in the Dieppe Raid; the British threatened to retaliate in kind.

183   **R. C. Sherriff, Siegfried Sassoon:** Two of the best-known writers about the First World War, Sherriff (1896–1975) for his play *Journey's End* (1929), Sassoon (1886–1967) for his many anti-war poems. (Sassoon was one of the original Sponsors of the PPU.)

183   **Germans, new defensive tactics:** On 8 October, the German High Command announced its decision to level Stalingrad with artillery, to reduce German loss of life in holding the city.

183   **Korda film of *War and Peace*:** Sir Alexander Korda (1893–1956), Chairman of MGM (London) Films, announced a project to produce a film based on Tolstoy's novel, but it was not made. In 1947 he produced a film adaptation of *Anna Karenina*.

183   **Tolstoy a pacifist:** In his later years, the great Russian writer (1828–1910) was a very influential pacifist.

184   **Lord Selborne:** R. C. Palmer, 3rd Earl (1887–1971), Conservative MP 1910–40, Minister of Economic Warfare 1942–45.

185   **Pollard's *Short History of the Great War*:** A. F. Pollard (1869–1948), Professor of History in the University of London, published this standard summary in 1920.

185   **Smuts:** Jan Smuts (1870–1950), South African soldier, statesman, botanist, philosopher; he was Prime Minister 1919–24 and 1939–48, and took his country into the War over the objections of Afrikaner nationalists.

185   **Mrs Roosevelt, arrival:** During her American lecture tour in 1937, VB had been invited to the White House by Eleanor Roosevelt (1884–1962), and also met the President. Mrs Roosevelt visited Britain in October 1942 as a guest of the King and Queen.

186   **Mountbattens:** Lord Louis Mountbatten (1900–79), grandson of Queen Victoria, and his wife Edwina (1901–60); he was Chief of Combined Operations 1942–43, Supreme Allied Commander in South East Asia 1943–46, and the last Viceroy of India 1947.

186   **Sir Harry Brittain:** A Conservative politician (1873–1974) unrelated to VB, he was an MP 1918–29 and a founder of the Anti-Socialist Union.

187   **Plowman's essay,** *The Right to Live*: This book of essays by Max Plowman (including "Stop Bombing!") was published by Andrew Dakers in 1942.

187   **large attack in Egypt:** The Second Battle of El Alamein was launched by the Eighth Army on 23 October: it turned the tide of the war in North Africa.

187   **Lord Gorell:** 3rd Baron (1884–1963), he served in the War Office 1918–20 and was Chairman of the Refugee Children Movement 1939–48.

187   **Max's book:** *The Right to Live*.

187   **James Maxton:** A prominent socialist politician (1885–1945), he was an

MP 1922–46, and Leader of the Independent Labour Party 1926–31 and 1934–39.

187 **Peter Pears, Benjamin Britten, Michelangelo sequence:** Benjamin Britten (1913–1976) composed *Seven Sonnets of Michelangelo*, a song-cycle for tenor and piano, in 1940; it was first performed in the Wigmore Hall, London, on 23 September 1942, by Britten's friend Peter Pears with the composer at the piano. Britten, a pacifist, later became a PPU Sponsor.

188 **President Wilson & Tumulty:** Joe Tumulty (1879–1954) was secretary and confidant of Woodrow Wilson (1856–1924), who helped to establish the League of Nations.

188 **feed the starving on Hoover's lines:** Herbert Hoover, 31st President of the United States 1929–33, had served as Head of the Commission for Relief in Belgium during the First World War. Over four years, the Commission fed about 10 million Belgian and French civilians.

188 *Daily Herald* **headlines:** Only three days later, Montgomery announced the unqualified victory in Egypt.

188 **Duke of Bedford:** The Marquess of Tavistock (Duke of Bedford 1940) believed that Hitler had been unjustly treated and that the War was a Jewish plot, so he had sought to mediate between the British and German Governments 1939–40.

188 **the *respectable* Food Relief Committee:** Unlike the Famine Relief Committee chaired by the Bishop of Chichester, the PPU's Food Relief Committee did not boast any Establishment figures among its members.

189 **Lady Mayer:** Dorothy, wife of Sir Robert Mayer, was a Quaker, and both were supportive of VB's "Letters to Peace Lovers". During the War they were Honorary British Representatives in New York to the Save the Children Federation.

189 **"great victory" in Egypt:** The British Eighth Army breached Axis defences at El Alamein and took 30,000 German and Italian prisoners, including Rommel's deputy and eight other generals.

189 **Curtice Hitchcock:** Director of the publishing company Reynal and Hitchcock (1892–1946), he represented American publishers and the Office of War Information on a special mission to England in November–December 1942.

190 **American landings:** The Allied landings in North Africa (Operation Torch) had the objective of gaining control of West Africa, to establish a base for operations against the occupying German forces of Southern Europe, notably France, and to achieve strategic freedom in the Mediterranean. The landings were politically delicate, with the Americans being given a high profile, since the British had, on 3 July 1940, attacked the French Mediterranean squadron near Oran, Algeria, to prevent it falling into German hands.

190 **Vichy-France putting up resistance:** The French puppet-government broke off relations with the United States following the North African action.

190   **fourth swing of the pendulum:** The North African campaign saw a number of advances and retreats by both sides before Montgomery's decisive victory at El Alamein.

190   **Algeria submits:** On 10 November, Admiral Darlan (1881–1942), who was appointed Commander-in-Chief of the French Navy in 1939 and then served Vichy until April 1942 as Minister of Marine, happened to be in Algiers when the Allies invaded on 8 November. He agreed to co-operate with the Americans, a decision apparently aided by Hitler's occupation of most of hitherto-unoccupied France from 11 November.

191   **paratroops to Tunis:** Axis forces retreated to Tunisia, which had been surrendered by the French.

192   **Tobruk back:** British troops reached and reconquered Tobruk on 12 November 1942. General Montgomery's Order of the Day to the Eighth Army was, "We have completely smashed the German and Italian armies."

192   **Benghazi:** Capital of Cyrenaica, one of the two provinces of Libya annexed by Italy in 1911, it was captured by the Allies on 19 November.

192   **French collaborating with the Allies:** On 13 November, the American General Dwight Eisenhower (1890–1969), Commander of the Allied invasion of French North Africa, flew to Algiers to confer with Darlan.

192   **Church bells ringing:** On 13 June 1940, church bells had been silenced, only to be rung by the police or the military to warn of an airborne assault. This ringing of the bells was therefore charged with emotional significance.

192   **Harold Latham:** An old American acquaintance (1887–1969), he was a director and vice-president of Macmillan of New York.

193   **large victory over the Japanese navy:** American and Japanese naval forces inflicted heavy losses on one another, but the losses sustained by the Japanese prevented them from resupplying their troops on Guadalcanal. Altogether the Japanese lost 12 large destroyers or cruisers, 2 transports and a cargo ship; the Americans lost the cruiser *Northampton*, and some other vessels were damaged.

193   **Tunisia, Germans landed there:** Towards the end of 1942, the Axis concentrated an entire Army Group, under General von Arnim, in Tunisia, together with many new tanks, aircraft and other equipment.

193   **Tagore's poem:** Rabindranath Tagore (1861–1941) was admired internationally as poet and sage.

194   **political row, us & U.S.A.:** On 13 November Eisenhower and Darlan agreed that the latter should become head of the civil government in French North Africa to rival Pétain. This move was unpopular with the British, and with the leader of the Free French forces, General Charles de Gaulle (1890–1970), who was disliked by Roosevelt.

194   **raid on Turin:** This attack, on 20 November, was one of the heaviest wartime bombing raids on an Italian city.

194   **Cripps out of War Cabinet:** He had emerged as a leading critic of

Churchill and wanted to take over as Prime Minister — which he might have managed if the fortunes of war had not so dramatically improved for the Allies. On 3 October 1942, Cripps told Churchill that his fundamental disagreement over defence policies was so great that he would have resigned if national fortunes had not been at so low an ebb. Following El Alamein, however, the tables began to turn and Churchill demanded Cripps' resignation.

194 **Herbert Morrison in place of Cripps:** The appointment of Morrison was widely applauded and he remained a member of the Cabinet until the War ended.

195 **French Fleet scuttled:** The French Admiralty ordered the scuttling of the fleet to prevent it falling into German hands; Vichy civilian politicians tried of course to dissuade the Navy from taking this action.

195 **synthetic foodstuffs:** Severe shortages of fresh fruit, fats and animal protein were partly offset by careful management of available supplies and the national diet, but also by adulterating foods and developing a variety of substitutes.

196 **M.S.J.'s latest novel:** In 1942 Storm Jameson published the novel *Then We Shall Hear Singing: A Fantasy in C Major*.

196 **Philip Toynbee:** (Theodore) Philip Toynbee (1916–81), son of the widely influential historian Arnold Toynbee, was a writer, critic, and foreign correspondent of the *Observer*.

196 **Beveridge Report published:** This "Report on Social Insurance and Allied Services" proposed a comprehensive scheme of social insurance and became the basis of the social legislation of the Labour Government of 1945–50.

196 **Beryl Chapman:** A member of the Blackheath PPU Group, she helped to distribute VB's "Letter to Peace Lovers".

197 **Tunis:** The Axis forces were fighting a desperate rearguard action to avoid being pushed into the sea.

197 **Anderson Shelter:** These shelters (named after Sir John Anderson, Minister of Home Security 1939–40) were intended to protect six occupants against all bomb-blasts except direct hits; they were made of corrugated steel, with an entrance protected by a steel shield, and were sunk three feet into the ground and covered with over a foot of earth. More than two million had been distributed by the Government by September 1940. They were issued free of charge to those with incomes of less than £250 per annum.

198 **stories of Nazi treatment of Jews:** The British Government reacted very slowly to information about the systematic extermination of the Jewish people. On 17 December Eden told the House of Commons that the Nazis were attempting genocide — the first public statement by the Government on the matter.

199 **Clement Davies MP:** An eminent statesman and jurist (1884–1962), Liberal MP 1929–62, he became Leader of the Liberal Parliamentary Party 1945–56.

199   **Lord Addison:** Christopher Addison, 1st Viscount (1869–1951), served as Minister of Munitions 1916–17, of Reconstruction 1917–19 and of Health 1919–21.

199   **Roy Harrod:** A well-known economist (1900–78), he served in the Prime Minister's Office 1940–42 and was statistical adviser to the Admiralty 1943–45.

199   **M. Maisky:** Ivan Maisky (1884–1975), Soviet Ambassador to Britain 1932–43.

199   **Armistice Campaign:** There was considerable uncertainty within the PPU about the wisdom of launching a nation-wide campaign for an armistice, although 59 PPU groups were in favour and 23 against (3 were divided, and 16 wanted instead a campaign to support Indian Independence). It was agreed that the campaign should have as its purpose the task of educating public opinion to accept an armistice. By March 1943, however — not least because the tide of war had turned in favour of the Allies — the PPU's Armistice Campaign had scaled down its objective to educating opinion to favour negotiation rather than an immediate armistice.

200   **horrors, Nazi behaviour:** The propaganda campaigns of the two World Wars made many sceptical about news that Jews were being systematically exterminated in Europe.

200   **Stuart Morris arrested:** Morris had received confidential Government documents outlining plans for dealing with any rebellion by Gandhi and his supporters.

200   **Howard Fox:** A PPU member, he was Secretary of the London Regional Board for Conscientious Objectors.

201   **Darlan assassinated:** He was attacked by Bonnier de la Chapelle, a royalist fanatic, on 24 December 1942.

201   **Goebbels:** Joseph Goebbels (1897–1945) was Hitler's powerful Minister of Enlightenment and Propaganda.

201   **war mystery:** The American Government maintained diplomatic relations with the Vichy regime but was also willing to deal with Darlan (who had collaborated with the Nazis) and appointed him head of the civil government in French North Africa. Churchill held a low opinion of Darlan and, after the British attack, in July 1940, on the French fleet at Oran, Darlan hated the British. Much remains unexplained about Darlan's death, but his assassin almost certainly acted alone.

202   **Giraud elected in N. Africa :** After Darlan's death, General Henri Giraud (1879–1949) was appointed high commissioner in French North Africa and Commander-in-Chief of French forces there. He was politically malleable, whilst de Gaulle was disliked by Roosevelt and Cordell Hull, the American Secretary of State, for his aloof independence.

202   **Harold Macmillan in North Africa:** He served as Minister Resident in North Africa 1942–45.

202   **Murphy:** Robert D. Murphy (1891–1975), the American representative in

Algiers 1943–44; a right-wing politician, Irish American and Anglophobic, he had considerable sympathy for Pétain.

1943

203 **stalemate in Tunis:** 1943 opened with very heavy fighting in both North Africa and on the Eastern Front.

203 **anthology,** *Above All Nations*: This collection of stories about "Acts of kindness done to enemies, in the war, by men of many nations" was first published in England in 1945, as edited by VB, Catlin, Gollancz and Sheila Hodges. With additional stories contributed by a German and an American editor, it was republished in the USA in 1949.

204 **Alan Staniland:** A member of the PPU and deputy editor of *Peace News*.

204 **Howard Kershner:** Dr Howard Kershner (b. 1891) was Director of Relief in Europe 1939–42 for the American Friends' Service Committee.

204 **6,000 Jews escaped from France to Spain:** In April 1943 an Anglo-American conference, convened in Bermuda to discuss the problem of refugees, agreed that some 21,000 (including 5,000 Jews) should be transferred from Spain to North Africa.

205 **Gollancz, *Let My People Go*:** Victor Gollancz published his powerful short book — *"Let My People Go": Some practical proposals for dealing with Hitler's massacre of the Jews and an appeal to the British public* — in 1943.

205 **Howard Whitten:** A militant member of the PPU (b. 1916), his registration as CO was conditional on his working in civil defence or agriculture. During the Blitz he was a stretcher-bearer, but then was imprisoned four times, for making anti-war speeches and for breaking his registration condition by working for the PPU's Food Relief Campaign. After the War he worked for Reuters, in Europe, Ethiopia and Pakistan.

206 **emotions re John:** The passenger plane between neutral Lisbon and London had been shot down by the Germans on 10 January, with the loss of its 13 passengers (including the actor Leslie Howard). This had filled VB with misgivings about John's imminent return route.

207 **Mr Justice [Hallett]:** (Sir) Hugh Hallett (1886–1967) was Judge of the High Court, Queen's Bench Division, 1939–57.

208 **Archbishops of Canterbury and Westminster:** The Anglican leader William Temple (1881–1944), Archbishop of York 1929–42, Archbishop of Canterbury 1942–44; and the Roman Catholic leader Arthur Hinsley, Archbishop of Westminster from 1935, who died later in 1943.

208 **personal pamphlet:** *One of These Little Ones* was published both by Andrew Dakers and the FoR in 1943.

208 **daylight raid, LCC school bombed:** The 44 deaths during this attack on a school in Lewisham — 39 children, 5 teachers — caused deep shock after a "long period of virtual immunity from heavy raids on London".

209 **fall of Tripoli:** British forces entered the city on 23 January 1943 and received the formal surrender by the Vice-Governor of Libya.

209 **RIIA:** The Royal Institute of International Affairs, founded in 1920.

209 **Edith Pye, Famine Relief Committee:** Like the PPU's Food Relief Campaign Committee, the Famine Relief Committee — of which Edith Pye, a Quaker, was Secretary — sought to win concessions from the Government on food relief supplies for Occupied Europe. It was supported permanently by the Quakers and other church groups and was regarded as more "respectable" than the PPU's Food Relief Committee.

209 **Cornelia Sorabji:** An eminent Indian barrister and feminist (1866–1954).

210 *Free India:* A journal or pamphlet devoted to the cause of Indian Independence.

210 **Dennis Stoll, Sir Oswald Stoll:** Dennis Gray Stoll, a writer and broadcaster, whose first two books, published by Gollancz, were set in India — *Comedy in Chains* (1944) and *The Dove Found No Rest* (1946). His father (1866–1942) was an Australian-born cinema magnate.

210 **Fenner Brockway:** Later Baron, he was a prominent socialist, pacifist, journalist and politican (1888–1988) forceful in the struggle for colonial emancipation; an ILP member until 1946, he became a Labour MP 1950–64.

210 **Silverman, Fred Messer, MPs:** Samuel Sydney Silverman (1895–1968), a Labour MP 1935–68; Frederick Messer (1886–1971), a Labour MP 1929–31 and 1935–50.

210 **Edward Thompson:** A Fellow of Oriel College, Oxford, Thompson (1886–1946) had been an educational missionary in India, and wrote several books (including *Tagore: Poet and Dramatist*) on Indian topics.

210 **Roy Walker, six months in prison:** He served six months in Wormwood Scrubs for refusing to register with the Ministry of Labour.

210 **Churchill and Roosevelt at Casablanca:** This meeting took place 14–24 January 1943 in French Morocco. It was primarily concerned with strategy, defeating the U-boats, continuing aid to Russia, the invasion of Sicily, the escalation of the bombing offensive against Germany, the allocation of sufficient funds to the Pacific theatre, and the assembly of an invasion force in Britain. At the concluding press conference, Roosevelt called for the unconditional surrender of Germany, Italy and Japan. As VB observes, there was no mention of post-war aims, save that world peace was considered contingent on the unconditional surrender.

210 **German army encircled:** The German Sixth Army under General Friedrich von Paulus (later Field Marshal) was trapped in Stalingrad without rations and ammunition. Hitler had told Paulus that "Surrender is out of the question".

211 **Relief Service Unit:** Probably a unit of the Pacifist Service Corps formed by the PPU on the outbreak of the War to undertake social service and humanitarian relief work.

211   **bombed Berlin twice, proclamation of Hitler's announcement:** The RAF made its first daylight raid on Berlin, using Mosquito bombers, on the tenth anniversary of Hitler's coming to power. The Stalingrad crisis was probably responsible for Hitler's cancellation of his customary anniversary address.

211   **Goering:** Hermann Goering (1893–1946), Prime Minister of the Third Reich, and Air Minister.

211   **huge German armies getting defeated:** In all, some 247,000 German soldiers were killed in the battle, and 90,000 were taken prisoner. The latter included Paulus and 16 other German Generals. The battle for Stalingrad was the turning-point of the War on the Eastern Front.

211   **Charles Morgan:** A well-known novelist and playwright (1894–1958); he and his wife, the novelist Hilda Vaughan (1892–1965), were old friends of VB's.

212   **Baroness von Reitzenstein:** *The Enchanted Fountain* by Baroness Josephine von Reitzenstein, was published by New Vision Press in May 1945; in her Foreword, VB describes it as "'letters' written by a German refugee mother in England to her young daughter left behind in Germany".

212   **Leslie Artingstall:** He was General Secretary of the British FoR 1936–46.

213   **Bishop of Birmingham:** Ernest Barnes (1874–1953), Anglican Bishop of Birmingham 1924–53.

213   **an Al Capone:** VB's intemperate comparison of Churchill to the infamous Mafia gangster is the strongest of her comments on the increasingly vengeful references to the German people in his speeches.

214   **Steinbeck's *The Moon is Down*:** Set in the War, this novel by the American novelist (1902–68) had been published in 1942.

214   **fighting in Tunisia:** On 14 February the Germans launched a strong counter-offensive there, inflicting heavy losses on the inexperienced American II Corps.

215   **debate on Beveridge Report:** This debate identified the Labour Party with the Report's very popular proposals.

216   **Bernard Shaw:** The famous dramatist (1856–1950) was a prominent supporter of reformist causes.

217   **Fielden:** Lionel Fielden, a campaigner for Indian Independence, published a study about India called *Beggar My Neighbour* in 1943.

217   **Bishop of Southwark:** The Rt Revd Bertram Simpson (1883–1971) was Bishop of Southwark 1942–58.

217   **Wordsworth's "the first mild day of March":** From the first line of "To My Sister" (1798).

218   **strange and terrible accident:** 173 people died of suffocation and 61 were seriously injured after a crowd, hastening down steps to one of London's public shelters, during an air-raid alarm, began to fall over one of their

number in the blackout. Ironically no bombs fell in the area of the shelter that night.

219　**cutting, *Evening Standard*:** Alex Wood was quoted in this article as having written, in his letter printed in *Peace News*, that it had been a shock "to discover what Stuart had done, and a further shock to discover how lightly some members of the Council viewed it".

219　**Harry Emerson Fosdick:** The Minister of Riverside Church, New York, he (b. 1878) was a member of the FoR Advisory Council.

219　**old Nuremberg destroyed:** On Monday 8 March, a raid by several hundred bombers inflicted serious damage on major German factories in the city, including two that had manufactured aircraft components.

220　**Harold Balfour:** A Conservative politician (b. 1887), he was an MP 1929–45 and Parliamentary Under Secretary for Air 1938–44.

220　**Athanasius, *contra mundum*:** Bishop of Alexandria, St Athanasius (296–373) refused to compromise with the popular heresy of Arianism, so was beset with enemies and often in exile.

220　**"Stop Bombing Civilians!":** This pamphlet was published by the Bombing Restriction Committee in March 1943.

221　**M. Pierlot:** Hubert Pierlot (1883–1963), leader of the Social Christian Party, was Prime Minister of Belgium 1939–45.

221　**Dr Bigwood:** (Sir) Cecil Bigwood (1863–1947) was Deputy Lieutenant and JP for the County of London.

221　**Claude Cockburn:** He was a member of the British Communist Party and a *Daily Worker* journalist. His own satirical news-sheet, the *Week*, banned in January 1941, together with the *Daily Worker*, because of its opposition to the War, was permitted to circulate again after the Soviet Union became an ally of Britain.

221　**the German "Peace Offensive":** This was probably an interpretation of an article by Goebbels (reported in *The Times*, 20 March 1943) asserting that the real threat to the world was Bolshevism, and that only by accepting German leadership could that threat be averted.

222　**Capt. Larke:** Albert Larke, a United Church minister, was Chaplain to the 4th Canadian Armoured Division and left the Army in 1946 with the rank of major.

222　**Mareth line:** A series of old French fortifications which constituted the best defensible position in eastern Tunisia. By 28 March the British Eighth Army occupied the main positions on the line.

222　**battle in Tunisia, none too well:** The Axis and Allied forces inflicted heavy losses on one another around El Guettar and Djebel Naemia.

222　**Werth broadcast:** Alexander Werth (1901–59), who had been Paris correspondent of the *Manchester Guardian* 1931–40 and a regular contributor to the *New Statesman* 1932–40, was a Special Correspondent in Russia for the *Sunday Times* 1941–46.

223 **burning Berlin:** This was the heaviest raid on Berlin to date: more than 900 tons of incendiaries and high explosives were dropped. During March 1943 the RAF dropped 8,000 tons of bombs on enemy targets; the 8th USAAF dropped 1,666 tons.

223 **Tunisia, great victory:** The battle for Tunisia was in its final phase; the German surrender of 12 May was the biggest victory of the War to that point, and ended all organised Axis resistance in Tunisia.

223 **horrid paper, iniquities of the Ministry of Supply:** War Economy Standard Paper was of very poor quality. In 1943 the Ministry of Supply, because of paper shortage, sponsored book drives; 56 million books were collected by October, and 50 million pulped. Publishers were limited to 40 per cent of the paper they had used before the War.

224 **all women with nursing experience must register:** Ernest Bevin (1881–1951), Minister of Labour and National Service 1940–45, introduced a series of registers (the number and type of which were gradually expanded during the War) to facilitate the Ministry's power to direct the population towards essential work.

225 **"Dion Heyworth":** The protagonist of VB's original version of *Account Rendered* was loosely based on Leonard Lockhart.

226 **Hitler, mysterious fate:** In mid-March 1943 there were two failed attempts on Hitler's life by military officers.

226 **Tribunal:** The Government adopted a more liberal policy towards COs in the Second World War than in the First. CO status might be granted on the basis of political, religious or humanitarian grounds, and given unconditionally, or conditionally, dependent upon the fulfilment of alternative, non-military service decided by the Tribunal. These Tribunals were administered by the Ministry of Labour and consisted of a Chairman (who was to be a County Court judge) and four other members, one of whom was appointed after consultation with trade union officials.

227 *Serpo Pinto:* The Portuguese liner on which John and Shirley Brittain-Catlin were to return to Europe later in 1943.

230 **Polish officers murdered:** On 13 April 1943, Goebbels' Ministry of Propaganda announced the discovery by German forces of the mass graves of thousands of Polish Army officers who had been murdered in 1940 and buried in the Katyn Forest near Smolensk. A request by the Polish Government-in-Exile for an investigation by the International Red Cross prompted Stalin to break off diplomatic relations.

230 **British Restaurant:** 2,160 British Restaurants, providing 600,000 meals a day, were in operation by September 1943. They were intended to supply the population with inexpensive meals.

230 **Russian–Polish row:** Existing evidence points to Russian guilt for the massacre, as tacitly acknowledged by reports in Polish newspapers in 1988. Presumably the Soviets were trying to decapitate Poland's likely postwar leadership to facilitate easy control of the country. VB, questioning why the

Russians should break off relations if the Germans were responsible, highlights one of the otherwise inexplicable reactions by the Soviets to Katyn.

230   **Poles, climb down:** They were indeed made to climb down, by Churchill, who was desperately anxious to maintain unity in the Allied camp.

231   **Lady R.:** Lady Rhondda (1883–1958), founder of the feminist journal *Time and Tide*, and friend of Winifred Holtby and VB.

231   **Mrs Sidney Webb:** Beatrice (Potter) Webb (1858–1943), eminent political scientist and socialist writer; her husband (1816–98) had also been very influential.

231   **von Arnim captured:** On 12 May General Jurgen von Arnim surrendered to the British in the name of all Axis forces in North Africa. Some 238,000 prisoners were taken.

232   **our raids:** 16–17 May was the night of the famous Dam Busters raid on the Eder and Mohne dams in the Ruhr. The RAF Lancasters breached two dams that controlled two-thirds of the water supply of the Ruhr.

233   **Agnes, Mgt. Lewis:** Amy Burnett's widowed sister; Mrs Brittain's companion, who had been one of her servants.

233   **fall of Mussolini:** Mussolini's fall came when he was forced to resign by the King of Italy, Victor Emmanuel III (1869–1947) and Field Marshal Badoglio (a former Chief of Staff who had opposed Italy's entry into the War in 1940). Mussolini was imprisoned, but, rescued by German airborne troops, soon set up a republican fascist regime in the northern part of Italy, which was occupied by Germany.

233   **memorial to Arnold Bennett at Hanley:** This tribute to the popular and prolific novelist (1867–1931) was, appropriately, in one of the Five Towns of the Potteries that he had made famous.

234   **week of raids on Hamburg:** On the night of 27–28 July, the RAF launched a series of raids on the big port city, killing about 20,000 inhabitants and injuring 60,000. Almost two and a half thousand tons of bombs were dropped, with incendiaries creating firestorms with temperatures of 1,000° C and winds in excess of 150 mph. During July and August approximately one and a half million incendiary bombs were dropped by the RAF and the American Air Force on Hamburg alone.

234   **Lord Listowel:** W. T. Hare, 5th Earl of Listowel (b. 1906).

234   **Eleanor Rathbone, Cunningham-Reid:** She (1872–1946) was a prominent Independent MP 1929–46; he, A. S. Cunningham-Reid (1895–1977) was a Conservative (later Independent Conservative) MP 1932–45.

234   **Stuart, Anthology:** This arrangement, whereby Stuart Morris, out of prison after his nine-months' sentence but without a job, helped find appropriate writings for *Above All Nations*, was obviously of mutual benefit. He was to be accepted back as the PPU's General Secretary when Patrick Figgis, who filled the position for 3 years, resigned to return to the ministry. Morris then

continued as General Secretary for many years, working productively with VB when she became Chairman in 1949.

235 **landing near Salerno:** On 9 September the American Fifth Army landed at Salerno, near Naples, and was so hard pressed by Kesselring's XIV Panzer Corps that the beach-head was almost lost; but by 16 September it was secured.

235 **Cat and Mouse business:** VB felt that COs like Howard Whitten were being pursued in a similar way to the Suffragettes, for whom the original act so nicknamed (1913) was devised: those who refused to eat in prison were released on a licence that would be revoked if they committed a further offence. VB's letter to the *Manchester Guardian* on this topic (22 September 1943) has been reprinted in *Testament of a Generation*.

235 **Norman Angell:** Sir Ralph Lane, best known by his pseudonym Norman Angell (1874–1967), writer, lecturer and socialist politician; his anti-war book *The Great Illusion* (1910) was translated into 20 languages, and in 1933 he won the Nobel Peace Prize.

235 **Strabolgi:** The Hon. Montague Kenworthy, 10th Baron Strabolgi (1886–1953), a Liberal MP 1919–26 and Labour MP 1926–31.

236 **Churchill back:** This time Churchill had met Roosevelt in Quebec, 17–24 August, at a conference code-named Quadrant; they had discussed the Normandy landings, Burma campaign, Italian campaign, and research on the atomic bomb.

236 **Lady Wavell, Lady Layton:** The wives of Field Marshal Archibald Wavell, 1st Earl, who was shortly to leave for India as its new Governor-General 1943–47, and of Walter Layton, 1st Baron (1884–1966), who had been Editor of the *Economist* 1922–38 and later of the *News Chronicle* and was Chief Adviser on Programmes and Planning to the Ministry of Production 1942–43.

237 **George Davies:** Warden of an educational settlement in Wales, he was a member of the PPU Council and later preceded VB as Chairman.

237 **John, Harrow:** VB's son was sent to this leading public school a few miles north-west of London, rather than to Eton, because it was less rigid (at Eton John would have been required to take Latin, although he had not studied it at his American school).

237 **Martin Parr:** Robert Parr (1894–1979) was HM Consul-General for French Equatorial Africa 1940–43.

1944

239 **Second Front:** The decision to open a second front, taken at the August 1943 Quebec Conference, was finally put into effect on D Day, 6 June 1944.

239 **my bombing booklet:** *Seed of Chaos: What Mass Bombing Really Means*, which VB started writing towards the end of 1943. Published in April 1944, it was attacked by George Orwell.

239 **Russians, Polish frontier:** On 3 January 1944 Soviet troops pushed across the pre-war border into Poland.

239 **? rocket guns:** The American Air Force and the RAF launched raids on the launch sites of the V1 rockets.

239 **Minister of Economic Warfare:** Lord Selborne was Minister of Economic Warfare 1942–45.

239 **Hugh Lyon:** (Percy) Hugh Lyon (b. 1893), writer and poet (he published *Challenge to Youth* in 1940), had served in the First World War, and was Headmaster of Rugby from 1931.

239 **Bishop of Wakefield:** Campbell Hone (1873–1967) was Bishop of Wakefield 1938–45.

240 **Roughtons:** Travelling from North America on the *Serpo Pinto*, Shirley Brittain-Catlin had made friends with Rosemary Roughton, a girl of about her age.

241 **huge air battles:** In January 1944, Allied bombers launched Operation Pointblank against the German aircraft industry as part of the effort to secure aerial superiority prior to the European invasion. The principal targets were the aircraft factories at Oschersleben, Halberstadt, Brunswick and Klagenfurt. In all the 8th and 15th USAAF dropped 22,000 tons of bombs on enemy targets during January.

242 **Sofia "wiped off the map":** The city was fiercely attacked on 15 January, marking the beginning of raids on Balkan cities.

242 **M. Michaloczyc:** Stanislaw Mikolajczyk (1901–66), leader of the Polish Peasant Party, who succeeded Sikorski as Prime Minister in July 1943 and remained head of the Government-in-Exile until he resigned in November 1944.

242 **Russo-Polish row:** Tension between the Soviets and the Polish Government-in-Exile in London escalated as the Soviets pushed into Poland. On 26 January the Russians published their report on Katyn, holding the Germans responsible for the massacre, further increasing the tension.

242 **proposal for Poles:** To placate the Russians and the Poles, it was decided to shift Poland westward — a singularly unhappy solution to the Polish problem.

243 **day raid on Frankfurt:** On 29 January the American 8th Air Force attacked Frankfurt with 800 planes and dropped 1,900 tons of bombs.

243 **German bombers manoeuvring to avoid flak:** On January 21 and 29, German bombers attacked London, and 57 were downed. Civilian casualties in England for January were 107 killed and 260 injured.

244 **St Paul's:** St Paul's Girls' School, Hammersmith.

247 **Dorothy Thompson:** The well-known American journalist, lecturer and broadcaster (1894–1961).

248 **invasion of Europe:** The largest amphibious operation in military history:

176,000 troops were disembarked from 4,000 ships in less than 24 hours, protected by 600 warships and 9,500 aircraft.

249   **Jooss Ballet, "The Green Table":** The German dancer and choreographer Kurt Jooss (1901–79), known for his socially-conscious dance-drama, had taken refuge in England from the Nazis in 1934; "The Green Table" (1932), his expressionist anti-war "Dance of Death" in one act, is one of the most important dances created in the twentieth century.

249   **pilotless planes:** Germany began launching the V1 rocket (Vergeltungs-waffe-I or Reprisal Weapon-I) against England on 12–13 June 1944. A total of 8,000 were launched and of these 2,340 fell on London. The V1 had a maximum speed of 155 mph and carried a one-ton warhead. The bombs killed 5,475 people and injured almost three times that number; they also destroyed over a million houses. They were christened "doodle bugs" or "buzz bombs" because of the noise they made. VB also called them robots or p-planes (pilotless planes). The Cabinet ruled that they should be called flying-bombs. Intelligence provided by the Polish resistance had from May 1943 warned of German plans for long-range attack.

250   **robot on a church:** On 18 June the Guards' Chapel, Wellington Barracks, in central London, sustained a direct hit and 119 people (including many distinguished officers) were killed and 102 seriously injured.

251   **2,000-ton raid on Berlin:** The raid was by 1,000 bombers escorted by 1,200 fighters.

252   **Charles Morgan's *The House of Macmillan*:** This history of the publishing house by the eminent writer came out in 1943.

253   **Second Thirty Years' War:** The Thirty Years' War was a series of religio-political conflicts throughout Europe (1618–48). VB's bitter reference links the First and Second World Wars, implying a similiar period of European conflict between 1914 and 1944.

254   **French patriots, Paris:** Paris was liberated on 23 August 1944 as the French 2nd Armoured Division moved into the capital. The Germans attempted to retake it, but were repelled, and two days later General Charles de Gaulle entered Paris. Brigadier General Jacques Leclerc accepted the German surrender of the city at 3.15 pm.

254   **Romania has quit the War:** Soviet forces went into action across the Romanian border in August 1944, and in two weeks had overrun the country. Romania accepted the terms of a Russian armistice on 23 August 1944, and two days later declared war on her former ally Germany.

254   **Bulgaria suing for peace terms:** Bulgaria opened negotiations with the United States and Britain for an armistice in the vain hope of not falling under Russian control. Although Bulgaria had not declared war on Russia, or sent troops to the Soviet front, Russia nevertheless declared war and overran the country in four days. With their position now secure in Romania and Bulgaria, the way lay open for the Soviet Army to advance upon Yugoslavia, Hungary and Greece.

254   **V2 weapon:** The first V2 exploded over London on 8 September 1944. The

Government, anxious to avoid panic, instructed that the explosions caused by the bombs be described as town gas explosions; Londoners promptly dubbed Hitler's latest weapons "flying gas mains". The V2 was 45 feet long and weighed 14 tons. In all, some 2,724 people were killed by the V2s and 6,000 badly injured. Four of them fell on Croydon, destroying 2,000 houses.

255 **"rocket coast":** The northern coast of France was studded with approximately 100 launch-sites, and others were located in Holland.

255 **dispute over supplies to Warsaw:** On 1 August 1944, the Polish underground army, partly in response to Soviet requests, began a military rising against the German troops occupying Warsaw. The Soviets, under direct orders from Stalin, halted their advance on Warsaw and watched the Poles fight a heroic 63-day battle. By refusing Soviet aid to the Poles, and Allied efforts to give aid, until he was sure that the Poles were defeated, Stalin sought to facilitate Soviet plans to control postwar Poland.

256 **Patton:** General George Patton (1885–1945). As a colonel on the Western Front in the First World War, he sent the first American tanks into action at St Mihiel on 12 September 1918. In 1944 he was commanding the newly-formed Third Army which on 28 August crossed the Marne and in April 1945 entered Czechoslovakia.

256 **pick-a-back planes:** In September 1944 the Germans were releasing V1s from piloted planes (He. IIIs) but with very little success.

256 **A. J. Cummings:** A prominent journalist (d. 1957), he was Political Editor and Chief Commentator of the *News Chronicle* 1932–55.

257 **two terrific explosions:** "This was actually the first V2 rocket", VB explained in a note added to her diary on 11 October.

257 **a fortnight's rest and treatment:** The Coombs was a "nature-cure home" run by two naturopaths, Thomas and Dorothy Elliot; it had been recommended to VB by Stephen Hobhouse when she told him she felt close to a breakdown.

258 **"blueprint" for a new League of Nations:** The League of Nations was not formally dissolved until April 1946. Its successor, the United Nations Organisation, was to be composed of two bodies: the General Assembly, in which all nations, regardless of size, were equally represented; and the Security Council, with a restricted membership, the five Great Powers having permanent seats.

258 **Tintern Abbey:** The beautiful ruins of this Cistercian abbey on the Welsh border (founded in 1131) inspired Wordsworth's "Lines Composed a Few Miles Above Tintern Abbey" (1798).

1945

259 **6 Endsleigh Street:** The address of Dick Sheppard House, PPU headquarters.

261 **Gresham's School:** A boys' public school, founded in 1550 by Sir John Gresham.

261   **San Francisco Conference:** Delegates from 50 nations met between
15 April and 26 June 1945 to give final approval to the structure of the
United Nations Organisation and to draft its Charter.

261   **Peter Fraser, conscientious objectors:** Scottish-born, Fraser (1884–1950)
was imprisoned during the First World War for his opposition to conscription in New Zealand. In March 1940 he became leader of the country's
Labour Party, and Prime Minister. COs in New Zealand, as in Australia,
were treated much more severely than those in England, and VB had been
asked to plead their cause.

261   **Joe Brayshaw:** He was Organising Secretary of the CBCO.

262   **end like Lincoln's:** A week after winning the American Civil War,
President Abraham Lincoln (1809–65) was dead — assassinated.

262   **Torgau:** On 25 April patrols of the Russian 59th Guards Division and the
American 69th Division met near Torgau: the first contact of Eastern and
Western ground forces.

262   **Goering has fled:** On 25 April Hitler ordered that he be stripped of all
authority, and next day ordered his arrest. Goering surrendered to the
Americans on 8 May, in Austria.

262   **Sheila Hodges:** A director of Victor Gollancz Ltd, she had been one of the
four editors of the British edition of *Above All Nations*. VB saw the book's high
sales as an indication that the people had been uneasy about war policies like
the blockade and area-bombing.

263   **execution of Mussolini:** on 28 April Mussolini was shot by Italian
partisans on the shores of Lake Como. His body, with that of his mistress
Clara Petacci, was hung upside down, on public display, in Milan.

263   **Himmler:** Heinrich Himmler (1900–45), head of the Gestapo and the
Secret Service, Minister of the Interior 1943–45. He made his offer of
surrender to the British and Americans on 23–24 April but was told that
armistice talks would have to include the Soviets. He was captured later by
the British, and committed suicide whilst in captivity.

263   **Count Bernadotte:** Count Folke Bernadotte (1895–1948) was nephew of
King Gustavus V of Sweden and President of the Swedish Red Cross. In
both World Wars he arranged exchanges of POWs, and Himmler's
choosing him as intermediary was well calculated.

263   **rumour that Hitler has died mad:** Hitler committed suicide on 30 April
1945 by shooting himself through the mouth. His health had declined
rapidly in his final days, and he was subject to frequent maniacal rages.

263   **Liddell Hart:** A military theorist, writer and publicist, Sir Basil Liddell
Hart (1895–1970) was military correspondent of the *Daily Telegraph* 1925–35
and *The Times* 1935, and published histories of both World Wars.

263   **appointment of Doenitz:** Karl Doenitz (1891–1980), Grand Admiral of the
German Navy 1943–45, was appointed President of the German Reich by
Hitler in his final testament, drawn up on 28 April 1945. He had been a U-
boat commander in the First World War and C-in-C of the Submarine Fleet

1939–43. He was sentenced to ten years' imprisonment for war crimes in
1946.

263   **split between Doenitz and Himmler:** Hitler chose the ruthless Doenitz as
his successor in an effort to ensure that his last wishes were carried out. He
had expelled Himmler and Goering from the Nazi Party for seeking peace
settlements with the Allies. However, Doenitz too sought peace, sending
envoys to Field Marshal Montgomery's Headquarters in the hope of
negotiating a separate peace with the West.

264   **surrender to Alexander:** Harold Alexander, later Earl Alexander of Tunis
(1891–1969), Supreme Allied Commander in the Mediterranean 1944–45,
accepted the unconditional surrender of the German armies in Italy on
2 May. After the War, he was Governor-General of Canada 1946–52.

264   **fall of Berlin to the Russians:** Russian troops entered Berlin on 21 April
1945 and had taken the city by 1 May. The fighting for the city was
murderous and its collapse brought an orgy of excesses by Soviet troops in
revenge for Nazi cruelties on Russian soil.

264   **no trace of Hitler or Goebbels:** The bodies of Hitler and his mistress Eva
Braun were burned in the garden of the Chancellery by his aides, in
accordance with his last wishes. Joseph Goebbels and his wife poisoned their
six children and then Goebbels shot her and himself.

264   **Nazi forces surrendered to Montgomery:** The approximately one million
German troops in Holland, Denmark and North-Western Germany surrendered unconditionally to Field Marshal Montgomery (1887–1976) on
4 May 1945, to become effective at 8 am on 5 May.

265   *South Riding* **film:** The successful 1938 film of Winifred Holtby's novel
starred Edna Best, Ralph Richardson, Marie Lohr and Ann Todd.

265   **Germany's total surrender:** On 7 May 1945 German forces surrendered
unconditionally to the Western Allies and to Russia. The instrument of
surrender was signed by the German Chief of Staff, General Jodl, at 2.41 am
at General Eisenhower's Headquarters in Rheims and ratified in Berlin the
next day. Operations ceased at 23.01 hours on 8 May. In all some 38 million
people lost their lives in the War; losses were almost equally divided between
soldiers and civilians.

266   **Gollancz's "What Buchenwald *Really* Means":** This powerful pamphlet
about the notorious concentration-camp was published in 1945.

266   **Keitel:** Field Marshal Wilhelm Keitel was Hitler's Chief of Staff, chosen
largely because he was pliable. In 1946 he was condemned to death by the
Nuremberg International Military Tribunal.

266   **great peace-meeting:** The National Peace Council arranged a mass
meeting at the Central Hall, Westminster, to express support for the
demand "Real Peace This Time". Around 5,000 people assembled, and the
meeting "turned into one of the largest demonstrations ever known in the
history of the peace movement". VB herself spoke four times that evening,
on the last occasion at Hyde Park.

267   **General Election:** On 25 May, Churchill had resigned after the National

Government began to disintegrate, with recriminations between Conservative and Labour members (like Brendan Bracken and Ernest Bevin).

267 **Hiroshima:** The world's first atomic bomb was dropped on the Japanese city of Hiroshima on 6 August 1945. It has been estimated that between 78,000 and 100,000 people were killed and a further 90,000 seriously wounded. (The Allied raid on Dresden of 14 February 1945, the most intense incendiary bombing attack of the War, caused around 135,000 deaths.)

267 **"poor Catherine" fairy tale:** VB used as Preface to *Testament of Youth* an extract from this tale whose heroine chooses a happy old age rather than a happy youth.

268 **Dean of St Albans:** The Very Revd Cuthbert Thicknesse (1887–1971), who had been a chaplain in the First World War and Chaplain to the King 1935–36.

268 **Maude Royden Shaw — of all people:** Now married, Maude Royden (1876–1956) had been a leading pacifist and feminist before the War.

268 **"Born 1925":** VB's final novel, it was conceived and begun at The Coombs (which it uses as a setting), and published in 1948.

268 **Foreign Office support for Denmark lectures:** Having been repeatedly denied an exit permit during the War, VB now found all restrictions suddenly lifted and the FO supportive of her Scandinavian tour.

268 **Myrtle Wright:** A Quaker, she had been caught in Oslo by the Nazi invasion in April 1940, and remained in Norway until the end of the War.

268 **"Letters to Peace-Lovers":** VB's selected edition of the Letters was not published because, as indicated by a note added later to this entry, Dakers was advised that it would have poor sales in the aftermath of the War. (The letters up to 4 April 1940 had been published in that year, as *War-Time Letters to Peace Lovers*, by the PPU's Peace Book Company.)

269 **John Marsh:** The Press Officer of the Help Holland Council, which had arranged the visit, he acted as escort.

269 **Henrietta Leslie, Dr Schutze:** A novelist and playwright, Leslie (1881–1946) was married to Harrie Schutze (1882–1946), a bacteriologist; they were old acquaintances of VB's.

269 **M. Bowen:** Marjorie Bowen was the pseudonym of (Margaret) Gabrielle Long (1888–1952); *The Vipers of Milan* (1917) is the best known of her historical novels, some of which are set in Holland.

269 **Godfrey Winn:** A popular writer, journalist, broadcaster and lecturer (1908–71).

269 **Olaf Stapledon:** (William) Olaf Stapledon (1886–1950) had served in the FAU 1915–19, and was a writer and lecturer, mainly on philosophical themes.

269 **Arnhem bridge:** The Battle of Arnhem (17–20 September 1944) was part of a plan to outflank the Siegfried Line; but paratroops could not capture the bridge despite bitter fighting.

269 **Prof. Leo Polak:** VB had stayed with this Jewish–Dutch Professor of Philosophy, his feminist wife and three daughters, when she visited Groningen during a lecture-tour of Holland in April 1936.

270 **Ravensbrück:** The notorious concentration camp for women, fifty miles north of Berlin.

INDEX

VB: Vera Brittain. For British Government ministries, departments and administrative measures, see "Government". For London boroughs, addresses and other locations, see "London".